"Pretends to Be Free"

"Pretends to Be Free"

Runaway Slave Advertisements
from Colonial and Revolutionary
New York and New Jersey

Edited by
Graham Russell Gao Hodges
and Alan Edward Brown

Fordham University Press
New York   2019

Copyright © 1994, 2019 Graham Russell Gao Hodges and Alan Edward Brown

All rights reserved. No part of this publication may be reproduced, stored in a retrieval system, or transmitted in any form or by any means—electronic, mechanical, photocopy, recording, or any other—except for brief quotations in printed reviews, without the prior permission of the publisher.

Original edition published 1994 by Garland Publishing, Inc.
Fordham University edition published 2019.

Fordham University Press has no responsibility for the persistence or accuracy of URLs for external or third-party Internet websites referred to in this publication and does not guarantee that any content on such websites is, or will remain, accurate or appropriate.

Fordham University Press also publishes its books in a variety of electronic formats. Some content that appears in print may not be available in electronic books.

Visit us online at www.fordhampress.com.

Library of Congress Control Number: 2018962098

Printed in the United States of America
21 20 19   5 4 3 2 1
Revised and expanded edition

Contents

List of Illustrations vii

List of Tables in Appendix 1 ix

Acknowledgments xi

Introduction xiii

A Note on the Text xli

A Note on Colonial and Revolutionary Newspapers xliii

Introduction to the Twenty-fifth Anniversary Edition xlvii

Teacher's Guide to "Pretends to Be Free" liii

Foreword by Edward E. Baptist lix

Runaway Slave Advertisements 1

Appendix 1: Tables 305

Appendix 2: Hues and Cries 321

Glossary 329

Selected Bibliography 335

Subject Index 345

Name Index 351

Illustrations

Following page 194

A Map of the Province of New-York ... by Claude Joseph Sauthier ... Engraved by William Faden, 1776. Courtesy of the Cornell University Rare Book Room.

Lester, Cæsar, Isaac, and Mingo, from *The New-York Gazette; or, The Weekly Post-Boy*, #1086, October 27, 1763.

Ben, from *The New-York Gazette; or, The Weekly Post-Boy*, #1235, September 4, 1766.

Bood, from *The New-York Gazette; or, The Weekly Post-Boy*, #1251, December 25, 1766.

Jem, from *The Pennsylvania Chronicle*, #235, July 1, 1771. Courtesy of the American Antiquarian Society.

Mark and Jenney, from *The New-York Journal; or, The General Advertiser*, #167, January 12, 1775.

Titus, from *The Pennsylvania Gazette*, November 22, 1775. Courtesy of the American Antiquarian Society.

Eastman Johnson, *A Ride for Liberty-The Fugitive Slaves*, circa 1862. Oil on board. Gift of Miss Gwendolyn O.L. Conkling. Courtesy of the Brooklyn Museum.

Tables

Comprising Appendix 1

1. Number and Gender of Fugitive Slaves, 1716–1783
2. Ages of Fugitive Slaves, 1716–1783
3. African-American Population for New York and East-Jersey, 1703–1775
4. Origins and Destinations of Runaways
5. Month of Escape of Runaways
6. Listed Skills of Runaways
7. Escape Strategies of Runaway Slaves
8. Language Abilities of Runaway Slaves
9. Masters' Comments on Appearance & Personalities

Acknowledgments

Preparation of a volume of this scope required the assistance of the highly capable and thoughtful professionals at the Colgate University Library and Interlibrary Loan Service, Olin Library and the Rare Book Room of Cornell University, Syracuse University Library, New-York Historical Society, New-Jersey Historical Society, Monmouth County Historical Association, Monmouth County Parks System, Bergen County Historical Society, New York Public Library, New York State Library and Archives, the American Antiquarian Society, the State Archives and Library-Trenton, and the Rutgers University Library.

There are a number of philanthropic societies, government agencies, and university programs which deserve recognition. They include the Colgate University Faculty Development Grants, American Council of Learned Societies Major Grant Program, New Jersey Historical Commission; National Endowment for the Humanities Summer Stipend and Travel to Collections Programs; New York State Library Visit to Collections Program. Special thanks goes to the Colgate University Student Assistance Program. This invaluable enterprise introduced Hodges to diligent Colgate students who created the initial transcripts of these advertisements. Students who helped immensely on this book include Paul Townend, Marianne Humphrey, Charles M. Grieco, Lisa Macquarrie, Matt Baldacci, JoEllen Kelleher, Melanie Sargeant, Matt Pardy, and Will Galloway.

At Garland Publishers, Leo Balk, Claudia Hirsch, and Rob McKenzie were patient, cheerful and highly supportive editors. Warren Wheeler contributed his extraordinary talents by photographing several of the notices. Special thanks is due to Reverend and Mrs. Graham R. Hodges, Margaret Washington, James and Celeste Creel, and Merlin Washington-Hodges. Jeanne Kellogg, Director of Colgate University's Academic Computer Center, has been a great friend and supporter of Mr. Brown's.

Introduction

This collection of 662 fugitive advertisements culled from the newspapers of colonial and revolutionary New York and New Jersey offers rich evidence of African American resistance to servitude and of a nascent black culture.* We tender this bountiful harvest of information to help students of early American history learn more about the dimly-understood world of African Americans in and around New York City. While discovering the texture of the urban and small farm milieu of the colonial and revolutionary North, we became aware of a unique African American culture, producing mobile, articulate, and assertive bondspeople surviving in a tough servile system. One manifestation of the maturation of black culture in two colonies where few African Americans enjoyed civil liberties, was that many fugitives would "pretend to be free."

Our introduction to the notices serves two purposes. First we set the context for the notices with a survey of the history of slavery in colonial and revolutionary New York and New Jersey. Because this description is not intended to be comprehensive, we have emphasized conditions which caused slaves to flee from their masters. Accordingly, we discuss initial African interactions with the two primary European ethnic groups in the region, the Dutch and English. Next we describe the demographic effects of the external and internal slave trades and the codification of slavery and African resistance, examine the contours of work and living patterns as they changed over time, and scrutinize the interweaving of sacred and secular cultures among slaves. We conclude with a brief analysis of how the American Revolution affected African Americans and slavery in the region.

Our second intention is to interpret the immense variety of evidence within the runaway notices. Since Carter G. Woodson published fifty-three pages of runaway notices in the second issue of the *Journal of Negro History* in 1916, historians have mined fugitive advertisements for evidence of slave resistance and culture.[1] There are two interlocking paradigms. First and foremost, runaway notices are evidence of slave resistance. As Peter Wood has remarked "no single act of self-assertion was more significant among slaves or more disconcerting among whites than that of running away." Escape hurt masters economically. Studying African runaways, Paul Lovejoy has shown that flight was an effective means of destroying property because escape represented an absolute loss of valuable property. Even if recaptured, the worth of slaves was reduced because they had been fugitives. Slaves usually departed during the busiest times of the agricultural calendar — cultivation and harvest — when their absence was inconvenient and disruptive. Fugitives also sabotaged property by destroying and stealing animals, equipment, and crops. Above all, flight was the most effective individual means of struggle against slavery; through escape, slaves were active agents who undermined the system of subjugation.[2]

Flight had political impact, combining what John K. Thornton has described as *petit* and *grand marronnage*. Grand marronnage involved slaves seeking to break free from the control of their masters either to found their own society elsewhere, or to seek refuge in a society that would give them greater freedom and opportunity. It extended to rebellions and plots which sought the complete overthrow of the system of colonial slavery and the replacement of the master's government with one led by the former slaves. Petit marronnage referred to slaves who absented themselves temporarily to take a holiday or to bargain with their masters for better working conditions. This was part of the "day-day-resistance," which, Raymond and Alice Bauer observed more than fifty years ago, undermined their masters' economies and domination. Just as slaves shirked at tasks, pilfered produce and destroyed crops, flight, even for a very short time, exasperated masters, and often wrecked their plans.[3]

Recently, scholars have examined runaway notices to rediscover slave culture. As perusal of the notices will quickly reveal, no single quality or group of characteristics encapsulated the cultures of the slaves of New York and New Jersey. Their national origins and ethnicities ranged

Introduction   xv

from West African to West Indian to locally-born mullatos sufficiently fair-skinned to pass as Caucasian. Their work cultures crossed urban and rural mentalities, with skills useful in town or country. A murmur of trans-Atlantic culture rippled among slaves, who were fluent in African, English, Spanish, French, Indian, High, Low, and Negro Dutch. We may also discern the personal styles and appearances of common people, interpret their gestures and speech for glimpses of the personalities behind the mask of servitude, and glean some understanding of their motivations and intentions for flight. Runaway advertisements give hints of the interior lives of slaves by indicating their religious beliefs, announcing their vices, or, as Michael Mullin has demonstrated, what body gestures and vocal intonations tell us about slave personality.[4] We learn, from the subjective opinions masters placed in the notices, what the ruling class perceived of their slaves' characters. In brief, the notices are the chief mode of evidence for assembling individual or group portraits of African Americans of the eighteenth-century North.

The 662 notices describe 753 fugitive slaves, an average of more than eleven per year between 1716 and 1783. Yet the advertisements published in this book do not constitute all the fugitive bondspeople of early New York and New Jersey. We have not included, for reasons of length, all the available notices in every colonial newspaper. Moreover, published runaway advertisements, as Peter Wood has explained, "represent little more than the top of an ill-defined iceberg." Although masters sometimes rushed their notices into print, often the time lag between date of disappearance and the advertisement indicated that a notice was only a last resort. Some slaves undoubtedly were caught quickly or returned home voluntarily; an unknown number, more apparent during the revolutionary period, when other methods of counting were available, vanished so completely that the expense of an advertisement was not worthwhile.[5]

Distance and scarcity of venues were additional factors. For virtually the entire colonial period the only newspapers in the region were in New York City or Philadelphia. Although rural masters hired agents or asked friends and relatives to reclaim fugitives and pay rewards, the process was easier for prosperous city-dwellers, and hampered slave owners on the frontier. Despite this, the overall patterns suggest that most slaves fled from the rural environs of New Jersey and New York. Of 729 instances in which masters indicated the place of flight, 418 or over 57 percent were in the country. Even during the chaos of the Revolutionary War, when masters outside of New York City had extreme difficulty placing an advertisement, notices by rural masters nearly matched those placed in the city, where three newspapers operated.

A second anomaly is the infrequency of advertisements in the first half of the eighteenth century. Only seventy-nine or 12 percent of the circulars date before 1750. Still, the historical record of slave resistance before 1750 undercuts any suggestion that slaves were quiescent or effectively corralled by their masters. A major revolt in 1712, failed but dangerous conspiracies in 1734 and 1741, and repeated acts of such individual slave violence against masters as ax-murder, rape, and arson deny any presumptions of slave deference.[6] Rather than sustained policing of slaves, the scarcity of the print medium on the frontier probably caused the paucity of notices before 1750. Having considered these limitations, runaway notices remain our best approach to early slave culture and resistance.

Africans first became slaves in the territory under Dutch rule during the first half of the seventeenth century. Seeking laborers to construct its new colony, the Dutch West India Company purchased sixteen Angolan males in 1626 from West Indian pirates. Four years later the company settled a number of slaves on a plantation in Pavonia, on the site of present-day Jersey City, planting an African presence in New Jersey. Although the Dutch West India Company eventually freed the first generation of slaves in the 1640s, it simultaneously planned to capture the slave market for North America; by 1655 New Amsterdam was the leading slave port on the continent. As the New Netherlands' economy privatized and Dutch settlements spread around the hinterlands of New York City into New Jersey, on Long Island and up the Hudson River valley, farmers and patroons alike eagerly purchased slaves to clear forests, construct small farm villages, labor in the seaborne economy of the city, and toil as domestics.[7]

Initially, the legal status of Africans in the two colonies was unclear. Slavery lacked statutory power in Holland and evolved more by custom than law in New Netherlands. Although there was a small class of free blacks, after 1650 most newly arrived Africans were enslaved. By 1664 there were at least eight hundred blacks in the colony, of whom around seventy-five were free people, who stood as examples to the slaves and with whom the unfree could conspire for liberty. The influence of these early decades of settlement was powerful. Even though the English vanquished the Dutch colonial government in 1664, Dutch settlers retained significant influence in the development of slavery as owners and, later, as opponents of abolition efforts. Above all, the Dutch, as artisans in the city, and owners of small, subsistence farms in the countryside, were perhaps the largest and most dedicated slave owners throughout the eighteenth century.

Forced African migration to the region did not end after Dutch imperial power ceased. In the late seventeenth century, Africans arrived in small parcels, or involuntarily accompanied masters migrating from Barbados; these were seasoned slaves originally from the Gold Coast, the Bight of Benin, and Angola. Pirates brought others from Madagascar. Although the Royal African Company, which held the monopoly over the supply of slaves to North America, initially ignored the northern colonies, by the eighteenth century, local slave owners actively embraced the international slave trade. Between 1700 and 1774, merchants in New York and Perth Amboy, New Jersey's slave port, imported over eight thousand Africans and seasoned West Indian slaves. Most transactions with the West Indies involved young males, purchased in small lots. They came from Jamaica, Barbados and Antigua, all colonies characterized by heavy slave mortality, frequent revolts, and little cultural interaction between whites and blacks. Slaves sent to New York were often known as "refuse" slaves, a term denoting troublesome slaves prone to flight and rebellion.[8]

Other slaves came in large shipments directly from Africa. Slave traders practiced "coasting" by which they purchased available slaves from a series of African ports. At various moments during the eighteenth century, New York's slave traders arrived in the city with several hundred imports from Africa. "Salt-water" slaves came from the Gold Coast factories of Whydah and Elmina, producing Kwa, Ewe, and Fanti nationals; from the Senegambia came Mandingoes, Fulas, Wolofs, and Jolas. From Benin came Aja and Yourba. In the Angolan and Congolese regions, dealers along a "moving frontier of slavery," bought slaves scoured from the Kasanje, Mbondo, and Mbailundu regions. As the slave trade pushed further and further inland, new African political powers replaced older cultures. The African societies producing these slaves were undergoing sharp social dislocation during the eighteenth century. Many of the slaves brought to New York and New Jersey were refugees from turmoil in Africa, worsened by the hazards of the middle passage. They were survivors of succeeding catastrophes, grimly resolute against the terrors of existence.[9] Although some arrived in America broken in body and spirit, others, determined to survive, quickly fled unpleasant masters.

Once in America, slaves were sold in an active, internal slave market. Local trafficking of slaves occurred at merchant houses, at the Meal Market in New York City, and among farmers in the hinterlands. Although some masters let favored slaves choose new owners, too frequently, local slave trading broke up marriages and families, and tore slaves from familiar surroundings. When life with a new master proved unacceptable, flight was a common response. As evidence of this, we note that on eighty-three occasions, masters listed in their advertisements, former owners or past residences of their eloped slaves, hoping to recapture their chattel hiding near family and friends.

The churning effects of the slave trade and local dependence upon slaves as the principal labor force produced a rapidly growing African population. By the third decade of the eighteenth century, Africans constituted over sixteen per cent of New York's population and over ten per cent of the inhabitants of East-Jersey. In certain counties the proportions were higher. In 1749, blacks, nearly all enslaved, were over one-third of the residents of heavily Dutch Kings County; across the river in Bergen County, another Dutch stronghold, blacks were twenty per cent of its folk. By 1750, over ten thousand slaves lived within fifty miles of Manhattan Island, the largest such congregation north of the Chesapeake. By the eve of the American Revolution, it may be estimated that over twenty thousand slaves worked in the region. Use of slaves for farm labor in rural regions meant an over-abundance of males, with a fifty-seven per cent majority in Kings by 1749. In the city, heavy use of black females as domestics produced a narrow majority of women. Meeting members of the opposite sex or sustaining families and culture often meant taking the risks of escape. For restless young males living and working on farms, escape was a promising option with little to lose.[10]

To control a growing, disorderly slave population, the English colonial governors of New York and New Jersey gradually established a slave code comparable in severity to ordinances in South Carolina or the West Indies. Initial laws defined blackness as a condition of slavery by limiting the terms served by white indentured servants and prohibiting, with varying success, the enslavement of Indians. Further laws limited black mobility and civil rights. In the 1680s local statutes required that slaves carry passes from their masters before leaving home. Succeeding ordinances forbade marketing by slaves, penalized those who traded with them, barred slaves from working as carters and porters, and banned assemblages by more than three slaves. As frequent prosecutions for these crimes indicate, slaves contested these laws.[11]

In 1702, colonial assemblies in New York and New Jersey passed comprehensive legislations establishing slavery. A substantial portion of the new laws focused on fugitive slaves, and firmly identified flight with insurrection. New York's omnibus legislation specifically addressed masters' anxieties about fugitive slaves. Recognizing that slaves in New York and Albany "have been oftentimes guilty of Confederating together in running away," the assembly outlawed gatherings of more than three bondspeople. The laws penalized anyone who harbored runaways with a £5 fine and made those who caused the loss of a slave liable for full value. In 1705 the New York Assembly passed a law mandating the death penalty for any slave found more than forty miles north of Albany. Although northern masters did not advertise for fugitives "dead or alive," as was the case in South Carolina, recaptured slaves faced severe penalties. Gradually the two colonies foreclosed any hope for black freedom. After an unsuccessful slave revolt in New York City in 1712, the two colonies limited future manumissions by requiring £200 bonds as security for emancipated blacks. These laws retained power past the American Revolution. Rather than moderate over the years, severe punishments magnified in times of crisis. After the slave revolt in New York in 1712, slaves were broken on the wheel, burnt alive, or gibbetted. In the aftermath of the failed 1741 conspiracy, dozens of slaves were burnt at the stake, hanged, or gibbetted. More fortunate ones were exiled to the West Indies. The rarity of manumissions, the lack of sympathy for abolition displayed by colonial legislatures, churches, and citizens insured that freedom-minded slaves could look only to occasional rebellions and conspiracies, or, less dangerously, to individual flight. [12]

Patterns of residence prefigured a rebellious slave population. There were two principal configurations of slavery in the regional economy. The first was rural, either on large private farms, where such local gentry as Frederick Phillipse, the second Lord of Phillipsburg Manor, owned forty-six slaves, or more commonly, a few slaves on small farms of less than one hundred acres.[13] While some of these farms were isolated, the vast majority were in agricultural communities. In the late seventeenth century, Dutch, Scottish, Huguenot, and English yeomen established pastoral communities in rural New York and New Jersey. Throughout the eighteenth century, slaves constituted a significant portion of the wealth of these small farmers.[14] Except those who lived on large farms, rural slaves rarely numbered more than five in each household. Such scattering impaired black family development, increased the possibility of sale of kinfolk, and exacerbated conditions for escape among isolated young men and women. Despite claims by eighteenth-century masters that the region's slaves were well-treated and contented, on such subsistence homesteads, life was harsh, monotonous, and unrewarding. Slaves used every opportunity to flock to the city on the weekends and holidays where taverns, markets and dance contests alleviated the tedium of home life.[15]

New York City was the center of slave culture in the region. Here at the markets, public squares and taverns, blacks congregated on weekends and holidays. On New Year's Day, Easter, and *Pinkster* (Pentecost Sunday), slaves clustered in friendly pubs, at the homes of free blacks, and on the wharfs to plot insurrection, or, more routinely, their own escapes. Runaways coming to the city joined gangs, which played important roles in the conspiracy of 1741.[16]

Initial censuses in New York in the early eighteenth century showed pockets of slaves in the wealthier, merchant-dominated wards.[17] At the same time, artisans also employed slave labor, although many preferred to hire bondsmen when the need arose. By 1745, female domestics became the largest sector of bondspeople in the city, a majority which never relinquished. The growth of New York's mercantile economy in the 1750s spurred many masters to hire out their bondsmen as sailors. Masters were quite willing to lease slaves to sea captains for lengthy voyages. Other slaves worked on the wharfs and piers of the city where fugitives knew that sea captains and wharfingers enlisted crews with few questions about backgrounds. By mid-century, warnings to masters of vessels against harboring fugitives were standard clauses in runaway advertisements.[18]

By the mid-eighteenth century, slaves worked in all sectors and levels of the economy. Their type of work depended upon their current master, and runaway notices were often registers of a slave's employment history. For example, Stoffels, who ran away from Judith Vincent of Monmouth County, a farming region, was an experienced house carpenter, cooper, wheelwright and butcher. Most slaves possessed general skills as domestics and laborers. In New York and New Jersey, where the bulk of slaves were domestics and laborers, masters listed skills for only 123 of 753 getaways. Commonly mentioned were domestics, farmers, privateers or mariners followed in frequency by chimney-sweeps, blacksmiths, bakers, coopers, shoemakers, and carpenters and tailors, weavers, and barbers. Millers, stable hands, accountants, sugar makers, and a wagon maker, armorer, potash masher, brassfounder, goldsmith, collier, silversmith, sailmaker, butcher, and skinner comprised the remaining workers.[19]

The most frequently listed skill was fiddling, by which a slave might carve out a difficult yet personally satisfying living in the black tavern and dance hall community of New York City, or at rural frolics. Of 753 runaways between 1716 and 1783, forty-four, or 6 percent were fiddlers. When we add three drummers, two fifers, two singers, and a french horn player, we find that in 123 instances in which masters specified black skills, musicians accounted for 42 percent of the citations. A talented fiddler or, in African-American terminology, a "songster" or "music physicianer," could survive singing and playing for fellow blacks. "Songsters," an occupational term current by the late eighteenth century, bound together a broad range of secular music including social songs, comic songs, blues and ballads. Such professional demands required extensive travel. In Africa, professional musicians toured up and down the west coast, taking inspiration from polycultural sources. Similarly, in America, black travelling musicians drew from Scotch, Irish, and English vernacular musics as well as African. There were other fugitives with *luft-menchen* talents. Scattered among the runaways in the mid-eighteenth century were three ministers, three doctors and a dentist, two fortune tellers, a watch seller, and a magician.[20] Work and skill, however ordinary or exotic, were parts of the cultural talents of a young, restive slave population for whom labor could mean mobility, as well as drudgery.

Even the African American contact with European religion bred tendencies towards flight. Protestant

Introduction xxiii

denominations in America, seeking to ameliorate the grim lot of slaves and insure their spiritual salvation, sought to convert slaves and inculcate docility through acculturation. The Church of England offered catechismal classes to slaves throughout the colonial period; although only a minority of Africans in the two colonies attended the schools, they created an ethos which equated education with better conditions and potential liberty. Anglican requirements that Africans be literate before baptism stimulated a small class of literate slaves able to forge passes, an example which inspired others to seek the liberating quality of literacy. A major theological dispute was the catalyst for other fugitive slaves. In European religions, baptism traditionally mandated the emancipation of Christianized slaves. To assure anxious masters the New Jersey assembly in 1704 and New York's in 1706 passed legislation ruling that catechism and baptism of slaves did not alter their civil condition. Though this key plank offered sacred justification to slavery, Dutch and Huguenot masters regarded it as deceptive, religious imperialism. Slaves, in turn, regarded this split among the master class as proof of slave masters' corruption of Christianity. The dilemma affected Dutch Reformed positions on slavery. Reformed church officials supported enslavement because it introduced heathens to Christianity. Dutch slave owners, however, wary of Anglican desires to catechize and baptize their bondservants, needed to answer inquisitive slaves about their place within Christianity. Masters either had to instruct slaves at home, and reply to inevitable questions about the meaning of Christianity and slavery, or watch helplessly as provocative language of Christian liberation came from other denominations, itinerants, or the slaves themselves.

The third wave of faith to engulf Africans came from dissenting congregations. First, the Society of Friends sought to cleanse the colonies of slavery; then Methodists and Presbyterians enlarged Christian conversion and attracted blacks through evangelical experience. Methodists made Africans charter members of congregations. Although evangelical ministers preached slave docility, the thrust of their message, their egalitarian spirit of salvation, and the pronounced abolitionism of the Society of Friends undermined Christian support for slavery. Last was the independent, religious experience of blacks themselves. Our fugitive slave notices reveal occasional examples of black religious leadership. Ministers appeared on the road occasionally as did Bible readers. One of the most interesting religious figures was Andrew Saxon, a slave carpenter who abandoned Jacobus Van Cortlandt in 1733. Saxon was dressed in shirts marked with a Cross and "professeth himself to be a Roman Catholic."[21]

In sum, slaves found that every sector of the economies and societies of New York and New Jersey contained, however inadvertently, reasons or inspiration for flight. Harsh laws sharply limited the potential for emancipation. Newly-arrived Africans and seasoned West Indian slaves came from turbulent, fragmented societies, where flight was common. In the Mid Atlantic colonies, repeated sales diminished loyalty to master or mistress. Gender imbalances between town and country virtually necessitated flight for any slave desiring to preserve or create a family. The multiple religious denominations in the two colonies either sustained dogmatic contradictions about the place of slaves in Christianity, or planted and nurtured ideals of liberty. Finally, whether by major revolt, or a constant stream of individual acts of defiance, Africans in New York and New Jersey experienced an unending river of courageous opposition to slavery.

Given these conditions, and because outright rebellion occurred only a few times in northern colonial history, it is not surprising that slaves and servants in New York and New Jersey resisted their conditions by running away. The first indications surface in 1648 when the General Council of New Netherlands passed an ordinance forbidding harboring of fugitive servants, revealing that refugee bondservants found succor among sympathetic colonists. Although newspapers in London began advertising for fugitive servants in the 1660s, the colonies, where no weekly journal existed until nearly the eighteenth century, used the "hue and cry" method to canvass for runaways.[22] In his initial message in 1664 following the English conquest, Governor

Introduction xxv

Richard Nicolls made the first known "hue and cry." He ordered that "all persons within my government to bee ayding and assisting [to Mr. Yarmouth of New England] to find out said Negroe....to seize him and return him." In his proclamation Nicolls offered the first available description of a slave and his clothing: "The Negroe is a lusty young fellow about 20 years of age, hee was cloathed in a red waistecoat, a pair of linen breeches, somewhat worne, a grey felt hat, but no shoes or stockings."[23] Other "hues and cries" occurred shortly afterwards. Jacob, who spoke, "Good English, Dutch, good Mohawk and Mohegan," ran away from his master, Sven Theunisse who offered a reward in either "Indian or Christian territory."[24] A few weeks later Cornelius Van Boorsen of Westchester County recorded the escape of a black family," A Negro Man and Woman with an Infant Child." Van Boorsen complained of some "evil Persons" inveigling the family. He believed the family "maybee on board some Shipp in the Harbor or Road outwards bound, thinking thereby to make their escape." The slave spoke good English and took with him "besides his ordinary habit, a red cart livery coat." A week later on October 2, 1679 the colony council responded to masters' complaints by passing a law establishing a large fine of £25 for harboring runaways and neglecting to send them home or to the magistrates.[25] An early example of maroons surfaced in 1690 when residents of Harlem complained of "a band of Negroes, who have runaway from their masters at New York and commit depredations on the inhabitants of the said village."[26]

In the early eighteenth century, colonial masters recorded "blacks who stole themselves," in newly-established newspapers. These reports indicate that a slave's disappearance could be both spontaneous and well-planned. One slave prepared by changing his name; Jacob, of Upper Freehold, New Jersey, "has several times changed his name, calling himself James Start, and James Pratt, &ct ... he passes himself as an Indian." He vanished much more suddenly. His master reported that "he went from work at his plough and was without shoe or stocking and no other clothes but an Oznabrig Shirt and Trowsers, an Old ragged waistcoat and an old hat." Bondsmen escaped despite drastic measures by their masters. Caesar ran away from Isaac Freeman of Woodbridge, New Jersey in February, 1756, then escaped again in August, 1756. Caesar wore a "pair of iron pothooks around his neck with a chain fastened to it that reached his feet." Quaco fled in 1761 wearing an "iron collar with two hooks to it, round his neck, a pair of Handcuffs with a chain to them, six feet long."[27]

Once beyond the master's property, slaves demonstrated extraordinary mobility as revealed by the notices sheriffs posted to masters of captured fugitives held. Masters had a designated time to collect their chattel from jail and pay expenses before the slave was auctioned. In 1751, Thomas Smith, sheriff of Cape May County in southern New Jersey, picked up Jupiter Hazard, a twenty-seven-year-old slave recently escaped from Piscataway, Rhode Island. After giving particulars of Hazard's appearance, Smith noted that Hazard "seems to have travlle'd pretty much, for he gives a good account of Rhode Island, New York, Pennsylvania, Shrewsbury and other places." Masters in southern colonies understood that their slaves could travel to New York through pathways in the Appalachian Mountains. Harry, who changed his named to Arnold, fled from his master in South Carolina and was "supposed to be in this province." Even newly arrived Africans could manage in the wilderness. Pero and Nero, "new negroes from the River Gambia," escaped from John Gartner of North Carolina, despite little skill in English. They were arrested in Shrewsbury, New Jersey in November, 1765. Eight months later they escaped from John Morris, their jailer, "in a small boat, 16 feet keel, a black bottom and her wales painted brown, had 4 oars on board."[28]

Perhaps the best means to avoid arrest on the road was a pass. During a century of indeterminate literacy, forged and outdated passes helped protect fugitives. Masters attempted to combat this method by warning the public of deception. For example, Henry and Joseph Robinson warned that Benjamin Moore, a black indentured servant, carried old contracts and "shows them for a pass, pretending to be a free Negro." Jenney, who fled with her husband, Mark, from

Major Prevost, in 1775 used another method. She obtained a "note to look for a Master, its likely she may make a travelling pass of it." [29] Other slaves used masquerade to escape capture. A favorite means was changing names. Jem, the slave of Isaac Wilkins of Newark "calls himself by the several names of James, Gaul, Mingo, Mink and Jim." Others found refuge among free blacks. Mary Ferrari, of New York City, mistress of Cate, guessed that her escaped slave, "is harbored by some of the Free Negroes." One slave faked his own death. Ben, slave of Elizabeth Finn of Bergen County, left his clothes by the shore of the Hackensack River, "which gives reason to suppose he took that method to deceive his master and prevent a search."[30]

Failure did not darken a slave's pursuit of freedom. Bood appears at least three times in our record. We first meet him in June 1759 when he and three other slaves ran away from masters in Hopewell, New Jersey. William Hunt, his master, pointed out that Bood probably was leading the quartet to the "Indian towns upon Sasquehanna," where the slave stayed on a previous flight some years before. Four years later, Hunt advertised again for Bood, now thirty years old. In 1766 Bood decamped a last time. Described as around thirty-eight years old, and a "remarkable stout, cunning, artful fellow," Bood's body recorded the hard life of the fugitive: "his great toes have been froze, and have only little Pieces of Nails on them."[31]

Other advertisements indicated the slaves' dedication to freedom. Frank of Morris County, who spoke English, Dutch, Spanish and Danish, was "artful and cunning" and escaped "twice from Persons who took him up." Frank received assistance from "two of Capt. Kennedy's Negroes." Sampson, slave of John Phillips of New York City, "has made a practice of running away and sculking in the woods near plantations." Pompey, slave of Robert Benson of New York City, was "sculking about the docks ever since his running away and wants to go a privateering." Arch, from Somerset County, New Jersey, went "some back way to Albany, to meet some yellow free Negroes, which went by water at the same time, or else try to get aboard some vessel, as he attempted about 3 years ago below Philadelphia." Arch could write his own pass and read the Bible.[32]

Slaves on the run joined forces with white indentured servants. At the bottom of society, racial difference counted for little among what Peter Linebaugh has called the picaresque proletariat. For example, four servants, "a white man and three Negroes," stole a large two-masted boat from George Mumford of Fisher's Island. Joseph Heday, a ruddy-complexioned native of Newark, wore a "red Whitney Great Coat, red and white flower'd serge jacket, a swan skin strip'd [jacket], a pair of leather breeches, a pair of trowsers and other clothes." One of the blacks, Fortune, wore similar clothing including "a new cloth coloured Fly-Coat with a red lining, a Kersey Great Coat, three Kersey Jackets and breeches of a dark colour, a new pair of Chocolate coloured corded Drugges breeches, a pair of blue and white check'd trowsers, two pair of shoes, one of them new, several pair of stockings a Castor and a new felt hat." The others carried similar amounts of clothing. The quartet stole "a firkin of butter, weighs about sixty pounds, two cheeses weights 64 pounds and bread for the same."[33] Masters believed that servants enticed slaves to run away. Sam, of Trenton, was "enticed by one Isaac Randall, an apprentice;" the pair stole a bay gelding to escape to New York or Philadelphia where they hoped to get on a privateer.[34] Men and women ran away to form interracial families. "A short chubby fellow" ran away from John Decker of Staten Island to be with "a negro wench of middle size, with child. It is supposed they went together." Runaway combinations revealed interracial marriages. Ned of Lancaster County, Pennsylvania, ran away with Mary Woods, a white woman from New Jersey "by whom he had a child near 3 months old." Ned could read and write and " 'tis very likely he has procured a pass for them as man and wife." Domingo, a "Spanish Negro Man," fled in 1748 to hide in the swamps of Manhattan Island, near the home of Mary Carrey, "a white woman who used to harbour him at her lodgings near the Stockade."[35]

A slave's destination greatly affected chances for success. While Eugene Genovese has argued that runaways in the Old South occupied unfavorable terrain with only minimum security with few chances to forge a viable community life,[36] the evidence in New York and New Jersey suggests that fugitives had a good chance of success. In the first place, masters in New York and New Jersey rarely knew where their slaves fled. In the 662 notices, only 123 destinations are indicated, with 71 of those coming during the Revolutionary War, when knowledge of a slave's whereabouts seldom insured recapture across enemy lines. Indeed, the largest single destination was the military, from which a master had little hope of recouping losses. Few could reasonably hope to seize slaves who left for the Indian territories, or for the sea. Of similar difficulty was finding a slave in the city. Of thirty-eight slaves fleeing to New York, twenty-two or fifty-seven per cent escaped from masters living in the city.[37]

We have noticed that escaped slaves found work in the city working on the wharfs and ships. There were opportunities in other sectors as well. Abandoned masters warned endlessly against unlawful employment of their chattel, indicating the frequency of the practice. Joe fled from Augustine Reid in 1764 to New York City where he "hired himself as a free man to a Butcher, in whose service he stayed that winter." The next year Joe hired himself to "Mr. Oakley in Westchester for a year and a half. Reid, hearing about his slave in 1766, went to take him up, but "he getting notice of it, went off and is probably lurking or concealed in the Neighborhood of Long Island or New York." The customs of slave hiring enabled literate slaves who used fake passes to deceive potential captors. Claus, 35 year old slave of Cornelius Newkirk of New York City, could "read and write both English and Dutch," and "it's likely will forge a pass." Caesar ran away from John Hobart of Eaton, Suffolk County in 1765 in the company of "one Thomas Cornwall...who it is feared has forged a pass for the Negro."[38]

The western frontiers beckoned to escaped slaves, who wished to leave colonial society behind completely. The two colonies did not penetrate far into the interior of the continent and American Indians rarely returned escaped slaves, particularly those with mixed blood. The general laws on slave flight stemmed from the 1680s when colonial authorities worried about fugitive slaves aligning with nearby Indian tribes.[39] Throughout the eighteenth century, colonial authorities asked Iroquois chiefs to return slaves or to pursue runaways, with little success.[40]

Nations in conflict with the English often enticed slaves. During the Seven Years' War masters suspected the French of enticing blacks with promises of freedom. A report in 1756 worried about "too great intimacy between the Negro slaves and the French neutrals in this province which "may at this time tend to stir up the negroes to an insurrection when such numbers of our militia are detached to the frontiers against the French."[41] In Albany officials reported that slaves "are grown very insolent and have intimated, that if they receive ill usage from their masters, they will runaway to Canada, where they will be free." In 1745 the New York council revived the old law which required harsh penalties for blacks fleeing north to the French and Indians.[42]

Thus far, we have noted the vast evidence of slave resistance within the runaway notices. Slaves were also individuals, with unique characteristics. Taken together, their styles and personalities formed the elements of an early African American lifestyle, which we may view more closely using the notices. The thumbnail portraits masters drew tell us much about the visual appearances of slaves. As owners hopeful of regaining valuable property recorded these bursts to freedom, they provided capsule descriptions of little-known people at critical moments in their lives. While the quality of the masters' comments was often very subjective, they doubtless knew some facts about their chattel. Thus we know that over 86 percent of the runaways were young males, a figure similar to the patterns in other colonies.[43] Masters were also reasonably objective about slave linguistic abilities. Bilingual speakers of Dutch and English abounded, with a few multilinguists knowing Spanish, French, Indian, and African tongues.[44] An inability to speak fluent English often dampened a fugitive's chances for success, as illustrated in the sheriffs' notices. At the same time, comments on vocal intonations are rare. Kate, mentioned

Introduction xxxi

above, had a shrill voice. Usually, observations about verbal qualities alluded to degrees of sincerity. Many fugitives were smooth-tongued, bold, convincing, or artful. Respected slaves were slow, serious talkers.

The assurance of masters' comments slipped as they recalled slaves' names. Masters undoubtedly believed they knew their chattel's identity, though they acknowledged that a name was often the first badge of enslavement to be discarded. The most common were single English names, such as Will, Dick, and Sam. The quality of other names made slave desires for a quick transformation unsurprising. Many masters avoided names potentially used by family members and so labelled their slaves with comic and classical names. More neutral were biblical names. Demonstrating personal selection, fifty-seven slaves had African surnames.[45]

Appearance and personality are more subjective, yet it is striking how masters in the North avoided such judgements as "down look," "smooth-tongued," and "bold." Rather they described clearly distinguished aspects such as scars, small-pox pits, disabilities, and lost teeth, or commented on vices such as drinking and smoking. Similarly the standard references to race was negro with occasional mentions of black, mullato, yellow and Indian.[46]

The comments masters made about physical characteristics are testimony to the injury, disease, and rough usage of slaves. During the 1740s and 1750s slaves were commonly described as "pock-marked," showing scars of smallpox epidemics. Others showed signs of physical abuse. Ralph, who fled from a sloop in New York harbor, had many dents in the top of his head, possibly caused by the "Ward-end of a key." Others showed the traditional marks of bondage. Scipio, who fled with his arms pinioned behind him, had "Buttocks pretty well marked with the Lash." Even more common were the scars or evidence of such injuries as broken legs and arms, missing teeth, lameness, partial blindness or verbal tics such as stuttering.[47]

The greatest information concerns the slaves' outer aspects — especially their clothing, hair-styles, and hats. Masters were able to recall in extraordinary detail the clothing slaves wore, owned, or stole. Except for a few privileged servants, slave dress was distinctly ordinary and usually homemade. By referring to the endless procession of tow cloth shirts and trousers, buckskin breeches, and beaver hats, we may reconstruct the vocabulary of male slave garments; for women, the evidence is scantier, but petticoats, gowns, and caps made up standard attire. Slaves did steal clothing to sell on the used market in New York or to disguise their appearance, but most seem to have deserted their masters with only one outfit. Comments on hair-style are less common, but masters did make distinctions between African, or closely-cropped, tightly curled hair, and "bushy" or Indian hair. A few hair-styles were distinctive. Dick "takes uncommon pains with his short wooly hair, which he wears cut on the forepart of his Head." Anthony Frost combed his "bushy" hair "very high in the shape of a roll." Kate "generally wears her hair very high and straight up, over a roll, with a great deal of pomatum." Hats were commonly made of beaver or an imitation; only in the revolutionary years did fashionable "maccaroni" hats appear.

Overall, the individual styles and appearances of the slaves described in the advertisements fit well with the group portraits drawn earlier. Among the runaways, we find restless, bored young men and women, doubtless tired of the physical and psychological maltreatment suffered on small, rural farms or from abusive mistresses in the city. Their clothing reflected the deprived existences they led on the frontier or in the city. Clearly fugitives hoped to exchange their buckskin britches and tow cloth shirts for sailors' uniforms or finer, urban dress. Those dreams came closest to reality during the American Revolution.

Slave flight quickened during the War for Independence. Whether inspired by political debate, inspired by abolitionist appeals of the Society of Friends, or opportunistically following the warring armies, slaves fled their masters in greater numbers than ever before. Unlike previous eras, government and military authorities actually sanctioned flight. Governor Lord Dunmore of Virginia proclaimed in 1775 that all "indented servants and Negroes" willing to

Introduction *xxxiii*

serve His Majesty's armies to put down the American rebellion would receive freedom in exchange for service. Around New York, British commanders William Howe and Henry Clinton repeated versions of Dunmore's proclamation later in the war. Americans could not make such open statements and retain unity with southern colonies, but many blacks understood or believed that military service in the Patriot army mandated emancipation. In a very few cases, they were correct.

Beyond official calls, the war provided cover for fugitives. In this collection, 288 or forty-two per cent of the 675 notices occurred between 1775 and 1783, nearly half as many as in the previous sixty years. A greater number of women fled their masters and mistresses during the war than in the previous six decades; of the 650 male fugitives listed between 1716 and 1783, 250 or thirty-nine per cent escaped in the tumult of the war. A glance at the timing of flight further shows the emancipating effect of the war. Generally slaves left their masters in the warmer months, avoiding wintry exposure. During the revolution, however, as the British occupants of Philadelphia and New York sought soldiers, foragers, wagoners, and servants, slaves fled throughout the year; eighty-four or forty percent of runaways during the war absconded between October and March. Slaves also fled from Loyalist and British masters. Servants and military support workers decamped whenever they chose.[48]

During the American Revolution, slave flight became universal. In the American South, tens of thousands of fugitives followed armies, formed their own battalions, and practiced a guerilla war against the slavocracy.[49] The British occupied New York City throughout the war and used it as a headquarters; after the defeat of Lord Cornwallis at Yorktown, black refugees flooded north to the city. In 1782 alone, over two thousand fugitives arrived from southern ports to join hundreds of blacks who fled across the Hudson River or from Long Island, creating the largest black community which had ever existed in the city. In addition to the 314 slaves listed in the advertisements, hundreds more escaped into the city, and were later registered as part of the black exodus to Nova Scotia. In all, the 3,000 former slaves and free blacks who left New York with the British took part in the largest single flight by chattel slaves in American history.[50]

Two runaways symbolized the military and political transformations of the black American Revolution. Titus, who escaped from John Corlis on November 8, 1775 joined Lord Dunmore's famous Ethiopian Regiment in Virginia and later returned to the New York region to become Colonel Tye, leading an interracial guerilla force in several battles, and impressing Americans and British alike with his leadership and courage.[51] Adam, advertised by David Cowell, in early 1783 declared himself free and debated his status with his former master in a remarkable series of newspaper articles. The public debate began after Cowell advertised Adam for sale as an "able-bodied Negro man," with excellent skills as a manager of horses. In a succeeding issue of the *New Jersey Gazette*, Adam challenged Cowell's ownership, arguing that he had been promised his freedom. The extraordinary debate raged on for a number of weeks; our notice is a part of the legal battle between the two, which ended only after Cowell's death just before Christmas, 1783. Perhaps, as Cowell claimed, Adam was merely a tool of "quaking authors," but what is significant is that revolutionary rhetoric provoked direct defiance by the slave in print.[52]

Slavery did not end in New York and New Jersey immediately after the American Revolution. The two states with the largest number of African Americans north of the Chesapeake pursued a halting process of emancipation. In state legislatures, political parties, societies and churches, free white men cautiously approached every step toward black freedom. Not until 1799 in New York and 1804 in New Jersey did the two states initiate gradual abolition, with newly-born slaves required to serve masters more than two decades without any compensation. New York did not finally extinguish slavery until 1827; New Jersey transformed remaining slaves to indentured servants in 1846, but slavery actually did not cease in the state until passage of the Thirteenth Amendment in 1865.

Introduction *xxxv*

As this painfully slow process unfolded, lawmakers debated the end of slavery in the legislature; societies and churches campaigned against human bondage. Black churches and societies were especially diligent in their efforts. Throughout the lengthy process however, many African American slaves used methods honed during the colonial period and simply ran away from their masters and slavery. Shane White, chronicler of the close of slavery in New York during the early national period, has counted 1,232 fugitives in a partial survey of newspapers between 1771 and 1805. White notes that, allowing for population differences, the average of thirty-five runaway slaves in New York surpasses the frequencies uncovered in studies of black fugitives in the South.[53] By fusing White's research with the sizable evidence in this volume, we can discern an ageless tradition of slave protest and action against bondage.

Despite the rapid decline of slavery in the two states in the 1820s, blacks in the two states, trapped in the receding shadow of gradual emancipation, used flight to secure freedom owned by an increasing number of African Americans. Astonishingly, fugitive slave notices appeared in Monmouth County, New Jersey as late as 1840 when Daniel Conover of Middletown, advertised the flight of two slave brothers, Aaron and Abram,[54] an indication of how flight remained a popular method for seizing freedom for northern blacks long after the American Revolution. During the colonial era and during the American Revolution, the self-emancipated slaves, who pretended to be free, and whose stories appear in the pages that follow, blazed the trails which their descendants like Aaron and Abram would follow.

Notes

* In addition to the runaway slave advertisements the collection includes sixteen sheriffs' detention notices of suspected runaways, two notices by private individuals, two legal notices, and ten advertisements for fugitive black indentured servants.

[1]. "Eighteenth-Century Slaves as Advertised by their Masters," *Journal of Negro History* 1 (1916), 163-216.

[2]. For quote see Peter H. Wood, *Black Majority: Negroes in Colonial South Carolina from 1670 through the Stono Rebellion.* (New York, 1974), 239. For comments see Paul Lovejoy, "Fugitive Slaves: Resistance to Slavery in the Sokoto Caliphate," in Gary Y. Okihiro, *In Resistance:Studies in African, Caribbean, and Afro-American History* (Amherst, Mass., 1986), 71-4. For comment on timing of flight see Barbara Jeanne Fields, *Slavery and Freedom on the Middle Ground: Maryland during the Nineteenth Century* (New Haven, Ct., 1985), 16. For an opposing opinion see Gerald Mullin, *Flight and Rebellion: Slave Resistance in Eighteenth Century Virginia* (New York, 1972), 192n.

[3]. John K. Thornton, *Africa and Africans in the Making of the Atlantic World, 1400-1680* (New York, 1992), 272-74; Raymond and Alice Bauer, "Day-to-Day Resistance to Slavery," *Journal of Negro History* 27 (1942), 388-420.

[4]. For questions of style see Shane White, *Somewhat More Independent: The End of Slavery in New York City, 1770-1810* (Athens, Ga., 1991), 185-207 and Jonathan Prude, "To Look Upon the 'Lower Sort': Runaway Ads and the Appearance of Unfree Laborers in America, 1750-1800," in *Journal of American History* 78 (1991), 124-60. For personality see Michael Mullin, *Africa in America: Slave Acculturation and Resistance in the American South and the British Caribbean, 1736-1831* (Urbana, Il., 1992) and Freddie Lee Parker, *Running for Freedom: Slave Runaways in North Carolina, 1775-1840* (New York, 1993), 123-73.

[5]. Wood, *Black Majority*, 240.

[6]. For the 1741 conspiracy see T. J. Davis, ed., *The New York Conspiracy by Daniel Horsmanden*, (New York, 1971); for enumeration of acts of violence see Graham Hodges, *Root and Branch: African-Americans in New York and East-Jersey, 1613-1863*, forthcoming.

[7]. For a general overview of slavery under the Dutch see Joyce D. Goodfriend, " Burghers and Blacks: The Evolution of a Slave Society at New Amsterdam," *New York History* 59 (1978), 125-144.

8. James G. Lydon, "New York and the Slave Trade, 1700-1774," *William and Mary Quarterly*, 3rd ser., 35 (1978), 375-95. For character of slaves from islands see Orlando Patterson, *The Sociology of Slavery: An Analysis of the Origins, Development, and Structure of Negro Slaves Society in Jamaica* (London, 1967), 113-32, 160-99; Hilary Beckles, *White Servitude and Black Slavery in Barbados, 1627-1715* (Knoxville, Tenn., 1989); David Barry Gaspar, *Bondsmen and Rebels, A Study of Master-Slave Relations in Antigua with Implications for Colonial British America* (Baltimore, Md., 1985).

9. For analysis of the social changes in Africa and their effects see, among others, J.K. Flynn, *Asante and its Neighbors, 1700-1807* (Chicago, Il., 1971), 20-44 and Joseph C. Miller, *Way of Death, Merchant Capitalism and the Angolan Slave Trade, 1730-1830* (Madison, Wis., 1989).

10. For population figures see Appendix, I, table 3 and Peter O. Wacker, *Land & People: A Cultural Geography of Preindustrial New Jersey Origins and Settlement Patterns*, (New Brunswick, N.J., 1975), 200-01.

11. A. Leon Higgenbotham, *In the Matter of Color, Race & the American Legal Process: The Colonial Period* (New York, 1978), 115-116 and *Minutes of the Common Council of the City of New York, 1675-1776*, 8 vols., New York, 1905), I, 86-6, 93, 139, 223-4, 277.

12. *Colonial Laws of New York from the Year 1664 to the Revolution*. 5 vols. (Albany, N.Y, 1894-96) I, 157-158, 582-584, 880; Edgar McManus, *History of Negro Slavery in New York* (Syracuse,N.Y., 1968), 80-82; McManus, *Black Bondage in the North* (Syracuse, N.Y., 1973), 83-84; Douglas Greenberg, *Crime and Law Enforcement in the Colony of New York, 1691-1776* (Ithaca, NY, 1976), 33, 46; Herbert Scofield Cooley, *A Study of Slavery in New Jersey* (Baltimore, 1986), 32-35; Clement Alexander Price, *Freedom Not Far Distant, A Documentary History of Afro-Americans in New Jersey* (Newark, N.J., 1980), 1-15.

13. David E. Narrett, *Inheritance and Family Life in Colonial New York City* (Ithaca, N.Y., 1992), 188.

14. David Steven Cohen, *The Dutch-American Farm* (New York, 1992). For discussion of the significance of slaves as wealth see Narrett, *Inheritance and Family Life*, 52-65 and Graham R. Hodges, *African-Americans in Monmouth County, New Jersey, 1784-1860* (Lincroft, N.J., 1992).

15. For effects of scattering see Fields, *Slavery and Freedom*, 28-32.

16. For gangs see Davis, *New York Conspiracy*, xiii, xv, 67, 93. For discussion of tendency of runaways to form gangs see Philip J.

Schwarz, *Twice Condemned: Slaves and the Criminal Laws of Virginia, 1705-1865* (Baton Rouge, La., 1988), 66-67, *passim*.

[17]. For concentrations see Thomas J. Archdeacon, *New York City, 1664-1710 Conquest and Change* (Ithaca, N.Y., 1976), 89-89; Thelma J. Foote, "Black Life in Colonial Manhattan, 1664-1786," Ph.D. diss, Harvard University, 1992, 78-82.

[18]. For use of slaves as artisans and domestics see Gary B. Nash, *The Urban Crucible: Social Change, Political Consciousness, and the Origins of the American Revolution* (Cambridge, Mass., 1979), 108-09. For sailors see William Jeffrey Bolster, "African-American Seamen: Race, seafaring work, and the Atlantic Maritime culture, 1750-1860," Ph.D. diss., Johns Hopkins University, 1991.

[19]. For Stoffels see *New-York Gazette*, June 24, 1734. For full list of skills see Appendix 1, table 6.

[20]. For discussion of "songsters" see Paul Oliver, *Songsters and Saints Vocal Traditions on Race Records.* (New York, 1984), 22-25. The frequency of fiddlers in a black population was not unusual. In the South, Sterling A. Stuckey argues, fiddlers constituted one out of every ten slaves and were essential to black music and dance traditions. See Sterling A. Stuckey, *Slave Culture Nationalist Theory & the Foundations of Black America* (New York, 1987), 18, 21, 107, 370 n159. See also Mullin, *Flight and Rebellion*, 93.

[21]. *The New-York Gazette*, October 1, 1745.

[22]. For English newspapers see Daniel Meaders, *Fugitive Slaves and Indentured Servants before 1800* (New York, 1993), 7-8. For definition of "hue and cry," see Julius Goebel and T. Raymond Naughton, *Law Enforcement in Colonial New York, A Study in Criminal Procedure (1664-1776)* (New York, 1944), 421.

[23]. For full text of these and following hues and cries, see Appendix 2. See also *State Library Bulletin History, #2, May 1899: Colonial Records of New York, General Entries, 1664-1665* (Albany, 1899), 122. For other hues and cries see Peter Christoph, et. al. eds, *The Andros Papers 1674-1688: Files of the Provincial Secretary of New York During the Administration of Governor Sir Edmund Andros, 1674-1688.* 3 vols. Syracuse, N.Y.: Syracuse University Press, 1989-1991. II, 189, 191-192, 200, 202, 204; III, 140-141, 440.

[24]. New York State Library Miscellaneous Manuscripts (NYSL Misc. Mss.), XXVIII, 127.

[25]. NYSL Misc. Mss. XXVIII, 129, 142; XXXVIII, 3; XXXV, 113.

[26]. NYSL Misc. Mss., XXXVI, 14.

[27]. For Jacob see *New York Mercury*, September 10, 1764; for Caesar see *Weekly Post-Boy*, August 30, 1756; for Quaco see *Pennsylvania Journal*, August 20, 1761. For other uses of iron collars see Harry,

Weekly Post-Boy, December 31, 1759 and Cyrus, *Weekly Post-Boy*, October 15, 1761.

28. For Lott see *Weekly Post-Boy*, October 15, 1750; for Jupiter Hazard, *Pennsylvania Gazette*, June 13, 1751; for Arnold see *Weekly Post-Boy*, November 20, 1760; for Nero and Pero see *Pennsylvania Gazette*, November 8, 21, 1765, *Weekly Post-Boy*, June 5, 1766.

29. For Benjamin Moore see *Weekly Post-Boy*, February 6, 1766; for Jenney see *The New York Journal*, January 12, 1775.

30. For Jem see *Pennsylvania Chronicle*, July 8, 1771; for Ben see *Weekly Post-Boy*, September 4, 1766; for Cate see *Weekly Post-Boy*, June 27, 1765.

31. For Bood see *Pennsylvania Gazette*, June 21, 1759; *Weekly Post-Boy*, January 7, 1763 and *Weekly Post-Boy*, December 25, 1766. Bood may have fled earlier. See *The Pennsylvania Gazette*, May 3, 1753 for a fugitive with a very similar description and name. For other fugitives with multiple escapes see the name index.

32. For Frank see *New York Journal or General Advertiser*, December 8, 1768. For Sampson see *Pennsylvania Journal*, January 28, 1752; for Arch see *Pennsylvania Chronicle*, October 8, 1770.

33. For picaresque proletariat see Peter Linebaugh, *The London Hanged Crime and Civil Society in the Eighteenth Century* (New York, 1992), 151-52. For indentured servants see Sharon V. Salinger, *"To Serve Well and Faithfully": Labor and Indentured Servants in Pennsylvania, 1682-1800*, (New York, 1987).

34. For Sam and Isaac Randall see *Pennsylvania Gazette*, October 31, 1745; for servants and slave see *Pennsylvania Journal*, October 4, 1770.

35. For man and woman see *Weekly Post-Boy*, July 5, 1756; for Ned and Mary see *Pennsylvania Gazette*, October 31, 1771; for Domingo and Mary Carey see *Weekly Post-Boy*, June 27, 1748.

36. Eugene D. Genovese, *From Rebellion to Revolution: Afro-American Slave Revolts in the Making of the Modern World* (Baton Rouge, La., 1979), 77.

37. For full accounting see Appendix I, table 4.

38. For Joe see *New York Gazette or Weekly Post-Boy*, June 26, 1766; for Claus, see *Weekly Post-Boy*, July 4, 1757; for Caesar see *Weekly Post-Boy*, December 5, 1765.

39. *Colonial Laws of New York*, 1:157; *New Jersey Archives*, 13:22; Cooley, *Slavery in New Jersey*, 32; McManus, *Black Bondage in the North*, 108-111.

40. John Romeyn Brodhead, comp; E.B. O'Callaghan and B. Fernow, eds. *Documents Relating to the Colonial History of the State of New York*, 15 vols. (Albany, N.Y., 1856-87), V, 637, 639, 674, 794, 965.

41. "Parish Transcripts, Folder 160, August 17, 1756, N-YHS; David Jones to Archibald Kennedy, August 15, 1757, Fort Neck, Long Island, Emmett Collection, NYPL.

42. For law on flight see "Parish Transcripts," Folder 156, April 1745, N-YHS.

43. For full totals see appendices 1 & 2. For similar conclusions in other colonies about the average age of runaways see Daniel E. Meaders, "South Carolina Fugitives as Viewed Through Local Colonial Newspapers with an Emphasis on Runaway Notices, 1732-1801," *Journal of Negro History*, 60 (1975), 288-320; Lathan Algerna Windley, A Profile of Runaway Slaves in Virginia and South Carolina from 1730-1787 (New York, forthcoming); and Billy G. Smith and Richard Wojtowicz, *Blacks Who Stole Themselves: Advertisements for Runaways in the Pennsylvania Gazette, 1728-1790* (Philadelphia, 1989), 12-13.

44. For full totals see Appendix 1, table 8.

45. Among the notices are 351 single English names, 45 full English names, 81 classical, 57 African, 47 biblical, 28 comic, 28 Dutch, 9 French, 4 Spanish and 62 unnamed slaves.

46. See Appendix 1, table 9.

47. *Ibid*; for Ralph see *Weekly Post-Boy*, December 18, 1758; for Scipio see *Weekly Post-Boy*, August 29, 1757.

48. For timing of flight see Appendix 1, table 5.

49. Sylvia Frey, *Water from the Rock: Black Resistance in a Revolutionary Age* (Princeton, N.J., 1991).

50. For discussion see Foote, "Black Manhattan," 341-92; for numbers see Graham Hodges, "Black Revolt in New York and the Neutral Zone: 1775-83," in Paul A. Gilje and William Pencak, eds. *New York in the Age of the Constitution* (Cranbury, N.J., 1992), 20-47.

51. For Titus see *Pennsylvania Gazette*, November 22, 1775; for Colonel Tye and other black loyalists see Hodges, "Black Revolt."

52. For Adam see *New-Jersey Gazette*, June 25, 1783. For an extensive discussion of the case, with a different conclusion than mine, see White, *Somewhat More Independent*, 117-19.

53. White, *Somewhat More Independent*, 140-41.

54. Hodges, *African-Americans in Monmouth County*, iii.

A Note on the Text

In general we have followed the original wording of the advertisements. We have retained the original spelling, punctuation, and capitalization. Occasionally we have made silent alterations of the spacing of the notices. Illegible words from the original advertisements are indicated by brackets, as are letters added for clarity. Newspaper sources and dates are indicated in the top of each notice; any other date is either the date of submission of the advertisement or an estimate of the date of the escape. New style dating is used throughout. The subject and name indexes refer to the case numbers at the beginning of each advertisement. The glossary defines many contemporary terms in the notices.

A Note on Colonial and Revolutionary Newspapers

New York's first newspaper, *The New-York Gazette* did not commence publication until 1725. New Jersey lacked a regular, weekly newspaper until 1777 although earlier efforts appeared in Woodbridge (*The Constitutional Currant*) in 1765 and in Bridgeton (*The Plain-Dealer*) in 1775. *The New-Jersey Gazette*, published in Burlington in 1777 was the state's first public journal. Before *The New-York Gazette*, local slave masters had to advertise in newspapers in other colonies or use the hue and cry method. The following list identifies titles used in this collection and offers an introduction to name changes. Although it is a fairly complete list of New York and New Jersey newspapers for the colonial period, it does not pretend to list all the Connecticut, Massachusetts, and Pennsylvania journals. Nor is it a complete list of the timing of name changes and publishers. Interested students should consult Henry S. Parson, *A Check List of American Eighteenth Century Newspapers in the Library of Congress* (Washington: Government Printing Office, 1936) or Clarence Brigham, *History and Bibliography of American Newspapers, 1690-1820,* 2 vols., (Worcester, Mass.: American Antiquarian Society, 1947) for fuller histories of colonial imprints.

Massachusetts

The *Boston News-Letter and the New England Chronicle*, 1704-1763. Succeeded by the *Massachusetts Gazette and the Boston News-Letter*, 1767-1768 and by the *Massachusetts Gazette* and the *Boston Post-Boy and Advertiser*, 1770-1775.

New Jersey

The New-Jersey Gazette (Burlington), 1777-1778. Removed to Trenton, 1778-1786.

The New-Jersey Journal (Chatham), 1779-1783.

The New-York Gazette; and the Weekly Mercury, (Newark, New Jersey), 1776.

The Political Intelligencer, and New-Advertiser, (Trenton) 1783-1785.

New York

The New-York Evening Post, 1744-1752.

The New-York Gazette, 1725-1744. Succeeded by *The New-York Evening Post*.

The New-York Gazette, (Weyman's) 1759-1767. The newspaper was briefly discontinued during the Stamp Act Crisis of 1765.

The New-York Gazette: and the Weekly Mercury, 1768-1783. A continuation of the *New-York Mercury*, beginning with the new title February 1, 1768.

The New-York Gazette: or, The Weekly Post-Boy, 1747-1759. Continuation of *The New-York Weekly Post-boy*. Changed name to *Parker's New York Gazette; or, The Weekly Post-Boy* in 1759, then back to *The New-York gazette; or, The Weekly Post-Boy* from 1762 to 1773. For the complicated publishing history of this newspaper in the 1760s see Brigham, *History and Bibliography*, I: 635-36.

The New-York Journal, or, The General Advertiser, 1766-1776. Revived in *The New-York Journal and the General*

Advertiser (Kingston, New York), 1776-1777. Moved to Poughkeepsie, New York and revived, May 11, 1778.

The New-York Mercury, 1752-1768. Continued as *The New-York Gazette: and the Weekly Mercury*.

The New-York Packett, and the American Advertiser, (Fishkill, New York), 1777-1783. Moved back to New York City, November 13, 1783.

The New-York Weekly Journal, 1733-1751.

New York Weekly Post-Boy, 1743-1747.

Rivington's New-York Gazetteer; or The Connecticut, Hudson's-River, New Jersey, and Quebec weekly advertiser, 1773-1777. Continued by *Rivington's New York Loyal Gazette*, 1777, and by *The Royal Gazette*, 1777-1783.

Royal American Gazette, 1777-1780.

Pennsylvania

American Weekly Mercury (Philadelphia), 1719-1749.

Pennsylvania Chronicle (Philadelphia), 1767-1774.

Pennsylvania Gazette (Philadelphia), 1728-1815.

Pennsylvania Journal, and the Weekly Advertiser (Philadelphia), 1742-1791.

Pennsylvania Packett (Philadelphia), 1771-1790.

Introduction to the Twenty-Fifth Anniversary Edition

This Introduction to the new edition of *"Pretends to Be Free"* reviews important new studies that affect our understanding and use of fugitive slave notices. The original Introduction retains its value as a guide to interpretations current in 1994, many of which hold their value today. In the quarter-century since the first publication of *"Pretends to Free,"* the study of slavery and black life in North America has undergone sizable improvement and taken numerous new directions. Several scholars have issued new collections of self-emancipation notices, greatly expanding their accessibility and knowledge about slavery and resistance. Antonio Bly, for example, has compiled examples of self-emancipation through flight in colonial Virginia and New England. Ed Baptist heads an ambitious plan to digitize all extant fugitive slave notices over two centuries into one database, a feat that would allow extraordinary detail and analysis about the self-emancipated.[1]

Scholars now link enslaved flight with major military events. Cassandra Pybus has shown the global dimensions of enslaved flight during the American Revolution, detailing how black loyalists migrated, under British protection, to Nova Scotia, Bermuda, Sierra Leone, Europe, and Australia and how many of them became permanent soldiers in the Imperial Army.[2] Pybus's study is part of a new, generally accepted understanding of the important role of enslaved blacks during the American Revolution. As historians connect the broad struggle for freedom between the American Revolution, the War of 1812, the Mexican-American War, and, ultimately, the Civil War, fugitive slave notices become all the more important as evidence of black resistance.[3]

Locating this collection of fugitive slave notices shows their renewed importance in national debates about slavery and freedom in American history. Ira Berlin's several books covering the vast impact of slavery and black life have instituted the importance of time and place in interpreting the African American experience. Within the context of time and place, Berlin has argued persuasively about the importance of the American Revolution and the impact of black self-emancipation through flight. Berlin's work, along with more regional studies, has illuminated the importance of chattel bondage in the northern colonies and states.[4]

Fugitive slave notices are now important for understanding how ordinary blacks resisted slavery and created their own brand of abolitionism. Manisha Sinha's massive reinterpretation of the history of abolition places the self-emancipated slave as the most important factor in the movement's eighteenth-century origins and development.[5]

While slavery created America's racial hierarchy, it was also about money. Scholars Ed Baptist, Walter Johnson, Sven Beckert, and Daina Rainy Berry have reconnected the histories of slavery and capitalism. Such studies naturally point with renewed interest to the values of the rewards for recapture of self-emancipated slaves.[6]

If those interpretations involve the external power of slavery, fugitive slave notices can also help us understand the internal dynamics of the master–slave relationship. One of the most perceptive and deeply researched analyses of a fugitive slave notice is David Waldstreicher's article, which later appeared as a chapter in his book *Runaway America: Benjamin Franklin, Slavery, and the American Revolution*. Focusing on the escaped bond man Charles Roberts, also known as German (notice #201 in this book), Waldstreicher emphasizes the importance of locality for using fugitive slave notices as evidence of "self-fashioning" by early American blacks. Fixing his attention on clothing, skills and trades, linguistic ability, and ethnic or racial identity found in hundreds of fugitive slave notices printed in Benjamin Franklin's famous newspaper the *Pennsylvania Gazette*, between 1729 and 1755, Waldstreicher moved far beyond simple calculations of these traits. Using collective biography at times or focusing on Charles Roberts, or German, Waldstreicher teased insights into black cultural resistance. Eschewing standard perceptions of runaways as positive resisters of bondage, Waldstreicher argued that many took on roles as tricksters or confidence men, by "pretending to be free." By pushing his research far beyond the words of the notice, Waldstreicher learned that John Holt, the noted colonial printer and Charles Roberts's or German's aggrieved owner, was not all he pretended to be. By looking closely at Holt's past commercial relations, Waldstreicher found that the printer was regarded as a debtor, a drunk, and a liar, many of the traits that the bitter master had ascribed to Charles Roberts. As I note in the Teacher's Guide, instructors should always investigate masters as well as the self-emancipated.[7]

Waldstreicher and others have benefited from the first modern publication in *"Pretends to Be Free"* of the runaway advertisement (#111) of the flight of Venture Smith in 1754 from his master, George Mumford of Fisher's Island. Venture Smith has become the subject of considerable interest among scholars for his narrative and his self-purchase, capitalist work ethic, and his extraordinary strength. In this complicated, rich notice, Venture fled from Mumford along with Joseph Heday, a white servant from Newark, and three other enslaved blacks. The group used a two-masted boat with plans for head for Mississippi, then part of Spanish West Florida, or to Native American country. In the advertisement, Venture is described as a "very tall fellow, 6 feet 2 inches high. thick square shoulders, large bon'd, marked in the face or scar'd with a knife in his own country." He wore or had with him an assortment of clothing, including several jackets, pants, coats, and shoes. This advertisement reveals interracial escapes and extraordinary means and plans, and it offers an introduction to one of the most famous self-emancipated enslaved people before Frederick Douglass.[8]

The most important book published in the past quarter-century about self-emancipation through flight is the collaboration by John Hope Franklin and Loren Schweninger, *Runaway Slaves: Rebels on the Plantation*. Looking at a vast array of fugitive slave advertisements and court records drawn from across the antebellum slave states, Franklin and Schweninger drew many conclusions useful for interpreting this volume. They found, for example, that many enslaved people sought refuge in cities, just as many detailed in this book gained freedom by flight to New York City. The authors of *Runaway Slaves* chronicled how enslaved people in flight often fled to nearby spots, sometimes adjacent to their plantation, before moving much greater distances. They often conspired and collaborated, were helped by free blacks and sympathetic whites, and found work to support themselves while securing their liberty. Many runaways, as did those in this volume, fled after sales broke up their families and were capable of violence as a means to maintain the newfound freedoms. Belying older arguments that southern enslaved people rarely fled because of police-state governance, Franklin and Schweninger uncovered sizable rates of success. Overall, the authors concluded that flight had a powerful impact on slavery and distorted national politics, an argument that is commonly accepted today.[9]

What Franklin and Schweninger and other scholars have demonstrated is that collections such as this one are even more valuable for anyone interested in enslaved resistance and in the quotidian worlds of early America. They are, as the Teacher's Guide will tell, highly useful for teaching about early Americans.

Notes

[1]. Antonio Bly and Tamla Haywood, eds., *Escaping Servitude: A Documentary History of Runaway Servants in Eighteenth-Century Virginia*, second edition (Lanham, Md.: Lexington Books, 2016); Bly, *Escaping Bondage: A Documentary History of Runaway Slaves in Eighteenth-Century New England, 1700–1789* (Lanham, Md.: Lexington Books, 2012); Daniel Meaders, ed., *Advertisements for Runaway Slaves in Virginia, 1801–1820* (New York: Routledge, 1997); Freddy L. Parker, *Running for Freedom: Slave Runaways in North Carolina, 1775–1840* (New York: Routledge, 1993). For Baptist's database, see http://freedomonthemove.org. A sample of other useful online databases includes the Texas Runaway Slave Project (http://digital.sfasu.edu/cdm/landingpage/collection/RSP); the National Humanities Center Resource Toobox (http://nationalhumanitiescenter.org/pds/maai/enslavement/text8/virginiarunawayads.pdf); and the Colonial Williamsburg Transcription of Virginia Gazette Runaway Advertisements (http://www.history.org/history/teaching/runaway.cfm).

[2]. Cassandra Pybus, *Epic Journeys of Freedom: Runaway Slaves of the American Revolution and Their Global Quest for Liberty* (Boston: Beacon Books, 2007).

[3]. Graham Russell Hodges, *Root & Branch: African Americans in New York and East Jersey, 1613–1863* (Chapel Hill: University of North Carolina Press, 1999), chapter 5; Hodges, *Slavery and Freedom in the Rural*

North: African Americans in Monmouth County, New Jersey, 1660–1865 (Madison: Madison House Books, 1997); Gary B. Nash, *The Forgotten Fifth: African Americans in the Age of Revolution* (Cambridge, Mass.: Harvard University Press, 2006); Douglas R. Egerton, *Death or Liberty: African Americans and Revolutionary America* (New York: Oxford University Press, 2011); Woody Holton, *Forced Founders: Indians, Debtors, Slaves, and the Making of the American Revolution in Virginia* (Chapel Hill: University of North Carolina Press for the Omohundro Institute of Early American History and Culture, 1999); Alan Taylor, *The Internal Enemy: Slavery and War in Virginia, 1772–1832* (New York: W. W. Norton, 2013); Steven Hahn, *The Political Worlds of Slavery and Freedom* (Cambridge, Mass.: Harvard University Press, 2009), chapters 1 and 2; Ira Berlin, *The Long Emancipation: The Demise of Slavery in the United States* (Cambridge, Mass.: Harvard University Press, 2015); Sarah E. Cornell, "Citizens of Nowhere: Fugitive Slaves and Free African Americans in Mexico, 1833–1857," *Journal of American History* 100:1 (September 2013), 351–374.

[4]. Ira Berlin, *Many Thousands Gone: The First Two Centuries of Slavery in North America* (Cambridge, Mass.: Harvard University Press, 1999); Berlin, *Generations of Captivity: A History of American Slaves* (Cambridge, Mass.: Harvard University Press, 2004); Berlin, *The Making of African America: The Four Great Migrations* (New York: Viking, 2010); Berlin, *The Long Emancipation.*

[5]. Manisha Sinha, *The Slave's Cause: A History of Abolition* (New Haven, Conn.: Yale University Press, 2016); For an important step toward this interpretation see David Brion Davis, *The Problem of Slavery in the Age of Emancipation* (New York: Knopf, 2014), 232–248.

[6]. Edward E. Baptist, *The Half Has Never Been Told: Slavery and the Making of American Capitalism* (New York: Basic Books, 2014); Sven Beckert, *Cotton: A Global History* (New York: Knopf, 2014); Beckert and Seth Rockman, eds., *Slavery's Capitalism: A New History of American Development* (Philadelphia: University of Pennsylvania Press, 2016); Walter Johnson, *River of Dark Dreams: Slavery and Empire in the Cotton Kingdom* (Cambridge, Mass.: Harvard University Press, 2013); Daina Ramey Berry, *The Price for Their Pound of Flesh: The Value of the Enslaved, from Womb to Grave, in the Building of a Nation* (Boston: Beacon Press, 2007).

[7]. David Waldstreicher, "Reading the Runaways: Self-Fashioning, Print Culture, and Confidence in Slavery in the Eighteenth-Century Mid-Atlantic," *William and Mary Quarterly*, 56: 2 (April 1999), 243–272, later adapted as a chapter in his *Runaway America: Benjamin Franklin, Slavery, and the American Revolution* (New York: Hill & Wang, 2005).

[8]. See Waldstreicher, "Reading the Runaways"; the essays in James Brewer Smith, ed., *Venture Smith and the Business of Slavery* (Amherst:

University of Massachusetts Press, 2010); Chandler B. Saint et al., *Making Freedom: The Extraordinary Life of Venture Smith* (Middletown, Conn.: Garnet Books, 2009); Robert E. Desroches, "Not Fade Away": The Narrative of Venture Smith, an African American in the Early Republic," *Journal of American History*, 84:1 (1997), 40–66; and the chapter on Smith in Russell Shorto, *Revolution Song, A Story of American Freedom* (New York: W. W. Norton, 2017).

[9]. John Hope Franklin and Loren Schweninger, *Runaway Slaves: Rebels on the Plantation* (New York: Oxford University Press, 1999).

Teacher's Guide to *"Pretends to Be Free"*

This guide is intended to offer suggestions to instructors wanting to help students understand the daily worlds of early America and human beings beyond such widely known figures as George Washington, Benjamin Franklin, and Thomas Jefferson. One of the first concerns is learning what early Americans, especially enslaved African Americans, looked like. These fugitive slave notices provide valuable insight to a seemingly intractable problem, an absence of images. Instructors hoping to teach their students what ordinary people looked like in early America in the times before the advent of photography have little with which to work. There exist very few images of enslaved colonial whites or of African Americans, other than a handful of images of enslaved people regarded as kitchen members of wealthy plantation families or, exceptionally rarely, images of such enslaved narrators as Olaudah Equiano or the recently discovered image of Ayuba Suleiman Diallo. Depictions of ordinary, identifiable enslaved people are almost unknown. One of the most interesting re-creations of enslaved people are included in the pictorial section of Bernard Bailyn's book *Voyagers to the West*.[1]

Lacking direct imagery. scholars have mined, as the Introduction to the first edition of this book does, fugitive slave notices for data telling of the enslaveds' clothing, hairstyles, body marks, speech patterns, skills, and even personalities. These verbal snapshots may be used credibly. Masters seeking recapture of their escaped bond people had little incentive to mislead about appearance or skills. In this collection, the most commonly listed skill was fiddling, a talent that allowed such musicians to earn cash at taverns, at docksides, or at country gatherings. In the case of more practical skills, instructors may compare enslaved work at blacksmithing, servant, carpentry, and the like with their masters' zeal to recapture them. Their comments about enslaved personality may lead to lively classroom discussions about the master's perceptions and the enslaved person's need to disguise his or her true feelings. Instructors may suggest comparison of any number of the notices to uncover similarities in appearance or, in the master's or mistress's sense of betrayal, that a person they often perceived as a member of their family would escape their grasp.

Once instructors and students have become proficient with identifying the enslaved's listed traits in appearance, personality, or skills, classes can consider creating collective portraits of the self-emancipated. Instructors may consult the subject index of this volume to find multiple examples of self-emancipated people with similar traits. There are, for example, thirteen different notices regarding sailors; nine describing people who stutter; and twelve who bore African body marks, including scarification, ear holes, and filed teeth. While male escapers from slavery dominate the colonial period, it is worth noticing that women constitute a sizable fraction of those from the era of the American Revolution and ask what that means.

Each of the notices announces a reward for the return of the escaped enslaved people. There was no standard currency in colonial or revolutionary America. Masters promised rewards in Spanish dollars, in English pounds or shillings, and, during the Revolution, in Continental dollars. Translating these currencies into modern money is very difficult because of massive differences in economic and social standards and the availability of money (many Americans rarely if ever saw actual coins). Even though questions about relative value are very common from visitors to Colonial Williamsburg, for example, there are few if any reliable guides. John McCusker's book *How Much Is That in Real Money? A Historical Price Index for Use as a Deflator of Money Values in the Economy of the United States* is useful, though older. Instructors may find it still useful to discuss in notice #175 in 1759 why several masters were willing to pay £20 for the return of Bood, but only £5 for Tom, who escaped at the same time. It would be useful as well to discuss who would chase escaped slaves and how those who sought to recapture self-emancipated people shaped racial hierarchies in early America.[2]

One of the most vigorous areas of recent scholarship concerns the Underground Railroad (UGRR), which is also one of the most popular of public histories. While scholars have been reluctant to extend arguments about the UGRR to eras before the antebellum period, still increasingly they uncover evidence of it during the constitutional and early national period. Acclaimed historian Eric Foner has argued that the UGRR may not have been a "highly organized system with tunnels, codes, and clearly defined routes and stations" but rather was an "interlocking system of local networks, each of whose fortunes rose and fell over time," and which helped a substantial number of self-emancipated blacks find freedom in the free states and Canada.[3] Instructors can ask what constituted the pre-history of the UGRR. Page 346 of the index to this book indicates numerous fugitives who ran away as couples, with Native Americans, with other blacks, with white indentured servants, or with other whites. UGRR survivors were known to change their names during flight to avoid detection; there are over twenty-five examples in the index for the colonial and revolutionary periods. Traditional views of UGRR operators include benevolent members of the Society of Friends, Congregationalists, Presbyterians, or other religious groups with anti-slavery attitudes. During the colonial and revolutionary periods, these faiths had not yet moved to add UGRR activism to their anti-slavery beliefs. Masters in early America regarded all enablers of fugitive slaves dimly. Captains of sea vessels or mine operators were routinely warned against "harboring" or employing fugitive slaves. How captains and mine owner fit into the roles of UGRR operators is a good question for class discussion. Similarly, the goals and destinations of fugitives are worthy of discussion and written assignments. What did it mean for a fugitive to seek refuge "with the enemy" or to go back to their families? Note that several sought refuges in the "swamps." Were these the beginnings of Maroon or independent, isolated communities of the self-emancipated?

    David Waldstreicher's profound analysis of advertisement #201 could provoke similar classroom investigations of the people mentioned in the fugitive slave notices in this edition. By googling personal names in the index, or by using such databases as America's Historical Newspapers or Newspaper.com, students might learn, for example, that David Ogden, Esquire, who advertised for the return of Bristol in notice #109, dated December 3, 1753, was a member of the colonial New Jersey Supreme Court and was later a loyalist in the American Revolution, fled to Britain after the war, and later returned to America. Such a connection will show students how slave ownership was evident in the highest levels of colonial law.

Instructors may find this last suggestion for classroom use too controversial, but I include it here because of the artist's creative employment of fugitive slave notices. In 1993, Glenn Ligon, a famed African American artist often concerned with questions about black identity and particularly masculinity, asked a number of his friends to use the common template for early American fugitive slave notices and to supply their own description of him in the body of the notice. Ligon then created ten such images and issued them in a portfolio. The Metropolitan Museum of Art, the Museum of Modern Art, and the Whitney Museum in New York City; the Walker Museum in Minneapolis; and the Harvard University Art Museums in Cambridge, Massachusetts, are just a few of the noted archives that have made Ligon's portfolio part of their permanent collections. MoMA in particular often exhibits the entire group. Harvard University Art Museums graciously allowed reproduction of one of the notices. Teachers may use Ligon's art as a means to discuss the contemporary relevance of fugitive slave notices. It may well be that an artist's creative freedom can conflict with classroom realities, but Ligon's work is too fascinating not to mention here.

Ligon's work, the constant use of fugitive slave notices in histories of early America and their signal importance in major works on slavery, indicates their continued relevance. I have often used them in classrooms at my college and found students to be fascinated by the information included in these succinct, evocative word-portraits of the enslaved of early America. I encourage you to do the same.

Ran away, Glenn Ligon. He's a shortish broad-shouldered black man, pretty dark-skinned, with glasses. Kind of stocky, tends to look down and turn in when he walks. Real short hair, almost none. Clothes non-descript, something button-down and plaid, maybe, and shorts and sandals. Wide lower face and narrow upper face. Nice teeth.

African American Artist Glenn Ligon's modern appropriation of a runaway advertisement for a self-emancipated man subverts the master's power over the enslaved's appearance, provides more ability to self-identify, and makes the advertisement more a freedom notice than a wanted poster for someone who had criminally escaped from slavery. (Glenn Ligon, Ran away, Glenn Ligon. 1993. Harvard Art Museums/Fogg Museum, Margaret Fisher Fund, 2008.95.9; Imaging Department © President and Fellows of Harvard College)

Notes

1. For a good, recent discussion of available images, see Alex Bontemps, ed., "Representing Slavery: A Roundtable Discussion in *Common-place.org*" at http://www.common-place-archives.org/vol-01/no-04/slavery/bontemps.shtml; for creative imagery, see Bernard Bailyn, *Voyagers to the West: A Passage in the Peopling of America on the Eve of the Revolution* (New York: Knopf, 1986).

2. John McCusker, *How Much Is That in Real Money? A Historical Price Index for Use as a Deflator of Money Values in the Economy of the United States* (1992; reprinted, 1993; second edition, revised, 2001, American Antiquarian Society). A good guide to translating values across currencies can be found at https://coins.nd.edu/ColCurrency/CurrencyIntros/IntroValue.html.

3. Eric Foner, *Gateway to Freedom: The Hidden History of the Underground Railroad* (New York: W. W. Norton, 2015). See also Manisha Sinha, *The Slave's Cause: A History of Abolition* (New Haven, Conn.: Yale University Press, 2016), 421–461, for a full discussion of the politics of fugitive slave abolitionism.

Foreword

Twenty-five years ago, the first publication of Graham Russell Gao Hodges and Alan Brown's co-edited volume *"Pretends to Be Free": Runaway Slave Advertisements from Colonial and Revolutionary New York and New Jersey* helped initiate and accelerate an important trend in the study of African American history. This collection of 662 newspaper advertisements, placed by enslavers who wanted to recapture the freedom-seeking enslaved people who had escaped from them, wasn't the only such collection. At least ten such volumes appeared between 1983 and 2015.[1]

"Pretends to Be Free" is one of the most carefully edited, patiently produced of these editions. Its editors recorded the available documentation on fugitives from enslavement in New York and New Jersey, whether their pursuers placed advertisements in those colonies' newspapers or in those of neighboring colonies.

For instance, advertisement #321, appearing in a New York City newspaper on August 22, 1768, asks readers to help Hendrick Colyer of New Jersey capture a "a Negro Fellow named Ishmael, by trade a Blacksmith." Each such advertisement opens a perspective, a window, on a narrative of resistance: one that the enslaver who placed the ad was trying to control. Yet control of this story had (at least temporarily) slipped out of their grasp—otherwise there would be no ad.

The stories, or pieces of stories, found here breathe and bubble with real detail about the people who sought to seize some freedom. Ishmael, for instance, was "much pitted with the Small Pox, Has a blemish on one eye." And the most interesting details were not physical—he was also "a great fid[d]ler," who not only made magic with music but was "often shewing sleight of hand tricks." We get at his relationships: He "has a Squaw for a wife"; and of his history—he had toiled in the ironworks near Middletown, New Jersey, hiring out with permission from his enslaver. From there, Colyer believed, Ishmael—perhaps with his wife—had headed toward Pennsylvania.

From the personal, to the collective, the advertisements can teach us things about freedom-seeking people—things that we could not otherwise learn. One particularly useful feature of this volume is the Appendices, which compile quantifiable and qualitative data about many of the fugitives. Such pieces of information reveal the way the enslaver kept track of only a few aspects of a whole person (age, skills, height)—specifically those which could affect the commodifiable value of human beings, ways to put a price on a person. But these pieces of information also are in most cases the only traces that remain of those enslaved individuals' lives. And such data points made their way onto the historical record because of these individuals' resistance. They wrote themselves into the record by fighting with their feet. Also helpful to the volume are the glossary and the two indices, as well as a Teacher's Guide.

The volume made, and now in this revised and reprinted version can make again, an important contribution to the history of resistance to slavery. Historians' works written in the 1970s and 1980s often emphasized culture and community as modes of protection and pushback against enslavers' attempts to bend and brutalize African people into mere commodities. Runaways, fugitives, freedom-seeking people—the men, women, and children advertised in *"Pretends to Be Free"* had communities and cultures, but they also acted as individuals. They risked all in their rebellion-by-movement against slavery, no matter the kind of freedom they sought. *"Pretends to Be Free"* thus reads well with the next generation of studies of black resistance to slavery/quests for freedom that has been emerging in the years since its publication—works like Stephanie Camp's *Closer to Freedom*, Marisa Fuentes' *Dispossessed Lives*, or Alex Byrd's *Captives and Voyagers*.

"Pretends to Be Free" also first appeared at a time when readers could find only a few histories of African slavery in the northern colonies. Many textbooks relegated northern slavery to a footnote, or little more than that. Students, even those who majored in history at the undergraduate level, could go through decades of schooling without even realizing that whites in the northern colonies had imported almost 27,000 enslaved Africans. Graham Hodges himself would soon publish *Root and Branch*, while scholars like Emma

Lapsansky, Gary Nash, Leslie Patrick-Stamp, Billy G. Smith, Graham White, Shane White, and others were even then producing innovative work on northern colonial- and Revolutionary-era slavery. Their projects built in turn on the earlier scholarship of historians like Lorenzo Greene. But in the years since the first edition of this volume appeared, new generations of work on northern colonial slavery have appeared. Scholars like Craig Wilder, Leslie Harris, Joanne Pope Melish, Antonio Bly, Nicole Maskiell, Simon Newman, Wendy Warren, Karen Clark-Pujara, and others make it impossible to ignore either slavery in the North, or African people's resistance to it.

As we try to understand the long-term impact of enslavement on the contemporary United States, it becomes more and more crucial to reckon with the fact that slavery existed in every one of the thirteen colonies. In most cases, if we reckon with the years between initial colonization and the Civil War, slavery existed for longer than did freedom. Just as important, as we try to understand the long-term impact of black resistance to racism, settler colonialism, and all of the other aspects of slavery's lives and afterlives, we also have to reckon with those who resisted slavery in the northern colonies—in particular the kinds of stories of freedom-seeking people we find here in *"Pretends to Be Free."*

Edward E. Baptist

Note

[1]. Billy G. Smith and Richard Wojtowicz, *Blacks Who Stole Themselves: Advertisements for Runaways in the Pennsylvania Gazette, 1728–1790.* Philadelphia: University of Pennsylvania Press, 1989; Daniel Meaders, *Advertisements for Runaway Slaves in Virginia, 1801–1820.* New York: Garland, 1997; Lathan A. Windley, *Runaway Slave Advertisements: A Documentary History from the 1730s to 1790.* 4 vols. Westport, Conn.: Greenwood Press, 1983; Freddie L. Parker, ed., *Stealing a Little Freedom: Advertisements for Slave Runaways in North Carolina, 1791–1840.* New York: Garland, 1994; Thomas Brown and Leah Sims, *Fugitive Slave Advertisements in the City Gazette: Charleston, South Carolina,*

1787–1797. Lanham, Md.: Lexington Books, 2015; Graham Russell Hodges and Alan Edward Brown, eds., *"Pretends to Be Free": Runaway Slave Advertisements from Colonial and Revolutionary New York and New Jersey.* New York: Garland, 1994; Antonio T. Bly, *Escaping Bondage: A Documentary History of Runaway Slaves in Eighteenth-Century New England, 1700–1789.* Lanham, Md.: Lexington Books, 2012.

Runaway Slave Advertisements

1. *The Boston Newsletter*, #641, July 23, 1716.

This is to give notice that on the 16th of July, 1716, Runaway from his Master, David Lyell, an Indian Man named Nim, he lately belonged to Mr. James Moore, he is about one and twenty years of Age and is a short broad shouldered Fellow his hair hath lately been cut off, he has a swelling on the back of his right hand, and can do something in the Carpenters trade, he hath with him two new shirts, a new wastecoat, and breeches of white course linnen, and the same of blew striped; a homespun Coat, wears a Hat, Shoes, stockings. 'Tis believed he endeavours to get on board some Vessel. Whoever takes up the said Indian in the Jerseys, and brings him to his said Master shall have forty shillings and charges and if in any other government Five pounds if they give but notice where his is, so that his Master may have him again. Direct to David Lyell in New-York or at Amboy in New-Jersey.

2. *The American Weekly Mercury* (Philadelphia), #153, November 15, 1722.

Runaway from William Yard of Trenton in West-Jersey, the Fifth Day of this Instant November, a Negroe Man named Fransh Manuel, but commonly called Manuel, of a pretty tall stature, and speaks indifferent English. He wears a dark coloured homespun coat, an Ozenbrig Jacket, old Leather breeches, Sheep-russet Stockings, new Shoes and an old Beveret hat. He pretended formerly to be a Freeman and had Passes; but he did belong to one John Raymond of Fairfield in New England and I bought him of said Raymond. And the said Negro boy has told since he has run away, That he found a Quantity of Ore for his Master, and that his Master had given him Free. Whoever takes up the said Negroe, secures him and brings him to Mr. William Bradford of New York, or to Mr. William Burge of Philadelphia or to his said Master at Trenton, shall have forty shillings Reward, beside all reasonable charges, paid by me, William Yard.

3. *The American Weekly Mercury*
   (Philadelphia), #190, August 1, 1723.

Runaway about the 15th of June last, from Gabriel Stelle of Shrewsbury, an Negro Man named Jack, of small stature, he had on an Osenbrigs shirt and a woollen shirt, a pair of Leather Breeches, a dark homespun Jacket, a dark Cloase bodied fashionable Coat with a brown Kersey Great-Coat, an Old Beaver hat, a pair of square toed shoes with wooden heels, he is a Madagascar Negro. Whoever takes up the said Negro and brings him to his said Master or to Issac Stelle in Allens Town, shall have two Pistoles as a Reward besides Reasonable Charges.

4. *The American Weekly Mercury*
   (Philadelphia), #239, July 9, 1724.

Runaway on the 9th instant from Alexander Morgan Pensawkin Creek, in the County of Glouster in West New Jersey, a servant Lad named Richard Boon, a well set full Fac'd short brown Hair, aged 18 years, also a Negroe boy named Cæsar, Aged about 10 years, they took a Wherry with two Sailes, the White Boy has on a homespun brown Kersey Coat, a felt Hat, and a Leather Jacket. Whosoever shall take up the said Lads and secure them, so that their Master may have them again, shall have 40 Shillings as a Reward for each and Reasonable Charges.

5. *The American Weekly Mercury*
   (Philadelphia), #249, September 17, 1724.

Runaway from the Plantation of Cornelius Van Horne on Rariton River a Malisgasco Negroe Man, named Tom, he is a black likely fellow, pretty Tall, a grave Look, has on a Homespun brown jacket, and lined the same, has brass Buttons.
   Whoever takes up the said Negroe and delivers him to his said Master Cornelius Van Horne, in New York or in

Amboy goal, shall have Three Pounds as a Reward plus reasonable charges.

6. *The American Weekly Mercury* (Philadelphia), #343, July 14, 1726.

Notice is hereby given, That there is come to the House of John Leonards at south River Bridge, near Amboy, in the Eastern Division of the Province of New Jersey, a Negroe Man, who was forced to the said House for want of Sustenance; he is a middle sized Man, talks no English or feigns that he cannot, he calls himself PoPaw, his teeth seem to be Fil'd or Whet Sharp; he will not tell his Masters Name. Whoever Ownes the said Negroe may have him from the said Leonard on coming or sending for, paying according to Reward (if any be) or if not, according to the Laws of this Province and also reasonably for his Diet 'till fetched.

7. *The American Weekly Mercury* (Philadelphia), #378, April 6, 1727.

There is in custody of William Nichols, Esq; High Sheriff of the County of Monmouth, a likely young Negroe man about 24 years old; he calls himself James, speaks little English and can given no account where he came from or who he belongs to. Any person that owns said Negro paying Charges may have him.

8. *The American Weekly Mercury* (Philadelphia), #386, June 1, 1727.

Run Away the 21st Day of May last, from James Leonard of Somerset in New Jersey, a Negroe Man named Will, aged about 26 years and has with him an old Lightish color'd Great Coat and Leather Breeches, and two Shirts and old pair of black and white Stockings and 'tis supposed that he has a Gun with him, he speaks good English. Whoever takes up the said Negroe and secures him so that his said Master may have him shall be well Rewarded, by said James Leonard.

9. *The American Weekly Mercury* (Philadelphia), #487, May 1, 1729.

These are to be given Notice that on the First Day of this Instant May, 1729, was taken up a Negroeman, about forty-three Years of Age and put into the Gaol at Burlington, for Stealing from Several persons sundry sorts of Goods; the Negroe Man saith he belongs to one Roger Mathews living in Baltimore County in Maryland, brother-in-law to one Edward Hall.

    N.B. The said Negroe man formerly belonged to Governeur Markham and was sold down at Maryland by Mr. Reneir, Attorney at Law.

10. *The American Weekly Mercury* (Philadelphia), #511, October 16, 1729.

Burlington, October 20, 1729. Broke out of the Gaol at Burlington, the 20th Day of October, Two Men. One named Aristoblus Christopher, about Thirty years of age, of a Swarthy Complexion, thick Brown Hair, about five feet and eight Inches high, Shipwright by Trade.

    The other a Malato and goes by the name of Malato John, about Forty Years of age about six Feet and two Inches high and well set, and smooth Fac'd, short Brown Hair, he pretends to be a Housecarpenter by Trade. Whosoever takes up the said Persons or either of them and bring them to Burlington shall have Forty Shillings Reward for Each and Reasonable charges paid by Thomas Hunlock.

Advertisements

11. *The New-York Gazette*, #238, May 18, 1730.

Ran Away, a Negro Man named Quash, from his master Cornelius DePeyster of New York City. The said Negro has thick lips, and has lost a foretooth. Whoever can take up said negro man and bring him to his Master, or secure him and give Notice, so that his Master can get him again, shall have *forty shillings* reward and all reasonable Charges.

12. *The New-York Gazette*, #239, May 25, 1730.

Run away from *Soloman Bates of Elizabeth-Town* a Negroe man named *Clause*, aged about 27 years old, has got with him a Homespun Coat of Linen and Wool, with Brass Buttons, an Ozenbrig Vest with black Buttons and Buttonholes, and an old striped vest, Leather Breeches, new homespun Worsted Stockings, black shoes with Buckles, he has a Hat and Cap and he can play upon the Fiddle and speaks English and Dutch. Whoever can take up the said Negroe and bring him to his said Master, or secure him and give Notice, so that his Master can have him again, shall have *reasonable satisfaction* besides all reasonable charges.

13. *The New-York Gazette*, #253, August 31, 1730.

Run Away last Tuesday two Negro Men, both branded RN on their shoulders; one remarkably scarrified over the forehead, clothed with trousers, The other with a coat and trousers. Whoever brings the said Negroes to Jason Vaughn in New-York, shall have thirty shillings and all reasonable charges paid.

14. *The New-York Gazette*, #329, January 30, 1732.

Run away about 10 o'clock Thursday last, from John Cannon, New York City, three Negroes with a sloop belonging to said Cannon, burthen about 35 tons. Whoever takes up and returns said Negroe Men and the Sloop shall receive Twenty Pounds and all reasonable Charges from
John Cannon.

15. *The New-York Gazette*, # 342, May 8, 1732.

Run Away from *Solomon Baites* of *Elizabeth Town* in New-Jersey, a Negro Man named Clauss, about 28 years old, but he sometimes calls himself Nicolas, he formerly belonged to *Daniel Bagley*. He has taken with him a grey Home spun Drugget Coat trim'd with Black, a homespun Kearsey Vest, a Pair of Leather Breeches with red Puffs and Shoes and Stockings, he can play on a Fiddle tolerable well, He is of a middle Stature. Whoever takes up the said Negro and give Notice, so that his Master can have him again, shall have *a reasonable reward* besides reasonable Charge. And all persons are hereby forbid to entertain said Negro as they will answer at the utmost Severity of the Law.

16. *The New-York Gazette*, #369, November 13, 1732.

Ran away from Joseph Reade of New York City, merchant, the 14th of November, 1732, a likely mullatto servant woman, named Sarah. She is about 24 years of age, and she has taken with her a callico Suit of Cloathes, a striped Satteen silk wastecoat, Two Homespun waste-Coates and Petty-coat; she is a handy Wench, can do all sorts of House-work, speaks good English and some Dutch. Whoever takes up the said Servant, and will bring her to her late Master, shall have five pounds as a Reward and all reasonable Charges paid.

17. *The New-York Gazette*, #415, October 1, 1733.

Ran away the 18th of August, 1733 from Jacobus Van Cortlandt, New York City, a Negro man slave named Andrew Saxon, a tall lusty fellow, is very black, walks stooping and somewhat lamish with his left leg; the thumb of his left hand is somewhat stiff by a wound he had in his hand; the shirts he had with him and on his back are marked with a Cross on the left breast; he professeth himself to be a Roman Catholic, speaks very good English, is a carpenter and a cooper by trade and has a Broad-Ax with him, a Two-foot rule and a Howell-hovel. He had on a pair of linnen or ozenbrig breeches, and an old coat, but 'tis uncertain what other Cloathes he has with him. Whoever takes up and secures the said Negro Man, and gives Notice to his said Master, so that he may be had again, shall have Forty Shillings if taken within Ten Miles of the City of New-York, and Three Pounds if further, as a Reward, and all reasonable Charges paid by   Jacob Van Cortlandt.

18. *The New-York Gazette*, #416, October 8, 1733.

Ran Away from Robert Pierson of Notingham near Trentown, a Negro Man, named Jack, a lusty stout well set Fellow, a little Pock-broken, aged 30 years: He had on when he went away, a dark brown straight bodied Coat with Brass buttons, a light coloured great Coat, two homespun Tow Shirts, two Pair of Drawers, a Pair of Orange coloured Stockings and indifferent Pair of Shoes, a good Felt Hat. Whoever shall take up the said Negro man, and secure him or bring him to his said Master, or given Notice to Mr. Samuel Bayard in New York, shall have Forty Shillings reward, besides all reasonable charges, per me. Robert Pierson.

19. ***The New-York Weekly Journal*, #21, June 10, 1734.**

Hackingsack, June 7, 1734.
RUN out of the Goal of the County of *Bergin* last Night, one *Jacob Powelse* of *Hackingsack*, aged 40 Years or thereabouts, middle Stature, Molatto Man, lame in one of his Finger, he had on when he went away a yellow Coat with old Buttons, and homespun Holland Westcoat and Bretches. Whoever takes up and secures the said Jacob Powelse so that he may be brought back to the Goal at Hackingsack, shall have 3 Pounds Reward paid by me
        Par. Parmyter, *Sheriff.*

20. ***The New-York Gazette*, #452, June 24, 1734.**

Runaway last Wednesday from Judith Vincent in Monmouth County in New Jersey an Indian Man, named Stoffels, speaks good English, about Forty years of age, he is a House Carpenter, a Cooper, a Wheelwright and is a good Butcher also. There is also two others gone along with him, one being half Indian and half Negro and the other a Mulatto about 30 years of age & plays upon the violin and has it with him. Whoever takes up & secures said Fellow so that he may be had again shall have forty shillings as a reward and all reasonable charges paid by the said Judith Vincent.
 N.B. It is supposed'd they are all going together in a Canow towards Connecticut or Rhode Island.

21. ***The New-York Weekly Journal*, #43, August 26, 1734.**

Run away from *Johanna Kelsall* of the City of *New-York*, a Negroe Man known by the Name of Johnsey here in Town, but writes his Name *Jonathan Stow*, about 25 Years of Age, of short Stature, bandy Legs, blubber Lips, yellow Complexion, his Hair is neither right Negro nor Indian, but between both, and pretty long, he had on when he went away a homespun Jacket, a pair of Trowsers, and a speckled Shirt.

Whoever takes up the said Negro and secures him, or brings him to his Mistress, shall have 40 Shillings Reward and all Reasonable Charges paid by me
Johanna Kelsall.

22. *American Weekly Mercury* **(Philadelphia), #773, October 24, 1734.**

Run away the 26 of June last, from Samuel Leonard of Perth Amboy in New Jersey, a thick short Fellow, having but one Eye, he is half Indian half Negro tho's as black as most Negroes; he had on when he went away a blue Coat; his name is Wan, he plays on the Fiddle and speaks good English and this country Indian. Any person bringing this said Fellow to his Master shall have Three Pounds reward with reasonable charges paid by Samuel Leonard.

23. *The New-York Weekly Journal,* **#100, October 6, 1735.**

Run away from Arent Bradt of Schinectady in the County of Albany, on Sunday the 28th of September last, a Negro Man, named William Smith, he is an indented Servant and no Slave; he is a pretty lusty well set Fellow, full fac'd, and in Colour like the Madagascar Negroes, speaks English, High and Low Dut[c]h, understands all Sorts of Husbandry Work, and something of the Trade of a Black-Smith; had on when he went away a Linnen Wastcoat and Breeches, homespun Stockings, and English Shoes, and carried with him a light coloured Frize Jacket, and a Pair of Linnen Breeches. Any Person that takes up the said Negro Man Servant, and secures so that his Master may have him again, shall have five Pounds Reward and all reasonable Charges.

24. *The New-York Gazette*, #523, October 27, 1735.

Ran Away from Zebulon Stout of *Somerset County*, a Negro Man named *Tom*, He is about Thirty-five years Old, and is a well set Fellow, but of a thin Visage. He speaks good English; he went away in a brown home-spun Vest lined with Orange coloured Shalune, an old Bever Hat, gray Yarn Stockins and New Shoes. This Negro is well known at Woodbridge and Elizabeth-Town. Whoever takes up the said Negro and gives notice to his Master, so that he can have him again, shall have Twenty Shillings Reward and all reasonable Charges paid them. Zebulon Stout.

25. *The New-York Weekly Journal*, #131, May 10, 1736.

Run away, 2d of this instant May a Servant Man named John Watson aged about 40 Years, is a short thick Man, fair Complexion, born near New-Castle on Delaware lately redeemed out of Bergin County Goal by Cornelius Wynkoop and Elizabeth Antony, storekeepers, of the said County, for a Considerable Sum of Money, he had on when he went away a Duroys Coat light brown, a Kersey Coat, dark Brown, with Brass Buttons, a Striped Holland Wastcoat and Britches of the same, wears a Wigg or Cap, is very subject to Drink, it is supposed that he has with him a Negro Man named Johnny a middle Sized slender Fellow, Pock broken, about 35 Years of Age, is a very good Cooper, speaks English, French and Dutch and can read and Write, had on an Iron Gray Great Coat, what other Cloath is uncertain, his Master's Name is Peter Valleau. There is also with them another Negro Fellow, named Cato, aged about 22 Years a likely Fellow——some thing taller than the above described and some thing thicker a Native of Madagascar, speaks good English and Dutch had on when he went away, a black homespun Coat with Brass Buttons, a striped homespun jacket and homespun Stockins. had with him 2 pair of new Shooes.

26. *The American Weekly Mercury* (Philadelphia), #933, November 10, 1737.

Ran-away the 3rd of this Inst. of November from Alexander Morgan of Waterford Township in Gloucester County in West New Jersey; a Negro Man named Cesar aged about 24 years, a tall slim Fellow with small leggs & Great Feet, had on when he went away a felt Hat, a Cotton Cap, a Homespun Coat with brass Buttons, a West-coat without sleeves, an Oznabrigs Shirt, Leather Breeches with Brass Buttons, a pair of worsted Stockings and a pair of yarn ones, two pair of peak'd toe'd Shoes; he took with him some Bedding in particular a new gray Blanket. He took a boat and went to Philadelphia, and ty'd the Boat to the backside of Anthony Morris's Wharf and is supposed he will Endeavour to get Aboard of some Vessel to go to Sea and pass for a free Negro.

Whoever takes up said Negro and secures him so that his master may have him again shall have Twenty Shillings Reward paid by Alexander Morgan.

N.B. All persons are hereby forewarn'd of Entertaining him. He ran away about a month before and had got in a Sailors dress in order to get aboard a Vessel to go as he said to Barbadoes.

27. *The New-York Gazette*, #634, December 19, 1737.

Ran away from John Bell, of New York City, carpenter, one Negro woman named Jenney, 14-15 years, born in *New York*, speaks English and some Dutch. She has a flat Nose, thick Lips, and full faced; had on when she went away, a Birds eyed Waistcoat and Pettycoat of a darkish colour, and a Callico Waistcoat with a large red flower, and a broad stripe, a Callico Pettycoat with small stripes and small red flowers. Whoever shall take up said Negro Wench and bring her to said John Bell, or secure her and give Notice, so that he can have her again, shall have *Three Pounds* as a Reward, and all reasonable Charges.

28. *The New-York Gazette*, #664, July 24, 1738.

Ran away from James Thompson of Piscattaway in New-Jersey, a lusty Madagascar man, of a yallowish Complexion, has a small Scar on his nose, and talks good English. He formerly belonged to Capt. *John Reid* of Monmouth County. He had on when he went away, a Flannel Shirt, and old torn Breeches. Whoever shall take up said Negro Man and convey him to his Master, or secure him and give Notice, so that his Master can have him again, shall have Twenty-Five Shillings, besides reasonable Charges, paid by James Thompson.

29. *The New-York Gazette*, #664, July 24, 1738.

Ran Away from John Hunt of Hopewell in the County of Hunterdon and Province of West-New-Jersey, on the 25th Day of this Instant *July*, a Negro Man named *Peet*, he had on when he went away, a Gray home-spun Coat with Brass Buttons, and a gadfel Hatt, a Tow Shirt and Breeches, with Shoes and Stockings. He is a Lusty well sett Fellow, about 28 years of Age, and was born upon Long-Island and speaks and reads good English.

    Whoever takes up the said Negro and secures him, so that the said John Hunt may have him again, shall have Three Pounds Reward, and reasonable charges paid by John Hunt.

    N.B. The said Negro calls himself Peter Waldren, and pretends to be a Free-Man.

30. *The New-York Weekly Journal*, #253, October 2, 1738.

Run away from Frederick Zepperly of Rheinbeck in Dutchess County Black Smith, a copper coloured Negro fellow named Jack, aged about 30 years, speaks nothing but

English and has been much used to the Sea, Short of Stature, thin Face, strong bearded and hair longer than Negroes commonly have and reads English, he had on when he went away an Orange Coloured Drugget Fly Coat somewhat faded, with brass Buttons a Homespun Linnen Coat, two striped Linsey Wolsey Waistcoats and two pair of Breeches the same also one pair of Leather Breeches a pair of Worsted Stockings and a pair of New Blew Yarn stockings, New square toes Shoes with Brass Buckles two homespun Shirts and a very good Hat.

Whoever takes up said Run away and secures him so that his Master may have him again or gives notice of him to Henry Beekman, Esq or to John Peter Zenger shall have Forty Shillings reward and all reasonable Charges.

31. *The New-York Weekly Journal*, #318, January 14, 1740.

Run away from Gabriel Cooke, a Negro Man named Jupiter of middle Stature, about 25 years of age; had on when he went away a Carfey Coat and Jacket, a Pair of Yellow Leather Britches, good Shoes and Stockings. Whosoever will take up and Secure the said Negro Man so that his Master may have him again shall have 30 Shillings as a reward and all reasonable Charges.

32. *The New-York Weekly Journal*, #342, June 23, 1740.

Run away from *Thomas White* of *Shrewsbury* a certain lusty Negroe Fellow named *James*, he has had his Right Shoulder out and still so which by lifting up his Arm may be soon discover'd; he had on when he went away a Homespun Coat, thread Stockings, and a new pair of Pumps. Whosoever takes up the said Negroe and Secures him so that his Master may have him again shall have *Twenty Shillings* as a Reward and all Reasonable Charges paid by Thomas White.

33. *The Pennsylvania Gazette* (Philadelphia), #613, September 11, 1740.

Run away on the 23rd past, from *James Leonard* of *Kingston* in *Middlesex County, East-New-Jersey* a Negroe Man named *Simon*, aged about 40 years, is a well-set Fellow, about 5 feet 10 inches high, has large Eyes, and a Foot 12 inches long; he was bred and born in this Country, talks good *English*, can read and write, is very slow in his Speech, can bleed and draw Teeth, Pretending to be a great Doctor and very religious and says he is a Churchman. Had on a dark grey Broadcloth Coat, with other good Apparel, and peeked toe'd Shoes. He took with him a black Horse, about 13 hands and a half high, a Star in his forehead, branded with 2 on the near Thigh or Shoulder and trots, also a black hunting saddle, about half worn.

Whoever takes up and secures the said Negro so that his Master may have him again, shall have *Three Pounds* Reward and reasonable charges, paid by James Leonard.

34. *The New-York Weekly Journal*, #360, October 27, 1740.

Run away the first of October, 1740, from *John Breese*, of the City of *New-York*, Leather Dresser, a Mullatto *Indian Slave* Named, *Galloway*. Aged 21 Years, about five foot four Inches high, a thin body, face markt with Small-Pox, he was born in the fort at *Albany*, can speak Dutch, and lived many Years with *Paul Richards*, Esq; some Years Mayor of this City; had on when he went away a dark gray homespun Jacket lin'd with the same, a pair of Linnen Breeches, and new Shoes; on the 3 Instant he was seen and challenged at Coll. *Phillipse's* Mill, and escaped by asserting he was sent in pursuit of a *Cuba* Man Run away, and took the Road towards *New-England*, he loves Rum and other strong liquors and when Tipsey, is a brave fellow and very abusive; Whoever Secures the said Slave so that his Master

or his Attorney may dispose of him shall have *Forty Shillings,* Reward and Reasonable Charges paid by,
John Breese.

35. ***American Weekly Mercury*** **(Philadelphia), #1131, August 27, 1741.**

Run away on the 23rd of August past from Philip French of New-Brunswick, in East-New-Jersey, a Negro Man named Claus, of middle Stature, yellowish Complexion, about 45 years of age, speaks Dutch and good English. He had on when he went away, a brown Kersey Wastecoat lined with red Peniston, a black Stock with a silver clasp, a pair of Oznabrigs Trowsers, and Breeches, an Oznabrigs Shirt, a striped Woollen Cap, square Toed Shoes, and an old Hat. He took with him a red double-breasted Wastecoat lined with blue Shalloon and trim'd with black. He is a Fiddler and took his Fiddle with him, he uses the Bow with his left Hand.
Whoever shall take up the said Negro Man and bring or send him to his Master above mentioned, shall have a Reward of Three Pounds, and all reasonable Charges, paid by Philip French.

36. ***The New-York Weekly Journal,*** **#461, September 27, 1742.**

Run away for Johannes Van Houten of Bergin in the Province of New-Jersey, a Malagasco yellow Negro wench, aged about 41 years, of middle Stature, well-set, a Scar on her right Cheek from her Ear to her Chin, she speaks very good Dutch. Whoever takes up the said Wench and brings her to her Master at Bergen, or to William Rome, Esq. in New-York, shall have 20 Shillings and all reasonable Charges.

37. *The Pennsylvania Gazette* (Philadelphia), #799, April 5, 1744.

Run away the 2nd Instant from Joseph Taylor, of Freehold Township, Monmouth County, East New Jersey, a lusty Negro Man, named Robin, about 20 Years of Age, with a small Wart upon his neck, large Hands and Feet, Had on when he went away, a Brown coloured Fly Coat and Jacket with Pewter Buttons, felt Hat, white homespun Shirt, old homespun Breeches, a Pair of white and black worsted Stockings, a Pair of good Country Shoes. He took with him a brown Mare.
    Whoever takes up and secures the Negro so that his Master may have him again, or brings him to his Master, shall have Twenty Shillings, or if Negro and Mare, Thirty Shillings Reward, and reasonable Charges, paid by Joseph Taylor.

38. *The New-York Weekly Journal*, #559, July 30, 1744.

Ran away on Wednesday the 11th of July fom Gabriel Leggett, West Chester County, a Mollato servant Man of the darkest hue, half Indian, half Negro, named James, a lusty stout fellow, 28, somewhat of a hitch in his walking, which may be seen by taking notice, had on a brown jacket and breeches, a tow-cloth shirt, but poor shoes, and an old shirt. Whoever takes up and secures said negroe so that his master may have him again shall receive forty shillings and reasonable expenses.

39. *The New-York Weekly Journal*, #599, May 6, 1745.

Run away from Robert Sharer of Dutchess County a Negro Man named Harry, 40, slender body, a wollen hat, two broad-cloth'd jackets, one darkish, the other a bright colour, gun metal buttons, leather breeches, a pair of trowsers and grey colour'd stockings Whoever shall secure said Negro Man in any Gaol, so that his Master may get him again, shall receive Forty Shillings Reward, and all reasonable Charges. N.B. He is supposed to be lurking about the city.

40. *The New-York Weekly Journal*, #602, May 27, 1745.

Run away the 20th of April from Joseph Hawkhurst on Long Island, a Negro Man named Tom, 26, of middle stature wearing an old beaver hat, a red duffil jacket, an Ozenbrig shirt and blew breeches and is much given to drink. Whoever will secure the said Negro Man so that his Master may have him again, shall receive Twenty Shillings and all reasonable Charges.

41. *New-York Weekly Post-Boy*, #146, November 4, 1745.

Run away the 26th of October last from Thomas Billow, a Negro Man named Mingo, aged 20 years, this country born, speaks very good English, of middle stature or rather spare, not very black, is a very active strong fellow; has a scar on the inside of his left thigh, which is not quite healed: Had on when he went away, a Beaver hat about half worn, a very god drugget coat full long for him, Ozenbrig waistcoat and Trowsers, a pair of thin wash-leather breeches, light grey worsted stockings and good coarse shoes. Whoever takes up and secures said Negro and gives notice thereof, so that he may be had again, shall have 40*s*. and all reasonable charges, paid by Thomas Billop. N.B. It is thought he will make for some seaport, in order to enter on board a privateer, 'Tis at their peril who entertains him.

42. *The New-York Weekly Journal*, #649, May 19, 1746.

Run away from John Willet, junr. of Flushing, the 24th of April, a Negro fellow of about 21 years of age, his name is Primus but alters his Name frequently, he is about 6 feet high, and well-proportioned, he is of a Malagasco complexion and it is observed that he will lye to that he is not to be believed or depended upon in that respect. Whoever takes up the said Negro and brings him to his Master or secures him so that his Master may have him again, shall be very well rewarded and all reasonable charges paid by me.

43. *The Pennsylvania Gazette* (Philadelphia), #916, July 3, 1746.

Philadelphia July 3, 1746. Runaway on the 19th of June last, from Hugh Martin, of Lebanon, in the County of Hunterdon, a Negroe Man named Jack, about 22 years of age, short, well-made and pitted with the Small-pox. Had on when he went away, a blue Linsey Woollsey Jacket, Tow Shirt and Drawers and an old Felt Hat. Whoever takes up and secures said Negro so that his Master may have him again shall have Twenty Shillings and all Reasonable charges paid by Hugh Martin.

44. *New-York Weekly Post-Boy*, #187, August 18, 1746.

Run away on Sunday the 10th instant from Captain George Hall, of this city, a tall likely young Negroe man named Quaw; he is a cunning and artful fellow, Jamaica born, stutters very much and has one of his ears cropt; he stole away a £5, 12*s*. and £3 Johannes Pieces and was seen going towards Kingsbridge. Whoever takes up said Negro and brings him to his master, shall have fifty shillings reward and all reasonable charges paid by George Hall.

45. *New-York Weekly Post-Boy*, #190, September 8, 1746.

Run away about 3 weeks ago, from Samuel Clowse, jun. at Jamaica on Long-Island, a Negro man named Frank, about 5 feet and a half high, of a yellow complexion, down Look, pretty much pock broken, pretends to play on the fiddle; had on when he went away an old blue Broadcloth Coat, the other Cloaths unknown and was bred at Mr. Rappelie's at New York Ferry; Whoever takes up and secures said Slave, so that he may be had again, shall have forty shillings reward, paid by Samuel Clowes, jun.

46. *The New-York Gazette, Revived in The Weekly Post-Boy*, #227, April 20, 1747.

Run away from Theunis De Klerk of Tappan in Orange County, a Negro Man named Sippee, about 30 years of age, of a middle size, is well-set, speaks good and proper English, and has a hoarse voice: Had on when he went away, a brown short watch-coat, a light colour'd red Jacket, a white Jacket bound round the edges with some other colour, and a Felt hat cock'd up and flattened on the Crown. Whoever takes up said Negro and brings him to his Master, or unto William Vredenburgh of New York shall have 40*s* reward and all reasonable charges paid by Theunis De Klerk.

47. *The New-York Weekly Journal*, #701, May 25, 1747.

New York, May 23, 1747 Made his escape from on board the Privateer Brig, Pollux, on the 20th inst, a Mulatto man named Storde, a Bermudian Born, aged about 23 years, pretty tall and pock broken, but not very much, but pretty large pits in his face, pretty fair, with his Head commonly shaved in order to make himself pass for a white man, by trade a carpenter; the cloathes he used to wear before he left the vessel, was a check'd shirt, a striped Flannel Jacket, a pair of Oznabrig trousers, a red and white worsted cap, and some other cloathes, but can't say what they were and believe, that he carried with him both shoes and stockings, with a large pair of silver shoe buckles and a silver stock buckle and also a pair of Gold Sleeve buttons, when in Bermuda, which without doubt he had with him, and which, 'tis thought he will offer to sell. It is very likely that he may be well dress'd as he had good cloath when he left Bermuda. The above mentioned Buckles and Buttons given him by his Master Mr. Thomas Hunt of Bermuda. Whoever takes up the said Mullatto slave and delivers him to Mr. Daniel Stiles at Captain John Waldron's at New York or to Mr. Philip Wilkinson, merchant at New-Port, Rhode Island, shall have ten pounds, as a reward and all reasonable charges paid by either. Daniel Stiles or Philip Wilkinson.

48. *The New-York Gazette, Revived in The Weekly Post-Boy*, #230, June 15, 1747.

RUN away from Andrew Reed of Trenton, the 30th of May last, a likely Negro Man named Isaac, about 30 Years of Age, of a middle Stature, and well set; he can play upon a Fiddle: Took with him when he went away, a light colour'd Broad Cloath Jacket, and a Drugget One about the same Colour, a Pair of Leather Breeches, two Ozenbrigg Shirts, and one fine Linnen One with Ruffels at the Breast; a Pair of dark colour'd Yarn Stockings, and a Pair of Shoes half worn: It is supposed he has got more Cloaths with him. Whoever takes up and secures the above Negro Man, so that his Master may have him again, shall have Forty Shillings Reward, paid   by   Andrew Reed.

49. *The New-York Gazette, Revived in The Weekly Post-Boy*, #231, June 22, 1747.

Run away from Samuel Tingley, a Negro Man named Andrew; had on when he went away, a blue Cloth Waistcoat, and green Breeches. Whoever takes up the said

Negro, and brings him home, shall have Thirty Shillings Reward, and reasonable charges, paid by Samuel Tingley.

50. *The New-York Gazette, Revived in The Weekly Post-Boy, #232, June 30, 1747.*

RUN away on Saturday the 20th of june past, from Thomas Tindall, of Trenton, in New-Jersey, a Negro Man named Sam; a pretty tall likely Fellow, has lately had the Small-Pox, and is pitted with it pretty much, aged about 28 Years: Had on when he went away, a light colour'd Cloth Jacket, Ozenbrigs Trousers, a Pair of Worsted Stockings, half worn Shoes, or Pumps, and an indifferent good Beaver hat; but it's tho't has got other Apparel with him, and changed.

Whoever takes up and secures said Negro, so that his Master may have him again, shall have Fifty Shillings Reward, and all reasonable Charges paid by THOMAS TINDALL.

51. *The New-York Gazette, Revived in The Weekly Post-Boy, #233, July 6, 1747.*

Ran away for his master Leonard Huff, on the 30th of last month, a Negro man named York, had on when he went away a Linsey woolsey great coat and jacket, the sleeves of his jacket are made of blue drudget shirt and narrow trowsers made of homespun linnen and a pair of shoes with double soals, grey coarse yarn stockings, an old coarse hat cut in the shape of a sailor's leather cap. Whoever shall cause the slave to be Brought to his master at Middletown, Monmouth County, shall receive Forty Shillings and all reasonable charges, paid by me   Leonard Huff.

52. *The New-York Gazette, Revived in The Weekly Post-Boy*, #252, November 16, 1747.

Run away on the first of October last, from the Widow of Alderman Van Gelder, a Negro Man named Frank, of a tawny complexion, speaks good English and Dutch; had on when he went away, a striped Flannel Jacket, Ozenbrig trousers, old shoes, but no stockings; he has since changed his Cloaths and has seen since his Elopement, to wear a red Duffels great Coat. Whoever takes up said Negro, and brings him to his Mistress, or to Victor Hyer, living near the English Church, shall have forty shillings reward, and all reasonable charges.

53. *The New-York Gazette, Revived in The Weekly Post-Boy*, #257, December 21, 1747.

RUN away from Robert Sherer, of the Fish-Kills, in Dutchess County, and Colony of New-York, A Negro Slave named Harry, aged upwards of 40 Years; had on when he went away, a woollen Hat, a worsted Cap, homespun Shirt half worn, homespun Coat, Flannel Waistcoat, homespun Breeches, blue Stockings, pretty good Shoes; he has been gone upwards of 3 Months, and it is supposed that he is conveyed or carried off by some ill minded and malicious Persons. Whoever can find out, or take up and secure said Slave, and give Notice thereof, so that his Master may have him again, shall have Three Pounds Reward, paid by ROBERT SHERER.

N. B. He was taken up and put in New-York Goal, last May was a two Years.

54. *The New-York Gazette, Revived in The Weekly Post-Boy,* #257, December 21, 1747.

Ran away from George Ryerson, Jr. of Peckquenock, East-New Jersey, the 18th Day of November, a young Negro Man named Harry, 20, of a middle stature and well-set. Had on when he went away an old Kersey jacket and a Tow linnen jacket under it, a tow linnen shirt and old breeches, black stockings and a pair of shoes. Whoever takes up and secures him so that his Master may have him again, shall receive Twenty Shillings and all reasonable Charges, paid by
George Ryerson.

55. *The New-York Gazette, Revived in The Weekly Post-Boy,* #258, December 28, 1747.

RUN away from John Coryell of Amwell, in New-Jersey, the 22d Day of November last, at Albany, a Negro Man named James Rouse: Had on Soldier's cloathing, but pretty bare, is lame in one of his Knees, and a Scar on his Upper-Lip: Whoever takes up the said Negro (if above the Highlands, shall have Forty Shillings) and if this Side the Highlands, Thirty Shillings Reward, and all reasonable Charges, paid by
John Coryell.

56. *The New-York Gazette, Revived in The Weekly Post-Boy,* #278, May 16, 1748.

Run away the 8th of this instant, from Colonel Francis Brett of the Fish Kills, in Ulster County, a Mollatto slave named Peter, 20, 6 feet high, pretty fair for a Mullato but Negro hair, a scar over both his eyes had on a yellowish Fly Coat of a Broad Cloth, Leather Breeches, grey homespun Stockings, a Beaver Hat, a grey homespun Jacket, a Linnen Shirt, and a Tow Cloth Shirt. Whoever takes up said Negro, and gives Notice to his said Master, or to the Printer hereof, so that he may be had again, shall have Forty Shillings Reward, and all reasonable Charges, paid by Francis Brett.

57. *The New-York Gazette, Revived in The Weekly Post-Boy*, #281, June 6, 1748.

Run-Away on Friday morning from Resolved Waldron of this City, baker, a Negro Man named Wan, by trade a baker, a yellow fellow about 25, much pock mark'd, and goes a little limp. Had on when he went away, a white Cloth Pea Jacket lined with blue, an Ozenbrig shirt, Sailor's trowsers, a pretty old Hat and shoes.

Whoever takes up and secures the said Negro Man, so that his master may have him again, shall have Forty Shillings Reward, and all reasonable charges, paid by Resolved Waldron.

58. *The New-York Gazette, Revived in The Weekly Post-Boy*, #284, June 27, 1748.

Run away from the Executors of Captain Beezley, a Spanish Negro Man, named Domingo, about 40, pitted with small pox, but a scar under his left eye brow, speaks bad English; had on when he went away a Brown cloth Jacket, a check shirt, an old hat flapt, a striped blue and white cotton trowsers, is supposed to harbour in or about the swamp, having frequently been seen near Mary Carrey, a white woman, that frequently used to harbour him at her lodgings near the Stockade. Whoever takes up said negro, and secures him, so that he may be had again, shall receive Twenty Shillings Reward by James Mills.

59. *The New-York Gazette, Revived in The Weekly Post-Boy*, #286, July 11, 1748.

Run away from Samuel Wickham of Goshen County of Orange, the 5th of June last, a Negro man named Jack, about 22 years of age, 5 feet high, very black, this country born, and speaks good English: Had on when he went away, an old felt hat, two new tow shirts and a fine one, one pair of old trowsers, a pair of thread stockings, one old grey kersey coat, a new homespun Duroy coat, a [linnen] jacket and a Holland Cap. Whoever takes up or secures said fellow, so that his Master may have [him] again, shall have Forty Shillings Reward, and all Reasonable Charges, paid by me, Samuel Wickham. N.B. It is thought he took with him a bay mare.

60. *The New-York Gazette, Revived in The Weekly Post-Boy,* **#286, July 11, 1748.**

Run away from his master Eleazer Tyng at Dunstable the 26th of May inst, a Negro Man servant called Robbin, almost the complexion of an Indian, short thick square shouldered fellow, a very short neck and thick legs, about 28, talks good English, can read and write and plays on the fiddle, he was born at Dunstable and it is thought he had been entered into the service at Philadelphia. Had on when he went away a striped cotton, Linnen blue and white Jacket, red Breeches, with Brass Buttons, blue Yarn stockings, a fine Shirt, a red Cap, a Beaver Hat with a mourning red in it, and sometimes wears a wig. Whoever will apprehend said Negro and secure him, so that his Master may have him again, or bring him to the Ware-House or Messrs. Alford and Tyng in Boston, shall have a Reward of Ten Pounds old Tenor, and all reasonable charges.

N.B. And All Masters of Vessels or others, are hereby caution'd against harbouring, concealing, or carrying off said Servant, on Penalty of the Law.

61. *The New-York Gazette, Revived in The Weekly Post-Boy,* **#287, July 18, 1748.**

Run away from Peter Kemble, New Brunswick, N.J., a Mullatto slave named Tom, 22, long visaged, a thick set broad-shouldered, walks as if one leg is shorter that the other, had on when he went away, an ash coloured Kersey Jacket pretty well worn, a Castor hat, and is bare legged: Whoever takes up the said Runaway or secures him in any Goal, so that his master may have him again, shall have Forty Shillings Reward, and all Reasonable Charges paid by Peter Kemble.

62. *The New-York Gazette, Revived in The Weekly Post-Boy,* #287, July 18, 1748.

Run away the 12th inst from Alexander Allaire of New Rochelle, two Negro boys, one aged 10, a tall slim fellow, his eyes look red—and speaks tolerable good English, had on a hat printed red, an Olive coloured coat, with close sleeves and a large pair of Coarse Trowsers. The other, aged about 16 or 17, a short thick set fellow, with a blue ragged jacket, coarse Trowsers and speaks but bad English. Whoever secures the said Negroes shall be well rewarded for their Pains by Alexander Allaire.

63. *The New-York Gazette, Revived in The Weekly Post-Boy,* #294, September 5, 1748.

Run away from Adam Allen of Kinderhook, the 21st of August last, a Negro Man named Hannibal, aged about twenty five years, is a square, well-set fellow, 5 and a half feet high and much pock-marked, especially about the nose, has a scar above his right eye. It is uncertain what cloathes he has on. Whoever takes up said negro, and secures him so that his Master may have him again, shall have Three Pounds reward, and reasonable charges paid by Adam Van Allen.

64. *The New-York Gazette, Revived in The Weekly Post-Boy,* #301, October 24, 1748.

Run away from the subscriber about a fortnight ago, a Negro Man Jack, 5 feet 8 inches, speaks hoarse and was Drummer aboard the Ship *Brave-Hawk*. Had on when he went away a light-coloured jacket, double breasted, a speckled shirt striped Holland trowsers, new Worsted Cap, an old Felt Hat and Shoes and Stockings. Whoever takes up and secures said negroe, so that his Master may have him again, shall have Forty Shillings Reward, and all Reasonable Charges paid by Joseph Haynes.

65. *The New-York Gazette, Revived in The Weekly Post-Boy,* #302, October 31, 1748.

Run away about 3 weeks ago from Emanuel Cocker of Newark in East-New Jersey, a Negro Man named Charles, aged about 35 years, and speaks broken English: Had on when he went away a red Jacket with white Metal Buttons, an old Felt Hat, a new Tow Shirt and old trowsers. Whoever takes up and secures the said Negroe, so that his master may have him again, shall have Three Pounds Reward, and all reasonable charges paid by Emanuel Cocker.

66. *The New-York Gazette, Revived in The Weekly Post-Boy,* #304, November 14, 1748.

Run away from John Pell of the Mannor of Pelham, a Negro wench named Bell, a boy named Janneau, a girl named Tamar, another named Dianah, another named Isabel, also a Negro Man named Lewis. Whoever will take up said Negroes, and bring them to John Pell aforesaid, shall have Five Pounds Reward, and all reasonable charges, paid by John Pell.

67. *The New-York Gazette, Revived in The Weekly Post-Boy*, #305, November 21, 1748.

Run away from Luykas John Wyngard of this city, merchant, a certain Negro Man, Simon, of a middle-stature, a slender spry fellow, has a handsome smooth Face, and thick Legs, speaks very good English. Had on when he went away a blue Cloth Great Coat. Whoever takes up the said Negro, and brings him to his Master, or to Mr. John Livingston, at New-York, shall receive Three Pounds, New-York Money, and all reasonable Costs and Charges, paid by John Livingston.

68. *The New-York Gazette, Revived in The Weekly Post-Boy*, #307, December 5, 1748.

Run away on the first of November last from John Tuthill of the Oyster Ponds at the East End of Long Island, a Mollatto man slave named Toney, 19, had on when he went away a Felt Hat, a brown Camblet coat, a red Jacket and speckled Trowsers. Also seen in company with him, an Indian man named Jack, belonging to John Petty of the same place, aged 18, had his hair cut off. Had on when he went away an old Beaver hat, a lightish colour'd close-bodied Coat, a red jacket, leather breeches and speckled trowsers. Whoever takes up the said Toney, and sends him to his said Master, or to Obadiah Wells in New-York, shall have Forty Shillings as a Reward, and Twenty Shillings for doing the same with the said Jack, and all reasonable Charges paid by John Tuthill, John Petty, or Obadiah Wells.

69. *The New-York Gazette, Revived in The Weekly Post-Boy*, #328, May 1, 1749.

Run away from Samuel Moore and Francis Bloodgood of Woodbridge, in New-Jersey, two Negro Men; one of which is a lusty young black fellow named Mando, aged about 20 Years; the other a yellow Madagascar Fellow named Tom, about 40 Years, of a Middle size, well set, and can read: We hear he has got a sort of an Indenture with him under the Pretence of being free. Whoever takes up the said Negroes, or either of them and secures them, so that his or their Masters may have him or them again, shall have Three Pounds Reward for each of them and all reasonable charges paid by us. Samuel Moore. Francis Bloodgood.

N.B. 'tis thought they are gone toward Albany and that there is another Fellow in company with them belonging to Samuel Nevill, short and well-set, half Negro and Half Indian, near 30 Years old.

70. *The New-York Gazette, Revived in The Weekly Post-Boy*, #332, May 29, 1749.

Run away on Monday the 15th instant May, from Jores Ramson, of New-York, a likely Negro Fellow named York, about 17 Years of Age, of middling Stature, speaks good English; had on when he went away, a blue and white streaked Woolen Jacket, coarse Ozenbrigs Shirt, an old Hat, and a pair of coarse Ozenbrigs Breeches. Whoever takes up the said Negro, and brings him home, or secures him so that his Master may have him again, shall have a Reward of Twenty Shillings, and all reasonable Charges paid by me
JORES RAMSON.

71. *The New-York Gazette, Revived in The Weekly Post-Boy*, #334, June 12, 1749.

RUN away on Sunday the 28th of May last, from Thomas Clark, at Little Egg Harbor, a Negro Man named Titus, aged about 27 Years, near Six Foot high:—Speaks good English, and can read; Had on a check Flannel Shirt, a grey Jacket, and a large Pair of Trowsers: He was brought up in Lime, in Connecticut, and is supposed will make that Way. Whoever takes up and secures him in Goal, and gives Notice to his

Master, or to the Printer hereof, shall have Twenty Shillings Reward, and all reasonable Charges.

72. *The New-York Gazette, Revived in The Weekly Post-Boy*, #337, July 3, 1749.

Run away on the 26th of June last, from Mr. John Zabriskie at Hackinsack, a Negroe Man named Robin, about 20 Years of Age and of a yellow Complexion: had on when he went away, a Linnen Jacket, short Trousers and Leather Hat: This is therefore to forewarn all Masters of Vessels to take the said Fellow on Board. And if any Person takes said Negroe and brings him to the Work House, they shall have Twenty Shilling Reward and all reasonable charges paid by John Zabriskie.

73. *The New-York Gazette, Revived in The Weekly Post-Boy*, #338, July 10, 1749.

Run away from Cornelius Vandervere of Middletown in New-Jersey, a Negro Fellow named Tony: Had on when he went away, a coarse Jacket and Linnen Breeches, an old Felt Hat, and old Ozenbrigs Shirt. He is a middle-sized Fellow, pretty full faced; can do all manner of Farmer's Labour and can play pretty well on the Fiddle. Whoever takes up and secures him again, so that his Master shall have him again, shall have Forty Shillings Reward, and all reasonable charges paid by Cornelius Vandervere.

74. *The New-York Gazette, Revived in The Weekly Post-Boy*, #338, July 10, 1749.

Run away the 21st Instant from William and Benjamin Hawxhurst, of Oyster-Bay, on Long-Island, a Negro Man named Tom, a middle size yellow Fellow, and is pretty well cloath'd: Took with him a black Horse with a white Snip or

Spot on his Nose. Whoever takes up and secures the said Negro and Horse, shall have a reasonable Reward paid by
WILLIAM *and* BENJAMIN HAWXSHURST.

75. *The New-York Gazette, Revived in The Weekly Post-Boy,* #346, September 4, 1749.

Run-away about two Months ago, from James Mills, of this City, a Negro Man named Bolton, a short ill looking Fellow, about 30 Years of Age, flat Nose, and Teeth black with Tobacco, he is a Chimney-sweeper, and had but very ordinary Cloaths on when he went away: Whoever takes up the said Negro Man, and brings him to his Master, shall have Three Pounds Reward, and all reasonable Charges paid by JAMES MILLS.

76. *The New-York Gazette, Revived in The Weekly Post-Boy,* #349, September 25, 1749.

Run-away on the 17th inst. from John Betts, of Jamaica, on Long-Island, a Mullatto Fellow named Isaac, aged about 24 Years, of a middle Size; Had on when he went away, a very good Head of Hair, a good Felt Hat, a brown Coat, Linnen Vest and Breeches, a Pair of blue Yarn Stockings, and good Shoes. Whoever takes up the said Fellow, and brings him to the Owner, or secures him shall have Three Pounds Reward, and all reasonable Charges paid them, by JOHN BETTS.

77. *The New-York Gazette, Revived in The Weekly Post-Boy,* #350, October 2, 1749.

RUN away on Monday the 25th of September last, from George Marple of Goshen Neck, Burlington County, in New-Jersey, a Spanish Mulatto Fellow, named George, about 26 Years of Age, middling Stature, well set, no Hair, speaks but indifferent English: Had on when he went away, a green Cloth Jacket about half worn, Beaver Hat, Check Shirt and Trowsers, light coloured Worsted Stockings, and old Shoes new soal'd, with large Brass Buckles, and is a Shoemaker by Trade: Took with him another Check Shirt, and two Silk Handerchiefs; he formerly belonged to Charles Reade, Esq; and has been a privateering; and 'tis likely may endeavor to get on board some Vessel; for which Reason all Masters are forewarned taking him on board at their Peril. Whoever takes up and secures said Fellow, so that his Master may have him again, shall have Forty Shillings Reward, and all reasonable Charges. paid by

GEORGE MARPLE.

78. *The New-York Gazette, Revived in The Weekly Post-Boy*, #352, October 16, 1749.

Run-away from Peter De Lancey, Saturday the 7th of October, inst. a Negro Man named Sam, of about 27 Years of Age: He is a tall Fellow, with thick Lips, has a flat Nose, is bow Legged and speaks English: Had on when he went away, a homespun Coat, and a short pair of Trowsers. Whoever takes up the said Fellow, or secures him so that his Master gets him again, shall have Thirty Shillings Reward; if taken out of the Government, Three Pounds, and all reasonable Charges, paid by

PETER DE LANCEY

79. *The New-York Gazette, Revived in The Weekly Post-Boy*, #353, October 23, 1749.

Run-away from Adrian Ryersz, on Staten-Island, the 12th of October Inst. a Negro Man named Hector, speaks good English, is about five Foot six Inches high, well set, with a Scar on his left Hand, and has a down Look: Had on when he went away a good Beaver Hat, a blue Coat lin'd with light colour'd Shalloon, a white Jacket and Shirt, a good Pair of Calf Skin Shoes, and a blue Pair of

Stockings.Whoever takes up and secures the said Negro, so that his Master may have him again, shall have Forty Shillings Reward, and all reasonable Charges paid by
ADRIAN RYERSZ.

80. *The New-York Gazette, Revived in The Weekly Post-Boy*, #378, April 16, 1750.

Run-away on the 25th of March last, from James Banks, of Newark, in the County of Essex, an Irish Servant Man named Arthur Harvey, (formerly Servant to Solomon Comes of Staten-Island) is about 20 Years of Age, of short Stature, has a down Look, with short dark Hair: Had on a brown great Coat, and a Snuff coloured Pea Jacket. Also run away with him, a Negro Man about the same Age, has a long Face, strait Nose, of a middle Stature, and had on a good red great Coat, a Butter-nut coloured Coat and Jacket, with some other Cloaths besides and has taken with him a Gun. Likewise run off, a Lad named Nathaniel Ward, Son to Nathaniel Ward of Newark, is of tall Stature, aged about 16 Years, and has white Hair; Had on a light blue Camblet Coat, and a deep blue Frize Jacket. Whoever takes up and secures all or either of the said Persons, so that their respective Owners may have them again, shall have for each THREE POUNDS, and all reasonable Charges paid by James Banks, Jonathan Sergeant, and Nathaniel Ward.

81. *The New-York Gazette: or, The Weekly Post-Boy*, #380, April 30, 1750.

RUN away from Thomas Day, of Hanover, a Negro Fellow, named Esop, who lately belonged to Jonathan Sergeant of Newark; he is of a middling Size, aged about 20 Years, long visag'd and a straight Nose: It is likely he had on a light blue Jacket and Leather Breeches. Whoever takes up and secures said Negro, so that his Master may have him again, shall have Three Pounds Reward, and all reasonable Charges, paid by

THOMAS DAY

82. *The New-York Weekly Journal,* **#867, August 6, 1750.**

Run away the 26th of this Instant from Mr. Joseph Shippen Iron Works formerly called Canby's Iron works, two servant men and a Negroe man, the one of the white servants is named Philip Mugguire, a carpenter by trade, 4 feet 9 inches high, a likely fellow and a black beard. Had on when he went away an old bengall jacket without sleeves, a felt hatt, tow breeches, a check'd shirt, white stockings, new pumps with brass buckles. The said servant is supposed to have a quantity of Money with him.

The other's name is John Coffey of middle stature, had on when he went away an ozenbrigs shirt and trowsers, with a new linsey woolsey blue jacket, a felt hatt, good shoes with brass buckles.

The above said Negroe had on a ozenbrig shirt and trowsers, a new linsey-woolsey jacket, a felt hat, good shoes with brass buckles, and handerchief; likewise the Negroe has stolen from his master a new broadcloth jacket of a lightish colour and a fine holland check'd shirt and trowsers, and a fine white shirt and two cambrick cravats and a pair of blewish white stockings. Whoever takes up the said servants and negroe man and secures them in any gaol, or brings them to the place aforesaid, shall have six pounds reward, and all reasonable charges, paid by us

John Mills
Alex Murray
Richard Harris

83. *The New-York Gazette, Revived in The Weekly Post-Boy*, #395, August 13, 1750.

Run away on the 5th Day of August Inst. from Jacob Ford, of Morris-town and County, East-New-Jersey, a Negroe boy named Ishmael, aged about 16 Years, short and thick, full Fac'd, has a very large foot, born in the Country, and has a sly Look: Had on when he went away a Flannel Jacket, dyed with Logwood of a purple colour, two woolen Shirts, one Tow shirt, and a Dowles Shirt, a new Felt Hat, Leather Breeches and Oznabrigs Trowsers.

Whoever takes up and secures said Boy so that his Master may have him again, shall have Three Pounds Reward and all reasonable charges, paid by Jacob Ford.

N.B. He went away with a Negro fellow already advertised by Shadreck Hatheway.

84. *The New-York Gazette, Revived in The Weekly Post-Boy*, #395, August 13, 1750.

Run away about four weeks ago, from Simon Cregier of the City of New York, a Negro wench named Phoebe aged about 45 years, middle sized, and formerly belonged to Dr. Cornelius Van Wyck at Great Neck; she is well known at that part of Long Island, and about Flushing; she had a note with her to look for a master, but has not returned again; her cloaths uncertain. Whoever takes up and secures said Negro wench, so that her Master may have her again, shall have forty shillings reward and all reasonable charges paid by Simon Cregier.

85. *The New-York Gazette, Revived in The Weekly Post-Boy*, #401, September 24, 1750.

Run away the 10th of September Inst. from John Cooper, of Elizabeth-Town in East-New-Jersey, a young Negroe Man, named Cæsar, between twenty and twenty-five Years of

Age, is small of stature, and speaks good English; he is almost as black as any in the land. Had on when he went away a grey Linsey Woolsey Waist-Coat, with one or two buttons on the Sleeve; a pair of Tow Trowsers and a Leather Jockey Cap instead of a Hat. Whoever takes up said Negro and delivers him to his said Master or to Obadiah Wells, Shop-Keeper in the Fly-Market in New-York shall have Forty Shillings Reward and all reasonable charges paid by John Cooper.

86. *The New-York Gazette, Revived in The Weekly Post-Boy*, #403, October 8, 1750.

Run away from Cornelia Rutgers of the City of New York, a Negro Man, called Hector, well-set, thick and of middle stature, thick lips and fatt; he formerly belonged to Mr. Newcome at Poughkeepsie in Dutchess County: it is supposed he had on when he went away, a light colour'd Kersey Pea Jacket, lined with red, an ozenbrig shirt and trowsers and shoes and stockings. Whoever takes up and secures the said Negro to his said Mistress, shall have thirty shillings reward, if taken with in the City and County of New York and if without the said County, three pounds reward and all reasonable charges paid by the said Cornelia Rutgers.

87. *The New-York Gazette, Revived in The Weekly Post-Boy*, #421, February 11, 1751.

Run away on Sunday night, the 3rd Instant, from Judah Hays, a Negro Wench, named Sarah, aged about 30 Years; she is a likely Wench of a Mulatto complexion, was brought up at Amboy in Colonel Hamilton's family, and has had several Masters in the Jerseys: She dresses very well, has a good Parcel of Cloathes and speaks good English. Whoever takes up said Wench, and brings her to her masters or secures her in any Country Gaol, so that he may have her

again, shall receive Forty Shillings Reward and all reasonable charges. Whoever entertains said Wench shall be prosecuted to the utmost Rigour of the Law. All Masters of Vessels, Boat Men &ct, are forewarned of conveying said Wench away as they shall answer the same. Judah Hays.
    N.B. Said Wench has robb'd her said Master in apparel &ct upwards of fifty Pounds.

88. *The Pennsylvania Gazette* (Philadelphia), #1169, May 9, 1751.

Run-away in July last, from Nicolas Everson, living in East-New-Jersey, two miles from Perth Amboy ferry, A Mullatto Negroe named Tom, about 37 Years of age, short, well-set, thick lips, flat-nose, black curled hair and can play well on the fiddle; Had on when he went away, a red-coloured watch-coat, without a cape, a brown coloured leather Jacket, a hat, blue and white twisted yarn leggings; speaks good English and Dutch, and is a good Shoemaker; his said master has been informed that he intends to cut off his watch-coat, to make him Indian stockings, and to cut off his hair, and get a blanket, to pass for an Indian; that he enquired for one John and Thomas Nutus, Indians at Susquehanna, and about the Moravians, and the way there.Whoever secures him in the nearest goal or otherwise, so that his Master may have him again, shall have Forty Shillings reward and reasonable charges paid by Nicolas Everson.

89. *The New-York Gazette, Revived in The Weekly Post-Boy*, #446, August 5, 1751.

Run away the 30th Day of June last, from Philip Smith of the Fish Kills in Dutchess County, in the Province of New-York, a Negro Fellow named Harry, aged about 20 years, of a short stature, well-set and very black: He had with him when he went away, one linnen shirt, two tow shirts, and a wollen shirt, a pair of Tow breeches and three pair of wollen stockings:—Whoever takes up and secures the said Negro so that his Master may have him again, shall have Thirty Shillings Reward, and all reasonable charges: And 'tis at their Peril who entertains him. Philip Smith.

90. ***The New-York Gazette, Revived in The Weekly Post-Boy, #451, September 9, 1751.***

Run away on the 3rd Instant, from John Willet of Hamstead Plains, a Negro Man named Holiday, a likely fellow, about 23 years of age, speaks good English: Had on when he went away, a whitish linnen coat with green cuffs, and a small cape to it; he is about 5 feet high and thin made. Whoever takes up said Fellow and secures him in the gaol at Jamaica, or the Work-house at New-York, or delivers him to said Willet, shall receive Twenty Shillings reward from John Willet.

91. ***The New-York Gazette, Revived in The Weekly Post-Boy, #461, November 18, 1751.***

RUN away from Thomas Van Wyck, of Oysterbay on Long-Island, the 8th of this Instant, a Negroe Man named Cæsar, aged about 23 Years, a pretty black bold Face, with large whites in his Eyes, and may pretend to be free; his right Hand has been bruised, by which Means 'tis not so big as the other: Had on when he went away, a Felt Hat, white Wollen Cap, a grey Kersey Coat, a homespun Check Shirt, a pair of wide Trousers, [ ] Leather Breeches under them, bluish Stockings, and new shoes. Whoever takes up and secures said Negroe, so that his Master may have him again, shall have Forty Shillings Reward, and reasonable.Charges paid by   THOMAS VAN WYCK.

92. The New-York Gazette, Revived in The Weekly Post-Boy, #461, November 18, 1751.

RUN away from Elijah Bond, at Trentown, in West New-Jersey, a Negro Man named Lott, about five Feet nine Inches high, a down Look, a well-set Lusty Fellow, about 24 Years of Age: Had on when he went away a red great Coat; his other cloaths are suppos'd to be chang'd, or wore out. He is supposed to be in Stamford, in New England. He went from Egg-Harbour in a Shingle-Shallop, or some other Vessel.—Whoever takes up the said Negro, and secures him so tha his Master may have him again, shall have THREE POUNDS Reward, by me,

ELIJAH BOND.

93. The New-York Gazette, Revived in The Weekly Post-Boy, #467, December 30, 1751.

New-York, 16th December, 1751.
RUN away, from John Willet, of Flushing, a lusty yellow Wench, aged about 26 Years; She has lost the two first joints of one of her little Fingers, and has been gone about 18 months. If any Person will inform her Master where she is, so that he may have her again, they shall be well rewarded.

94. Pennsylvania Journal, and the Weekly Advertiser (Philadelphia), #480, January 28, 1752.

Run away from John Phillips of this City, 4th of May last, a Negroe man named Sampson, about 40 Years of age, a short well set Fellow, much pitted with the small pox. has a very old look, had one when he went away a blue fearnothing jacket, Ozenbrig shirt and Trowsers and an old Felt hat. He has made a practice of running away and sculking in the woods near plantations, he was taken up last Year and put in

Amboy gaol. Whoever takes up and secures said Negroe so that his master may have him again shall have Five Pounds and reasonable charges paid by John Philips.

95. *The New-York Gazette, Revived in The Weekly Post-Boy*, #478, May 18, 1752.

Run away, a Spanish Negro Man, named Tone, who lately belonged to William Lanen, of this city, Butcher, of a small stature, between 20 and 30 years of age, by Trade a butcher, but understands something of the Tayloring Business. Whoever takes up said Negro, and brings him to John Marston at Flushing, in Queen's County, or to Whitehead Hicks at New York, (or secures him so that either of them do get him) shall be well rewarded and all reasonable charges paid. N.B. All Masters of Vessels are forewarned carrying him off, and whoever conceals him, may expect to be prosecuted with the utmost Rigour of the Law.

96. *The New-York Gazette, Revived in The Weekly Post-Boy*, #490, June 8, 1752.

Run away last Saturday, a likely Mulatto fellow, named Crook, aged about 22, speaks French and English, pretends to be free; had on a brown home spun jacket, Homespun Shirt, a blue flowered Handerchief on his head, no Hat, and is barefoot. THIRTY SHILLINGS reward will be given for taking him up, or securing him in jail, paid by WILLIAM BAYARD.

97. *The New-York Gazette, Revived in The Weekly Post-Boy*, #492, June 12, 1752.

Run away, on the 2nd of this Instant June from DANIEL LAWRENCE, of Flushing, on Long Island, a short thick Negro Fellow, named Anthony, with thick lips, is of a yellow Complexion, and plays on the Violin: Whoever takes up the said Negro, and secures him, so that his Master may have him again, and gives notice thereof to Ralph Hylton, of New York, shall be very handsomely rewarded for their trouble.

98. *The New-York Gazette, Revived in The Weekly Post-Boy, # 495, July 13, 1752.*

Run away, from Adrian Ryersz, of Staten Island, on the seventh of this Inst. July; a Negro man named Hector, about 5 feet 6 inches high, speaks good English, and has a scar on his left Hand near his little Finger; has taken with him, two Pair of Trowsers and one shirt: Whoever takes up said Negro, and secures him, so that his Master may have him again, shall have Forty Shillings reward, and all reasonable charges paid by ADRIAN RYERSZ.

99. *The New-York Gazette, Revived in The Weekly Post-Boy, #509, October 30, 1752.*

Run away some time in August last, from ABRAHAM VAN BUSKIRK, of Bergen County in New Jersey, a Negro Man, named Jack, aged about 25 years, middle siz'd, and not very black, pretty thick Lips, speaks very slow, and talks both English and Dutch, and 'tis suppos'd he has a false Pass: Had on a grey homespun Linsey Wolsey Coat, red Linsey Wolsey jacket, a Tan shirt, and Linnen shirt; and has three Pairs of Breeche with him; white Woolen Stockings, and a Leather Hat. Whoever takes up said Negro, and secures him, so that his Master may have him again, shall have THREE POUNDS reward, and all reasonable charges paid by ABRAHAM VAN BUSKIRK.

100. The New-York Gazette, Revived in The Weekly Post-Boy, #509, October 30, 1752.

Run away on the 15th of October, from David Kent, of Woodbridge in East-New-Jersey, A Negro Man named Cæsar, a middling thick short Fellow, his right Foot twisting and the Toe of the same inclining to turn outward as he walks, and his right Knee bending inward towards the Left; He talks but poor English, and is about 22 years of age: Had on when he went away an old blue coat, a Felt Hat, a Homespun Linnen Shirt, a Pair of Tow-Cloth Trowsers, a Pair of old Stockings, and a pair of Shoes something too large for his feet. Whoever takes up said Negroe and brings him to his Master shall have Thirty Shillings reward and all reasonable Charges paid by David Kent.

101. The New-York Gazette, Revived in The Weekly Post-Boy, #510, November 6, 1752.

Run away from Philip Livings[t]on, of New York, on the 28th of October last; a Negro Man, lately imported from Africa, his Hair or wool is curled in locks, in a very remarkable manner; he is a very likely lusty fellow, and cannot speak a word of English, or Dutch, or any other language but that of his own country. He was seen last Monday on New York Island, and is supposed now to be in the Woods near Harlem. whoever takes up said Fellow, and delivers him to his said master shall receive THREE POUNDS as a reward, from PHILIP LIVINGSTON.

102. The New-York Gazette: or, The Weekly Post-Boy, #519, January 8, 1753.

Run away on the 26th of December last, from the Subscriber, living in Freehold, E. New Jersey, a Mulatto Servant Fellow, named Lawrence Smith, a short, thick, well-set Person, round shoulder'd, and a down look: Had on when he went away, a brown Coat and Jacket, the coat lin'd with red Shalloon, and the Jacket with old grey Broadcloth, with flat white buttons to both, a pair of old Leather Breeches, grey Yarn Stockings, old Ozenbrigs Shirt, and a check-linnen Shirt, a good pair of shoes, and a pair of Calf-skin pumps, and has taken away a good Beaver hat, wide brim'd, a new brown Wigg, a Pair of Blue Sale Worsted stockings; he has also with him, an old Indenture, with his Mother's name to it, and his own, Mary Smith and Lawrence Smith, or their marks. Whoever takes up the said Servant and secures him, so that his master may have him again, shall have forty shillings reward, and all reasonable charges paid by me, JOHN THROCKMORTON.

103. *The New-York Gazette: or, The Weekly Post-Boy*, #534, April 23, 1753.

Run away the 12th Instant April, from ISAAC KINGSLAND of Saddle River, in Bergen County, East New Jersey, a Negro Wench named Nell, who formerly belonged to Robert J. Livingston, Merchant in New York: she is a tall slim Wench, has three Diamonds in her face, one on each side and the other on her Forehead: had on and taken with her when she went away, three Petticoats, one is an old quilted one, and the other two homespun, one striped and the other mixed, a blue and white striped short gown, a bluish homespun Waistcoat, and an Ozenbrigs shirt, with Homespun sleeves, a short blue cloke, a new pair of Blue Stockings, a pair of old crooked shoes, and several other Things too tedious to mention. These are therefore to Forewarn all Masters of Vessels and others, of carrying off, concealing or harbouring said Wench, as they will answer it at their peril with the utmost Rigour of the Law. Whoever takes up the foremention'd Negroe, and secures her in any Goal, so that her master may have her again, shall have Forty Shillings reward, and all reasonable charges paid by ISAAC KINGSLAND.

104. *The Pennsylvania Gazette* **(Philadelphia), #1271, May 3, 1753.**

Run away on the 28th ult. from the subscriber, living Amwell, A Molatto man, named Boot, about 25 years of age, about 5 feet ten inches high, and has had the small pox: Had on when he went away, a light colour'd jacket, pretty ragged, and a mouse colour'd jacket under it, the skirts has been cut short, good buckskin breeches, with brass buttons, some of the tops of them are off, blue grey yarn stockings, good shoes, and felt hat, torn in the brim. Whoever takes up said slave, and secures him, so that his master may have him again, shall have Forty Shillings reward, and if above 20 miles from home, Three Pounds, and all reasonable charges, paid by

Thomas Hunt.

105. *The New-York Gazette: or, The Weekly Post-Boy*, **#542, June 18, 1753.**

Run away on Sunday the 3rd day of May last, from Jacobus Bruyne, of Bruynswick, in the county of Ulster and province of New York, a Negroe Man Slave, named Andrew, aged near 40 years, he is of middle Stature, black skin'd, speaks good English and Dutch: had on when he went away, a coarse Linnen jacket and Trowsers, old shoes and stockings, he has been formerly out a Privateering with Capt. Tingley, and it is supposed he may attempt to get on board some Vessel to go out; these are to forewarn all Masters of Vessels carrying him off at their peril. Whoever takes up and secures Said Negroe, so that his master may have him again, shall have Forty Shillings reward, and all reasonable Charges paid by JACOBUS BRUYNE.

106. *The New-York Gazette: or, The Weekly Post-Boy*, #558, October 15, 1753.

Run away on Sabbath Day evening, Sept. 2, 1753, from his Master Chauncy Graham, of Rumbout, in Dutchess County, a likely Negroe Man named Cuff, about 30 years old, well set, has had the Small Pox, is very black, speaks English pretty well for a Guinea Negroe, and very flippant; he is a plausible smooth Tongue Fellow. Had with him a pair of greenish plush breeches about two-thirds worn, and a Pair of russel ditto flowered green and yellow, two white shirts, two Pair of middling short Tow Trowsers, one pair of Thread Stockings knit in Squares, one Pair of blue fine wool ditto flowered, one Diaper Cap, one white Cotton ditto, one blue Broad Cloth Jacket with red lining, one blue homespun coat lined with streak'd Lindsey Woolsey, or woolen, &c. &c. &c. He is a strong Smoaker. 'Tis supposed he was seduced away by one Samuel Stanberry, alias Joseph Linley, a white fellow that run away with him, and 'tis very likely this white man has wrote the Negro a pass; for 'tis said he has been in Norwalk in Conecticut, and passed there for a free Negro, by the name of Joseph Jennings, and that he was making toward the Eastward. Whoever shall take up and secure said Servant, so that his Master may have him again, shall have FORTY SHILLINGS New-York Money Reward, and all reasonable charges paid by CHAUNCY GRAHAM. N.B. All Masters of Vessels are forbid to carry off said Servant, as they would not escape the utmost Rigour of the Law in that case made and provided.

107. *The New-York Gazette: or, The Weekly Post-Boy*, #562, November 5, 1753.

FORTY SHILLINGS Reward To be paid to any person who shall take up and return to the Subscriber, a Negro Slave, called Lewis, sometimes Lewis Francois. He lately belonged to Mr. Francis Philips, after that to Mr. Henry Cuyler, to whom he came not long since from Jamaica. He is about 5 feet 6 inches tall, very thin, talks English and French, walks very nimbly, and is quite black. Had on a white Linen shirt, brown Yarn Stockings, large square Brass Buckles on his shoes, a light brown cloth breeches, with Silk Knee Bands, a yellow Cloth Jacket, with double gilt buttons. He has been seen lurking about the Town, and is supposed to be harboured by West-India Negroes of his Acquaintance. WILLIAM SMITH, jun.

108. *The New-York Gazette: or, The Weekly Post-Boy,* **#566, December 3, 1753.**

Run away the 12th Instant November, at night, from PATRICK MOTT, of Hempstead, on Long Island; a Mullato Fellow Named Tom, is about 30 years of age, and is a short well-set Fellow, about 5 feet and a Half high, full fac'd, with black curl'd hair: Had on when he went away, a brown homespun Coat and jacket, a Pair of Leather Breeches, a Pair of Linnen Breeches, two shirts, one of white Linnen, and the other a check'd Woollen, an old Beaver or Castor Hat, speaks good English, and plays well on the violin. Whoever takes up said Mullato, and brings him to his Master, or secures him, so that he may have him again, shall have Three Pounds reward, and all reasonable Charges, paid by me PATRICK MOTT.

109. *The New-York Gazette: or, The Weekly Post-Boy,* **#567, December 10, 1753.**

Run away on the 28th Instant from the subscriber living at Newark Mountains, a Negroe Man named Bristol, about 5 feet 6 inches high, not very Black, was bred at the East End of Long-Islands, and lately belonged to David Ogden, Esq. at Newark: Had on when he went away, a grey Bearskin Watch-coat, a yellow Duroy tight bodies Coat, Leather Breeches, black and white speckled Yarn Stockings and a Hat about half-worn. Whoever takes up said Negroe of that his Master may have him again, shall have Forty Shillings Jersey Money and all reasonable charges. Joseph Heddin.

110. *The New-York Gazette; or, The Weekly Post-Boy*, #580, March 11, 1754.

Run away the 10th of January last, from John Wardell of Shrewsbury, a small Negro Fellow named Ash; he took with him a red Duffil Watch-coat, good bearskin Under-Coat, Camblet Jacket and Kersey Breeches with Brass Buckles on them. Whoever takes up and secures said Man, so that his Master may have him again, shall have Forty Shillings Reward and all reasonable charges paid, by John Wardell.

111. *The New-York Gazette: or, The Weekly Post-Boy*, #583, April 1, 1754.

Run away from George Mumford of Fisher's-Island, the 27th Instant, four Men Servants, a white Man and Three Negroes, who hath taken a large two-mast Boat, with a square Stern, and a large white Pine Canoe; the Boat's Timbers are chiefly red Cedar. The White Man named Joseph Heday, says he is a Native of Newark, in the Jerseys, a short well set fellow of a rudy complection; his cloathing when he went away was a red Whitney Great Coat, red and white flower'd Serge Jacket, a Swan-Skin strip'd ditto, lapell'd, a Pair of Leather Breeches, a Pair of Trowsers, old Shoes & ct. The Negroes are named Fortune, Venture and Isaac; Fortune is a tall, slim comely well spoken fellow, had on a Kersey Great Coat, three Kersey Jackets, and breeches of a dark colour, a new cloth coloured Fly-Coat, with a red lining, a blue serge jacket, with red lining, a new Pair of Chocolate colour'd corded Drugges Breeches, a Pair of blue and white check'd trowsers, two pairs of shoes, one of them new, several Pair of Stockings, a Castor and a new felt hat. Venture had a Kersey dark colour'd Great Coat, three Kersey jackets, two pair of Breeches of the same, a new cloth coloured Fly-Coat, with red shaloon lining, a green ratteen Jacket almost new, a crimson birded stuff ditto, a pair of large Ozenbrigs Trowsers, a new felt hat, two pairs of shoes, one pair new, several pair of Stockings; he is a very tall fellow, 6 feet 2 inches high, thick square shoulders, large bon'd, mark'd in the face, or scar'd with a knife in his own country. Isaac is a Mustee, a short Fellow, seemingly clumsy and stiff in his Gate, bushy Head of Hair, sower Countenance, had on a Kersey Great Coat, Jacket and Breeches as aforesaid, a new cloth colour'd Fly-Coat, with Lining, a Pair of Trowsers, of Guinea Cloth, a new Felt Hat, shoes and stockings as above. Stole and carried away with them, a Firkin of Butter, weighs about 60 pound, two Cheeses weighs 64 pounds, and Bread for the same.

Whoever takes up and secures said Run-aways, so that their Master may have them again, shall have TWENTY POUNDS, New-York Currency, Reward and all reasonable charges paid, or equivalent for either of them; or secure the Boat, that the Owner may have her again, shall be well rewarded by GEORGE MUMFORD.

112. *The New-York Gazette: or, The Weekly Post-Boy*, #585, April 15, 1754.

Run away from the Subscriber, living at Piscataway 19th Day of February Last, a Negro fellow named Primus, of a yellow complexion, near six foot high, speaks good English: had on when he went away, a grey Jacket and Breeches, white stockings and good shoes. Whoever takes up and secures said Negro, so that his Master may have him again, shall receive three pounds reward, and all reasonable Charges, paid by John Martin.

113. *The Pennsylvania Gazette* (Philadelphia), #1337, August 8, 1754.

Runaway on the 28th of July last, from Derrick Aten of Readens Town, Hunterdon County, in New Jersey, a Negroe Man, named Jack, about 30 years of age, near five feet high, has a flat nose, much pock-marked, a lover of white women, and a great smoker: Had on when he went away, a red strait bodied coat, striped homespun jacket, and another whitish ditto. Whoever takes up and secures said Negroe so that his master may have him again, shall have Three Pounds Reward and reasonable charges paid by Derrick Aten.

114. *The New-York Gazette: or, The Weekly Post-Boy*, #613, October 28, 1754.

Runaway the 27th of September past from George Reyerse, of Pequanek, in the County of Bergen, a Negro man called Robin, of middle Stature, and about 40 years of age, not very Black, had on when he went away a white Homespun woolen Jacket, a pare of Leather Britches, no Shoes, an old Beaver Hatt, and had about Forty Shillings in money with him, as it is thought. Whoever takes up said Negro and secures him so that his Master may have him again, shall have Forty Shillings Reward, besides all reasonable costs and Charges paid by me George Reyerse.

115. *The New-York Gazette: or, The Weekly Post-Boy*, #635, March 3, 1755.

Run away from the Heirs of Barent Van Cleek, of Poughkeepsie, deceased on Tuesday the 23rd Instant March, a Mulatto colour'd Man Slave named Tom, pock-broken, about 5 feet 10 inches high, a well set likely Fellow, plays well on the Fiddle, and can read and write; perhaps he may have a false Pass: Had on when he went away, a red plush breeches, a full trim'd Coat, a cloth Jacket, and it's supposed several other clothes: took with him a bay Horse about 13 hands and a half high with a [ ] on his fore head, bridle and sadle: whoever takes up said Negroe, and delivers him to Poughkeepsie, or secures him in a gaol, and gives notice thereof to Leonard Van Cleek, or Myndert Veile, of Duchess County, shall receive five Pounds Reward, and all reasonable charges paid by LEONARD VAN CLEEK and MYNDERT VEILE.

116. The New-York Gazette: or, The Weekly Post-Boy, #635, March 3, 1755.

Run away the 21st Instant from Godfrey Mallbone Esq., and Capt. Robert Stoddard, two Mullato Fellows in Company with each other, named Jeremy and the other Anthony: the first mentioned carried with him, two blue Coats, turn'd up with red, and a Silver laced hat, with sundry other Clothes; one of his Hands is considerably less than the other; is supposed to be 21 years of age and five feet ten inches high. The other had on a darkish Bearskin coat, light cloth jacket and breeches, and a Blue jacket with Brass Buttons, a pair of red breeches, and a castor hat, with sundry other Clothes; about 18 years of age, supposed to be about 5 foot 8 inches high. Both speak good English. Whoever shall take up said Runaways, and bring them to their above mentioned Masters, shall have twenty Pounds Reward for each, and all necessary charges paid by GODFREY MALLBONE AND ROBERT STODDARD.

117. The New-York Gazette: or, The Weekly Post-Boy, #647, June 23, 1755.

A Mulatto Negro named Tom, Run away from Joseph Harris, of Beekman's Precinct, in Duchess County, being the same Fellow formerly advertised, that then belonged to the Heirs of Barent Van Cleek, deceased and a reward offered by Mynder Viele and Leonard Van Cleek, who since sold him to said Harris; he went away on the first Instant, and had on a half worn Beaver Hat, a blue and white Cotton Cap, a greenish homespun Coat, a blue cloth Jacket, a white linnen Shirt: he took also with him a linen jacket and breeches, also a red plush breeches; he is lusty and well built, full of Freckles, talks English and Dutch, can read, write, and Cypher, play well on the Violin: Whoever takes up Said Negro, and secures him in any goal shall receive five Pounds, York Currency, and all reasonable charges paid, and if any takes extraordinary Trouble and secures him, an honourable allowance shall be further paid by Joseph Harris.

118. *The New-York Gazette: or, The Weekly Post-Boy*, #650, Aug 10, 1755.

Run away the 10th of this Instant from John Shepherd of Shrewsbury, a Mullatto Fellow called Tom, and who formerly belonged to Dr. Mills; he is of a middle size, with middling long hair and is 24 Years old. Had on when he went away a garey Homespun Jacket, an old Beaver Hat, Oznabrig Shirt, Buckskin Breeches and a Pair of old Shoes and Stockings. Whoever takes up and secures the said Mullato so that his Master may have him again, shall have Forty Shillings reward and reasonable charges paid by John Shepherd.

119. *The New-York Gazette: or, The Weekly Post-Boy*, #653, September 1, 1755.

Run away from Joseph Webb, of Wethersfield, on the 23rd day of June last, a Negro Servant man about 30 years of age, about 6 feet high, straight limbed and well set. Had on him when he went away, a pair of Deer Skin Breeches, with flat Metal buttons, and Straps on the knees: carried away a new pair of Tow Cloth Trousers, a check Woolen Shirt, a brown Jacket with the Sleeves partly off, and talks but poorly, and has a hole in each ear, and generally wears Pegs of wood in them; his Fore Teeth somewhat rotten, whoever takes up and secures the said negro, and conveys him to his said master at Weathersfield, or confines him in any of his masters gaols, shall have Five Dollars reward, and all reasonable charges paid by Joseph Webb.

120. *The New-York Gazette: or, The Weekly Post-Boy*, #655, September 15, 1755.

Run away from Samuel Fowler, living in Ulster county on the west side of Hudson's River, near Newbourgh, a short well set Negro fellow, between 30 and 40 years of age, and halts a little with his Right leg. Had with him when he went away a good yellowish colour'd coat, double breasted, a blue Camblet Jacket, a pair of Tow Trousers, and a Pair of new shoes. Whoever takes him up and secures him so that his Master may have him again, shall have Three Pounds Reward and reasonable charges paid by Sam Fowler.

121. *The New-York Gazette: or The Weekly Post-Boy*, #666, October 27, 1755.

Run away from the subscriber, since Saturday the 4th instant, a negro man named Holliday, a likely fellow, middle siz'd, about 25 years of age: had on a homespun Kersey jacket, a felt hat and Shoes and Stockings; he is well known in this Town and is suppposed to be secreted by some of his Acquaintance. Whoever brings him to the subscriber shall have Twenty Shillings reward and all reasonable charges paid by John Willet.

122. *The New-York Gazette; or, The Weekly Post-Boy*, #669, November 17, 1755.

Run away on the 5th of November 1755, from Abraham Vandorn, of Freehold, in Monmouth County, in New-Jersey, a negro man named Toney, about 5 feet 9 or 10 inches high, well set of a yellowish Colour, and flat Nose, has a Scar on his nose just by his Eye; had on when he went away, an old beaver Hat, a coarse Shirt, two Jackets, one brownish and the other stript without sleeves, a pair of trousers and half worn Shoes. Whoever takes up the said Negro and secures him so that his Mistress might have him again shall have Twenty Shillings reward and all reasonable charges payed by me, Anne Vandorn, widow.

123. *The New-York Gazette: or The Weekly Post-Boy*, #670, December 1, 1755.

Run away from Lawrence Janse Van Buskerk, near Hackinsack, a negroe man who was lately advertised in the Mercury, named Æsop. He is of a middling size a round forehead a straight Nose and has a very guilty look: Had on when he went away, a grey Jacket and a green Jacket underneath it, a pair of stripped Trowsers and an old Beaver Hat; he is aged about 25 Years. Whoever takes up and secures said Negro so that his master may have him again shall have Forty Shillings and all reasonable charges, paid by Lawrense Janse Van Buskerk.

124. *The New-York Gazette: or, The Weekly Post-Boy*, #673, December 15, 1755.

Run away in this city on Friday the 10th instant, December, from Ezekial Ball, of Elizabeth Town Farms, a likely negro man, about 22 years of age is of middle Size, and long visag'd. Had on when he went away a new felt Hat, blue cloth Jacket without Buttons, Home spun shirt, old Leather Breeches with Trousers over them, brown Stockings and half worn Shoes. He pretends to be a free Man and formerly belonged to Mr. Thomas Grant in New-York.

Whoever takes up the said negro and brings him to the workhouse in New York City, shall have three Dollars reward and all charges paid by Ezekial Ball.

125. *The New-York Gazette: or, The Weekly Post-Boy*, #677, January 12, 1756.

Run away on Thursday night the 8th instant of January from Mrs. Elizabeth Carpenter, a negro boy named Venture, has a remarkably surly Look, had on when he went away a blue Watch-Coat, a pair of Buckskin Breeches, a striped Waistcoat with Metal Buttons, a very dirty old homespun Shirt, a pair of mixed Hose, and a pair of large Buckles on his shoes. Whoever takes up the said negro and brings him to said Mrs. Elizabeth Carpenter shall have forty shillings together with all reasonable charges.

126. *The New-York Gazette: or, The Weekly Post-Boy*, #683, February 16, 1756.

Run away the 24th Day of January last, from Isaac Freeman, of the Township of Woodbridge, in East-New-Jersey, a middle-sized thick squat Negro Fellow named Cæsar, aged about 22 years; Had on when he went away, a Wool-Hat, a double Worsted Cap, a Flannel Shirt, a red Broad Cloth Jacket, and a light-coloured cloudy-like Linnen and Woollen Jacket, and a Pair of white Leather Allom-dress'd Sheep-Skin Breeches; a pair of black and white Stockings, and half-worn Shoes with Buckles in them: 'Tis thought he has also with him, a Linsey-Woolsey Breeches of the same sort as the Jacket, and a coarse Linnen Shirt.

    Whoever takes up said Negro, and secures him, and give Notice, so that his Master may have him again, shall have Twenty Shillings Reward, or if he is brought home to his Master, Forty-Shillings Reward, and all reasonable Charges, paid by ISAAC FREEMAN.

127. *The New-York Gazette: or, The Weekly Post-Boy*, #685, March 1, 1756.

Run away on the 14th of February last, from Josiah Halsted, of Shrewsbury, Monmouth County, East-New-Jersey, a Servant Man named Johan Jeremiah Myer, about 5 feet 4 inches high, well set, something pitted with the Small Pox, speaks very broken English, pretends to be a Black-Smith, is about 21 Years of Age: had on when he went away, a Felt Hat, an old curled Wig or white Cap, a Garlix or Flannel

Shirt, and a half-worn Bear-Skin Coat, and a long brown Jacket, with Cuff-Sleves; had with him a new striped Holland Vest, a Pair of black Plush, a Pair of Buckskin, and a Pair of Dimity Breeches, a Pair of Grey Worsted, and a Pair of Coarse Yarn Stocking, and old shoes with Buckles. He has broke open his Master's Barr, and robb'd him of a considerable Sum of Money, It's Suppos'd he went away with a Molatto Man named Tom, Belonging to John Sheppard of said Place, and formerly the Property of Doctor Mills. Whoever secures said Servant, so that his Master may have him again, shall have FIVE POUNDS Reward, and all reasonable Charges paid by me, JOSEPH HALSTEAD.

128. *The New-York Gazette: or, The Weekly Post-Boy*, **#690, April 5, 1756.**

Run away on Monday morning the 29th of March last, from Peter DeLancey, Esq., West Chester, a middle fixed mulatto negro called Hannibal, about 5 feet 8 inches high, sharp featured, and speaks very good english. Had on when he went away a homespun coat and 2 pairs of Breeches, 2 pairs of homespun stockings, 2 [   ] one homespun, the other Ozenbrigs [   ]. Whoever takes up the said negro and delivers him to Goal or York Work-House shall have a reward of forty shillings and all reasonable charges paid by Peter DeLancey.

129. *The New-York Gazette: or, The Weekly Post-Boy*, **#690, April 5, 1756.**

Run away from his master, Christopher Youngs of Southhold, on Friday the 26th instant, a mulatto slave named Cæsar, about 24 years old, 5 feet 8 or 9 inches high, pretty well set, of a light Complexion, is sometimes taken for an Indian and has a large Mole under his left Eye. Had on when he went away a dark coloured Great Coat, leather breeches, a Body Coat of blue and white Colour, old shoes capt, a new Felt Hat, but Hair pretty short and straight. Whoever takes up and secures said Slave so that his master might have him again shall have a Forty Shillings reward and all reasonable charges paid by Christopher Young. N.B. All masters of vessels are forbidden to carry him off.

130. *The Pennsylvania Gazette* (Philadelphia), #1425, April 15, 1756.

Runaway from the subscriber living at Middletown, in East-New-Jersey, the 9th of January last, a Negro man named Cato, alias Toby, aged about 30 years, a lusty well set fellow, full fac'd: Had on when he went away a plain-made Bear-skin coat, with flat Metal Buttons, a white woollen vest; wool hat and cap, a brown Tow Shirt, Buckskin Breeches, wool stockings, a pair of pumps with large brass buckles: he was branded when a boy in Jamaica, in the West Indies, with a B (and I think) C on his left shoulder blade; he is sly artful fellow and deceives the credulous by pretending to tell fortunes, and pretends to be free, speaks English as well as if country born, and plays on the Fiddle; it is thought he is gone towards the Cedar Swamps, and that some base Person has given him a Pass. Whoever apprehends said slave, and secures him, so that his master may have him again, shall receive Forty Shillings reward and reasonable charges paid by Richard Stillwell.

131. *The New-York Gazette: or, The Weekly Post-Boy*, #698, May 31, 1756.

Runaway on Monday the 20th Instant from Dennis Hicks of this city, Shipwright, a likely Negro Lad of about 14 years old, a short chubby fellow, full faced: Had on a blue sailors jacket with a striped Homespun one under it, an old brown Cloth pair of Breeches, an old Hat and Cap. Whoever takes up and secures said Negro, in that he may be had again, shall have Twenty Shillings reward and charges paid by Dennis Hicks.

N.B. He was seen on the Saturday following and is supposed to be still skulking in the town. All persons are forewarn'd to harbour him, or carry him off. His name is Pompey.

132. *The New-York Gazette: or, The Weekly Post-Boy,* **#699, June 14, 1756.**

Run away the 10th of May last, from the subscriber, then lodging at the Widow Marth's, at Perth-Amboy, a Negro Man named Frank, a likely smooth-tongu'd Fellow, about five feet, five inches high, well-set and has lost two of his fore teeth: He had on a Great Coat, an old Jacket, Leather breeches, Old stockings and Shoes: 'Tis supposed he has plenty of Money, and will travel only in the Night: He has been run away a considerable time, was just taken up at a great Distance, and was upon the Road home, when he made his Escape again. He had his Wife with him at first, but two days after his escape his wife was taken in the Woods near Amboy, and himself seen, but got off, 'Tis likely he may change his Name, and pretend to be free. Whoever takes up the said Negro, and secures him so that he may be had again shall have FORTY SHILLINGS Reward, and all reasonable charges paid by the Widow Marth or the subscriber James Rowen.

133. *The New-York Gazette: or, The Weekly Post-Boy,* **#702, June 28, 1756.**

Run away the 20th day of June instant, 1756, from Henry Allen, of Great-Neck on Nassau Island, a mulatto fellow named Licum, aged about 24 years, and about 5 feet, 9 inches high, well set, walks stooping, with a down-look, and black curl'd hair: Had on when he went away, a felt hat about half worn, a brown Tow Shirt, and Tow trousers, a brown Jacket, with blue Worsted Lining, one shirt of Irish Linnen, and a Pair of half-worn brown broad-cloth breeches. Whoever takes up and secures said Fellow in any of his Majesty's Goals, so that his Master may have him again, shall have Forty Shillings Reward and all reasonable charges, by me HENRY ALLEN.

134. *The New-York Gazette: or, The Weekly Post-Boy*, #703, July 5, 1756.

Run away the 2d instant July, from John Decker, of Staten Island, a negro Man, being a short chubby fellow, with extraordinary bushy Hair, is barefoot, and has a Soldier's red Great Coat on. Also ran away from the Widow Haughwout, of the said Island, a negro wench, of Middle Size, is with child, and speaks broken English, and has a bundle of Clothes with her. It is supposed they went together. Whoever takes up the said negro Man and Wench, and secures them so that they may be had again, shall have Forty Shillings Reward, and Charges paid by the Owners, John Decker, and Widow Haughwout.

135. *The New-York Gazette: or, The Weekly Post-Boy*, #706, July 26, 1756.

Run away on the 15th instant July, from Mrs. Mary Elliston, of the City of New York, a Negro Man named Titus, is a well set fellow, of between 29 and 30 years of age: Had on when he went away, an Olive colour'd Jacket, black Breeches, a Pair of white Stockings, half-worn Pumps: Took with him two homespun Jackets, and a heavy Jacket lined with red. He is full of Talk, and can read and write well. Whoever takes up and secures said Negro, so that his Mistress may have him again, shall have Twenty Shillings, if taken in this City, and if out of it Thirty Shillings Reward, and all reasonable Charges paid by MARY ELLISTON.

136. *The New-York Gazette: or The Weekly Post-Boy*, #706, July 26, 1756.

Run away from the subscriber, a Negro Man belonging to Mr. Robert Benson, named Pompey, about 25 years of age, can speak both Dutch and English, is square well set Fellow, somewhat of a yellowish Complexion, and is exceeding well known in this City, having been used ago with the Beer Waggon for some Years past. Whoever apprehends said Negro, so that the Subscriber may have him again, shall have Twenty Shillings Reward. He has been sculking about the Docks ever since his running away, and wants to go a privateering. This is also to forewarn all Persons from harbouring said Negro at their Peril. LODEWICK PAMPER

N.B. He is supposed to have been carried off some days ago to Stamford in New-England, having been seen on board the Sloop of Abraham Demeld.

137. *The New-York Gazette: or, The Weekly Post-Boy*, #707, August 2, 1756.

Run away from Samuel Fowler, living on the West Side of the Hudson River in Ulster County near Newbergen a negro man between 30 and 40 years old, is a short well set Fellow; had on when he went away a yellow coloured Coat, double-breasted, a Scotch Bonnet on his head, a new Tow shirt and trousers and halts a little with his right leg and pretends to be a Doctor: Whoever apprehends the said negro so that his master may have him again shall have Three Pounds reward, and all reasonable charges paid by Samuel Fowler.

138. *The New-York Gazette: or, The Weekly Post-Boy*, #709, August 16, 1756.

Run away on the 9th day of August instant from William Mott of Great-Neck in the town of Hampstead in Queens County on Nassau Island, a negro man slave named Joe; a middle sized well set likely Fellow, middling full-faced and black, had a small round Scar on his left cheek, born here and speaks good english, about 29 or 30 years of age: had on when he went away a gray homespun coat with Pewter Buttons, a white Linnen jacket, a white homespun linnen shirt, a speckled Linnen handkerchief wound about his Neck, a Felt Hat, Tow Trousers, a Pair of old pumps, with buckles, carried with him a Jacket the same as his coat. Whoever takes up and secures the said negro fellow so that his master may have him again shall have three pounds reward and all reasonable charges paid by William Mott. N. B. All Commanders of Vessels are forbid carrying off the said Negro.

139. *The New-York Gazette: or, The Weekly Post-Boy*, #709, August 16, 1756.

Run away on Monday the 2nd instant from Sam Nutman, of Newark a middle sized Negro Fellow named Bristol, about 35 years old: had on a black Linsey Woolsey Coat, a Pair of Leather Breeches and Tow Trousers. It is suspected he has a Pass with him, and being an artful Fellow will attempt to impose on the most Careful: Took with him a yellow coloured Camblet coat, and two good white shirts. Whoever apprehends and secures said negro so that his master may have him again shall have Five Pounds reward and all reasonable Charges paid by Samuel Nutman.

140. *The New-York Gazette: or, The Weekly Post-Boy*, #711, August 30, 1756.

Run away on Tuesday the 20th instant from Thomas Hamersley, of the city of New-York, Goldsmith, a negro fellow named Duke, about 5 feet 5 inches high, has very thick lips and of a yellow Complexion, and can work at the Gold Smith's business, had on when he went away a speckled Shirt and Trousers. Whoever takes up the former said negro fellow so that his Master may have him again shall have twenty shillings if taken in town; if off the Island, forty shillings, and all reasonable charges paid by Thomas Hamersley.

141. *The New-York Gazette: or, The Weekly Post-Boy*, **#711, August 30, 1756.**

Run away the 16th day of this instant August, from Isaac Freeman of the Township of Woodbridge in East New Jersey, a middle fixed squat negro named Cæsar, aged 22 years: Had on when he went away an old Beaver Hat and old wig, a Tow cloth shirt, and Tow-Trousers, a dark coloured homespun woolen jacket, and an old pair of shoes: When he went away he had a pair of Iron Pot-Hooks around his neck with a chain fastened to it that reached his feet, but may possibly have gotten it off. Whoever takes up said negro and secures him and gives Notice, so that his master may have him again shall have Twenty Shillings reward, or if he is brought to his Master Forty Shillings Reward and all reasonable Charges, paid by Isaac Freeman.

142. *Pennsylvania Journal, and the Weekly Advertiser* **(Philadelphia), #728, November 18, 1756.**

Runaway a Negro woman named Molly, about three weeks out of the small-pox, is about 32 years of age, born and bred in the Island of Bermuda, speaks good English, and has been used to the House, its supposed she went in to the Jerseys, any person that will deliver the said Negro wench to the work-house in Philadelphia, or give certain information that she may be had again, shall have Twenty Shillings reward, paid at the London Coffee House.

143. *The New-York Gazette: or The Weekly Post-Boy*, #726, December 13, 1756.

Run away from Joseph Harris, of Beekman's Precinct, in Dutchess County, on the 3rd of September last, a Mulatto Fellow named Tom, about 5 feet eight inches high, is thick and well set, can talk good Dutch and English, and can play very well upon the fiddle.—can read, write and cypher and has some Freckles. He first listed himself in the Boston Forces and was seen in Albany about a fortnight ago with the Forces so that it is likely he has gone toward Boston or other Parts of New England. Whoever takes up and secures the said servant fellow so that his master might have him again shall have Ten Pounds New York currency reward and all reasonable charges paid by Joseph Harris.

N.B. Whoever secures him send notice to Balrus Van Kleek in the city of New York; or the said Joseph Harris.

144. *The New-York Gazette: or, The Weekly Post-Boy*, #733, January 31, 1757.

Run away from Caleb Ferris of East-Chester, in the Province of New York, sometime before last Christmas; a lusty likely man slave named Joe, aged about 25 years old, he is of a yellow complexion being mixed Indian and Negro, much of an Indian countenance, he speaks altogether English and is well set every Way, about five feet ten inches high, understands all sorts of Plantation Work and is an excellent Hand to make a Stone-Wall, he was born of a slave and brought up by Martha Clarks of W. Chester and upon her death he is so often running about, he sometimes pretends to be free and it is supposed that some vile person has given him a pass, he is a great Fiddler and when he went away he took his Fiddle and a bundle of cloth. Whoever will take up the said Servant and secure him so that his Master may have him again shall have three pounds reward and all reasonable charges paid by me, Caleb Ferris.

All persons are hereby forewarned from harbouring or carrying off said servant.

145. The New-York Gazette: or, The Weekly Post-Boy, #747, May 9, 1757.

New-York, April 21, 1757.
Run away from Jacob Van Shaick, jun. a negro man named Reick. Had on when he went away: Leather Breeches, striped woolen trousers and shirt of the same, a Yellowish Vest, old Shoes, and no hat. Whoever takes up the said Negro and brings him to Henry Dumont, of this city shall be rewarded for the same by me, Jacob Van Schaick. N.B. If he returns of his own Accord, his faults shall be forgiven.

146. The New-York Gazette: or, The Weekly Post-Boy, #748, May 16, 1757.

Run away on Sunday the 3rd day of this Inst. from George Armstrong of Morris-Town in Morris County, East-New-Jersey, a likely young Negro Fellow named Rantus, about 18 or 19 years of age, but pretty lusty for his age—Had on when he went away, an old Hat, a good light coloured homespun Cloth Coat with Metal Buttons and light homespun lining, thick Leather Breeches and Trowsers over them, a coarse homespun Tow Shirt; brown Yarn stockings, without feet and good shoes but run on one Side. He had also a black velvet Stock or neckcloth, speaks good English and understands Country Business. Whoever takes up and secures the said Negro Fellow and gives notice so that his master may have him again shall have three Spanish milled Dollars Reward and all reasonable Charges paid by George Armstrong.

147. The New-York Gazette: or, The Weekly Post-Boy, #748, May 16, 1757.

Run away the 25th of April last, from Thomas Robinson of Brookhaven in the County of Suffolk, on Long Island, a negro man named Ned, about 23 years old, he stole a Barge and was seen on the Thursday following in the Sound opposite to Lloyd's Neck, steering to the Westward. The Barge has lost part of her stem and several of her Timbers broke. He has a crooked Knee. Had on when he went away a new grey Kersey Coat, a new Pair of Pumps. The said negro can both read and write, and probably has wrote himself a Pass. Whoever takes up the said negro and secures him so that his master may have him again shall have Twenty Shillings Reward and all reasonable Charges paid by Thomas Robinson, jun.

148. *The New-York Gazette: or, The Weekly Post-Boy, #750, May 30, 1757.*

Five Pound Reward. Run away on Thursday the 26th Inst. from Rachel Low of this City a negro man named Charles, aged about 23 years, about 5 feet 6 inches high pretty likely and well set, speaks pretty good English and some Dutch, this country born, had on when he went away an oznabrig shirt and trousers, blue jacket without sleeves, a Castor Hat, also took with him a blue cloth coat, red vest, and red Everlag Breeches, several shirts, and other wearing apparel. Whoever takes up the said Negro or secures him so that his Mistress may have him again shall receive five pounds reward and all reasonable charges paid by applying to the said Rachael Low, to Peggy Low in Broad Street or Henry Kip, near the Merchants Coffee House. N.B. All Commanders of Vessels are forwarned to conceal or harbour said negro.

149. *The New-York Gazette: or, The Weekly Post-Boy, #750, May 30, 1757.*

Run away from Moses Clement at Queensbury, a negro man named George, about 25 years of age, he is a tall lusty fellow, and has a swelling on one knee: He had on when he went away a new blue great coat and a handkerchief tied around his head. Whoever takes up the said negro and brings him to his master living in New-York opposite

Oswego-Market shall have Twenty Shillings reward and all reasonable charges paid by Moses Clement.

150. *The New-York Gazette: or, The Weekly Post-Boy*, #751, June 6, 1757.

Run away together the 26th of May last the following Negroes Men: from Jacob Mersereau, living in Richmond County Staten Island: A negro man named Jack, about 5 feet 9 inches high, speaks good English and Dutch, and is a Weaver by trade, had on when he went away a Homespun coat, a striped blue and white Vest, about 21 or 22 years of age. From Jacob Van Horne in Bergen County a negro man named Jack, about 5 feet 9 inches high, and is much the colour of an Indian: had on when he went away homespun cloaths. From Jacob Van Buskirk of Bergen County aforesaid, a negro man named Cuff, about 5 feet 3 inches high, had on Homespun Cloaths and can play upon the Fiddle. Whoever takes up and secures any or all of the said Negroes or will deliver them to Mr. Otis Vantile or Rem Symonson at the ferry or Staten Island or to their respective masters shall have five pounds reward and all reasonable charges paid by said Vantile and Symonson on their delivery, or their Owners.

151. *The New-York Gazette: or, The Weekly Post-Boy*, #751, June 6, 1757.

Run away on Wednesday morning the 24 of May last from the sloop Ranger Benjamin Bethall, Master, a Negro Man named Frank, about 5 feet 6 inches high, had on when he went away an Ozenbrigs shirt, speckled Shirt, Shoes and Stockings, he is Bermuda born. Whoever takes him up and brings him to the Printer or to the said Master Bethall, shall have Five Pounds Reward and all reasonable Charges paid by Benjamin Bethall.

152. The New-York Gazette: or, The Weekly Post-Boy, #755, July 4, 1757.

Run away from Cornelius Newkerk, a lusty Negro Man named Claus, about 35 years old, is much Pock-broken, can read and write both English and Dutch, pretends to cypher, and has a very heavy Gate. Had on a light colour'd silk-Camblet Coat, lin'd with Shalloon, a flower'd Stuff Waistcoat lin'd with the same as the Outside, a Wash-Leather Breeches, almost white with wearing and Washing, light colour'd Worsted Stockings, one Pair of homespun blue Woolen Stockings; took two Pair of shoes, big Brass Buckles; Brass Knee Buckles; one fine Garlix Linnen Shirt one Homespun Shirt, a Beaver Hat much worn; had a Quantity of small Silver with him, and its likely will forge a Pass. Whoever takes up the said Negro, and gives Notice thereof to Andrew Breasted, sen. or Isaac Ryckman, in New-York, and secures him so that his Master may have him again, shall have THREE POUNDS Reward, and all reasonable Charges paid by CORNELIUS NEWKERK.

153. The New York Mercury, #251, May 30, 1757.

Run-Away from Frind Lucas, at the Mines, near Second-River, an Indian slave, named Wan, about 30 years of age, a little slim fellow, about 4 feet 4 or 5 inches high, thick short hair, which was cut off last fall: He was seen at Elizabeth-Town with a bluish great coat, and a rusty beaver hat, and offer'd to list as a soldier and am informed, was since at Amboy. Whoever takes up and secures said Indian, so that his Master may have him again, shall have forty shillings reward, and reasonable charges paid by Frind Lucas.

154. *The New-York Gazette: or, The Weekly Post-Boy*, #762, August 29, 1757.

Middletown, Monmouth County, East-New-Jersey, August 1, 1757. Runaway from the subscriber the first of January, twelve months past, a Negroe Man, named Cato, who has since his elopement changed his name several times: Had on when he went away a Pair of Buckskin breeches, fine brown linen shirt, a plain made whitish Camblet Coat, dark Yarn stockings, new shoes, and a wool hat. He is a short well-set Fellow, understands Husbandry in all its parts, an excellent hand with a scythe in grass or grain, speaks English as if country born, and pretends to be free. Underneath his right-shoulder blade he was branded in Jamaica when a Boy with the letters BC, which are plain to be seen. He plays poorly on the fiddle and pretends to tell fortunes. It is supposed he has a forged pass. Whoever secures the said Negroe so that his Master may have him again, shall receive a reward of Five Pounds and reasonable charges paid by Richard Stillwell.

155. *The New-York Gazette: or, The Weekly Post-Boy*, #762, August 29, 1757.

New-York, August 23, 1757. Run or let away this Day from Lane's Ferry, a Negro Man who had his Hands pinioned behind him, and belonged to the Sloop Margaret and Mary, John Baddeley, Master of So. Carolina. His Name is *Scipio*, about five feet five inches high, of a middling Bulk, a little Pock-markt, his Mouth extends more than common, has a large Bump over one of his Eyes, his Buttocks pretty well marked with the Lash, speaks pretty good English, though somewhat thick, was born at St. Christophers, and says he understands something of the Cooper's Business. Had on when he went away, an Oznabrigs Frock and Trowsers, and a Worsted Cap. Whoever takes up the said Negro, and delivers him to Capt. John Schermerhorn, in New-York, shall receive Three Pounds Reward, and all reasonable Charges. Any Person that harbours or carries the said Negro off in any Boat, Barque, or Vessel whatever, may depend on being prosecuted to the utmost Rigour of the Law.

156. *The New-York Gazette: or, The Weekly Post-Boy*, #768, October 10, 1757.

Run away from Caleb Ferris, of East-Chester, a Negro Man slave called Joe, aged about 25 years. He is a lusty well fed Fellow every Way, about five Feet Ten inches, thick shoulder'd, full round Face, speaks altogether English, his Hair frizzled, being half Indian. He has been voyage privateering, and is a great Fiddler. He has a large Leg and broad Foot, and commonly wears Sailors Habit. He was born at Westchester, and sometimes pretends to be free.

Whoever takes up the above described Slave, and will secure him so that his Master can have him again, shall have Six Pounds Reward, paid by CALEB FERRIS.

N.B I hereby forbid and forwarn all Persons dealing with, entertaining, or employing him, under any pretence whatsoever. And I further forwarn all Masters of Vessels, Captains of Privateers, from taking him on board, or carrying him off under any Pretence whatsoever.
September 25, 1757.

157. *The New-York Gazette: or, The Weekly Post-Boy*, #774, Nov. 21, 1757.

Ran away on the 8th of November, Inst. from James Carrol, of this City, a Negro Wench, aged about five or six and thirty Years old, or thereabouts, called Rose, formerly called Grace, talks but very indifferent English. Had on when she went away, a striped Homespun Joseph, an old red Cloth Petticoat, white Yarn Stockings, and old Shoes, lame in one of her Legs, with a broken Shin. Whoever secures the said Wench, shall have Twenty shillings Reward, and all reasonable charges paid by JAMES CARROLL. November 21, 1757.

158. *The Pennsylvania Gazette* (Philadelphia), #1512, December 15, 1757.

Philadelphia, December 9, 1757. Runaway last Monday from the subscriber, living in Cranberry, in the County of Middlesex, in New Jersey, a Spanish Negroe Man, named John Juster, about 5 feet 7 or 8 inches high, a well-built fellow of a yellow Complexion; had on when he went away an old Felt Hat and a Worsted Cap, an old brown coat and blue Jacket, old blue Plush Breeches, Yarn and Worsted stockings and old Shoes. Whoever takes up and secures said Negroe, so that his Master may have him again, shall have Thirty Shillings reward, and reasonable charges paid by John Reid, junior.

N. B. He served Four Years at Lawrence's Farm in said County, and has his old indentures with him which may be used of for a Pass. All Masters of Vessels are forbid to carry him off at their Peril.

159. *The New-York Gazette: or, The Weekly Post-Boy*, #779, December 26, 1757.

New-York, Decemb. 24th, 1757, Ran away last Night from the Sloop Walter, William Price, Master, lying in Rotten Row; a Negro Man, named Ralph; about 25 years of Age, about 5 feet, 4 inches high, smooth-faced, thick lipped; speaks good English. Had on when he went away, a blue Jackett, and a Drab colour'd Do. and a white Flannel Waistcoat, a grey pair of Stockings, much worn, with a pair of black worsted one's under them. Any Person taking up the said negro, and bringing him to Mr. Waddel Cunningham, Merchant, New-York, or to Mr. Alexander Hamilton, Merchant in Philadelphia, shall receive 5 dollars reward, and reasonable charges.

160. *The New-York Gazette: or, The Weekly Post-Boy*, #780, January 2, 1758.

Run away from the subscriber, about five weeks ago, a young negro man called Hanibal, alias Sandy, born at Barbados: He is about 5 feet long, thick lip'd, and thick cheek'd, has a down look, a scar under his chin; a fellow that will talk much; had on when he went away, a brown short jacket with hooks and eyes, a black and white strip'd homespun double-breasted jacket, a leather pair of breeches, and an old wigg and hat. Whoever secures the said negro, so that his master may have him again, shall have forty shillings reward and all reasonable charges paid by Cornelius Tiebout.

161. *The New-York Gazette: or, The Weekly Post-Boy*, #785, February 6, 1758.

Run away on Sunday last the 29th January, from Philip Duley, living in Bloomendall, on York-Island, a Negroe man, called Tom, late the Property of Jacobus Kip, about four Foot, five Inches high, well fed, speaks broken English; had on when he went away, a brown Cloth Coat, Buttons of the same, Buckskin Breeches, grey Yarn Stockings, Brass Buckles in his shoes, a good Felt Hat, with a Pewter Tutton on it, work'd like a Hair Button: Whoever takes up the same Negro and secures him so that his Master may have him again, shall have Twenty shillings Reward, and all reasonable charges by PHILIP DULEY.

162. *The New-York Gazette: or, The Weekly Post-Boy*, #789, March 6, 1758.

Run away from Edmund Matthews of Livingston's Manor about the Beginning of this Month, a Negro Fellow about 20 years of age, has a smooth face and has a very thick build; had on when he went away, a Bearskin coat, white cloth Breeches, a blue and white striped Holland shirt, and a grey

Pair of stockings. It is thought that he will try to go out in some of the Privateers. Whoever takes up and secures the said negro so that his Master may have him again or gives notice to James Carrol of the City of New York, Butcher, or at the New-Printing Office, in Beaver-Street, shall have Forty Shillings Reward and all charges paid.

163. *The New-York Gazette: or, The Weekly Post-Boy*, #798, May 8, 1758.

Run away on Monday last, from John Hastier, of this city, Goldsmith, a lusty well-set Negro Man, named Jasper, about 5 feet, 6 inches high, speaks good English and understands the Silversmith's trade. Had on when he went away, a brown Forest cloth coat with flat Pewter Buttons, blue Waistcoat, with same Sort of Buttons; a Leather Breeches, with the like Buttons, old Hat, broken Yarn stockings, and old shoes. Whoever takes up the said Negroe, and secures him so that his master may have him again, shall have Four Pounds reward and all reasonable charges paid by JOHN HASTIER.

164. *The New-York Gazette: or, The Weekly Post-Boy*, #809, July 3, 1758.

Run away from Mr. Thomas Scramshaire of this city, the 5th instant, a mulatto wench named Fanny about 5 feet 4 inches high, and talks good English has a smiling Countenance and black-curled Hair, full-breasted; she had on when she went away a small black silk Hat, a large cross barred blue and white striped Stuff gown and an old red quilted petticoat with a Bundle of several other Things, the Contents as yet unknown—Whoever takes up and secures or discovers where the said Fanny is harboured so that her Master may have her again shall receive 20 shillings reward if taken up in the town, and 40 shillings if cross'd any ferry, with all other reasonable charges that might arise thereupon: and whoever shall offer to harbour or entertain the said wench may depend upon being prosecuted to the utmost Rigour of the law by me, Thomas Scramshaire.

165. *The New-York Gazette: or, The Weekly Post-Boy*, #812, July 24, 1758.

Run away from Ide Meyer on the 20th of June last, a Mulatto Wench named Ohnech, but goes by the name Hannah and pretends to be free: She is about 4 feet 4 inches high and 28 years of age; is well set and speaks both English and Dutch very well, had on when she went away a home spun stole, a petticoat, Blue short cloak and white cap; whoever takes up and secures the said wench so that her master may have her again shall have Twenty shillings reward and all reasonable charges paid by me Ide Myer.

N.B. All persons are forewarned to entertain her and all masters of Vessels to carry her off at their peril.

166. *The New-York Gazette: or, The Weekly Post-Boy*, #812, July 24, 1758.

New-York, July 16, 1758. Run Away on the 10th of this inst. July from James Swan, of this city, pilot; a negro man named York, about 5 feet 8 inches high, of a slender make, talks pretty good English, is a good cook, can play on the violin, and shave, and dress wigs;—He had on when he went away, old shoes, and carv'd silver buckles, blue and red worsted plush breeches, old trowsers, check shirt, a blue jacket, a small-cropt hat, with yellow worsted ringing round it; and steps pretty long: He formerly belonged to Lawrence Lawrence, of this city, merchant.—Whoever takes up the said negro, and secures him so that his master may have him again, shall have, if within the city, 20*s*. if between it and King's-Bridge, 30*s*. and 40*s*. if farther, and all reasonable charges, paid by JAMES SWAN.

All master of vessels, and captains of privateers, are

Advertisements

forwarned from carrying him to Sea, or harbouring him on board their vessels, as they may expect to answer it at their peril.

167. *The New-York Gazette: or, The Weekly Post-Boy*, #817, August 28, 1758.

Run away on the 13th of August Instant, from William Peartree Smith, Esq., of Elizabeth-Town in New-Jersey; a Negro Man named Prince, had on a Leather cap, Linnen Waistcoat and breeches, coarse blue stockings, a thick pair of shoes, speaks Dutch and English, has lived in Jamaica in the West-Indies with Mr. Simon Parsco, and in Duchess County in New York with Mr. Nixon, has been lately seen in New York, and it is said passed King's Bridge, where he showed a pass and pretended that he belonged to a Butcher in New York, and was going in to the country to fetch cattle for his master: whoever secures him in any of his Majesty's Goals, so that his master may have him again, shall be well rewarded.

168. *The New-York Gazette: or, The Weekly Post-Boy*, #820, September 13, 1758.

Run away yesterday morning from Joseph Griswold of this city, distiller; a middle siz'd Negro man, aged about 40, speaks little or no English, as he mostly lived with the French: had on when he went away, a short blue sailor's jacket, and trowsers, a check shirt, and old hat. His name is Frank or Francois—Whoever takes up said Negro fellow, so that his master may have him again, shall have twenty shillings reward, and all reasonable charges paid by JOSEPH GRISWOLD, living in Pearl-Street.

169. *The New-York Gazette: or, The Weekly Post-Boy*, #820, September 13, 1758.

Run away from the Subscriber, living at Philipsburg, a Mulatto Servant Man, named Henry, aged 23 years, about 5 feet 8 inches high; has a Scar on his forehead; took with him a greasy Beaver Hat; wore a brown homespun Coat; took away with him a blue Jacket and several other things; he plays very well on the Violin.—Whoever secures the said Mulatto so that his Master may have him again, shall have 20 shillings reward and all reasonable charges paid by Samuel Devenport.

170. *The New York Mercury*, #321, October 9, 1758.

Run-away on Monday the second Instant, from Benjamin Williams, a Negro Man, named Bristol, about 5 feet 7 inches high, aged about 26 Years: Had on when he went away a red Jacket, brown Great-Coat, brown Camblet Breeches and wide trowsers, a pair of new shoes, with strings, and a new felt hat: Whoever takes up said Negro fellow and brings him to his said master at Newark or to Daniel Nap, in New York, shall have Forty Shillings Reward and all resonable charges paid by Benjamin Williams.

171. *The New-York Gazette: or, The Weekly Post-Boy*, #832, December 11, 1758.

Run away from Benjamin Williams, of Newark in East New Jersey, on Monday the 4th Instant; A Negro Man, about 26 years of age, five feet seven inches high; had on when he went away, a Jersey Provincial Coat, red Jacket, and wide trowsers; speaks good english, and plays well on the Violin. Whoever secures said Negro, and brings him to me, shall have Forty shillings reward, and all Charges paid, by BEN WILLIAMS.

Advertisements

172. *The New-York Gazette: or, The Weekly Post-Boy*, #833, December 18, 1758.

Run away on the 23rd of December, 1757, from the sloop Walter, of Maryland, then lying at Hunter's Quay, in New York; a Negro Fellow named RALPH, Maryland born; about 5 feet 6 inches high; speaks hoarse and thick, and is a great Chewer of Tobacco; flat nose and very thick lip'd, and wide mouth'd. He has been scalded on the Back of his left hand, and up his arm, by which the scar thereof appears; and is of a swarthy complexion: He has also a great many Dents in the Top of his Head, which seem to be the Ward-end of a key: he has the Use of his left Hand better than his Right; and is what is commonly called left-handed: he has had the Small-Pox, but not much pitted It's expected he is on board some of the Privateers belonging to this city. Whoever takes up and secures the above Negro, so that his master may have him again, shall have FIVE POUNDS Reward,—if in or near New York, the Reward will be paid by Samuel Bowne, Merchant;—if in Philadelphia, by Reefe Meredith, Merchant,—and if in Maryland, by James Campbell (the Owner) in Charles Country; besides all reasonable charges.

173. *Parker's New-York Gazette; or, The Weekly Post-Boy*, #838, January 22, 1759.

Ran away from Richard Harris, of Staten Island, the 14th Instant; a Negro man named Tom, speaks good English, about 30 years of age. Ran away at the same time a Negro Boy named Harry, 14 years old, has an Impediment in his speech, speaks good French, and has lost one of Fore Teeth: They both had light coloured Kersey jackets, with white flowered Metal Buttons; Harry had a cap on, such as Mariners generally wear, and Tom had a Great coat with a cap to it, that covered his head on Occasion. Whoever takes up and secures said Negroes, so that their Master can have them again, shall receive twenty shillings reward for each, and all reasonable Charges paid by RICHARD HARRIS.

174. Parker's New-York Gazette; or, The Weekly Post-Boy, #839, January 29, 1759.

TEN POUNDS Reward: Run away on Wednesday Night last, from the Subscriber, a Negro fellow named Jack, well-set, and not very black: Had on when he went away, a brown Pea-jacket, and a blue under one: He also took with him a Pair of Buck-skin Breeches. Whoever takes up and secures said Negro Fellow, so that his Master may have him again, shall receive TEN POUNDS Reward, and all reasonable charges paid by Wm. Brown John.

All Masters of Vessels and others, are forbid to carry off said Fellow, at their peril.

175. Parker's New-York Gazette; or, The Weekly Post-Boy, #858, May 28, 1759.

New-York, May 16, 1759. Run away from Nicholas Jones, and Luke Ryerson, of Paughquanack in the County of Bergen, on Sunday Night the 13th Instant, Two Negro Men Slaves, one named Peter, a lusty well set Fellow about 5 feet 6 inches high, had on when he went away, a linsey woolsey Jacket with Pewter Buttons, Leather Breeches, new Shoes with Brass Buckles, a worsted Cap and Felt Hat.

The other named York, is about 5 foot high, pretty much pock-broken, he had on when he went off, a greenish homespun Jacket, a Castor Hat almost new, and a worsted Cap; they also took with them sundry other Cloaths, a Dog, a Gun, and a Fiddle: Whoever apprehends the above mentioned Negroes, and secures them in any Goal so that their Masters may have them again, shall receive FORTY SHILLINGS Reward for each, and all reasonable Charges paid, by NICHOLAS JONES, And LUKE RYERSON.

N.B. All masters of Vessels, Captains of Privateers and others, are forbid to entertain, or carry off said Fellows at their Peril.

176. *Parker's New-York Gazette; or, The Weekly Post-Boy*, #860, June 21, 1759.

Forty-Five Pounds, Proclamation Money, Reward. Runaway last night from the subscribers living in Hopewell, In New Jersey, one Mulatto, and three Negroe Men, viz. The Mulatto named Bood and a Negroe named Bristol, the property of William Hunt, is about five feet ten inches high and pretty well set; they each had a dark colour'd coat, several Shirts and Pairs of Shoes, Stockings and Breeches: for taking up and bringing back to his Master, Twenty Pounds Reward for Bood and Ten Pounds for Bristol.

A Negroe Man named Jack, thick and well set, the property of John Hart, took with him a Cloth Coloured Kersey Coat, several Shirts and Pairs of Breeches, Shoes and Stockings: Ten Pounds will be given for taking him up and bringing him back to his Master.

Also a Negro man named Tom, short and well set, the property of Joseph Calder, took with him a dark coloured coat, several shirts, Pairs of Breeches, Shoes and Stockings. Five Pounds reward will be given for taking him up and returning him to his Master.

It is supposed they all went away and will travel together, and that they are gone to some of the Indian Towns upon Sasquehannah, the Mollatto Bood, having been entertained by the Indians there several months, some years ago; they took two Guns, two or three Hatchets and several Blankets with them. William Hunt, John Hart, Joseph Calder.

177. *Parker's New-York Gazette; or, The Weekly Post-Boy*, #865, July 30, 1759.

RUN-AWAY, On Friday the 18th Day of May, from JAMES I. ROSS of the Nine-Partners in Dutchess-County, a Negro Man Named Dick, but sometimes called Martin, speaks good English and Dutch, about Thirty or Thirty-three years of Age, a middling tall slim Negro; had on when he went away, a woolen check Shirt, and took with him a linnen check Shirt, a purple blue napt Jacket, lined with yellow Flannel, a Pair of Linnen Trousers; and took with him a Pair of Check Trousers, a Pair of black and white Stockings, a Thread of white and a Thread of Black twisted together, a Pair of grey Stockings, a great Coat of a Yellowish Brown, and a worsted Cap:—Whoever takes and secures said Negro, so that his Master may have him again, shall have THREE POUNDS Reward, and all reasonable Charges paid, by Dutchess-County, May 18, 1759. JAMES I. ROSS.

178. *Parker's New-York Gazette; or, The Weekly Post-Boy*, #868, August 20, 1759.

Run away on the 6th Instant, from Joshua Hatfield, of the White Plains, in West-chester County, Province of New-York, a negro man named Will; he is about 26 Years of Age, thin visag'd, and slim Bodied;—Had on when he went away, a home-spun Jacket, of different colours, but may change his Cloaths perhaps, and talks good English.—whoever takes up said negro, and will secure him so that his master may have him again, or will bring him to Capt. Abraham Hatfield, or Dr. Graham, of the White-Plains aforesaid, shall receive, if taken within Twelve miles of the said Plains, 16 Shillings, and if farther, 40 Shillings Reward, and all reasonable Charges paid by me Joshua Hatfield. N.B. All masters of Vessels, or Captains of Privateers are here by forwarned from carrying off said Negro, as they may expect to answer the same at their Peril.

179. *Parker's New-York Gazette, or, The Weekly Post-Boy*, #869, August 27, 1759.

Run away from Dennis Hicks, of Phillipsbourg, in Westchester County and the Province of New York, a mulatto man named Bill, aged about 20 years. Had on a brown Camblet waistcoat without sleeves and one Camblet ditto lined with silk, a pair of new blue stockings, a pair of new shoes, a pair of Leather Breeches and old Trousers, and one pair of striped ditto, a coarse felt hat stitched around the brim with white yarn. he has a long sharp nose with a black Mole on the Right side of his face near his Nose; has very large Ears, speaks good English and pretends to be free, he says that he has a White Mother and was born in New England. He is of middle size and has a thin visage with his hair cut off. All persons are forbid to harbour him and all masters of vessels are forbid to carry him off, as they will answer it at their peril. Forty shillings reward for securing him in any gaol, or bringing him to me so that I may have him again, and reasonable charges paid by Dennis Hicks.

N.B. This fellow was advertised in the New York papers on the 5th of June, and in Newhaven the 11th of June, and was afterwards taken up in Waterbury, and was put into Litchfield gaol and from thence he was brought to Bedford, and there made his escape from his master again. Those who apprehend him are desired to secure him in Irons. He was taken up by Moses Foote of North Waterbury in New-England. It is likely he will change his clothes as he did before. The Mole above mentioned is something Long.

180. *Parker's New-York Gazette; or, The Weekly Post-Boy*, **#874**, October 1, 1759.

Run away from the subscriber, living at the great Nine Partners in Dutchess County, a negro man named Jack Green, about 5 feet 8 inches high, well made and a strong fellow: Had on when he went away, a blue Jacket and Check Trousers. Whoever takes up and secures the said negro so that his master may have him again, shall receive Twenty Shillings reward and all reasonable charges paid by Joel Gillet. N.B. He took a dark Bay Horse with him.

181. Parker's New-York Gazette; or, The Weekly Post-Boy, #874, October 1, 1759.

Run away on Wednesday the 26th of September last, from Captain Thomas Davies of the City of New-York, a mulatto wench named Fanny, with her young child about 8 months old, the said Wench is pretty tall and had on when she went away a red and white striped Cotten Gown, a striped blue and white Petticoat, and a Cap without any Border: Whoever takes up the said Wench and brings her to the said Thomas Davies at the sign of the Harlequin at the Whitehall Slip, shall have Twenty Shillings reward and all reasonable charges paid by Thomas Davies. October 1, 1759.

182. Parker's New-York Gazette; or, The Weekly Post-Boy, #881, November 19, 1759.

Run away on the 29th day of October from Richard Barnes of Harrison's Purchase in West-Chester County and the Province of New York, a negro man named Peter, but he may perhaps change his name, he is about 26 years of age, is short and well set, has had the Small-pox but had it easy and turns his Toes within as he Walks, he is a fine bold sulking Fellow. Had on when he went away a good Felt Hat, a new Woolen Jacket of a dark Colour almost new and an old Bearskin Jacket under it, one or two Shirts and a pair of Wollen Britches and one Pair of blue Stockings, but it is very likely he may Change his Apparell. Whoever takes up the said negro so that his Master may have him again shall have Twenty Shillings reward if taken within 20 miles, and Forty Shillings if taken farther off paid by me, Richard Barnes. N.B. It is supposed he will go either to the army or sea; therefore all Captains of Vessels are forbidden to carry him off at their Peril.

Advertisements

183. *Parker's New-York Gazette; or, The Weekly Post-Boy*, #889, December 31, 1759.

New-York, December 31, 1759, RUN-AWAY, from Charles Lewis, of the City of New-York, Mariner, the 20th Instant, a negro fellow named Harry, about 5 feet nine Inches high: Had on when he went away, an old green Jacket, and a white one under it, wore a Cap, and Woolen ribb'd Stockings, and had an Iron Collar round his neck, which is not visible without examination. Whoever takes up said Negro Fellow and secures him so that his Master may have him again, shall receive Twenty Shillings reward, and all reasonable Charges paid, by CHARLES LEWIS.

184. *Parker's New-York Gazette; or, The Weekly Post-Boy*, #894, February 18, 1760.

Run away on Friday the Eighth of February inst. From John Sebastian Stephany, Chymist, a Negroe Man, named Pompey, he had a wooden Leg on when he went away, a white Coat, an Ozenbrigs Shirt, tow Cloth Trowsers: Whoever takes up the Said Negroe, and brings him to his said Master, shall have Twenty Shillings Reward, paid by JOHN SEBASTIAN STEPHANY.
    N.B. He inclines to go to Sea, all Masters of Vessels are forbid to carry him away, as they shall answer it at their Perril.

185. *Parker's New-York Gazette; or, The Weekly Post-Boy*, #898, March 17, 1760.

New-York, March 17, 1760. Saturday Evening Run-away from on Board the Snow *Sadler*, a Negroe Boy named Glasgow, aged about 18 Years, has got several Cuts in his Forehead, has a very clumsy Walk, and talks very broken English: Had on when he went away, a blue great Coat, a plain white Swan-skin Jacket, a pair of Trowsers, a pair of light blue Stockings joined in the Middle, and new pair of Shoes. Whoever takes up the said Boy, and brings him to his Master, shall have a Reward of THREE POUNDS, and all reasonable Charges paid by Captain WILLIAM FITZHERBERT, now living at the New-Dock.

N.B. All House-Keepers and Masters of Vessels are forbid to harbour the said Boy, for if they do, they may depend on being prosecuted according to Law.

186. *Parker's New-York Gazette; or, The Weekly Post-Boy*, #901, April 14, 1760.

FLUSHING, on LONG-ISLAND, March 30, 1760. RUN-AWAY from Barnabus Ryder a Negro Man named Cæsar, aged about 25 Years, this country born, he is not a right Black, has a little of the Yellowish Cast, a pretty lusty Fellow, Talks good English, but Stutters a little in common, and if frightened he stutters very much; He is Remarkable for losing one of his Fore Teeth: Had on when he went away a light colour'd Devonshire-kersy Coat, a Soldiers Red Jacket, Breeches and Hat, a pair of old Shoes. Whoever takes upon the said negro Man and bring him to his said Master, shall have 40 Shillings Reward, and all reasonable Charges paid, by BARNABUS RYDER, now living at Flushing.

N.B. All House-keepers and Masters of Vessels are forbid to harbour said Negro Man; if they do, they may depend on being Prosecuted according to Law.

187. *The Pennsylvania Gazette* (Philadelphia), #1644, June 26, 1760.

Upper-Freehold, June 16, 1760 Runaway from the subscriber, last night, a Negroe Man, named Abraham, aboput five feet ten inches high, 21 years of age and of a very black Colour: Had on when he went away, a brown Jacket, with Pewter Buttons, a half worn Felt Hat, one Pair of half worn Shoes, and one pair of Worsted Stockings. He also took with him two Pair of Trowsers, four Shirts, one pair of Cotton Stockings and one Crape Neckcloth. Whoever takes up and secures said Negro so that his Master may have him again, shall have Forty Shillings reward, and reasonable charges paid by me. John Cox.

188. *Parker's New-York Gazette; or, The Weekly Post-Boy,* **#912, June 30, 1760.**

Run away on Friday the 6th of June, from Roger Barnes, a negro boy named Tom, aged 14 or 15 years, born in New-York, pretty black. Had on when he went away a felt hat, an Osnabrigs shirt and trousers, deep blue broad cloth jacket, the Fore-parts lined in two Colours, red and brown cloth, with white Buttons. Whoever takes up the said negro so that his Master may have him again shall receive Forty Shillings reward and all reasonable charges paid by Roger Barnes. N.B. All persons are forbid to harbour said negro.

189. *The New York Mercury,* **#416, August 4, 1760.**

Run-Away from the Subscriber living at Bergen in New-Jersey on Wednesday the 30th of July, a Negro fellow named Robin, about 25 years of age, five feet 8 inches high, and speaks good Dutch and English, this Country born, is a slim yellow Fellow and had a down look: Had on when he went away, a blue Cloth Jacket and Tow Trowsers. Whoever takes up and secures said Fellow, if in New York, shall have Forty Shillings, and if out of the Province of New York, Three Pounds and all reasonable charges paid by Thomas Brown in New-York or George Codiments.

N.B. All Masters of Vessels and others are forbid to carry him off or harbour him.

190. *Parker's New-York Gazette; or, The Weekly Post-Boy,* **#931, November 6, 1760.**

Run away from John Waddell the 6th Instant, a negro man named Charles, about 24 years old, a likely middle fine Fellow, talks good English, this Country born; he formerly belonged to Colonel Moore, is well known in town and in Harlaem, and was seen last Saturday night in Harlaem. Whoever takes up said negro and brings him to his master shall have Five Pounds reward paid by John Waddell.

N.B. He reports that he is a free negro and has a Counterfeit pass or Certificate, in order to induce any Commander of a vessel to take him off.

191. *Parker's New-York Gazette; or, The Weekly Post-Boy,* **#933, November 20, 1760.**

Forty Dollars reward and all reasonable charges shall be paid to any person that secures and brings to William Kelly of the City of New York, merchant, a negro man named Norton Minors who ran away from his masters, Messrs. Bodkin and Farrall on the Island of St. Croix, on the first Day of July last; is by trade a Caulker and Ship Carpenter, has lived at Newbury in New England, was the property of Mr. Mark Quayne, who sold him to Mr. Craddock at Nevis, from whom the above gentlemen bought him about three years ago, is about five feet eight inches high, aged about 37, speaks English, reads and writes, and is a very sensible fellow.

192. *Parker's New-York Gazette; or, The Weekly Post-Boy,* **#940, January 8, 1761.**

New-York, December 24, 1760, Ran away the 24th of September last, from John Mersereau, Carpenter, of Staten-Island, a Negro Man named Hank, aged about 25 Years, five Feet, seven Inches high, is partly black, and has a Hair Mole, on his right Cheek; he speaks better Dutch than English, had on a brown homespun Cloth Coat, full made, and a pair of Trowsers:—He formerly belonged to one Mr. LeRoux, and also to one Mr. Campbell, both of Tapan, in Bergen County, and it is strongly suspected that he is still lurking or concealed either at Tapan or Kakeat, in the said County. Whoever takes up, and secures the said Negro, so that his Master may have him again, shall have FIVE POUNDS Reward, and all reasonable Charges. And if any One will give certain Intelligence of his being entertained or concealed so that the Offender may be brought to justice, He shall have FIFTEEN POUNDS Reward, upon Conviction, besides all reasonable Charges, paid by JOHN MERSEREAU.

193. *The New-York Gazette* (Weyman's), #108, February 16, 1761.

RUN AWAY from the Subscriber, on the 20th of December last, a Negro or Mulatto Man Servant, aged about 28 Years, named Mark Edward, born near Byram River, in the County of Westchester; a well set Fellow, near six Feet high, talks good English, plays well on a Fiddle, calls himself a free Fellow, goes commonly with his Head shaved, hath two Crowns on the top of his Head, small black specks or moles in his Eyes, with a scar near the middle of his Breast, and a mole on his left Breast. Had on when he went away, a good pair of Leather Breeches, a blue Broadcloth Jacket, a red Jacket under it without sleeves, a good Beaver Hat. Whoever takes up and secures said Fellow, shall have FIVE POUNDS New-York Money Reward, and all reasonable Charges paid, by me ABNER SMITH, of New-Haven, in the Colony of Connecticut.

N.B. All House-keepers, and Masters of Vessels, are hereby forbid to harbour, conceal, or carry off said Fellow, as they may depend on being prosecuted according to Law.
ABNER SMITH

194. Parker's New-York Gazette; or, The Weekly Post-Boy, #947, February 26, 1761.

Run away on Sunday Evening the first of February, a Molatto Wench named Suck, aged about 20 Years, formerly belonging to Boshirks, Had on when she went off a Homespun Short Gown with different coloured Stripes, a Blue and white Handkerchief, a quilted petticoat, one side Light coloured the other side Black, with white Woollen Stockings; a short, and inclining to fat Wench. Likewise Run away on Monday February the 16th, a Negro Man named Prince, had on when he went off a Brown Bearskin Pea Jacket Double Breast Lapel, lined with light coloured Cloth, a short Double Breasted Red Waistcoat Brass Buttons, a pair of Cloth Breeches, Olive Colour, Red Puffs and Button-Holes, 5 Foot 10 Inches high, straight, much pitted with the small Pox, late belonging to the Widow Phillips, brought up at West-Chester. Whoever takes up either of the said Negroes, so that their Masters may have them again, shall have Three Pounds for either of them if taken in the Country, and Thirty Shillings if taken in Town for either, and all reasonable Charges paid, by Capt. HUNTER and Capt. SAMUEL BAYARD.

195. Parker's New-York Gazette; or, The Weekly Post-Boy, #963, June 18, 1761.

RUN AWAY, on Tuesday the 9th Inst. from the Subscriber, living at Turtle-Bay, a Mulatto Wench named Lens, 17 Years old, can speak good Dutch and English, and sings a good Song; is a handsome Wench, and may pass for a free person, as she is very well featured all but her nose, and lips, which are thick and flat, has long black curld hair and a mould on her face: Had on when she went away a homespun Josey and Pettycoat, but no shoes nor stockings. Whoever takes up and secures said wench on the Island of New-York, so that she may be had again, shall have Forty

Shillings Reward, and if in another Government, Three Pounds paid by DAVID DEVORE,

N.B. All Persons are forbid to harbour or entertain said Wench at their peril. Likewise, all Masters of Vessels are forbid to carry her off.

196. *Parker's New-York Gazette; or, The Weekly Post-Boy,* **#968, July 23, 1761.**

RUN AWAY from JAMES BERNARD, Inn-holder at the King's Bridge, A Negro Man, named Windsor, About 23 Years of Age, short Stature, full faced, with Blotches in his Face, and walks bow-legged: Had on when he went away, a brown Frock Livery Coat with yellow Collar and Button-holes, white Shirt, and Waistcoat, black Shag Breeches, speckled Stockings, new Shoes, a Gold lac'd Hat, and had with him a new Beaver Hat. Whoever takes up and secures said Slave in the Work-house in New-York, shall have Twenty Shillings Reward. All Masters of Vessels and others, are warned not to harbour, conceal, or carry off the said Negro, as they will answer it at their peril.

197. *Pennsylvania Journal, and the Weekly Advertiser,* **(Philadelphia), #976, August 20, 1761.**

Run-away from the Subscriber a Negro Man named Quaco about five feet eight inches high, marked in the Face with sundry short strokes: Had on when he went away an old Light coloured Coat, old torn shirt, a white Pair of Trowsers, a pair of new shoes, with a Pair of brass Buckles in it, and a Pair of light coloured yarn Stockings: The said Negro had an iron Collar with two Hooks to it, round his neck, a pair of Hand-cuffs with a chain to them, six Feet long. Whosoever takes up said Negro and confines him to any Gaol, or conveys him to his Master shall have Forty Shillings Reward and all Necessary charges paid by me Joseph Carver.

N.B. It is supposed that he will make for Philadelphia, for he was taken from thence the 11th Instant. The Negro talks broken English. He is a of a black complexion, and a lusty fellow. All persons are forbid harbouring said Negro, if they do, they must expect penalty of the Law.

Please to enquire for the Owner at Daniel Cooper's Ferry.

198. *The New-York Gazette* (Weyman's), #145, October 13, 1761.

RUN away on the 4th of September, from *Elias Wood*, of *Elizabeth-Town*, in *New-Jersey*, a Negro Man named ROBIN, formerly lived with *John Zobriskey*, at *Hackensack*, and lately at *James Johnston's*, on Staten-Island, used to go in his Ferry-Boat: He is a middling tall strait-limb'd Fellow, Mark'd with the Small-pox, yellow Complexion, long curl'd Hair, a little Dutchified. Whoever secures him in any of his Majesty's Gaols, so that his Master may have him again, shall have EIGHT DOLLARS Reward, and all reasonable Charges paid. (It's supposed he has taken a Canoe out of Bown-Creek) N. B. All Masters of Vessels and others, are forbid carrying off said Servant.

199. *Parker's New-York Gazette; or, The Weekly Post-Boy*, #993, January 14, 1762.

Run away the 4th instant from David Anderson of North Castle, in New York Government, a Negro Man Servant named Tom, 28 years of age, 5 feet 6 inches high, or there about; well built, and very Square broad Shoulders, has a Scar on the right side of his Nose, another under his left Eye, also one on the left side of his Head, plain to be seen, given to him by a Horse as he says, speaks good English and Low Dutch, is a very artful and insinuating Fellow, and plays on the fiddle, had on when he went away, an old sail Hat, blue Jacket, red Great Coat, blue breeches with trowsers over them, tow shirt, white yarn stockings, old

Advertisements 91

Shoes and large Brass Buckles: Whoever apprehends him and brings him to his aforesaid Master, or secures him in any of his Majesty's Gaols so that his Master may have him again, shall have Twenty Shillings reward, and all necessary charges paid by David Anderson.
  N.B. All persons are forbiden to harbour the above said negro at their peril.

200. *The Pennsylvania Gazette* (**Philadelphia**), **#1739, April 22, 1762.**

Run away from the Subscriber hereof, on Thursday the 8th of April inst, a Negroe lad named Moses, about 18 years of age, born at Trenton, in East Jersey: Wore (when he went away from my home in Oxford Township in the County of Philadelphia) a striped Lincey inside Jacket, without any sleeves, a Buckskin outside Jacket, an old Felt Hat, a light coloured Pair of Cloth breeches pretty much worn, a Pair of old Shoes, an old Pair of greyish Stockings and plain Brass Buckles; he has also a remarkable scar across the Toes of his left foot. Any Person or Persons who will apprehend the said Negroe lad, and have him secured, so that the Owner may have him again, shall have Forty Shillings Reward, and all reasonable charges paid by me George Keen.

201. *Parker's New-York Gazette; or, The Weekly Post-Boy*, **#1008, April 29, 1762.**

Five pounds reward, run away on Monday the 12th instant from me the subscriber, a Mulatto Servant man named Charles, and known by the name of Charles Roberts, or German. He is a likely well set Fellow, 28 or 30 years of age, and about 5 feet 6 inches high, and has had the Small-Pox. He has a Variety of Clothes, some of them very good, and effects to dress very neat and genteel, and generally wears a Wig. He took with him two or three Coats or Suits, a dark brown or Chocolate coloured Cloth coat, pretty much worn, a dun or Dove coloured cloth, or fine Frize, but little worn, and a light blue grey Summer Coat of Grogam, Camblet, or some such stuff, a Straw coloured Waistcoat, edged with a Silver Cord, almost new; and several other Waistcoats, Breeches, and Pair of Stockings; a blue Great Coat, and a Fiddle. His behavior is excessively complaisent, obsequious, and insinuating; he speaks good English smoothly and plausibly, and generally with a cringe and a smile, he is extremely artful, and ready at inventing specious pretences to conceal villanous Actions or Designs. He plays on the Fiddle, can read and write tolerably well, and understands a little of Arithmetic and Accounts. I have reason to believe some evil minded Persons in town have encouraged and been Accomplices in his villanous Designs; it is probable he will contrive the most specious forgeries to give him the appearance of a free man: I have already been informed of a Writing he has shown for that Purpose and by which means he has imposed upon many people; who may all be easily satisfied he has no legal claim to freedom, even from slavery, nor any pretence, but by the very law which he is my servant for 40 years, as the record of the court at New Haven will witness. At that place where the former Owner of the said Slave lived, he was guilty of various Crimes and Felonies, for which he was several times publickly whipped, and only escaped the Gallows by want of Prosecution. When he became my servant I intended to have him shipped to the West Indies and sold him there, and kept him in prison till I should get an Opportunity, but on his earnest request solemn Promises of his Good Behavior, and seeming Penitence I took him into my Family upon trial, where for a Time he behaved well and was very servicable to me. Decieved by his seeming Reformation, I placed some Confidence in him, which he has villanously abused; having embezzled Money sent him to pay for Goods, borrowed money and taken up goods in my Name unknown to me, and also put on his own Account, pretending to be a Freeman. By this villanous proceeding I suppose he has collected a considerable Sum of Money; I am also apprehensive that he has been an Accomplice in some of the late Robberies commited in and near this City. Whoever will take up the said Servant and bring him to me or secure him in some of his Majesty's Gaols so that I can have him again, if taken up in the City of New York shall have Five Pounds reward and greater, if taken up at a greater Distance. Any persons who take him up are desired to be careful and to bring him before the Magistrate, and have him well searched, leaving all the Money and Goods found upon him except the necessary he has on in the Hands of the Magistrate, and to be very watchful against an Escape, or being deceived by him, for he is one of the most artful of Villains. John Holt.

202. *The Pennsylvania Journal, and the Weekly Advertiser* (Philadelphia), #1021, July 1, 1762.

July 1, 1762 Run-away from Moore Furman of Trenton on Saturday last, a Negro Man named Harry, he appears to be about 20 years of age, speaks low but proper and can read English, is about 5 feet 9 inches high, and slender made, stoops a little, or rather hangs his Head looks down and suspicious when he is spoke to; his Leggs are small and his Feet appear flatter than common tho' not large and when he walks turns his toes out pretty much and walks heavy; he had on when he went away, an old Bearskin Jacket much patched and mended, an Ozenbrig Shirt and Trowsers, but he has a Change of summer Cloathes with him chiefly made of fagoty or fustian of a pale yellow or snuff Colour, he may alter his Dress. Whoever takes up and secures said Negroe so that his Master may have him again, or will deliver him to the subscriber in Philadelphia, shall receive a reward of Forty Shillings and be paid all reasonable charges by Robert Lettis Cooper, jun.
N.B. He is not been used to hard labour.

203. *The New-York Gazette; or, The Weekly Post-Boy*, **#1018, July 8, 1762.**

Second River, June 30, 1762.
Run away from his Master a negro man named Frank, tall, slim, had on when he went away; a Tow shirt and Trousers, bare foot and bare legged, has a Scar on his Upper Lip, from his Nose downwards: Whoever takes up the said negro, and secures him, so that his Master may have him again shall have Forty Shillings reward, and all reasonable charges paid by John Kingsland.

204. *The New-York Gazette; or, The Weekly Post-Boy*, **#1024, August 19, 1762.**

New York, August 19, 1762. RUN away from the Subscriber, on Tuesday the 27th instant, a French Negro Man, about 30 Years of Age; speaks pretty good English of a short Stature yellow Complection, and has had the Small Pox, and doubtless will pretend to be a free Man.—Had on when he went away a Light colour'd cloth pair of breeches and Jacket with flash Sleeves, a Pair of long striped Trowsers, a Check Shirt with Chitterstrings, and wears Wings in his Ears: Whoever takes up and secures said Negro, so that his Master may have him again, shall have Forty Shillings Reward, and all reasonable Charges paid by BENJAMIN HALSTED.

205. *The New-York Gazette; or, The Weekly Post-Boy*, **#1025, August 26, 1762.**

RUN away on Sunday Evening the 22d Instant, from Mrs JANE DURHAM, a Negroe Fellow nam'd TOM, about five Feet and a Half, of a black Complexion; had on when he went away a light brown Sagathee Coat, crimson Waistcoat and Breeches, a pair of light grey Stockings, white Shirt and Felt Hat, he formerly lived at Chariss Hunt's, at Eastchester, where it is supposed he is gone to: he took with him a

Violin, as he play's on it: Whoever takes up said Negro and secures him, so that his Mistress may have him again, shall receive FIVE POUNDS Reward, and all reasonable Charges paid. All Persons are forwarned harbouring or entertaining him: and all Masters of Vessels are forbid carrying him off, as they shall answer at their Peril. JANE DURHAM.

206. *The Pennsylvania Gazette* (Philadelphia), #1759, September 9, 1762.

Run away from James Smith of Burlington, on the 3rd of this Inst. September; a Mullato Servant Man, named Jack, or John Johnson, about 24 Years of age; he had a bushy head of Hair, stoops as he walks, splaw footed: Had on when he went away, a light colour'd Home-spun Coat and Linen Jacket, with black Glass Buttons, light Fustian Breeches, or else blue Cloth ones, Ozenbrigs shirt, Worsted Stockings, good Pumps, with carved Brass Buckles in them. He formerly lived with Joseph Biddle of Springfield. He ran away on the 16th of June last and was committed to Chester Gaol. Any Person that takes him up and confines him in any Gaol, and send Word to his Master, shall have Three Pounds Reward and reasonable Charges, paid by James Smith.
  N.B. He has old indentures and other Papers with him that he may impose upon the Public with. It is supposed he wants to get on board a Privateer or some other Vessel. All Masters of Vessels are requested not to carry him off.

207. *The New-York Gazette; or, The Weekly Post-Boy*, #1027, September 9, 1762.

RUN away from the Subscriber, living at Egg Harbour, in the County of Gloster, and Province of New-Jersey, the 23d of August, a Mulatto Servant Man named JAMES, about 27 Years of Age, he is a short well set Fellow, speaks good English, with remarkable bushy Hair; had on when he went off, an Oznabrigs Shirt, Tow Trowsers and Frock; he also took with him a handsome Dog: Whoever takes up said Servant and gives Intelligence, or secures him in any of his Majesty's Gaols, so that his Master may have him, shall have FIVE POUNDS Reward, and all reasonable Charges paid by me RICHARD WESCOT.

208. *The New-York Gazette; or, The Weekly Post-Boy*, #1027, September 9, 1762.

New-York, Sept. 9, 1762. RAN away the 8th inst. a Negro Man named Jack, alias Salem, a short sett Fellow, a little lame on his right Foot, speaks good English, had on, when he went away, a blew Surtout Coat with yellow Buttons, black knit Breeches, black Stockings, and a Check-Shirt: Whoever brings said Negro to Christopher Heysham, in Kingstreet, shall have Two Dollars Reward if taken within the City, and Five Dollars if taken without, and all necessary Charges paid by said HEYSHAM. N.B. All Persons are forbid harbouring or carrying off said Negro at their Peril.

209. *The New-York Gazette; or, The Weekly Post-Boy*, #1027, September 9, 1762.

Taken up, a Runaway. ON Fryday the 27th of last Month was taken up, and is now confined in the Gaol at the City Hall Perth Amboy, a Negro Man who says his name is FRANK, and that he belongs to George Risoer, living at Pompton in East New Jersey. The Master of the said Negro, making his Property appear, may have him, on paying Charges, by applying to the Subscriber, Gaoler of the City Hall at Perth Amboy. JONATHON MILLS. Sept. 7th 1762.

210. *The New-York Gazette; or, The Weekly Post-Boy*, #1029, September 23, 1762.

New-York, September 22, 1762. RUN AWAY, ON Tuesday last a Negro Boy, named Jack, 13 or 14 Years of age about 5 Feet high, pretty well set, born at Martinico and speaks but little English, has something of a down, heavy look, not very Pleasant, and is not much given to talking. He had on a white Shirt, a Pair of black stocking Breeches (perhaps he may have a pair of Trowsers over them) a white Waistcoat next his shirt, above that a lightish brown stuff Waistcoat, with a dirty Silver Cord round the Edges, and no Sleeves, and above that a black Stocking Waistcoat, much too bigg and too long for him, a black silk Neck Cloth and a Castor Hat somewhat worn. He had no Shoes or Stockings. He always carried with him a short Hickory Stick with a ferrel, and a black String; He was seen on Wednesday Morning at the Ferry Stairs: Whoever will bring the Said Runaway to me, or secure him and gives me Notice shall have TWO DOLLARS Reward, and all reasonable Charges paid. All Persons are forbidden to harbour, or entertain him, or carry him out of the province, as they will answer it at their Peril. SAMUEL DEALL.

211. *The New-York Gazette; or, The Weekly Post-Boy*, #1030, September 30, 1762.

Tappan, Sept. 26, 1762. RUN away last Sunday Evening, from his Master, in Orange County, Johannes Blauveldt, Blacksmith, a Negro Fellow, named as he says, Adonia, but by us Duca, he is a yellow Complexion, being a mixed Breed, speaks and reads pretty good Low Dutch, and speaks little English: is a very good Black Smith by Trade, and can make Leather Shoes, and do some thing at the Carpenters Trade, is about 5 and a half Feet high, full Faced, black Hair, but cut off about one Inch long, is 20 or 22 Years old, had on, when he went away, homespun Trowsers, Shirt, gray Waistcoat, and Felt Hat; took with him a check Shirt and Trowsers, a white Shirt and a Pair of blue Cloth Breeches, and one home spun Waist Coat, he had been whip'd the day before he went off, which may be seen pretty much on his right side, he pretends to be free, and perhaps will get a Pass for that Purpose: Whoever takes up and secures the said Fellow, so that his Master may have him

again, shall have THREE POUNDS Reward, and all reasonable Charges paid by JOHANNES BLAUVELDT
 N.B. All Masters of Vessels and others are forbid to carry him away.

212. *The New-York Gazette; or, The Weekly Post-Boy*, #1030, September 30, 1762.

RUN away from the Hospital in New-York, a negro Man, named Pero, about 19 Years old, had Bobs in his Ears, and a white Jacket, strip'd Trowsers, a Hat, but no Shoes, is a French Negroe from Martinico, can talk but little English, is a handsome Fellow, straight, very polite, has been gone a Fort'night; but has been seen lately in Town: Whoever takes him up, and brings him to the Printer hereof, shall have TEN DOLLARS Reward, and all other Charges paid, by JOHN STEWART. N.B. All Persons are forewarned not to harbour him, and Masters of Vessels not to carry him off.

213. *The Pennsylvania Gazette* (Philadelphia), #1764, October 14, 1762.

Broke out of the Trenton Gaol, on Monday night, the Fourth of this Instant October, a Negroe Wench, named Venus, formerly the Property of Samuel Stout, junior, in Amwell: Had on when she went away, a Lincey Jacket and Petticoat; she is likely to have round her Head two or three Handkerchiefs. Whoever takes up said Wench, or secures her so that she may be delivered to John Allen, High Sherrif at Trenton, or the Gaol Keeper, shall have Three Pounds Reward, and reasonable charges paid by me, John Allen, High Sherrif,
 N.B. All Masters of Vessels are forbid to carry her off at their Peril.

214. *The New-York Gazette; or, The Weekly Post-Boy*, #1032, October 14, 1762.

RUN AWAY, A Negro Fellow, who answers to the Name of SALVANUS, he is about 22 Years of Age, 5 Feet 4 Inches high, well set, pretty Black and pitted with the Small Pox. His Teeth are filed, he Speaketh broken English, had on when he went away, a Light blue double breasted Jacket, lined white Flannel, a Pair of light colour'd Breeches, and an Oznabrig shirt: He is supposed to be about Town in the Day Time, carrying in Wood for the People, to support himself: Whoever will bring the said Negro to RICHARD WESTON, Bricklayer, in King George Street next Door to Mr. George Peakes, shall receive TEN SHILLINGS Reward.

215. *The New-York Gazette; or, The Weekly Post-Boy*, #1035, November 4, 1762.

DUBLIN, A Negro, well known in New-York; the Property of Mr. Roper Dawson, ran away from Staten-Island, the 13th inst. He is about Five Feet high, slender built, has a scar under one of his Eyes, very pert, active, and talkative, speaks English very plain; had on, when he went away, a new Watch Coat of drab Colour, yellow Buttons; check Shirt, a Pair of old Duck Trowsers, plain square Copper Buckles in his Shoes, a broad Gold Lac'd Hat, also a blue Scotch Bonnet: Whoever give Intelligence of, and secures him, shall receive FIVE DOLLARS Reward, and all Charges paid by his Master: New-York, Octob. 20, 1762.

216. *The New-York Gazette; or, The Weekly Post-Boy*, #1038, November 25, 1762.

RAN away from the Subscriber, the 14th inst. a lusty well built Negro Fellow, named Pompey, aged 24 Years, his left Legg is a wooden one. Whoever takes up said negro, or secures him in any of his Majesty's Gaols, so that his Master may have him again, shall receive FIVE DOLLARS, and all reasonable Charges paid by J. SEBASTIAN STEPHANY. Chemist near the New Dutch Church.

N.B. All Masters of Vessels, and others, are forbid harbouring, concealing, or carrying off the said Negro, as they shall answer it at their Peril.

217. *The New-York Gazette; or, The Weekly Post-Boy*, #1042, December 23, 1762.

New-York, Dec. 21, 1762. Run away from the subscriber, a Negro Man named Joe, about 24 years of age, of a yellow Complection, much Pock-marked, about 5 feet 7 inches high, has something of a down Look, had on when he went away, a brown Coat with red Lining, a red double breasted Vest, a pair of old Thicksett breeches, Felt Hat, is supposed to have gone towards Rariton as he has relations there. Whoever takes up and secures the said negro so that his master may have him again shall have Forty Shillings reward and all reasonable charges paid by Stephen Forman.

218. *The Pennsylvania Gazette* (Philadelphia), #1775, December 30, 1762.

Run away on the 22nd, of December Inst. from Samuel Parr, of Waterford Township, Gloucester County, West-New-Jersey, three miles from the new Bridge on Cooper's Creek, a Negroe Man, named Moses, about five feet three or four inches high: Had on when he went away, a new Cloth upper Jacket, an old red under Jacket and old Leather Breeches. Took with him a Wherry, with Oars and Sail and a Gun. he is Country Born, about 23 Years of Age, formerly belonging to Standish Ford, and afterward to George Keen, who sold him out of the Workhouse for running away. Whoever takes up said Negroe and brings him to his Master, shall have Three Pounds Reward paid by Samuel Parr.

All Masters of Vessels are forbid to carry him off.

Advertisements 101

219. The New-York Gazette; or, The Weekly Post-Boy, #1044, January 7, 1763.

Ran away the 22nd instant from Anthony Waters, a negro man named Siro, about five feet two inches high, yellow Complexion, black curl'd Hair and Bow legs; had on when he went away, a brown Coat, green Jacket, Leather Breeches, and blue Stockings, his shoes cut on the top and sew'd up again. Whoever takes up said servant and brings him to his master or secures him in any of his majesty's gaols so that his master may have him again, shall receive twenty shillings reward and all reasonable charges paid by Anthony Waters, jr., or Edward Waters.

220. The New-York Gazette; or, The Weekly Post-Boy, #1061, March 5, 1763.

Went away on Sunday morning, the 1st day of May instant, from the house of Adam States, a negro woman called Lucretia or Cretia, she is low in stature, has not been long in the country, and speaks broken Dutch and English, she has had the smallpox and is also great with Child: She had on when she went away, a black Petticoat mended or patched on both Sides, a white Apron and a speckled Handkerchief, a blue waistcoat and laced cap with a blue short Cloak: She is very slow in walking and is very black of Complexion: She was entrusted into the Care of the Subscriber to sell, and belongs to the Widow Mary Dauchy, New York. Any person who takes up and secures the said negro woman so that her Mistress or the subscriber may have her again, shall receive three pounds in New York money and all reasonable charges paid by Henry Jacob Pitts.

All masters of vessels are hereby forewarn'd not to carry her off as they will answer at their peril.

221. The Pennsylvania Journal, and the Weekly Advertiser (Philadelphia), #1066, May 12, 1763.

Run away from Samuel Meeker, a Negro Man, Sampson, about 6 feet 4 inches, aged 24 Years, speaks good English: Had on when he went away two dark colour'd homespun Jackets, Leather Breeches, brown Stockings. Whoever takes up and secures said Negro so that his Master may have him again, shall receive Twenty Shillings Reward and all reasonable charges paid by Samuel Meeker.

222. The New-York Gazette; or, The Weekly Post-Boy, #1064, May 26, 1763.

Run away from Wilson Hunt, in Maidenhead, near Trenton, a Negro man named Bood, about 30 years of age, five Feet nine Inches high, pretty well set, of a yellowish Complexion; had on a Felt Hat, a dark brown tweil'd Kersey Jacket, a white Flannel Shirt, Leather Breeches, yarn Stockings, and good Shoes. Whoever takes up and secures the said Negro Man in any of his Majesty's Gaols, or brings him to his said Master shall have, if taken up in the Province of New Jersey, six Pounds, if out of that province, Ten Pounds Reward paid by
    May 2, 1763.   Wilson Hunt.
    N.B. He is a smooth Tongued Fellow and will endeavour to make his Escape if not well secured.

223. The New-York Gazette; or, The Weekly Post-Boy, #1067, June 16, 1763.

RUN away, last Night, from Samuel Hallett, of Hallett's Cove, a Negro Girl, named Phill, belonging to James Neilson, Esq; of New-Brunswick, about five Feet high, well made, and pretty Black. Whoever will take up and secure the said Wench, or bring her to said Hallett, or James Abeel, in New-York, or to her said Master, at New-Brunswick, shall receive TWENTY SHILLINGS Reward, and all reasonable Charges, by either of the above mentioned Persons.

224. The Pennsylvania Journal, and the Weekly Advertiser (Philadelphia), #1072, June 23, 1763.

Run-away last night from the Ship Sarah, a young Negro Man, named Jack, about 6 feet high, very slim make, a very smooth face, his Eyes bloodshed, is a native of Guadaloupe, formerly belonged to Mr. Penell of that Island, speaks tolerable good English: Had on a brown Fustian Frock trimmed with red, a white Shirt, black Stock, Buckskin Breeches, wears Shoes with Brass Buckles and light blue worsted Stockings, and sometimes white Ditto; he has a green Waistcoat and one the same as his Frock. Whoever brings the said Negro to Messrs. Willing and Morris, or on board the said Ship, shall have Five Pounds reward. Thomas Dixon.

N.B. He was at Gloucester all Sunday night. It is supposed he is gone to New-York.

225. The New-York Gazette; or The Weekly Post-Boy, #1071, July 14, 1763.

Run away from Colonel John Read of Fairfield in Connecticut, two mulatto fellows, one named Titus, aged 22, of a middling Stature, longish visage, pale or tawny Complection his hair cut off, plays well on the fiddle, and had one with him, had on a Blue Flannel Coat and pewter buttons, a brown Camblet Vest, Horn Buttons—The other named Daniel, age 16, large of his age, broad face and high Cheek Bones, long black hair, cut off on the top of his head, had on a brown Camblet coat, red lining and white linen, and a mixt colour flannel Vest, both had blue Great Coats, with yellow Metal Buttons and Leather Breeches. Any person that will take and return them to their said master, or secure them so that he might have them shall have Five

Pounds New York Money reward or Fifty Shillings for either of them singly, and all needful charges paid. They had a gun with them and a forged pass.

Whoever takes them is desired to secure them well, or they will give him the slip, and also to search well for and secure said pass for which two Dollars will be added to the reward. All masters of vessels are forbid to carry them off. John Read. Fairfield, July 7, 1763.

226. *The New-York Gazette* (Weyman's), #240, July 18, 1763.

Whereas Isaac Johnson, formerly of the City of New-York, shop-keeper, but late of the Nevesinks, deceased, did by his Will, set at Liberty a Mollatto slave, called Thomas Jackson, and provided Security to render his Manumission effectual; but the Bond for that purpose hath been Destroyed, and an unjust Attempt lately made to sell him at Vendue; which induced certain Persons, from Motives of Humanity, to indemnify the City or Place he may reside in, whereby his Freedom is perfected: These are therefore to caution all persons against purchasing the said Thomas, if he should again be offered to sale. And threats having been Thrown out by Persons claiming the Estate of the said Issac Johnson, that they would dispose of the said Thomas beyond Sea, all Masters of Vessels are prohibited from carrying him off as they will answer it at their Peril, the Persons who have taken him into their Protection being Resolved to procure him Justice. He is about 14 Years of age, five feet high, of a slender Make, born in this Country, and can read and write.

227. *The New-York Gazette; or, The Weekly Post-Boy*, #1073, July 28, 1763.

Run away from the subscriber on Thursday night last, the 21st instant, three new negroes, two men and one woman, the woman talks a little English, is scarified on her face, and had on when she went away an Oznaburgh jersey and

Petticoat, with beads round her Arms and Neck, but it is supposed may alter her dress, as she took away several Things marked E, T, H, and others belonging to a negro wench in the House: the men had on Oznaburgh frocks and trousers, and one of them a brown cloth jacket without sleeves; as they are unacquainted with the Country it is probable that they have been enticed away by some evil minded Person or Persons: Whoever discovers and secures said negroes, so that the owner may have them again shall receive a pistole reward for each and all reasonable Charges. And for discovering the offender or offenders so that they may be brought to Justice, a reward of Ten Pounds, and all reasonable charges by applying to the Subscriber in Stone-Street. Peter Hile. New-York, July 26, 1763.

228. *The New-York Gazette; or, The Weekly Post-Boy*, #1073, July 28, 1763.

TAKEN UP AND committed to the Gaol in Perth-Amboy, a Black Boy, about 16 Years of Age, with Bushy Hair, not resembling the African Negroes; had on a Check Shirt, and Oznaburgs Trowsers; speaks pretty good English, says he was born in Bombay, in the East Indies; and that he came to New-York from Santa Croix, in the Snow Nancy, Cap. Hind.—As he is taken up upon suspicion of being a Runaway Slave, or Servant: If he is such, his Master by applying to the Gaoler in Amboy aforesaid, and paying the Charges, can have him. Perth-Amboy, July 20, 1763.

229. *The New-York Gazette* (Weyman's), #244, August 15, 1763.

RUN away on Saturday last, the 13th August, from the Subscriber, a well set Negro Fellow, named Pompey, about 20 Years of Age, has well made Legs, Scars on his Shins, a thick flat Foot, thick Neck, little Eyes, no Beard, short Fingers, and a Cast on his Hand which is also thick: He is about five Feet 8 Inches high, was bought out of Capt.

Richards, and his Name on board was Apollo. Had on a fine Check Shirt, having a white Patch on the Back of it; Linsey Woolsey double-breasted Jacket without Buttons on the Sleeves; a red Cap, long striped Trowsers that has a white Patch on one Thigh, and a Check one on the other; has no Shoes or Stockings, but a coarse bit of Linen for a Neckcloth: He has a Hole in each Ear, and a Resemblance of the Small-pox. All Masters of Vessels and others, are strictly forbid carrying him off, to harbour or conceal him, as they must assuredly answer it in Law. Whoever secures him in any of his Majesty's Gaols, so that he may be had again, shall have FIVE POUNDS Reward, with reasonable Charges, paid by, ARTHUR M'NEIL.

230. *The New-York Gazette; or, The Weekly Post-Boy*, #1076, August 18, 1763.

RUN away, a Negro Man named Tom, born in Jamaica, but last from Havannah, near thirty Years of Age, about 5 Feet ten Inches high, his Eyes set deep in his Head, halts in his Walk, he generally wears a Red Waistcoat, faced with white, other Times a grey Coat faced with Red; speaks the West-Indies Accent and a little Spanish, and pretends to be free. Whoever apprehends and will deliver him to me, at the City Arms, will receive a Reward of Two Pounds. GEORGE BURNS. All Master of Vessels, and others are cautioned against concealing him.

231. *The New-York Gazette; or, The Weekly Post-Boy*, #1076, August 18, 1763.

Committed to the Goal in Perth-Amboy, a likely Negro Man, about Six feet high, a Scar on his left Cheek Bone; has on a Pair of Leather Breeches, Flannel Shirt, an old Red Great Coat, says his Name is Daniel: He can give no intelligible Account of his Master, as he cannot speak English. His Master by applying to the Goaler in Amboy aforesaid, proving his property and paying Charges, can have him. Perth-Amboy, August 16, 1763.

232. The New-York Gazette; or, The Weekly Post-Boy, #1077, August 25, 1763.

New-York, August 14, 1763. TWENTY DOLLARS REWARD, RUN away from John Leake, a Negro Man nam'd Wall, about 40 Years of Age, five Feet six Inches high, yellowish Complection, one Leg a little thicker than the other, his Head bald, born at Oyster Bay, speaks good English; had on when he went away, a red Coat, a Manchester Velvet Jacket, white Thread Stockings, and new Shoes.—Whoever brings him to his said Master at New-York, shall have the above Reward, and all reasonable Charges.

233. The New-York Gazette; or, The Weekly Post-Boy, #1078, September 1, 1763.

THREE POUNDS REWARD. RUN away last Saturday, a Negro Man, Baptist, belonging to the Estate of the late Mr. Robert Kennedy. He is a French Negro about 40 Years old, 5 Feet 10 Inches high, pitted with the Small-Pox, and speaks bad English. He had good Cloaths, and generally wears a green Jacket, and striped, Holland skirts, Whoever takes up and secures said Fellow, and brings him to Mrs. Ferrara's, shall have Three Pounds paid them by GEORGE TRAILE. All Commanders of Vessels, &c. are forbid to carry him away.

234. The New-York Gazette (Weyman's), #247, September 6, 1763.

Fishkill, August 26, 1763
RUN away from his Master, the Rev. Mr. Chauncy Graham of the Fishkill, in the County of Dutchess, and Province of

New-York, a Negro Man named *Trace*, aged 25 Years [ ] spry well-built Fellow; bred in New-England; looks very brazen, prompt and likely; talks flippent; has a flat Forehead and the lower part of his Face something prominent; his Hair [ ] on the Top, with a Tupee Foretop; plays on the Violin: He took with him an old blue Great-Coat, a Pair Leather Breeches, ditto Trowsers, a white Shirt, ditto Check, ditto Ozenbrigs, a [ ] under Jacket, a new Castor Hat, a Pair blue and white Stockings. Whoever takes up and secures said Negro, so that his [ ] Master may have him again, shall have Forty Shilings Reward and all reasonable Charges paid by CHAUNCY GRAHAM.

N. B. All persons are hereby forbid to conceal, harbour, or carry off said Negro, as they shall answer it at their Peril.

235. *The New-York Gazette; or, The Weekly Post-Boy*, #1080, September 15, 1763.

TAKEN UP, On the 6th Instant, in a Wood near the House of the Subscriber in Shrewsbury, A Negro Man, about 5 Feet 9 Inches high, speaks but little English, and appears to be about 50 Years of Age: He had on, 2 Jackets, one of blue Cloth, the other Silk Camblet, both without Sleves; an old Pair of wide Trowsers, and a pretty good Felt Hat.—The Owner may have him, by applying to John Wordel, Esq; or the Subscriber in Shrewsbury. LOCHLIN M'INTOSH.

236. *The Pennsylvania Gazette* (Philadelphia), #1814. September 29, 1763.

Five Pounds Reward. Runaway the 12th of July last, from Abraham Hewlings in Evesham, West-New-Jersey, a negroe Man, named Moses, about 18 years of Age, about 5 feet 3 or 4 inches high, and has a Scar on the upper Side of one of his feet: Had on when he went away, An Ozenbrigs Shirt and Trowsers, a lightish coloured Cloth Jacket, with a Piece set in the Forebody, an old Felt hat and a Pair of strong Shoes. He took with him a sickle. Whoever takes up and secures said Servant, so as his Master may have him again, shall have the above reward, and reasonable charges paid by Abraham Hewlings. N.B. He formerly belonged to George Keen and it is supposed is harboured by some ordinary people, for while he belonged to said Keen, he was concealed by a Dutchman near Germantown.

237. *The New-York Gazette; or, The Weekly Post-Boy*, #1082, September 29, 1763.

RUN AWAY FROM the subscriber, at Verderica Hook, in Orange County, about Thirty Miles from New-York, on Tuesday the Twentieth Instant, a Negro Man named Harry, about Thirty Years of Age, Five Feet and a Half high, pretty well set, black Complexion, full Faced, has not had the Small Pox, speaks good English and Dutch; two Fingers on his left Hand are somewhat stiff, so that he can neither straighten them, nor shut them close; bred to farming Business:—Had a coarse white Linen Shirt, ruffled at the Boson; a narrow brimmed, half worn Beaver Hat; a blue broad Cloth Coat, about half worn, four Inches too long waisted for him; a striped linsy Waistcoat, and wide striped Cotton Trowsers; had with him a Pair of grey Worsted, and a Pair of old white Woolen Stockings, and a Pair of very remarkably large broad rim'd Brass Buckles—He carried with him several other wearing Clothes, viz. Two checked Woolen Shirts, blue and white; One or Two Pairs of coarse narrow homespun Tow Trowsers; and had some Money with him, wherewith he may have purchased other Clothes. Whoever secures the said Negro, giving me Notice so that I get him again, shall have Forty Shillings Reward, and all reasonable Charges paid by BENJAMIN KNAP.

N.B. Masters of Vessels, and all other Persons are desired not to carry off, conceal, or harbour the said Negro, as they will answer the Penalty of the Law, in such cases made and provided.

238. *The New-York Gazette; or, The Weekly Post-Boy*, #1082, September 29, 1763.

RUN AWAY, On the 5th Instant September from the Subscriber at the Province Arms, in New-York, A Negro Man named Sam, well Limb'd, round faced, about 30 Years of age, but looks younger; French born, but speaks pretty good English; is a good Cook, and was lately bought of Capt. James Delancy. He had on when he went away a narrow brimmed black Hat, somewhat worn, cock'd on one side, which he commonly wore behind; a light and brown Coat, Short Shirts; a Scarlet pair of Breeches, Pewter Buckles, and black Worsted Stockings.—But he may probably change his Dress. He is well known in this City, and it is supposed is now lurking, and concealed therein. Whoever will take up and secure the said negro, so that I may get him again shall have Forty Shillings Reward, paid by GEORGE BURNS. N.B. Master of Vessels, and all other persons, are desired not to carry off, conceal or harbour the said negro, as they will answer the Penalty of the Law, in such Cases made and provided.

239. *The Pennsylvania Journal, and the Weekly Advertiser* (Philadelphia), #1088, October 13, 1763.

Mr. Low's Cato Run-away from Raritan Landing, October 3, 1763, being a middle siz'd Mullatto slave, born in this country, about twenty years of age, has a very wide mouth, bushy hair (lately cut off), walks with his knees bending forward, his cloathes are a French soldier's coat, almost new which had been white but dyed, (not pressed) together with the lining of brown colour, bordering upon the olive, a new vest, lin'd with white, which had also been made for a French soldier, both alter'd to fit him, with brass buttons, also an old blue coat, and old leather jockey cap and trowsers of tow cloth.

He is an extream handy fellow at any common work, especially with horses, and carriages of almost any sort,

Advertisements 111

having been bred to it from a little boy, and to the loading and unloading of boats, a good deal used to a farm, can do all sorts of house work, and very fit to wait upon a gentleman, speaks very good English and Dutch, also pretty good High Dutch, is noted for his sense, and particularly for his activity at any things he takes in hand.

It is supposed he will endeavour to pass for a freeman, and get away in the country, or go with some vessel to any part, so as not to be overtaken; all persons are forbid harbouring of him, and all masters of vessels taking him on board.

Any person that will bring him to his Master Cornelius Low of Raritan-Landing, near New-Brunswick or secures him any of His Majesty's Gaols, giving notice thereof so that he may be had again, shall have ten dollars Reward and more if it can be reasonably demanded, with Proper charges.

240. *The New-York Gazette; or, The Weekly Post-Boy*, #1084, October 13, 1763.

FORTY SHILLINGS REWARD, RUN away from me the Subscriber, living at Rariton, a Negro Man named Aberdeen, between fifty and Sixty Years of Age, about five Feet six Inches high, speaks bad English, had on when he went off, a Tow Shirt and Trowser, but stole away a good many good Clothes, so that he may alter his Dress:— Whoever takes up and secures said negro, so that I may have him again, shall have the above Reward of Forty Shillings, and all reasonable Charges paid by me. JONATHAN RUNYAN. Rariton, Sept. 26, 1763.

241. *The New-York Gazette; or, The Weekly Post-Boy*, #1086, October 27, 1763.

RUN AWAY THE 18th Instant at Night from the Subscriber, in the City of New-York, four Negro Men, Viz. LESTER, about 40 years of age, had on a white Flannel Jacket and Drawers, Duck Trowsers and Home-spun Shirt.

CÆSAR, about 18 Years of Age, cloathed in the same Manner. ISAAC, aged 17 Years Cloathed in the same Manner, except that his Breeches were Leather; and MINGO, 15 Years of Age, with the same Clothing as the 2 first, all of them of a middling Size, Whoever delivers either of the said Negroes to the Subscriber, shall receive TWENTY SHILLINGS Reward for each beside all reasonable Charges. If any person can give Intelligence of their being harbour'd a reward of TEN POUNDS will be paid upon conviction of the Offender. All Masters of Vessels and others are forewarn's not to Transport them from the City, as I am resolved to prosecute as far as the law will allow. WILLIAM BULL.

N.B. If the Negroes return, they shall be pardon'd.

242. *The New-York Gazette* (Weyman's), #256, November 7, 1763.

About three weeks ago, a Negro Man came to the House of Thomas Letson at Black Point, in East New Jersey. He calls himself Sambo, is about $5\frac{1}{2}$ feet high, speaks English very indifferently says he belongs to one Allen; and is now sick. Whoever lays claim to said Negro and proves Property, may have him (on paying charges) by applying to said Thomas Letson.

243. *The New-York Gazette: or The Weekly Post-Boy*, #1099, January 25, 1764.

WHEREAS a Negro Man, named Cyrus, but calls himself Harry, had a Pass from the Subscriber, to go to Elizabeth Town, and return on Saturday the 7th inst. and is still absent: Whoever takes up the said Negro, and brings him to his Master, shall have Forty Shillings Reward, and all reasonable Charges paid by JEREMIAH STANTON. N.B. The said negro is 28 Years of Age, but looks much older; is about 5 Feet 2 Inches high, a good deal mark'd with the Small Pox, speaks Dutch, and very bad English, had on when he went away, a blue Watch Coat, with Brass Buttons, Leather Breeches, and a white Shirt. Staten Island, January 18, 1764.

244. *The Pennsylvania Gazette* (Philadelphia), #1831, January 26, 1764.

Ran away on the 16th of January inst. from the subscriber living in Middlesex County, near Cranbury, a Spanish Negroe Man, Named John Jeste: Had on and took with him, a Felt Hat, two yellowish coloured Jackets, one without sleeves, a homespun brown Tow shirt, old Leather Breeches, blue Yarn Stockings, and two Pair of old Shoes. Whoever takes up said Negroe and brings him home, or secures him so that his Master may have him again, shall have Three Pounds reward and reasonable charges paid by John Rees.
N.B. He ran away about six years ago and was take up at Capt. Elves's Place near the Lower Ferry. All Masters of Vessels and others are forbid to harbour or carry him off.

245. *The New-York Gazette: or The Weekly Post-Boy*, #1101, February 9, 1764.

RUN away, on Wednesday the 1st instant, from Alexander Leslie, of Little Queen Street, the Corner of the New Dutch Church, New-York, A Negro Wench, named Hannah; lately the Property of Mr. David Milligan: She is about nineteen Years old, had on, when she went away, a green Jacket, an old homespun Petticoat, a red and white Handkerchief about her Neck; Men's Shoes, and also carried with her an old black Crape Gown, an old flowered Apron, and a Check one; which she no doubt intends to Dress in, that she may not be known; She was born in this Country, speaks very good English, and is of an Olive Colour.
Whoever takes up and secures the said Wench, shall have Two dollars Reward, and all reasonable Charges paid.—And all Masters of Vessels, and others, are

forewarned not to carry off or harbour the said Wench, as they must expect to be prosecuted as the Law directs, by ALEXANDER LESLIE.

246. *The Pennsylvania Journal, and the Weekly Advertiser* (Philadelphia), #1107, February 23, 1764.

New-Brunswick February 9, 1764. Run-away yesterday morning from Brooke Farmer, Esq. post-master in New Brunswick, a Negro wench named Nell, between 30 and 40 years of age, middle sized, well-set, a very little pitted with the small-pox, is very handy and talkative. she formerly lived with the widow Prittons in Trentown. Had on when she went away, a homespun tow shift, a flower'd flannel under-petticoat, a homespun ditto, striped red, white and blue, a linsey woolsey jacket darn'd under the arms, and a stuff cross bared short gown, a pair of blue stockings footed with a different colour, low heeled shoes lately soaled, with white metal buckles. Whoever takes up said Wench and secures her that her master may have her again, shall have Forty Shillings reward and reasonable charges paid by Brooke Farmer.

247. *The New-York Mercury*, #646, March 12, 1764.

Runaway on Saturday the 24th of February a Negro fellow named Jack: He is about 5 feet 8 inches high, of a very black complexion, and pretty much pitted with the small pox; his hair pretty long and stares very much; was born at Hackensack; when he talks, he speaks very quick. He had on when he went away, a short scarlet Duffil Waistcoat, made without flaps, (out buttoning close round to the Waistband of his breeches) and a red watchcoat, a Pair of long trowsers. Whoever secures the said Negro so that his Master may have him again, shall have Five Dollars Reward and all reasonable charges, paid by me Edward Agar. N.B.

Advertisements

Since he first went away, he came privately into the House in the Night, and has take away the rest of his cloathes, viz. A blue camblet Coat, and a Pair of Leather Breeches, shoes and stockings, so that he may possibly change his dress and appear in them. All masters of Vessels, are hereby forewarned not to carry him off, and all Persons are forbid to harbour him, as they shall answer it at their peril.

248. *The New-York Gazette: or The Weekly Post-Boy*, #1106, March 15, 1764.

Easton, in the county of North-Hampton, and Province of Pennsylvania, Notice is hereby given that there are in the gaol of this county, three negroes, viz. a negro man named Jack, about 38 years old and about 5 feet 10 inches high and his wife named Jane, a tall wench, about 33 years old, and a negro boy of about 4 named Peter. They were all commited to this gaol on the 6th day of October, 1762. They speak some broken English and some broken low Dutch, they were advertised in the *Pennsylvania Gazette* in the month of November, 1762. And whereas no owner has appeared and I can learn nothing from them but that they come from Schenectady, and have thought proper to give this furthur notice that their owner may come and take them away, or they will soon be sold for the charges by Jacob Backman, Gaol Keeper.

249. *The New-York Gazette: or The Weekly Post-Boy*, #1107, March 22, 1764.

RUN-AWAY FROM Ralph Isaacs in New-Haven, in Connecticut, a lusty Negro Man, talks bad English, and broken French, had on when he went away, a Regimental Short Coat, checked Woolen Shirt, brown Cloth Breeches, took with him a blue Coat with a red Cape, and a white Shirt. Whoever shall secure the said Negro in any of his Majesty's Gaols so that the Owner may get him again, shall have Five Pounds New-York Money Reward, and all reasonable Charges paid. RALPH ISAACS.

250. *The New-York Gazette: or The Weekly Post-Boy*, #1107, March 22, 1764.

Albany, February 12, 1764. RUN-away on Friday the 10th Inst. a likely negro Man, named Jacob, belonging to George Wray, at Albany; the said Negro is about 24 Years old, 5 feet 6 3.4 Inches high without shoes, has a Scar on the right side of his Forehead, one on his left Temple; (both just on the Edge of his Hair) and another on the Crown of his head; two large Pock-marks on the upper Part of his left Cheekbones, crooked Legs, the Calves of his Legs remarkably high, a lump on each Shoulder by being flogg'd some time past, stoops forward in walking, and hangs down his Head; speaks good English, some French, and a little Spanish, but little or no Dutch; of an insinuating Address, very apt to feign plausible Stories, and may perhaps call himself a free Negro. He has been seen on the Road to New-England. Whoever apprehends the said Negro, and brings him to his Master above-mentioned, or to the Printer of this Paper, or secures him in any Gaol, giving his Master Notice of it, shall receive Five Dollars Reward, and all reasonable Charges. He had on when he went away, a Blanket Coat, green Leggings and Maccasins, Buckskin Breeches and a red Worsted Cap. It is supposed he had with him, a black and white spotted Dog, answering to the Name of Venture.

251. *The Pennsylvania Gazette* (Philadelphia), #1842, April 12, 1764.

Five Pounds Reward. Run away on the 26th of March last, from the subscriber, at Great Egg Harbour, a Spanish Indian Servant Man, named James Donbar, about 5 feet 3 or 4 inches high, his hair tied behind: Had on when he went away, a blue Jacket, lined with red, a Check Flannel Shirt, old Leather Breeches, and blue Stockings; there are a blue

Great Coat, and an Indian Blanket missing, and it is thought he will make toward the Forks of Delaware. Whoever takes up and secures said Runaway in any gaol so that his master may have him again, shall have the above Reward and all reasonable Charges, paid by Richard Wescot.

252. *The Pennsylvania Gazette* (Philadelphia), #1844, April 26, 1764.

Run away from the subscriber living at the Falls of Schuykill, a Negroe Woman, named Betty; it is uncertain what dress she will appear in as she had different sorts of clothes with her. She has a husband at Mr. Bard's Ironworks in Mount-holly, and it is thought she keeps thereabouts. Whoever takes up and secures said Negroe in the Workhouse in Philadelphia, shall have Thirty Shillings reward, paid by Jane Blackwood.
N.B. All Persons are forbid to harbour her at their Peril.

253. *The New-York Mercury*, #655, May 14, 1764.

Run-away on the 22nd of April last, from Samuel Cock, of the township of Mansfield Wood-House, Sussex-County, and Province of West-Jersey, a Negroe Man, by name Harry or Traso, about 5 feet 10 inches high, of a very black complexion, understands playing on a Fiddle, brought up in this Country, about 25 or 26 years old, a likely Fellow: Had on when he went away, a blue Kersey Coat, with a Cape, and old brown Jacket, without sleeves, an old Pair of Trowsers, a pair of blue breeches, made of Everlasting, and an old Felt Hat. Whoever takes up and secures said Fellow so that his Master may have him again, shall receive as a Reward, Two Dollars if taken in the Province of New Jersey and Three if in any other Province, and all reasonable charges paid by Samuel Cock, of the Township aforementioned; or Teunis Post in Somerset County.

254. *The New-York Gazette: or The Weekly Post-Boy*, #1115, May 17, 1764.

TAKEN UP IN South-Amboy, the 17th Instant, by Silyar Morrel, A Negro Woman who appears to be about 20 Years of Age, speaks no English, and seems to be lately arrived in the Country: She had on her, a striped Linen and Woolen PettyCoat, and a blue Duffel Jacket, The Owner by applying to the Gaoler in Perth-Amboy, proving his Property, and paying the Charges, can have her again. Dated April 23d, 1764.

255. *The New-York Mercury*, #657, May 28, 1764.

Run-away from the Subscriber living in Bound-Brook, Somerset County, East-New-Jersey, on Wednesday, the 8th of May inst. a lusty Negro Fellow named Fortune: Had on when he went away, a coarse red Frieze Jacket, with a crimson colour'd Shag Jacket under it, a Pair of Buckskin breeches, a new Felt Hat, Stockings without Feet and no Shoes. Any person taking up and securing said Negro so that his Master may have him again, shall have Four Dollars Reward and reasonable charges paid by Francis Baird.

256. *The Pennsylvania Gazette* **(Philadelphia),** #1849, May 31, 1764.

Cumberland County, West New-Jersey, May 28, 1764. Last Week was committed to the Gaol of this County, two Negroe Men: the one by name of Amos, about 30 Years old, who says he was born in Guiney, and is now the Property of Colonel Hopper of Queen Ann's County in Maryland; the other calls himself Daniel Rogers, says he is a free Negro and that he came from Cambridge in Dorset County, but as he hath no proper credentials, and his Companion declares him to be a Slave, these are to desire their Masters to fetch them away and pay Cost. Howell Powell, Sherrif.

Advertisements

257. *The Pennsylvania Gazette* **(Philadelphia), #1849, May 31, 1764.**

Runaway from the subscriber living in Upper-Freehold, Monmouth County, West-New-Jersey, on the 21st of this Inst. May two Negroe Men, one named Toby, a well-set fellow about 21 or 22 years of age, 5 feet 5 or 6 inches high, of a pleasant Countenance for a negroe, shews his Teeth frequently, which are very white, is square built, with bow legs, all the Toes on one foot are short as they have been froze, the Toe next to his Great Toe on the other Foot lies over his Great Toe, his Coat is redish brown, of bought Cloth, with a green Thick-set Lining, a new Ozenbrig shirt, a pretty good Felt Hat; had on Leather Breeches, much worn, which he may change; he can play upon the Violin, but not extraordinarily well. The other is named Abraham belonged once to Mr. Emlen in Philadelphia, to Joseph Staniard and to John Cox of Upper Freehold aforesaid; he can write and read, understands Planation business; he is old than the other and about 5 feet 9 or 10 inches high, well-built; it is likely he will forge a Pass, and pretend to want a new Master for himself and the other. Whoever takes up and secures said Negroes in any Gaol or either of them, so as their Masters may have them again or brings him them home, shall have Twenty Shillings Reward for each with reasonable Charges paid by Joseph Grover and Joseph Coward.

258. *The Pennsylvania Gazette* **(Philadelphia), #1851, June 14, 1764.**

Runaway from the subscriber living in Cranberry, Middlesex County, on the 20th of May last, a Negroe woman named Lucy alias Sue, about 30 years old, a slender, small woman, wants some of her Teeth, full eyed, her Dress uncertain; she took two quilted Petticoats, one red, the other blue; a blue and white China Gown, and a pair of Green Cloth shoes which she may change for others. It is supposed she went to Bucks County, to one Lambert Vandyke's near

Shaminy Meeting-house, where she has a Daughter; her mother and brother lived with Mr. Kemble in Brunswick; she speaks Dutch well. Whoever secures said Negroe so that her Master may have her again, shall have Twenty Shillings Reward with reasonable charges, paid by Patrick Hanlon.

259. *The Pennsylvania Gazette* (Philadelphia), #1853, June 28, 1764.

Runaway from the Subscriber living in Trenton, New-Jersey, on the 21st of June, a Negro man, named Tony, a thick chunky well-set Fellow, about 30 Years of Age, about 5 feet 7 or 8 inches high, has a remarkable Way of walking as if he was a little lame, and stoops a little forward: Had on when he went away, a light coloured Cloth Jacket, with Patches at the Elbows, Ozenbrigs Shirt and Trowsers, old Hat, old Shoes, has a bad Cut in his left Thumb, fresh cut just before he went away. Whoever takes up and secures said Negroe in any of His Majesty's Gaols, so that his Master may have him again, shall have Forty Shillings Reward and all reasonable Charges, paid by me William Lister.

260. *The New-York Gazette* (Weyman's), #291, July 2, 1764.

RUN away from WILLIAM DOUGLASS, of Staten-Island, a Negro Man, named GEORGE, aged about 22 Years, near 5 Feet 10 Inches high, slender built, talks a good deal upon the New-England Accent; large Eyes, with a good deal of White in them: Had on when he went away, a speckled Flannel Shirt, a Pair of twill'd bagging Trowsers piec'd, a Pair of black Stockings, new Pumps with carved Silver Buckles, a homespun brown upper Jacket, and a red Waistcoat without Sleeves under, lin'd with buff-colour'd Flannel, a Felt Hat not half worn. Any Person taking up, and securing the above Negro in any Gaol, so that his Master can have him again, shall receive the Sum of Forty

Shillings, and all reasonable Charges, paid by me WILLIAM DOUGLASS, living on Staten-Island.

261. *The New-York Gazette* (Weyman's), #294, July 23, 1764.

RAN-away on Wednesday the 18th Instant, from JOSEPH ANTHONY, of Courtland's Manor, a Negro Man, named, JACK; is very black, has no front upper Teeth, and talks good English. Had on when he went away, a Soldier's old red Jacket, check Shirt, an old Pair of Buckskin Breeches, with Ozenbrig Petticoat Trowsers over them. He is supposed to be gone to the House of Mr. John Coombs, at Jamaica, on Long-Island; or otherwise to Mr. Palmer's, at Whiteplains, Westchester County, from each of whom he has been sold. Captains of Vessels are desired to be careful in not carrying him away; and Ferrymen forbid to carry him across Ferries; as they must answer the Damages. Whoever takes up and secures the said Negro, so that his Master may have him again, shall have FORTY SHILLINGS Reward, and reasonable Charges paid by JOSEPH ANTHONY.

262. *The Pennsylvania Gazette* (Philadelphia), #1859, August 9, 1764.

Run away from Dr. Bern Budd, of Hanover, in Morris County, East New-Jersey, a likely well set Negroe Man, about 5 feet 9 or 10 inches high, of a yellow Complexion: Had on when he went away, a blue Broadcloth Coat, with Tortoise-Shell Buttons, a double breasted Broadcloth Jacket, with Mohair Buttons and Leather Breeches. He took with him 3 white Shirts, a check Ditto, a snuff coloured Manchester velvet Jacket, one striped ditto, and a pair of wide Trowsers. He speaks good English, understands all Sorts of Farmer's Work, and something of the Sea, and no Doubt will endeavour to pass for a free Negroe as he can write any Pass he thinks necessary. Whoever takes up the said Negro and confines him in any of His Majesty's Gaols, and sends his said Master notice, so that he may have him again, or brings him to his said Master, shall receive Ten Dollars Reward, and all reasonable charges paid by Bern Budd.

N.B. All Masters of Vessels and others are forbid, on their Peril, to carry him off, or harbour him.

263. *The New-York Gazette: or The Weekly Post-Boy*, #1132, September 13, 1764.

Run-away on Monday the 27th of last Month, August, from Gilbert Smith, of Upper Freehold, in Monmouth County, East-New-Jersey, a Slave, named Jacob, but has several Times changed his Name, calling himself James Start, and James Pratt, &ct. his Mother was a Negro and his Father an Indian, but he passes himself for an Indian, and is like one, of a yellowish Tawney colour, is about 23 years of age, 5 feet 4 or 5 inches high; his Hair cut short on his Crown, but curls around his neck; has a remarkable Scar on one of his Cheekbones, occasioned by a Scald or a Burn, and speaks good English. He is much addicted to Smoaking and Drinking. He went from his Work at the Plough and was without shoe or stocking, and had no other clothes but an Oznabrig Shirt and Trowsers, an old ragged Waistcoat and an old Hat. He came to New York on Wednesday Morning last, with one Aaron Buck, on a sloop from Barnegat or Tom's River and has since been seen in Town. Any person that will bring the said Run-away to Mr. John Talman in New York, Butcher, or Mr. Francis Field, on Golden Hill, or commit him to any public gaol will receive from either of them, Forty Shillings reward, and all reasonable charges. Gilbert Smith.

N.B. All Masters of Vessels are forbid to harbour conceal or carry him off as they will answer it at their peril.

264. The Pennsylvania Gazette (Philadelphia), #1864, September 13, 1764.

Burlington, September 6, 1764. Was committed to the gaol of this country on the Fourth Instant, a certain Negroe man, about 5 feet 9 or 10 inches high, of a yellow Complexion, speaks good English and says he was born in New England, and has been a little to the Sea; he had several sorts of Passes with him, which it thought he wrote himself. His Master is desired to come and pay Charges, and take him away, otherwise he will be sold for the same, by Ephraim Phillips, Gaoler.

265. The New-York Gazette: or The Weekly Post-Boy, #1132, September 13, 1764.

Jamaica, August 30, 1764.
This day I took up a Negro Man, he calls his name Cato and says he lives at Middletown Point in East New-Jersey; he is a young Fellow, something short, well set, and with a small Scar over his left Eye, has on a hat without Brims, a brown coat, and old stocking leggins, blue Breeches, no shoes, and speaks broken english; I shall put him in Gaol at Jamaica, where the owner may find and have him, if he doth not get from said gaol, he paying me for my Trouble and all Charges. The fellow says his master is John Hendricks. Daniel Hulet.

266. The New-York Gazette: or The Weekly Post-Boy, #1133, September 20, 1764.

Run away from the subscriber last Saturday night, a negro man named Harry, formerly belonging to Mr. Van Dollsen, Mason, in this city. He is well built, had on when he went away a light coloured double-breasted Jacket, a coarse white Linen shirt, short wide trousers, half-worn shoes, steel Buckles and a Scotch bonnet: he is apt to get drunk, stutters a bit, speaks very good English, Spanish, and French, and a little bit of other languages. N.B. He has left the first Joint of two of his toes next to his great Toe, by Frost. Whoever takes up the above Negro and brings him to his Master or secures him in any Gaol, shall have Twenty Shillings reward if taken in this city or on the island, and Forty Shillings if in another country or government. Aris Remsen.

267. *The New-York Gazette: or The Weekly Post-Boy*, #1133, September 20, 1764.

Run away from John Hendricks of Middletown, East New-Jersey, a negro man named Cato, who he took out of Jamaica Gaol on Long Island Sunday the 16th instant, and run away again on Monday the 17th, he is a short well set Negro, likely, speaks broken English had on an old Snuff coloured Coat, a small white Vest, a pair of blue Breeches, no Shoes, a pair of Leggings, and a Hat without a Brim. Whoever takes up the said Negro Man and secures him, so that his Master might have him again shall receive Thirty Shillings Reward and all reasonable charges paid by John Hendricks.

268. *The New-York Gazette* (Weyman's), #304, October 1, 1764.

TAKEN up on Staten-Island, and now in Goal at Richmond-Town, a Negro Fellow that appears to be about 30 Years of Age, is slim bodied, and has the usual Negro Cuts in his Face; says his Name is MINGO; has been about two Years in the Country; speaks bad English;—Has on a French Soldier's Coat turned up with Blue; says his Master's Name is William Bennet, and that his House was burned and he was put in Goal, and one John Abraham's took him out, with whom he lived about four Months, and then Run-away from him. The Owner can have him by applying to the Sheriff of Statten-Island, and paying the Charges.
New-York, September 17, 1764.

269. *The New-York Mercury*, #677, October 15, 1764.

Ran-away from the subscriber, living at Lamington, in the County of Somerset, a Negro Man, named Mount, about 20 years old, 5 feet 6 or 7 inches high: had on when he went away, a light coloured Sagothee Coat, a black Broadcloth Jacket, a homespun dark colour'd Jacket, also homespun Tow Trowsers, a new felt Hat, Shoes and Stockings; talks very broken English; he also took with him a light colour'd grey Horse, about 10 or 11 years old, 14 hands high, a natural Trotter, no Brand or other Mark, also, an old Saddle and Bridle. Any person takingup said Negro Man, and Horse, and securing them so that the Owner may have them again, shall have Thirty Shilling reward and all reasonable charges paid by me Robert Barkley.

270. *The New-York Gazette* (Weyman's), #307, October 22, 1764.

RAN-away the 12th of August last, from the Subscriber, living in Roxbury, County of Morris, two Negro Men, one about 20 Years of Age, named JOE, a sprightly well-set Fellow, understands all sorts of farming Work, and pretends to be a Fidler. The other about 30 Years of Age, named BEN, understands House-Work, as to baking, washing, and cooking; he knows but little about Farming; he is a thick clumsey Fellow, with a Scar near the Corner of his Eye. They had on when they went away, Tow Shirts and Trowsers; the young Fellow had a half worn wool Hat, a Soldier's red Coat, and bare Feet; the other had on an old light blue Kersey Vest, with thick grey Kersey Lining, half-worn Shoes, and no Hat. Whoever will takes up the aforesaid Negroes, so that I can have them again, shall have FIVE POUNDS Reward, or *Fifty Shillings* for either, and all reasonable Charges paid them by me, or Arnout Cannon, at the Sign of the Wheat-Sheaf, near the Ship-Yards. AUGUSTINE REID.

N. B. All Masters of Vessels and others, are strictly forbid either carry them off, or in any Manner to harbour them, as they will assuredly be obliged to answer a Prosecution. And if any Person can give Information whether they are gone off by Sea already, and by whom, shall be rewarded with *Thirty Shillings*, on the aforesaid Application.   Sept. 3, 1764.

271. *The New-York Gazette: or The Weekly Post-Boy*, #1140, November 8, 1764.

Run away on Tuesday night the 30th instant, two new negro men who speak no English;—Had on new blue Jackets and Breeches, new Stockings and Shoes without any Buckles—any person that brings 'em to the Printer of this Paper shall have Twenty Shillings reward, and all Masters of Vessels and others are forbid to carry them off, or harbour them at their Peril.

272. *The Pennsylvania Gazette* (Philadelphia), #1874, November 22, 1764.

Five Pounds Reward Runaway from the subscriber on Saturday, the 30th of June last, a young Mullato fellow, about 20 years of age, named Frank, about five feet five inches high, well set, full fac'd short black curled hair, very apt to swear when angry; had on and with him when he went away, a coarse homemade Tow shirt and Trowsers, a Woolen Jacket, homemade, old Hat and Stockings; it is supposed he has changed clothes and perhaps his Name by this time. It is also supposed he is somewhere in the Cedar Swamps in the Jerseys, down Delaware River as his Mother and others of his acquaintance, live near Cohansey, where the said Fellow I believe was bred. Whoever takes up and secures said Mulattoo in any Gaol, or brings him to his said Master, shall have the above Reward, besides reasonable charges, paid by Thomas Witherspoon.

Advertisements

273. *The New-York Gazette: or The Weekly Post-Boy,* **#1145, December 13, 1764.**

Run away the 12th of last month from the subscriber, living in Middletown in East New Jersey, a negro man named Jasper, about 25 years old and 5 feet 10 inches high (born in New York) had on when he went away a brown homespun jacket and breeches, the jacket cuffed with the same, a Tow shirt, White Yarn Stockings,a pair of pumps and a felt hat; he understands the farming Business. Whoever takes up said Negro and secures him in any Gaol, giving Notice therof to his Master so that he may have him again, shall have Three Pounds reward and reasonable charges paid by John Stevenson. Middleton, November 4, 1764.

274. *The New-York Gazette: or The Weekly Post-Boy,* **#1145, December 13, 1764.**

Run away, last night the 12th instant, from Rebeccah Morehouse, opposite to Alderman Benson at the shipyards, New York, a tall slim straight negro wench named Pegg, about 40 years of age, of yellowish complexion, has had the small-pox, but is smooth faced, and talks good English, has the middle finger of her left hand crooked and cannot straighten it, was born at Oyster Bay but has resided for several years in New York and formerly belonged to Mr. Pell, is sensible, cunning and artful and can wash iron and cook; had on a short red cloak a white hat and a pair of men's shoes and with her callico gown and a variety of cloathes. Whoever will bring home the said wench to her mistress or to the subscriber, ship carpenter at the ship yards, shall have a dollars reward if taken in town or three dollars if taken out of town, besides all reasonable charges. John Leversage.

275. *The New-York Gazette: or The Weekly Post-Boy*, #1150, January 17, 1765.

RUN-AWAY from John Thomas, jun. at Rye, in West-Chester County, about the middle of November last; A Negro Man called Joe, about thirty five Years of Age, he is near six Feet high, of a yellowish Complection, has had the Small-Pox, but hardly visible, has some Scars on his Breast, was born in Jersey, but since lived with Messenger Palmer, near Stanford, in Connecticut: Had on when he went away a brown Cloath Jacket, a Woolen Shirt; a Pair of Leather Breeches, a Pair of white Woollen Stockings. Whoever takes up said Negro and secures him so that his Master may have him again, shall receive Three Pounds Reward, and all reasonable Charges, paid by me JOHN THOMAS, jun. Rye, January 9, 1765.

276. *The New-York Gazette: or The Weekly Post-Boy*, #1163, April 18, 1765.

Run-away from JOHN VERMILLYE, at the New Bridge, on the West Chester Side, on Sunday the 7th of April, a Mulatto Fellow named TONEY, about 5 Feet 6 Inches, has short curl'd Hair, and has something of the New-England Way of expressing himself. Had on when he went away, a brown great Coat, a black and white mixed wove Prunelta ditto, a striped blue & white Jacket, two Pair of striped blue and white Trowsers, one knit blue Pair of Breeches, one white and one Check Shirt, a Pair of knit Stockings, and had a good Castor Hat. Whoever takes up and secures said Fellow, so that he may be had again, shall have FOUR POUNDS Reward, and reasonable Charges paid by JOHN VERMILLYE.

N.B. All Masters of Vessels are strictly forbid to carry away, or employ him, and all others to hire or harbour him, as they must answer such unlawful Proceedings. Those who apprehend and secure him any where near New-York, are desired to give Notice to the Printer hereof.

Advertisements 129

277. *The Pennsylvania Gazette* (Philadelphia), #1901, May 30, 1765.

Run away from the subscriber living in Roxbury, Morris County, East-Jersey, a Mullatoe Fellow, named Tom, about 30 Years of Age, about 5 feet 6 inches high; had on when he went away, a blue Waistcoat, a Pair of Buckskin Breeches, which it is likely he has changed. He has one extraordinary Mark, having no Toes on either of his Feet. Whoever takes up the said Mullatoe fellow and secures him, so that his Master may have him again, shall have Ten Pounds Reward and all reasonable Charges paid by John Vandorn.

278. *The New-York Gazette* (Weyman's), #339, June 3, 1765.

Run away from Augustine Reid of Morris County, New-Jersey, Two Negro Men, one named Ben, about 35 years of age, is a thick set fellow, and has a scar on one of his cheeks; born in Barbadoes, in the West-Indies, & has been over about two years and a half; the other is named Joe, about 20 years old; the white of his Eyes is of a reddish cast, has black specks in them, is a nimble active Fellow. Whoever takes up and secures the said Negroes so that their Master may have them again, shall receive Thirty Pounds Reward for Both or Fifteen Pounds for either and all reasonable charges, paid by Augustine Reid.

279. *The Pennsylvania Gazette* (Philadelphia), #1906, June 4, 1765.

Run away from the subscribers on Sunday, the 9th of last Month, two likely Negroe Fellows, the one named Begill, about 5 feet 10 inches high, slim built, has been in the Country near 4 years, speaks tolerable good English for the Time, aged about 35 or 40 years; had on when he went away a Linsey Coat, of black and blue Colours mixed, with Brass Buttons, a Felt Hat, white Shirt, Sheepskin Breeches,

Stockings of mixed Colours, and double soaled shoes. The other named Jerry, aged about 25 Years, near the Height and Size of the former, has been in the Country about 3 years, speaks very broken English; had on when he went away, a striped Linsey Waistcoat, white Shirt, and narrow short Trowsers, old Shoes, no Stockings, an old Felt Hat, with a red String or Garter around the Crown. Whoever takes up the said Negroes and brings them to the Subscribers in Reading, in Hunterdon County, New Jersey or secures them in any Gaol, giving Notice to the said Owners, so that they may have them again, shall have Six Dollars Reward, and reasonable charges or Three Dollars each paid by Samuel Herriot or Lawrence Pool.

280. *The New-York Gazette: or The Weekly Post-Boy*, **#1173, June 27, 1765.**

RUN-away on Monday last, from the Subscriber, a Negro Wench called CATE: She is a lusty, stout Wench, pretty Fat, and has thick Lips: had on when she went away, a strip'd Home-spun Petticoat, a double purple and white Callico short Gown, both sides alike, a Pair of old Stuff Shoes, without Stockings. It is supposed that she is harboured by some of the Free negroes, or others in Town. Whoever takes her up here, and secures her, shall have Forty Shillings Reward; and if taken in the Country, they shall have the same Reward, together with reasonable Charges for sending her to New-York. All Persons at their Peril, are forewarned from harbouring or carrying her off. MARY FERRARI.

281. *The New-York Gazette: or The Weekly Post-Boy*, **#1174, July 4, 1765.**

TWENTY SHILLINGS Reward, RAN away from William Johnson, of this City, Blacksmith, a Negro Man, named SHARP, about Twenty Years of Age, he is a tall slender made Fellow, of a yellowish Complexion, speaks very little English, had on when he went away, a blue Sailor's Jacket, a checked Shirt, Oznabrigs Trowsers, an old Beaver Hat, cock'd; a Pair of old Shoes, but no Stockings; he is somewhat marked with the small Pox, & is supposed to be skulking about Town. Whoever secures said Negro, and brings him to JOHN JOHNSON, of this City Sadler, shall have the above Reward; and all Master of Vessels and other Persons, are forbid from carrying off, or harbouring said Negro.

282. *The Pennsylvania Gazette* (Philadelphia), #1907, July 11, 1765.

Runaway from the subscriber living in Amwell Township, Hunterdon County, West Jersey, on the 20th of May last, a Negroe Man, named Sambo, about 30 Years of age, near 6 feet high, slim built, a single Mark on his Right Cheek; he is a New Negroe and can speak but little English; he is apt to speak the Words that are spoke to him again. It is supposed that he is either stolen or decoyed away. Whoever takes up said Negroe so that this Master may have him again, shall have Three Pounds reward, and if stolen, Ten Pounds provided the Thief is brought to Justice, with reasonable charges paid by Isiah Quinby.

283. *The New-York Gazette* (Weyman's), #350, August 8, 1765.

Perth-Amboy, August the 5th, 1765. In the Custody of the subscriber, two Negro Men, the one a yellow Fellow, named Jack, the other black, named Ezekiel, They say their Master's Name is Jacob Starne, and that he is the owner of a Forge in Muskenecunk. Their Master is desired to pay Charges and take them away. Richard Carnes.

284. *The New-York Gazette: or The Weekly Post-Boy*, #1175, July 11, 1765.

RUN-away from the subscriber, on Tuesday the 9th instant, a negro man named TOBY, this country born, yellow conplexion, about 5 feet 7 inches high, and about 21 Years of age; had on when he went away, a brown fustian jacket, ozenbrigs shirt and trowsers, and an old beaver hat. Whoever takes up and secures said negro, so that his master may have him again, shall receive 5 dollars reward, and all reasonable charges paid by AUGUSTINE VAN HORNE.

285. *The New-York Gazette: or The Weekly Post-Boy*, #1178, August 1, 1765.

Run away from James Barnard, inn-holder, on Philipsborough, in the county of West-Chester, on Friday the 19th of July, a negro man named Dublin; middle sized, about 35 years of age, slow of speech, thin faced; had on when he went away, an old bearskin jacket tow cloth shirt and trousers and an old hat. Whoever takes up and secures said negro, so that his master may have him again, shall have Twenty Shillings reward and all reasonable charges paid by James Barnard.

286. *The New-York Gazette: or The Weekly Post-Boy*, #1179, August 8, 1765.

Run away from the subscriber, at West Chester, on Sunday the 21st of July Last, a negro fellow named Mingo who I'm told has formerly gone by the name of Jim, he is well made, well-looking negro, of about 5 feet 6 inches high, is 27 years old, but appears rather older than he is, he understands all kinds of farming work and plays tolerably on the fiddle, He was born at Long Island, and was lately the property of one John Jones, blacksmith, at or near Harvest Straw, who had him from one Campbell of the same place. He had on (or with him) a deep blue broad cloth coat that had been turned, with blue buttons to it; a blue cloth waistcoat, a coarse brown linen waistcoat and an old black plush waistcoat, brown mixed color cloth breeches with a pair of blue worsted and a pair of white ribb'd threaded trousers. Whoever takes up and will secure the said fellow so that the master may have him again shall receive Forty Shillings Reward and all reasonable charges from Isaac Wilkins. Westchester, August 8, 1765.

287. *The Pennsylvania Gazette* **(Philadelphia), #1917, September 19, 1765.**

Five Dollars reward. Runaway from Greenwich Forge, in Sussex County, West New-Jersey, a Negro boy named Castello, about 20 Years of age; had on a white Shirt, half silk yellow jacket, yellow knit Worsted Breeches, red and white, speckeld worsted Stockings, new Shoes, with square Brass Buckles and a good Beaver Hat; the colour of his coat unknown; wears a Truss. Whoever secures said Negro in any Gaol, so as he may be had again, shall have the above Reward, by applying to John Hughes in Philadelphia or to Hugh Hughes in said Forge.

288. *The New-York Gazette: or The Weekly Post-Boy*, **#1186, September 26, 1765.**

Albany: Run away from the subscriber yesterday, a mulatto negro man, a Spaniard named Joseph, about 25 years old, a short well made fellow, speaks broken English (he went off with a big Spanish negro belonging to Mr. Bayard of New York, sent here to sell) He had on when he went away, a blue jacket, an old light colour'd ratteen ditto without sleeves, an oznabrigs shirt, old leather breeches, a pair of black ribbed stockings, a hat bound with worsted binding,a pair of new shoes with brass buckles. Whoever takes him up, and secures him in any of his Majesty's gaols, shall have forty shillings reward and all reasonable charges paid by Mr.

John Ernest, a merchant in New York, or the subscriber in Albany, Barent Ten Eyck.

All masters of vessels and others are forbidden to conceal, harbour, entertain or carry off the said servant, as they will answer at their peril.

289. *The New-York Gazette: or The Weekly Post-Boy*, #1186, September 26, 1765.

Run away on the 17th instant, September, from Abraham Douw, Esq., at Albany, a Spanish negro man named Tom, aged about 28 or 30 years: He is a very black likely tall fellow, his left ear cut off, and has lost one of his small toes by the frost, he pretends to be a free man and speaks very good English and Spanish, had on when he went away a blue vest, a duffle great coat, a pair of trousers, a handkerchief about his head, and a woolen hat. He went away in the company of a mulatto Spaniard belonging to Mr. Barent Ten Eyck, of Albany, and it is supposed they are gone to New-England: Whoever takes up or secures the said negro in any of his majesties gaols, giving notice so that his master may have him again shall receive Forty Shillings reward besides all reasonable charges paid by the subscriber in New-York, or the said Abraham Douw, Esq., in Albany. Nicholas Bayard.

290. *The Pennsylvania Gazette* (Philadelphia), #1926, November 21, 1765.

Taken up by the subscriber, two Negro Men, about five feet eight inches high, both new Negroes from the River Gambia. Upon examining of them they say, they belonged to John Gardner of North-Carolina, the Name of the Particular Place they won't tell; one of them speaks a little English, the other not. They call themselves Pompey and Nero. Pompey is the largest of them and Nero slender. They say they travelled through the Mountains from North-Carolina. The Master upon applying to the subscriber living in the Town of Shrewsbury and paying the charge he has been at, may have them. John Morris. Shrewsbury, New Jersey, November 8, 1765.

291. *The New-York Gazette: or The Weekly Post-Boy*, #1194, November 21, 1765.

Ran away on Thursday the last, the 14th instant, from the subscriber living in Newtown Long Island, a Negro Man Slave, about 30, five feet ten inches high, of a slender make, a yellowish colour, and a good Deal pitted by the Small Pox about the Nose. Had on when he went off, a white Cloth Jacket, a blue Duffil great Coat, much faded, with white flat Metal Buttons, breeches, black and white mixed Yarn Stockings, new Shoes, and a small old Wool hat. Whoever takes up said Slave and delivers him to me, or secures him so that I may have him again, shall have Three Dollars reward and all reasonable charges paid by Paul Burtus.
    N.B. All masters of vessels and others are forbidden to harbour, conceal or carry off said fellow, at their peril.

292. *The New-York Gazette: or The Weekly Post-Boy*, #1196, December 5, 1765.

Forty shillings reward. Ran away from the manor of Eaton, in Suffolk County, on the 18th of November, a negro man named Ceaser, about 40 years of age, 5 feet 8 inches high, has thick lips, bandy legs, walks lame and speaks very bad English; had on when he went away, a blue jacket, check flannel shirt, tow cloth trousers, black and white yarn stockings, half worn shoes, and an old felt hat; has formerly lived in some part of West Jersey where it is suspected he has gone; he went off in the company of one Thomas Cornwell, who calls himself a Bristol man and who it is feared has forged a pass for the negro. Whoever secures the negro so that the subscriber may have him again shall have the above reward and all reasonable charges paid by John Hobart.

N.B. All masters of vessels are forbidden to conceal or transport said negro.

293. *The New-York Gazette: or The Weekly Post-Boy*, #1197, December 12, 1765.

Taken up on Monday evening the 3rd instant by the watchmen of this city, committed to the work-house of this city by alderman Brinkerhoff, a negro who calls himself Ceaser, being a well-set black fellow and about 5 feet 4 inches high, says he was formerly the property of Cornelius Hatfield of Elizabethtown but now belongs to Mr. Hobbart on Long Island. His master, on applying to the above mentioned magistrate, and paying the charges, may have his servant again. New-York, December 12, 1765.

294. *The Pennsylvania Gazette* (Philadelphia), #1930, December 19, 1765.

Went away from Joseph Sharp of Salem County, West Jersey, the 10th of November last, a Negro Man, named Sambo, under pretence to get a Master; he is a thick short felow, limps with his Right Knee and one of his Buttocks is bigger than the other; about 40 years of age, talks much and cannot count above 15; if you ask him how much 10 and 5 is, he can't tell such Questions; he has had many masters, and lived at Mount-Holly, when the Furnace went, with Mr. Bard, it is thought he will endeavour to get to Philadelphia, or is gone to New York. Whoever takes up said Negroe and secures him in any Goal, so that his Master may have him again, shall have Three Pounds Reward; if taken in this County or Cumberland, Forty Shillings, paid by Joseph Sharp.

295. *The New-York Gazette: or, The Weekly Post-Boy*, #1201, January 16, 1766.

FIVE POUNDS Reward. RAN-AWAY from the subscriber, on Wenesday morning last; a French negro man, named JOHN, a likely well made black fellow, about 30 years of age, pitted with the small-pox, his eyes small and bloodshot, remarkable good teeth, and wide mouth, about 5 Feet 8 inches high, walks upright, and is complaisant:—Had on, a good castor hat, Ozenbrigs shirt, black crape cravat, brown bearskin great coat, cloth upper Jacket, lined through with red striped linsey, figured brass buttons, a green napt sailor's jacket, fore parts lined with greeen shalloon, back with Ozenbrigs, Philadelphia patterns brass buttons, leather breeches, yarn knit stockings, good shoes, and square steel buckles—He took with him one white shirt, one pair of stockings, and a leather cap, lined with fur. It is probable he may be found playing on his fiddle, which he took with him.

Whoever will bring him home, or give notice where he may be found, so that his master may have him again, shall be entitled to the above reward, by applying to John Franklin in New-York, or Enoch Story in Philadelphia.

296. *The New York Gazette: or, The Weekly Post-Boy*, #1205, February 6, 1766.

Forty Shillings Reward. Run-away on Wednesday the 25th day of December 1765, from us the subscribers, living in Freehold and county of Monmouth, in East New Jersey an indented Negro Man named Benjamin Moore, about forty years of age, five feet six inches high, a likely spry fellow. He took with him a grey and a red jacket, 1 pair of brown breeches, 1 pair of ribb'd blue stockings, and a good hat. He has taken with him sundry other clothes, and it is supposed he will change his dress. He was formerly an indented servant to Job Throckmorton and George Rhea at Freehold and has taken those old indentures of said Throckmorton and Rhea with him and shows them for a pass, pretending to be a free Negro. Whoever takes up said Negro and secures him so that his Master may have him again, shall have the above reward, and all reasonable charges paid by us. Henry and Joseph Robinson.

N.B. All masters of Vessels and other persons are forewarned not to harbour, conceal, or carry off the said Negro at their peril.

297. *The New-York Gazette: or, The Weekly Post-Boy,* #1216, April 24, 1766.

RUN AWAY from Isaac Man a Negro Wench named Sal. She is short and well set, pretty much mark'd with the small-Pox, about 28 Years of Age, had on a Purple Calico Gown, a striped Cotton short ditto, a purple and white Calico Joseph, an old plain Gown, a blue quilted petticoat, a green Penistone ditto, a red shirt Cloak, & a black Silk Hat. All Masters of Vessels are hereby forbid to carry her off, and all Persons are warned not to harbour her. Whoever takes up the said Wench, and delivers her to Messrs. Stanton and Teabrooke, Carpenters at the North River, shall receive Twenty Shillings Reward, and all reasonable Charges Paid.

298. *The New York Gazette; or, The Weekly Post-Boy,* #1217, May 1, 1766.

Forty Shillings Reward. Run-Away from the subscriber on Monday the 21st of April last, a yellowish Negro Fellow, named Bill, formerly belonging to Mr. Cornelius Clopper at Rariton Landing, in New-Jersey, appears to be about 20 or 22 Years of age, about 5 feet 6 inches in height, speaks good English and Low Dutch fluently, had on when he went away, an old red Cloth Jacket, a Pair of old Homespun Trowsers, and an Iron Collar; which last it is supposed he has found Assistance to get off. Whoever takes up and secures or secures him so that I may get him again shall have Forty Shillings Reward for their Trouble, besides all necessary Expenses. All Masters of Vessels and other Persons, are warned not to carry off, conceal or harbour the said Runaway, as they would avoid a Prosecution of the law. New York, May 1, 1766. John Klein.

299. *The New York Gazette; or, The Weekly Post-Boy*, #1222, June 5, 1766.

Six Pounds Reward Ran Away from the subscriber in Shrewsbury the two following Negroes, viz, Pompey, a lusty fellow, about 35 Years of age, 5 feet 8 or 9 inches high.—Had on red Duffel Trowsers, and Waistcoat, speaks pretty good English. Nero, a slender young fellow, about 25 Years of age, speaks very bad English; had on a red duffle Waistcoat, and brown Broadcloth Breeches. They went away in a small boat, 16 feet keel, a black bottom and her wales painted with Spanish-brown, had 4 Oars on Board. Whoever brings the said Negroes to any of his Majesty's Gaols, so that he may have them again, shall receive the above reward besides all reasonable charges from John Morris.

300. *The Pennsylvania Journal, and the Weekly Advertiser* (Philadelphia), #1228, June 19, 1766.

Two Pistoles Reward Run away from the Subscriber on Monday the 5th of May, a Negro Man, named Hannaball, a likely black fellow, has a pert look, and when talking is always either laughing or smiling, he is about 5 feet 7 or 8 inches high, he walks proper and straight without limping, but if examined will find one of his feet stiff and scarce be able to bend it from his ankle to his toes, his apparell not well known but such as is common for slaves, his over jacket was light coloured fearnot, it is supposed he has travelled toward Duck-Creek and from thence either to Philadelphia or the Jerseys, and may endeavour to pass for a free man and sailor, as he has been used to go by water. Whoever takes up the said fellow, and secures him so that his Owner may have him again, shall have the above reward and reasonable charges if brought home paid by Emory Fuetter.

301. *The New-York Gazette; or, The Weekly Post-Boy*, #1225, June 26, 1766.

Ran away from the subscriber living in New York, the beginning of June instant, a negro fellow named Charles, about five feet ten inches high, Pock-pitted, very black, and remarkable for his white teeth; speaks both French and English, Jamaica born, and marked under his left Breast P. le Count; had on when he went away, a brown Jacket, and a blue short waistcoat underneath it, a Pair of trowsers, and a sailor's round hat. Whoever takes up the said negro and secures him so that his master may have him again, shall have forty shillings reward and all reasonable charges paid by Andrew Myer, in Dock-Street.

N.B. All masters of vessels and others are hereby warned not to harbour or carry off said Servant at their Peril, as they will answer as the Law directs.

302. *The New York Gazette; or, The Weekly Post-Boy*, #1226, July 3, 1766.

Woodbridge, July 1, 1766 Ran away from the subscriber on Sunday the 15th of June last, a Negro Man, named Cuff, about 5 feet 9 inches high, and about 22 years of age, has a scar on his right great Toe and the Ends of several other of his Toes are cut off. Whoever takes up and secures said Negro so that his Master may have him again, shall have Four Dollars Reward, and all reasonable charges paid by Jonathan Clawson.

N.B. All persons are forewarned from harbouring, concealing or carrying off said Negro, as they will answer it at their peril. 'Tis supposed he has got a Pass with him.

303. The New-York Gazette; or, The Weekly Post-Boy, #1230, July 31, 1766.

Taken up by the subscriber, at Blooming Grove near Goshen, in Orange County, in the Province of New York, on Sunday the 13th of July instant, and put into Gaol at Goshen, a run away negro man who says his name is John Linch, that he is a free man and lived with Mr. Hannes Bush, at Schuylkill River Ferry in Chester County, in the Province of Pennsylvania: He is about 25 years of age, 5 feet 7 inches high, is mark'd on the Scull with one Scar on the right side and two on the Left; has a remarkable Scald on the inside calf of his leg, speaks good English and High Dutch, and has something of a stoppage in his Speech: He says that about 3 weeks before he was taken up, he had been a Prisoner in the Gaol at Sussex County and was released to enable him to pay his fees, but that one Joshua Taylor, a School Master, who had been a prisoner with him pursuaded him away from that Place. He says he can prove his Freedom by one Samuel Tucker, living at Trenton, in New Jersey; [but he is supposed to be one of the two Negroes that it is reported, were lately concerned with the Rape of two White Women, which occasioned the Death of one of them, one of whom it is said was brought to Justice and the other escaped.] Any person claiming the said negro, and proving his property, may have him on paying charges to John Hudson, Deputy Sheriff of Orange County.

304. The New-York Gazette; or, The Weekly Post-Boy, #1233, August 21, 1766.

Ran away about the Middle of July last from the Subscriber, living in King's Country, Long Island, a Negro man named Jack, he is about 35 years of age, slim made, about 5 Feet 8 Inches in height, speaks good English and Dutch, and has been used to tending in a Grist Mill.— Whoever secures him in any Gaol or brings him to me shall be well rewarded, and all reasonable Charges paid by ABRAHAM SCHENK. New-York, August 15, 1766.

305. The New-York Gazette (Weyman's), #386, September 1, 1766.

R U N A W A Y on Saturday the 16th Instant August, from Doctor William Bush, at Horse-Neck, in Connecticut—A Negro Man, named Jim, about 36 Years of Age, five Feet six Inches high, hangs down his Head when he walks, speaks good English, is very nimble and sprightly, and can do all Sorts of farming Business very handily.

He had on when he went away, an old Wool Hat, a dirty brown Kersey upper Jacket, with the Skirts sewed together all round; an under Jacket of red Coating, lapped over before, a new Tow Shirt, and long narrow Trowsers.

Whoever secures the said Negro, in any public Gaol, or brings him to Doctor James Murray, in New-York, or to his said Master in Connecticut, upon Application to either of them, receive a Reward of Forty Shillings New-York Money, if the said Negro is taken up in Connecticut, or of three Pounds, if taken up in the Province of New-York, besides all reasonable Charges.

New-York, 27th of August, 1766.

306. The New York Gazette; or, The Weekly Post-Boy, #1235, September 4, 1766.

Run away on Saturday the 23rd of August last, from Nathaniel Richards at Newark, a Negro Man named Ben, about 5 feet 8 or 9 inches high, aged 28, slim made, thin visage, yellow Complexion, and can speak good Dutch. He formerly belonged to Thomas Budde, at Morris-town in New Jersey, who several months ago sold him to the Widow Mrs. Elizabeth Finn at Prakenas in the County of Bergen, from whom he run away soon after, and being advertised, was taken and brought home to his Mistress, by whom he was sold soon after to the Subscriber. When he went away he pretended that he was going to swim, and as he never returned, and next day his Clothes were found near the Shore, he was supposed to be drown'd, till his Character was known, which gives Reason to suppose he took that

Method to deceive his Master and prevent a Search. It is not known whether he had any Clothes with him or not. Whoever returns him to his Master or secures him in any gaol, shall receive Eight Dollars Reward and all reasonable charges. Nathaniel Richards.

307. *The New-York Gazette; or, The Weekly Post-Boy*, #1236, September 11, 1766.

Run away from the Subscriber living at Jamaica, on Long Island, on Thursday last, a Negro fellow named Tony, about 5 feet 11 inches high, of a yellowish complexion, speaks both Dutch and English; had on when he went away, a brown Camblet coat and Waistcoat, a Pair of Plush Breeches and a Pair of Trowsers.—Whoever takes up said Negro, and secures him so that he may be had again, shall have Twenty Shillings Reward, and all reasonable Charges paid by DOW DITMES.
N.B. All persons are hereby forewarned not to harbour conceal, or carry away the said Negro, as they shall answer as the Law directs.

308. *The New-York Gazette; or, The Weekly Post-Boy*, #1251, December 25, 1766.

THIRTY DOLLARS REWARD: RUN-AWAY from the subscriber, the 16th of September last, a Negro Man named BOOD, about 38 Years old, 5 Feet 10 Inches high, yellow Complexion, thin Visage, has had the Small Pox; his great Toes have been froze, and have only little Pieces of Nails on them: He is much addicted to strong Liquor, and when drunk very noisy and troublesome. Whoever takes up said Slave, and brings him home, or secures him in Gaol, so that his Master may get him again, shall be intitled to the above Reward of THIRTY DOLLARS, paid by WILSON HUNT. Any Person who takes up said Negro, is cautioned to be particularly careful that he does not make his Escape, as he is a remarkable stout, cunning, artful Fellow. Hunterdon-County, Maidenhead, December 20, 1766.

309. *The New-York Mercury*, #811, May 18, 1767.

Run-away from the subscriber the 24th of March last, living at Middletown Point in New-Jersey, a Negro Man, named Joe, 6 feet high, long-visaged, with large eyes, a smooth-tongued fellow, 'tis likely he will change his name, and is about 30 years old: Had on when he went away, a grey homespun Jacket, and a red one under it, an Ozenbrigs Shirt, a Pair of light coloured Broad-cloth breeches, patched in many Places, grey woolen Stockings, and new Shoes. Whoever takes up and secures the said Fellow, so that he may be had again, shall receive Five Dollars Reward, paid by William Hendrickson.

310. *The Pennsylvania Gazette* (Philadelphia), #2004, May 21, 1767.

Somerset County, near Prince-town, New Jersey, May 9, 1767 Run away from the Subscriber about 23rd of April last, a Negroe Man, named Linden, about 33 years old, about 5 feet 9 or 10 inches high, yellow complexion, has had the Small-Pox, his fore Finger stiff, his Coat and Jacket of new homespun brown Broadcloth, good Leather Breeches, good stockings and good hat; it is supposed he has obtained a Pass, and will try to pass for a free Negroe; he is addicted to strong Liquor and when drunk troublesome. He pretends to be a Doctor. Whoever takes up and secures said Slave in any Gaol, so that his Master may get him again, shall be entitled to the above Reward. Any Person who takes up said Negroe is cautioned to be particularly careful that he does not make his Escape; he is remarkably stout, and a cunning artful Fellow. Gizebert Lane.

311. The New-York Journal, or, The General Advertiser, #1276, June 18, 1767.

New-York, June 13, 1767. Ran-away the 8th inst. June from the Subscriber at Ramapough, a Negro Man named Hack, about 30 Years of age, 5 feet 4 inches high, well-set, had on a white Broadcloth Coat, a black Calimanco Waistcoat, yellow Breeches and black Stockings; Whoever takes up and secures said Negro, and returns or secures him so that his Masters may have him again, shall have Forty Shillings New York Money Reward; and all persons are hereby warned not to entertain, conceal, or remove him away, as they will answer it at their Peril: Note he is suspected to be now in New-York. He speaks Dutch and English well. Lawrence Jacobus Van Buskirck.

312. The New-York Gazette; or, The Weekly Post-Boy, #1284, August 13, 1767.

RUN away from the Subscriber, on Saturday Night last, a likely Negro Man named Prime, about 25 Years of Age, and about Five Feet Four Inches high; he took with him when he went away, two striped linsey Wollsey Jackets, a red Cloth one, and a blue Camblet one: He was seen coming out of the Mouth of the Kills in a Canoe on Sunday Morning last, with an Intention of coming to New-York, in Order to get on Board some Vessel: Whoever takes up and secures said Negro, so that his Master may have him again, shall have a reward of Five Dollars and all reasonable Charges paid by JOHN MERCEREAU.

N.B. All Master of Vessels and others, are forbid to carry him off or harbour him at their Peril.—It is very likely he is gone to Mr. David Provost's Farm, about Six Miles from New-York, as he formerly lived there. Staten-Island, August 11, 1767.

313. *The Pennsylvania Gazette* (Philadelphia), #2015, August 6, 1767.

Runaway from the subscriber living in Upper Freehold, Monmouth County, near Imley's Town, on the 22nd of last Month, a servant Negroe Man half Indian named Charles but will probably alter his name, about 28 years of age, about 6 feet two inches high, well set, something knock-kneed, large feet, a scar on one of his cheeks, near his temple, a yellow complexion, long hair, very much curled, and thin on the top of his head; had on, when he went away, a light grey homespun coat, streaked lining, about half worn, his Jacket of a darker colour, and more worn, tow shirt and trowsers and felt hat and it is likely that he will change his clothes. Whoever secures said servant so that his master may have him again, shall have Three Pounds Reward, and reasonable charges, paid by Richard James.

314. *The New-York Journal, or, The General Advertiser*, #1292, October 8, 1767.

Middletown-Point, October 5, 1767. Run away from the Subscriber the 5th Instant, a Negro Man, named Cato, a short, thick fellow: He had on when he went away, a white hat, a brown Jacket, and a long red do. with a Short Skirts behind, black Breeches, with Long Trowsers over them, brown Stockings with white feet. Whoever takes up said Negro so that I may get him again, shall have Thirty Shillings Reward and all reasonable charges paid by John Hendricks, New York, September 25, 1767.

315. *The New-York Gazette; or, The Weekly Post-Boy*, #1306, January 11, 1768.

New-York, January 11, 1768. Run away about 2 Months ago, a French Negro Man, named John Baptist, speaks French, and broken English, pitted with the Small Pox, fat Nose, square built, about 5 feet 6 Inches high, his little

Finger of his Left Hand, stiff and straight, his Age about 45 or 50 Years: He has Holes in each Ear for Earing. Whoever takes up said Negro, and tends Word to the Subscriber, shall have FORTY SHILLINGS Reward, and all Charges paid by WILLIAM DARLINGTON.

316. *The Pennsylvania Journal, and the Weekly Advertiser* (Philadelphia), #1317, March 3, 1768.

Run-away from the subscriber on Wednesday the 24th February 1768, living in Middletown, Monmouth County, East-New Jersey, a Negro fellow named Lank, about 5 feet 8 or 9 inches high, slender made, about twenty-five years of age; had one when he went away a light colour'd homespun coat, an old hat, a grey homespun jacket, blue cloth breeches, and yarn stockings. Any person who takes up the said Runaway and brings him to me, shall have twenty shillings reward, and all reasonable charges, paid by William Hendricks.

317. *The New-York Journal; or, The General Advertiser*, #1324, May 19, 1768.

Run away May the 14th 1768 from the subscriber in Middletown, a Negro man named York, about five feet nine inches high, 18 years of age, well set, has one of his fore teeth broke near the gum; had on when he went away, a suit of homespun mixt grey clothes, shoes and stockings, brass buckles, and a cock'd set hat, with a white metal button. Whoever takes up said Negro and secures him, so that his master may have him again, shall have twenty shilling reward and all charges, paid by me, Cyrenius Van Mater.

318. *The Pennsylvania Chronicle* **(Philadelphia), #75, June 13, 1768.**

Woodbridge, June 9, 1768. Runaway from the Subscriber, the 29th ult. a Negroe Man named Cuff, about 5 feet 10 inches high, full faced, and thick set; has a large Scar on his great right Toe, cut within; had on when he went away, a Woolen Shirt, a Pair of Leather Breeches, a Grey Kersey Jacket, and Felt Hat, but may probably change his Dress. Whoever takes up said Negroe Man, and secures him so that his Master may have again shall have Three Dollars Reward, paid by the Subscriber. Jonathan Clawson.

319. *The New-York Gazette; and the Weekly Mercury*, **#868, June 20, 1768.**

Run-away from the Subscriber living at Pumpton in New-Jersey, on Saturday the 4th Instant, a Negro Man named Harry, 40 years old, much pitted with the Small-Pox, and can speak both Dutch and English, can play on the Violin and loves Grog: Had on when he went away a blue Broad cloth Coat, a blue and white Holland Jacket, red cloth Breeches, and new Shoes with brown Yarn Stockings. Whoever takes up and secures said Fellow so that he may be had again, shall receive Five Pounds reward and all reasonable Charges, from John Acton.

320. *The New-York Gazette; or, The Weekly Post-Boy*, **#1335, August 1, 1768.**

RUN away, on Friday Evening last, a negroe Man, named Norway about 33 Years of Age, but has an older Look near 5 feet high, marked with the Small-Pox, talks slowly, and very indifferent English; he sometime since lived with Mr. William Ralsten, Inn holder, in Philadelphia, but about a Year post with Mr. William Provest, in New-York: Had on, when he went away, a blue Coat, with Silver Thread Buttons, a reddish mix'd Colour Cloth Waistcoat, and white

Plush Breeches.Whoever brings the above negroe to Mr. Provest, in New-York, shall receive Five Dollars Reward with all reasonable Charges.

321. *The New-York Gazette; and the Weekly Mercury*, #877, August 22, 1768.

Ten Dollars Reward Run-away from Hendrick Coyler, of East-New-Jersey, a Negro Fellow named Ishmael, by trade a Blacksmith, is much pitted with the Small Pox. Has a Blemish in one eye, is a great fidler, and often shewing slight of Hand Tricks; has a Squaw for a wife. He got leave of his Master about 2 years since to get towards Middletown; it is said he has work'd some time at the Iron Works near Spotswood, 'tis thought he is since gone towards Pennsylvania; he has been acquainted about East-Town. Whoever takes up said Fellow and delivers him to Capt. Elias Dayton in Elizabeth-town, or said Colyer at Horses-Neck, shall have the above reward and all reasonable charges paid by Hendrick Colyer.

322. *The New-York Gazette; or, The Weekly Post-Boy*, #1339, August 29, 1768.

City of New-Brunswick, August 25, 1768 Notice is hereby given that on Monday the 22nd Inst. were taken up and committed to Gaol, two likely young Negroe Fellows; one calls himself London, about 5 feet 6 inches high; the other Robert, about 5 feet 3 inches: They pretend to be free, say that they did belong to a Gentleman a Merchant from St. Christopher's that they came with their Master to New-York, who lodged with the Widow Richardson on Rotten-Row, that their Master died there last Spring and before his Death gave them free. The chief Cloathing about them was contained in a good Ozenbrig Bag, marked P.R. #19, viz, a white Fustian Coat, lined with Shalloon, a pair of Leather Breeches, one White Linnen Jacket, 5 white Shirts, one pretty fine, marked W.I 2 pair of cloth breeches, 2 pair of

Trowsers, one a pair of Yarn, and 2 pair of Worsted ribb'd Stockings, one White Handerkerchief, one Duffields Great Coat, had on each a Beaver Hat, one about half-worn; Jackets, coarse Shirts and Trousers, pretty good and in Appearance belonged to a Gentleman. Whoever claims said Negroes are desired to be speedy in taking them out. Or if Mrs. Richardson or any other person knows them to be free, are desired to give Notice thereof, that upon paying charges, they may be set at Liberty.

323. *The New-York Gazette; or, The Weekly Post-Boy*, #1342, September 19, 1768.

Woodbridge, September 12, 1768. Broke out of the Gaol at Perth-Amboy, on the 9th Instant, a Mullatto Servant Man named Charles Lee, born in England, about 5 feet 9 inches high, slim built, has a Scar on one side of his nose, and wears his own hair; had on a light coloured silk Jacket and an old felt hat; he had run away from Maryland and was taken up and committed to said Gaol. He is a watchmaker by trade, and as he has been in the provincial service, it is suspected he is gone towards Albany. Whoever takes up said Servant and secures him in any Gaol, or brings him to the Subscriber in Woodbridge, shall have Seven Pounds reward and all reasonable charges paid by Nathaniel Heard.

324. *The New-York Gazette; and the Weekly Mercury*, #883, October 3, 1768.

Taken up a few Days ago and committed to the Gaol of the Borough of Elizabeth, in New-Jersey, by order of John Stites, Esq; Mayor, a Negro Man about 24 years old, very thick lips, talks both Dutch and English, says he is a free man, and that he lived some time at Bloomingdale, near New-York: When taken up he had on a blue Cloth Coat, old Shoes, without Stockings. The Owner may have him again, paying Charges, and proving his Property, by applying to the said John Stites, Esq. or the Gaoler, Benjamin Miller.

Advertisements 151

325. The New-York Gazette; and the Weekly Mercury, #900, January 23, 1769.

Run away in New-York, from the Subscriber, living at Middle-town Point in East New Jersey, last November, a Negro Man named Jim, speaks both English and Dutch, about 30 years old, a slim Fellow and much pitted with the small pox. Had on when he went away, an old red Watch Coat and Tow Trowsers. Whoever takes up and secures said Negro so that he may be had again, shall receive Thirty Shillings reward and reasonable charges from William Hyer.

326. The New-York Gazette; or, The Weekly Post-Boy, #1367, March 13, 1769.

On Monday night the 20th instant, made his escape or was taken off from one of the islands called Two Brothers, near Hell-Gate, a negro man named Jacob, belonging to Henry Brasier, and formerly known in this city by the name of the Fu-Fu Negro or Money Digger: He is between 40 and 50 years old, full face, large flat nose, a small scar on the lower part of it: His eyes very full, as if they were starting out of his head, he had on a red Duffle Jacket with blue lining, blue Breeches, a Felt Hat, and common Shoes and Stockings. He speaks both English and Dutch and was brought up in the Jersies a little above Brunswick. Whoever takes up he said Negro, and brings him to his master on the North Brother Island, shall have Forty Shillings Reward and all reasonable charges paid by Henry Brasier.

327. The New-York Gazette; and the Weekly Mercury, #917, May 22, 1769.

Run-away from the Subscriber, living at Newark, in New-Jersey, on Wednesday the 17th Instant, a Negro Man named Benjamin; but it is likely he will change his Name; he has a Mold on his cheek, has a down-look of a Yellow Cast, a Lively Fellow, and is about 5 feet 9 inches high: Had on when he went away, a short Ranger's Coat, grey or blue and a red Watch-coat. Whoever takes up and secures the said Run-away, so that he may be had again, shall receive five Dollars reward, and all reasonable charges paid by Nathaniel Richards.

328. *The New-York Gazette; and the Weekly Mercury*, #918, May 29, 1769.

Run-away from Elizabeth-town, Sunday night the 21st Inst. a likely Negro Fellow, about 20 years old, of middling stature: Had on when he went away a blue cloth coat, a brown jacket and waistcoat, and blue stockings, and took with him a brown coat. Whoever takes up the said Fellow and delivers him to Mr. Isaac Woodruff, Merchant, in Elizabeth-town, shall receive 40*sh* Reward.

329. *The New-York Journal; or, The General Advertiser*, #1380, June 15, 1769.

June 12, 1769 Run-away on Satuday the 10th of this Instant, from Leffert Waldron, at the 3 Mile Run, near new Brunswick, a yellowish Negro, named Ben, about 19 years old, about 5 feet 2 inches high, bushy Hair, speaks both low Dutch and English: Had on when he went away, a brown homespun Coat, with white Metal buttons, new homespun breeches, Felt Hat and sundry other Clothes. Also, at the same time, run away, a Negro Fellow, from Ernestus Van Harlingen, at Millstone, in the County of Somersett, at the Court-House, named Jack, about 21 years old, about 5 feet 9 inches high, well built, also yellowish, speaks both Dutch and English: Had on when he went away, a blue coat, brown jacket, half worn Leather Breeches and Felt Hat. Whoever will take up said Negroes and secure them so that their Masters may have them again, shall have Six Dollars reward if taken within the Province and Seven Dollars if taken without the Province, or half for each, paid by us. Leffert Waldron and Ernestus Van Harlingen.

P.S. The above Negroes are supposed to be gone off together as they were missing both together, at one time. It is supposed they have a false pass.

330. *The Pennsylvania Gazette* (Philadelphia), #2113, June 22, 1769.

Run away last night, from the Subscriber, living in Monmouth County, East-New Jersey, an indented servant man who calls himself William Kelly, he is a yellow fellow, part Indian and part Negroe, about 40 years of age. a well made strong fellow, about 5 feet 8 or 9 inches high; had on when he went away, an old beaver hat, a homespun light coloured cloth jacket, under ditto of the same striped flannel shirt, old leather breeches, old yarn stockings and old shoes; has a large scar on the outside of his right leg, cut by a scythe, is much given to drink, and is very talkative. Whoever takes up and secures said Servant so that his Master may have him again, shall receive Forty Shillings Reward, and reasonable charges, paid by Jos. Saltar. April 15, 1769.

331. *The Pennsylvania Chronicle* (Philadelphia), #131, July 10, 1769.

Somerset County, New-Jersey, July 15, 1769. Ran away from the subscriber, A Likely Negro Fellow, about five feet ten inches high, pitted with the small pox, has a nose more like a white than a black, speaks good English and writes a good hand. He took with him three jackets, one a fine brown cloth, another of homespun linsey woolsey, lined, the other double breasted, without sleeves and one pair of new trowsers. His other clothing is not known. Whoever takes up and secures said Negro so that his Master may have him again, shall have Three Pounds Reward, and all reasonable charges paid by William Cooke.

332. *The New-York Gazette; and the Weekly Mercury*, #924, July 10, 1769.

Five Dollars Reward Ran-away from the subscriber in Freehold, Monmouth County, in East-New-Jersey, on the 3rd Ultimo, a Negro Man named Frank, about 24 years old, about 5 feet 7 inches high; and walk nimble and light: Had on when he went away, a black Everlasting Jacket without sleeves, white Shirt, Tow Trowsers and Felt Hat bound with yellow. Whoever takes up said Negro and secures him to his Master, shall receive the above Reward and all reasonable Charges paid by Daniel Van Mater.

    N.B. He has a small round Scar on his cheek and it is thought he is to come to New-York and all Masters of Vessels is charged not to carry him off.

333. *The New-York Gazette; and the Weekly Mercury*, #933, September 11, 1769.

Three Dollars Reward Run-away from the subscriber at Elizabeth-Town on Tuesday the 22nd of August last, a likely young Negro Fellow called John: He is considerably upon the tawny colour, was born in this country; and bred in the family of the late Mr. Brockhurst at Pompton. It is conjectured that he may be lurking somewhere thereabouts or on Col. Philips Manor. Whoever shall secure the said Negro so that his master may have him again, shall receive the above recompense, and all charges paid by William P. Smith.

334. *The New-York Gazette; and the Weekly Mercury*, #936, October 2, 1769.

Run-away on Sunday night the 17th Inst. from the subscriber living in Newark, New-Jersey, a Negroe Man, named Ben; he is considerably on a tawney colour (it is likely that he will change his name as he is a crafty Fellow), he is about 30 years of age, 5 feet 8 or 9 inches high, well made, has a hair-mole on his cheek and lost two of his foreteeth, walks very quick, something stooping forward: Had on and took with him when he went away, one blue broad-cloth short coat with white buttons, a nankeen jacket laced behind, two check and two tow shirts, two pair of tow trowsers, one pair of wollen and one pair of worsted stockings, one pair of pumps, and a short gun, brass mounted, and a piece of brass along the upper part of the barrel, almost as far as the sight. Whoever shall secure the said Negroe so that his Master may have him again, shall have Five Dollars reward and all reasonable charges paid by Nathaniel Richards.

335. *The New-York Gazette; and the Weekly Mercury*, #939, October 23, 1769.

Runaway from the subscriber living at Canoe-Brook, Essex County, New-Jersey, two Negro Men Slaves; the one called Cato, but sometimes calls himself John. He is a likely slender fellow about 5 feet 7 inches high, 30 years of age, with a Scar on the hind part of his Head, about the bigness of a Two Shilling piece: he had on a Snuff coloured thick set Coat, a Beaver hat about half worn, with Jacket and homespun Trowsers, but it is probable he will change his Dress. The other named Scipio a short thick well-set Fellow, about 5 feet high, and about 25 years of age, has a Rupture plainly to be discovered: Had on a blue and white striped homespun double breasted under Jacket without sleeves, and a black and white striped Jacket with sleeves over it; a blue Duffils watch coat, and a Pair of long white homespun Trowsers. Whoever takes up and secures the said Runaways so that they may be had again, shall receive Four Dollars reward for each, and all reasonable charges paid by Jonathan Squire and John Williams.

336. The Pennsylvania Gazette (Philadelphia), #2131, October 26, 1769.

September 30, 1769. Twenty Dollars Reward for taking up and delivering to his Master, at Elizabeth-Town, a Negroe man slave, named Britt, this country born, about 30 years of age, near 6 feet high, a well set fellow; or Ten Dollars will be given if taken up and secured in Northampton gaol so that his Master, the subscriber may have him again; he was formerly the property of Nathaniel Salmon of Springfield in the Borough of Elizabeth, Essex County, and Province of New Jersey, who was taken in execution by William Barnett, Sherrif of said Borough and county, and was sold at public vendue, for the benefit of said Salmon's creditors, unto the subscriber, and is supposed to be taken off by his former master, and gone to Lahnawanack or Wyoming as he was seen with said Salmon, travelling on that road. These are therefore to warn all persons from harbouring entertaining or buying said Negro on their Peril, as they may depend, on being prosecuted, as the law directs (in such cases) for detaining or keeping said slave from his Master's service. JACAMIAH SMITH.

337. The New-York Gazette; or, The Weekly Post-Boy, #1410, January 8, 1770.

Albany, December 29, 1769 Five Pounds Reward Stolen in the Night Preceding the 28th Instant from Colonel Bradstreet, a strong well made black Horse, fifteen hands high, with a good saddle and Bridle, and supposed to be taken by a dark Mullatto or Negro Man, who made his escape out of the Gaol a Day or Two before, where he was confined for running away from his Master Mr. Nathaniel Richards, of Newark, in New Jersey. Said Mullatto or Negro is about 5 feet 10 inches high, thin made, large flat nose, with curled hair down each cheek, had on a grey surtout coat. Whoever takes up said Horse, with or without the Negro, shall have the above Reward, with reasonable charges, on bringing him to Col. Bradstreet, or securing him and wending Word thereof, and if the Negro is taken it is requested that he be secured in some Gaol. and Information thereof be given to Col. Bradstreet. His name is said to be Ben and that he has changed it to Bon or Bond.

N.B. An Irishman, commonly called Toby Quit, absconded the same night from Albany, and perhaps may have taken the horse. He is about 5 feet 9 inches high, fair short hair, tied behind, had on an old Hat, with a blue half worn surtout Coat, with brass buttons on each side and a double cape.

338. *The Pennsylvania Gazette* (Philadelphia), #2164, June 14, 1770.

Run away from the subscriber living on the Sea Shore near Metetekunk, in the County of Monmouth, Township of Dover, and Province of East-Jersey, a Negro Man, named Prince, 5 feet 8 or 10 inches high. Had on when he went away, an Iron Collar round his Neck, a Wool Hat, with a green Binding, Ozenbrigs Shirt and Trowsers, a brown Waistcoat, without Sleeves, and shoes, without Stockings. Whoever takes up said Negroe and secures him in any of His Majesty's Gaols, or brings him to his Master, shall have Twenty Shillings reward and reasonable charges paid by me Joseph Allen.

339. *The New-York Gazette; or, The Weekly Post-Boy*, #1443, June 18, 1770.

New-Jersey, June 12, 1770 Run away from the Subscriber living in Woodbridge, East New-Jersey, in the night of the 2nd Instant, a Negro Man called Dick, about five feet eight inches high, about 28 years of age, speaks very good English, is a well-looking, well-built fellow, somewhat on the Yellow; takes uncommon Pains with his short wooly Hair, which he wears cut on the fore Part of his Head: He took with him a blue coat, a black Velvet Jacket and Breeches, with sundry other very good Cloathes. It is likely that he may change his Name, and have a Pass: He has been seen in New-York a few days ago. Whoever takes up and secures the said Fellow so that his Master may have him again, shall receive Five Pounds New-York Currency and all reasonable charges paid by me David Edgar.

N.B. As he took with him a silk Cap, it is likely he may cut off his Hair. All Masters of Vessels and others are hereby forewarned of harbouring or carrying him off at their Peril.

340. *The Pennsylvania Chronicle* (Philadelphia), #196, October 8, 1770.

Forty Shilling reward Ran away on the 6th of this Instant October, from the subscriber, living in Somerset County, East N. Jersey, a Negro Man, named Arch, about 5 feet 8 inches high, and about 30 years of age, pretty black, walks very upright, and wears his hat right up. Had on when he went away, a brown coloured linsey coat, red vest, lined with white, buckskin breeches, and white stockings; also took with him a grey kersey jacket, with the sleeves turned up. It is imagined he is gone some back way to Albany, to meet some yellow free Negroes, which went by water at about the same time, or else try to get aboard some vessel, as he attempted about 3 years ago below Philadelphia, but was taken up. It is supposed he has got a false pass; he can read the bible very well. Whoever takes up said Negro, and secures him in any of his Majesty's gaols, so that his master may have him again, shall be paid the above reward, and all reasonable charges paid by Roelof Van Dike.

341. *The New-York Gazette; or, The Weekly Post-Boy*, #1458, December 10, 1770.

RUNAWAY from me the Subscriber, a Negro Boy, named SPIER; had on when he went away a blue Cloth Coat, with another short white Ditto under it, old knit yellow Breeches, Shoes and Stockings, and his Hat sewed up all round. He is

Advertisements 159

about Fifteen Years of Age, is remarkably black, large Nose, with Guinea Cuts on his Cheeks, has two very large Lubs near each Ear, is pretty well set, and a little knock knee'd, very apt to smile when spoken too. If taken up in Town One Dollar Reward, and if out of Town Two Dollars, and all reasonable Charges, will be paid by JOHN SLIDELL.

N.B. I do forewarn all Persons, from Harbouring, concealing or carrying off said Slave, at their Peril. He took with him a large white Blanket. New-York, Nov. 16, 1770.

342. *The New-York Gazette; or, The Weekly Post-Boy,* **#1472, March 18, 1771.**

RUN AWAY on Thursday the 7th of March, from Peter Low, a Mulatto Slave, named Syme, or Symon, (half Indian and half Negro Breed) aged about 24 Years, is a Chimney Sweeper: Had on when he went away, an old Thickset Coat, and old Beaver Hat, an old Watch-Coat, and other old Cloaths; had his Utensils for Sweeping with him: —He is short and wellset, has a heavy walk, speaks slow and thick, both Dutch and English: has short but straight Indian like Hair, and generally smiles when spoken to. Perhaps he may pretend to be free. Masters of Vessels and others are warned from carrying him off.

Whoever takes up the said Negro and secures him, so that his Master may have him again, shall have Two Dollars, and if taken out of the City of New York, Four Dollars Reward, with all reasonable Charges, paid by PETER LOW.

N.B. The said Peter Low, continues to make and sell, CHOCOLATTE at his House the upper end of Maiden-Lane.

343. *The New-York Gazette; and the Weekly Mercury,* **#1013, March 25, 1771.**

Twenty Dollars Reward. Run away about 18 months since from Springfield, near Elizabeth-Town, a certain Negro man named Brit: He is about 30 years old, near 6 feet high, stout and well made: He was taken by execution at the suit of Elias

Desbrosses, Esq. of New-York and sold at Vendue by the Sheriff of Essex County, and purchased by Jecamiah Smith. The said Fellow is supposed to be harboured at Wyoming, by his former Master, Nathaniel Salmon. All persons therefore are forbid to harbour or entertain said Negro, and any Person that will take him up, and bring him to the Subscriber, shall have the above reward or 10 dollars if taken and sent to any Gaol in the Province of Pennsylvania, New-Jersey or New-York, so that he may be had again. Jecamiah Smith.

344. *The New-York Gazette; and the Weekly Mercury*, #1028, June 8, 1771.

New York, June 14, 1771. Runaway from William Bayard's farm, Hoobock, opposite the City of New-York, a mullato servant man, named charles, about 40 years of age, five feet seven or eight inches high, much pock-broken, his head partly grey, wears a cap sometimes; speaks good English, rather thin, understands all kinds of farming business, is a good coachman and gardner, and tends well on a gentleman; has carried a number of cloathes with him so that he cannot well be described, as to what he wears; passes it is said for a freeman and has a forged pass with him. All masters of vessels are forbid to carry him off and all taverns and other houses from entertaining him. Whoever will secure the said fellow in the nearest gaol where he is taken up, and give the earliest intelligence to his Master, shall have Ten Dollars reward, and all reasonable charges paid by William Bayard.

345. *The Pennsylvania Journal, and the Weekly Advertiser* (Philadelphia), #1491, July 1, 1771.

Perth Amboy, July 4, 1771. Fifteen Pounds Reward Runaway from the subscriber, in the month of October, 1762, a Mullatoe Woman Slave, named Violet, about 35 years of age; she is very active and rather tall, sometimes afterwards she was seen in the company of one James Lock, somewhere on the Susquehannah, and by information was apprehended and committed to gaol, in the year 1764, in Frederick's Town, In Maryland, on suspicion of having runaway. From that gaol she was reported to have made an escape and two month's ago, was discovered about fifteen miles from Ball-Fryer's ferry, in Frederick's county, in Maryland aforesaid where she had three children, Edward Bonnel of Monmouth County, in the Province of New-Jersey, was formerly her owner, and after his decease she was sold by his executors to the subscriber. Any person who may take her up must secure her strictly or she will certainly escape again, being remarkably artful. Whoever delivers her and her children to the subscriber or Thomas Kean, Esq, in New Castle, on Delaware, shall receive the above reward, or ten pounds for the wench only, and reasonable charges from Philip Kearney.

346. *The Pennsylvania Chronicle* (Philadelphia), #235, July 1, 1771.

Twelve Dollars reward Ran away from the subscribers the 2nd Day of July instant, a Negro Man slave, who calls himself by the several names of James, Gaul, Mingo, Mink and Jem. His real name is Jem; he is about 5 feet 6 inches high, thick set, and not very black; he has a scar on his face, and is about 35 years old; he took with him two oznabrigs shirts and trowsers, a broadcloth coat, a coating waistcoat, a felt hat, and a violin. He is supposed to have gone off with a certain Patrick Johnson, who was born in Ireland, about 5 feet 10 inches high and 30 years old; he is thin about the flesh, having lately been sick; had on and took with him, one new check and two new oznabrigs shirts and trowsers, a felt hat, narrow-brim'd and bound with brown ferreting, an old fustian waistcoat without sleeves, fine short brown hair and is much addicted to strong liquors. They stole and took with them, a large brown Horse, about 12 years old, near 15 hands high, very strong made, paces and trots, and is branded, either on the shoulder or thigh with some letters not remembered. Whoever takes up and secures the said Negro and Horse and delivers them to the subscribers at Newark, in New-Jersey, shall be entitled to the above reward and well paid for extra charges, or Eight dollars for the Negro and Four Dollars for the Horse. Isaac Wilkins, Samuel Ogden. Newark, July 4, 1771.

347. *The New-York Gazette; or, The Weekly Post-Boy*, #1496, September 2, 1771.

New-York, August 15, 1771. RUNAWAY from the Subscriber, a negro Boy, of about 15 Years of Age, named BRISTOL, can speak both Low Dutch and English, is small of his age; had on when he went away, a Tow-Cloth Jacket and Trowsers, Oznabrigs Shirt, was barelegged. Whoever takes up said Negro Boy, and will bring him to me in Chappel Street, or to the Printers hereof, shall have TWO DOLLARS Reward, and all reasonable Charges, paid by AARON STOCKHOLM. All Persons are hereby forbid to harbour him, and Masters of Vessels forewarned carrying him away at their Peril.

348. *The New-York Gazette; or, The Weekly Post-Boy*, #1552, June 15, 1772.

RUN away from the Schooner Dove, Benjamin Crane Master, last week a Negro man Named JAMES, about six feet high, very black, speaks tolerable good English, had on when he went away, a brown jacket and a pair of stripped flannel trowsers very much tarr'd, a woolen check or stripped shirt; said negro was born in Jamaica, from whence he ran away about twelve months since, seems to understand the taylor's trade, and likewise driving a coach, is one of which capacities, he may likely offer his service to some gentlemen in this city, and likewise pretends he is free. Whoever apprehends said negro and delivers him to the subscriber living on Cromline's Wharf, shall receive five

Dollars reward and all reasonable charges paid by JOHN HOSMER. New-York, June 14th, 1772.

349. *The New-York Gazette; and the Weekly Mercury*, #1087, August 24, 1772.

RUN-AWAY from the Subscriber, living at Harlem, the 2d inst. a Negro Man named TOM: Had on when he went away, a Tow Shirt and Trowsers, Homespun Jacket lined with green, and an old Hat: walks upright, very thick Lips, about 5 Feet 9 Inches high, and very black. Whoever takes up the said Negro, and brings him to his Master, or secures him in any of his Majesty's Goals, shall have THIRTY SHILLINGS Reward, and all reasonable Charges, paid by the Subscriber. SAMSON BENSON, jun.

350. *The New-York Gazette; and the Weekly Mercury*, #1087, August 24, 1772.

RUN-AWAY from the Subscriber, living at Goshen, in Orange County, on Tuesday Night last, a Negro Fellow named Stephen, about 5 Feet 8 Inches high: Had on a Homespun Jacket, Tow Trowsers, and an old [ ]. Whoever takes up the said Negro, so that his Master may have him again, shall have THREE POUNDS Reward, and all reasonable Charges, paid by me, SILAS HORTON. August 3.

351. *The New-York Gazette; and the Weekly Mercury*, #1090, September 14, 1772.

RUN-away from the subscriber, living at Westchester, a negro lad named Claus, about 18 years old, and 5 feet 7 or 8 inches high: Had on when he went away, a white hat about half worn, a brown jacket without lining, tow shirt and trowsers, and an old pair of shoes: He speaks good English and Dutch. Whoever takes up the said negro and secures him, so that he may be had again, or delivered to his master, shall have Forty Shillings reward, and all reasonable charges, paid by ISAAC LEGGETT.

352. *The New-York Gazette; and the Weekly Mercury*, #1095, October 19, 1772.

RUN-AWAY from the subscriber, living in New-York, on Saturday morning the 8th inst. a negro man named CATO, of about 22 years old, and about 5 feet 9 inches high; he is very black, straight, and well-limb'd, looks grum, speaks pretty good English, a little lisping. Three months ago he belonged to Charles Tooker, of the borough of Elizabeth, county of Essex in the province of New-Jersey: It is supposed he is gone that way: Had on an ozenbrigs shirt, jacket, and trowsers, a new felt hat, shoes and stockings, he likewise took with him an ozenbrigs shirt, jacket and trowsers, and almost a new beaver hat, and a blue waistcoat half worn. Whoever takes up the said negro man, so that his master may have him again, shall receive 20*s.* reward, if on this island, and 40*s.* if taken elsewhere, and all reasonable charges, paid by JOHN DE PEYSTER, jun.

353. *The New-York Gazette; and the Weekly Mercury*, #1097, November 2, 1772.

Six Pounds Reward. RUN-away from Caleb Morgan, in East-Chester, the eighteenth day of October last, a negro man named Sambo, about 25 years of age, about five feet nine inches high, of a yellow complexion, pretty slim built, a sober looking fellow: Had on when he went away, a blue broad cloth coat, with red lining; a black Manchester velvet jacket without sleeves, a pair of buckskin breeches, and blue stockings, a good pair of thick shoes, two shirts, and an old felt hat; one of his fore fingers (the tip end) is bruised off, so that the skin grows fast to the bone; the other hand the middle finger is something crooked, so that he cannot open it so straight as the others. He talks very good English, and I believe he can talk Dutch, he being brought up among the Dutch the west side of the north river. It is mistrusted that a white man has carried him away in order to make sale of him, or has given him a pass; the man's name that is mistrusted is John Norris, about 30 years of age, often goes down to the Jerseys; perhaps he may have changed his name, he is a lusty man. If any person does discover any white man with the negro, and they have made sale, or does it to make sale of him, and takes up the white man with the negro, and secures them in any of his Majesty's goals, so that I can come get my negro again, and the white man brought to justice, shall have the above reward; or Five Pounds, and reasonable charges, for the negro alone; paid by CALEB MORGAN.

354. *The New-York Gazette; and the Weekly Mercury*, #1101, November 30, 1772.

FIVE DOLLARS REWARD, RUN-away from Samuel Ogden, of Boontown, in the County of Morris, and Province of New-Jersey, on Sunday the 18th of October last: A Negro Man named Mingo or Tim, he is about 30 Years of Age; has a scar either on his Nose or one of his Cheeks; is about 5 feet 7 or 8 Inches high, plays on the Violin, speaks good Dutch and English, and is much addicted to Strong drink: Had on when he went away a dark brown broad cloth Coat, with brass Philadelphia Buttons, a brown broad cloath waist-coat, with basket mohair Buttons, a Pair of red coating Trowsers, an ozenbrig Shirt and wool Hat. He was formerly the property of Isaac Wilkins, Esq; of West-Chester, about which Place it is not unlikely he may be lurking. Whoever apprehends said Negro and returns him to his Master, or secures him in any of his Majesty's Goals, shall be paid the above Reward, and all reasonable Charges by SAMUEL OGDEN.

355. The New-York Gazette; or, The Weekly Post-Boy, #1551, January 4, 1773.

RUNAWAY from the subscriber, on the 25th of December last, a Negro Wench, named PHILIS, late the property of William Smith, Esq; She had on when she went away, a light coloured calimanco gown, a check apron, black silk cloak, and a black peelong bonnet. Said Wench is marked in the forehead with a diamond, has lost several of her fingers on each hand, and also some of her toes. Whoever takes up and secures said Wench, so that she may be had again, shall receive TWENTY SHILLINGS reward, and all reasonable charges, paid by MARY EXCEEN.

All Masters of vessels are hereby forwarned carrying off said Wench, as they may depend upon being prosecuted with the utmost rigour of the law.

356. The New-York Gazette; and the Weekly Mercury, #1106, January 11, 1773.

RUN-AWAY from the subscriber, on Sunday Evening the 27th Day of December last, a Negro Man named JACK, about 33 Years old, a short spare Fellow: Had on when he went away, a brown double-breasted short Forrest Cloth Jacket, with plain Brass Buttons, lined with red Baize; a red Baize under jacket, Leather Breeches, and blue Yarn Stockings. He took with him a light Coat much wore of fine twilled Frize, the knap wore off, and a new blue Watch-coat of Coating, with white plated Buttons. He was purchased from Hendrick Emons, of Rockey-Hill, in New-Jersey, about 9 Years ago, and it is supposed he is either gone that Way, where he has a Mother, or else to anthony Ten Eyck's, at Albany, where he has a Wife.—Any Person that will take up said Negro and secure him, so that his Master mat have him again, shall have Forty Shillings Reward, and all reasonable Charges, paid by PETER KETELTAS.

357. *The New-York Gazette; and the Weekly Mercury*, #1106, January 11, 1773.

TWENTY SHILLINGS Reward. Absented himself from his Master, living in Hanover-Square, the 2d Inst. a Negro Man called Dick, aged 19 Years. He had on when he went away, a Beaver Hat, smartly cocked, a new light coloured Coat and Waistcoat, with Metal Buttons, green Linings, the Collar and Cuffs of the Coat turned up with Green; new Buckskin Breeches, a Pair of ribbed Stockings of a mixed Colour, and Silver Buckles in his Shoes. He is a likely, well-made Fellow, and speaks both English and Dutch. It is supposed that he has been seduced by bad Company during the late Holydays; and that he is lurking somewhere in the City, or its Environs. Whoever secures the said Negro, so that the Subscriber may have him again, shall receive Twenty Shillings Reward, from CHARLES INGLIS.

358. *The New-York Gazette; and the Weekly Mercury*, #1112, February 15, 1773.

RUN-AWAY from the subscriber on the 29th of August last, a negro man named SAM, aged about 26 years, is about 5 feet 10 or 11 inches high, has black smooth skin, streight built, and well limb'd; has a scar on one of his knees, can speak both English and Dutch, but sounds mostly on the latter: He is very strong and nimble, and does not want for wit; he can play well on the violin, and is fond of company: It is likely he may have a forged pass, and pretends to be free. All masters of vessels and others, are hereby forbid to harbour or carry off the said slave, or any wise to asist him. Whoever apprehends him, and delivers him to the subscriber in the Manor of Cortlandt, shall receive a reward of FIVE DOLLARS, with reasonable charges, if taken in Westchester County; and if taken out of said county, THREE POUNDS, with charges as above, paid by JOHN BRYAN.

359. The New-York Gazette; and the Weekly Mercury, #1124, May 10, 1773.

THIRTY DOLLARS Reward. RUN-AWAY from the subscriber, living at Connecticut Farms, near Elizabeth-Town, New-Jersey, the 13th of March, a negro man named BRET: He is the same fellow the Salmons have had at Weyoming for three years past; is stout and well made, near 6 feet high, about 33 years old: Had on when he went away, a red great coat half worn, a blue coat, and a Kersey jacket of the same colour, with flat white metal buttons, buckskin breeches, and black and white stockings. He can read and write, and 'tis supposed will forge a pass. Whoever takes up and secures the said fellow in either Philadelphia or Easton goal, so that his master may get him again, shall have the above reward, and all reasonable charges for bringing him to the subscriber. — 'Tis probable he may endeavor to get to the Mississippi; and in case taken there, and sent to New-York, the above reward will be paid by Hugh Gaine.— If apprehended, unless well secured, he will endeavor to make his escape, being strong and very artful. Those that harbour said fellow, may depend on being prosecuted by JECAMIAH SMITH.

360. The New-York Gazette; and the Weekly Mercury, #1126, May 24, 1773.

TEN DOLLARS Reward. RUN-AWAY from the subscriber, living in Morris county, New-Jersey, on Sunday night the 9th inst. a likely young negro wench named HAGER, about 20 years old: Had on when she went away, a black and white striped linsey woolsey short gown and pettycoat, with some other cloths which she took with her: She has stole some goods, and was under a warrant for stealing when she absented herself. Any person who takes up and secures her, so that she may be had again, shall have the above award of TEN DOLLARS, and all reasonable charges, paid by JACOB MORRELL.

N.B. All persons are forbid to harbour or conceal her, as they may depend on being prosecuted to the utmost rigour of the law.

361. ***Rivington's New-York Gazetteer; or The Connecticut, Hudson's-River, New-Jersey, and Quebec Weekly Advertiser,* (hereafter *Rivington's New-York Gazetteer*), #8, June 10, 1773.**

RUN away from the Subscriber about fourteen days past, a Negro man named *Pompey*, a well set Fellow about 5 Feet 8 inches high, speaks both English and Dutch, but something broken, had on when he went away, a claret coloured coat, a grey waistcoat, lined with flannel, blue broadcloth breeches, white linnen trowsers, one check, and two white shirts, is about 35 years of age: Whoever takes up said slave, and secures him in any of his Majesty's gaols, or returns him to his Master at Newark in New-Jersey, or to Captain Josiah Banks, at Hackinsack, in the county of Bergen, shall have four Dollars reward from me. May 11, 1773. DAVID OGDEN.

362. ***The New-York Gazette; or, The Weekly Post-Boy,* #1576, July 5, 1773.**

FORTY SHILLINGS REWARD, RUN-AWAY from the subscriber, living at Newark, Essex country New-Jersey, on the 3d inst. a Mulatto Fellow, called HARRY, about twenty years of age, five feet two inches high, straight black hair which he generally wears tied behind, speaks good English and understands the potash business: He had on when he went away, a blue cloth coat, white lining, brown linen waistcoat, striped trowsers, an old castor hat, newly dressed. Whoever takes up and secures the said Mulatto Fellow in any of his Majesty's goals, so that his master may have him again, shall receive the above reward. Newark, June 14, 1773, THOMAS BROWN.

It is supposed he will endeavour to get to the German Flats or parts adjacent: If he should be taken up in the county of Albany, and delivered to Capt. Peter Brott, in the city of Albany, he will pay the above reward.

363. *Rivington's New-York Gazetteer*, #12, July 8, 1773.

Five Dollars Reward, RUN away from the Subscriber living in Shrewsbury, a Negro servant man named BEN, otherwise called Cip, about 30 years of age, near 5 feet high, of a yellow complexion: had on when he went away, a pair of tow trowsers, linen shirt, with creepers to the bosom and wrists, a frize jacket, with cuffs to the sleeves, he has been in the army, and talks much when a little elevated with liquor. Whoever secures said Negro shall be entitled to the above reward, and all reasonable charges, paid by STEPHEN TALLMAN, jun. June 26, 1773.

364. *Rivington's New-York Gazetteer*, #17, October 21, 1773.

Run away from the subscriber living on Long Bridge Farm in the County of Middlesex, New Jersey, a negro man named Jack, he is of a brown colour, about 5 feet 11 inches high, rather slim made; had on when he went away, a broad cloth homespun jacket without sleeves, blue and red mixed, leather breeches about half worn, a flannel shirt, and an old wool hat. It is suspected he may have taken some other cloathes with him, but it is not certain. Whoever takes up and secures the said negro man and brings him to the subscriber, or secures him in any gaol, so that he may have him again, shall have eight dollars reward and all reasonable charges paid by Samuel Okeson. N.B. He has been gone about three weeks.

365. *Rivington's New-York Gazetteer*, #31, November 18, 1773.

Ten Dollars Reward, run away Tuesday night, from Michael Varien, a negro wench named Violet, about eighteen years old, of a yellowish colour about five feet high, she has a scar on her left arm where she was inoculated about the size of a shilling and a small blemish in one of her eyes: before she went off she took away a large quantity of cloathes belonging to her mistress consisting of chintz gowns, two black silk cloaks and hats, a red short cloak, laced caps, etc. Whoever brings the said wench to the Bull's Head in Bowery Lane shall receive the above reward.

366. *Rivington's New-York Gazetteer*, #50, March 31, 1774.

Woodbridge, in East-Jersey, April 1, 1774. FIVE DOLLARS Reward. RUN away on the 22nd day of March, at night, from the subscriber, living in the township of Woodbridge, in East-Jersey, a servant man, name JACK, about five feet seven inches high, Indian look, bushy hair, about thirty-two years of age, and can read; he has lost his upper foreteeth, and is to be seen on his left hand, a bruise done formerly by a stone: Had on when he went away, a linsey woolsey jacket and breeches, both grey coloured and much worn, black horn buttons on the jacket, and pewter buttons on his breeches, of different sorts, a striped outer jacket, with strings in his shoes. He may pretend himself a freeman, but he is a proper slave born in this province, has often runaway by drinking too much, and other misdemeanors. Whoever takes up the said servant so that his mastermay have him again, shall receive the above reward, and reasonable charges paid, by me ISAAC TAPPEN.

N.B. The abovementioned servant was seen to go through Baskinridge the 24th of March.

367. The New-York Gazette: and the Weekly Mercury, #1178, May 23, 1774.

FIVE DOLLARS Reward. RUN-away from the subscriber (the 27th of April last) living at King's-Bridge, an elderly negro fellow named Jack, about six feet high, bald pated, Guinea mark'd, &c, speaks good English, and has a smattering both of French and Dutch, lived formerly on Staten-Island : had on when he went away, a grey homespun jacket and breeches, with a pair of coarse tow-cloth trowsers. Any person that secures the said negro, so that the owner may have him again, shall be entitled to the above reward, and all reasonable charges, paid by I. G. TETARD. N.B. As the fellow has formerly been a sailor, he may probably take to sea; therefore all captains of vessels are forwarned carrying him off at their peril.

368. Rivington's New-York Gazetteer, #63, June 30, 1774.

Five Dollars Reward. RAN AWAY on the night of the 4th instant, from Abraham Lawrence, living at Flushing on Long-Island, a Negro man named GEORGE, about five feet eight inches high, very thin visaged, of a yellowish complexion, and has black bushy hair, which he commonly wears tied behind; had on and took with him a whitish linen coat, a grey homespun coat, blue jacket, buff-coloured half-worn velvet breeches, with some patches, black stockings, and old shoes, and most commonly wears his hat cocked, though may change his coat to a brown. Whoever takes up said run-away and returns him to his master, or secures him in any of his Majesty's gaols, with giving his master a notice thereof, shall have FIVE DOLLARS reward, and all reasonable charges paid by the subscriber. All masters of vessels and others, are forbid carrying off, or harbouring said run-away, as they will be dealt with according to law, ABRAHAM LAWRENCE.
Flushing, June 6, 1774.

N.B. He has been seen in New-York with a bundle of cloaths tied up in a handkerchief. which he stole the night before he came off. He came over Long-Island Ferry to New-York on Sunday the 5th instant, in company with a white man who paid his ferriage. It is supposed they are both gone to the Eastward.

369. *The New-York Gazette: and the Weekly Mercury*, #1184, July 4, 1774.

RUN-AWAY from the subscriber living at Paramus, in the County of Bergen, on or about the first of May last, a negro man named PRINCE, about 40 years of age, five feet nine inches high, a black looking fellow, with some grey hairs in his beard: Had on a red duffles great coat, a brown strait coat, tow trowsers, had neither stockings nor shoes with him. Whoever secures the said negro that his master may have him again, shall have FOUR DOLLARS reward, and all reasonable charges paid by ANDREW JOHN HOPPER.

370. *Rivington's New-York Gazetteer*, #72, September 2, 1774.

Five pounds reward. Run away from the subscriber, living in Scohary, the 6th of June last, a negro man named Bram, he is of a yellowish complexion, much pock-marked; about five feet six inches high, had on when he went away a white woolen homespun jacket, a wool hat, a woolen shirt, buckskin breeches, linen trousers, a pair of grey stockings, a good pair of shoes and plated buckles.

Whoever takes up the said negro and secures him in one of His Majesty's gaols so that his master may have him again or delivers him to Jacob Ten Eyck Esq. at Albany shall receive the above reward, and all reasonable charges. John Bacher.

N.B. All masters of vessels and others are hereby warned not to harbour him or carry him off.

371. *Rivington's New-York Gazetter*, #72, September 2, 1774.

Run away about four weeks ago from the farm of Charles Atkins, esq., at Harlaem a mulatto man named Pierot: he is about 5 feet 8 inches high, near 40 years old: he was born in the West Indies.
 Whoever takes him up and brings him to Mr. Lawrence Kortwright, in New York, shall have Twenty Shillings reward and all reasonable charges paid.

372. *Rivington's New-York Gazetteer*, #74, September 15, 1774.

TEN DOLLARS REWARD. RUN AWAY on Friday the 26th of August, 1774, from the subscriber, North-Castle, Westchester county, and province of New-York, A NEGRO MAN, Named WILL, about 27 years of age, about five feet six inches high, somewhat of a yellow complexion, a spry lively fellow, very talkative; had on when he went away, a butter-nut coloured coat, felt hat, tow cloth trowsers; he has part of his right ear cut off, and a mark on the backside of his right hand.
 Whosoever takes up said Negro and brings him to his master, or secures him in gaol, so that his master may have him again, shall have the above reward and all reasonable charges, paid by JAMES BANKS.
 N.B. Masters of vessels are hereby warned not to carry off the above Negro.

373. *Rivington's New-York Gazetteer*, #78, October 13, 1774.

Ten Pounds Reward. Run away from the Subscriber, about the 29th of Sept. 1772. A likely well set Negro Man, named Cæsar, About twenty-six Years of Age; he is a black Fellow, and speaks good Low Dutch, as well as English, is very much given to Liquor, and is quarrelsome in his Cups. It is supposed he will be for staying about the Island in New-York Government, amongst the Dutch, and probably pass for a Freeman; he has a Scar on one Side of his Face, the Resemblance of a C. He formerly belonged to John Goy, of Philadelphia, and is now my Property.

Whoever takes up the said Negro, and brings him to me, or so secures him, that he may be had by John Galloway, in Philadelphia, or Patrick Ewing, in Cecil County, in Maryland, shall receive the above Reward of either of them, or from me, WILLIAM EWING, in Sincastle County, Virginia.

374. *Rivington's New-York Gazetteer*, #78, October 13, 1774.

WESTCHESTER, Oct. 3. Run away from the Subscriber, A Negro Man, named CLOSS, about five Feet seven Inches high; had on when he went away, a brown homespun Jacket, coarse Tow Shirt, and stripped Trowsers, rather long; he speaks good low Dutch, and English. Whosoever takes up and secures the said Negro, so that his Master may have him again, shall have Five Dollars reward, and all reasonable Charges paid by SAMUEL WELL. All Masters of Vessels and others, are forwarned to harbour or carry off said Negro, as they will answer it at their peril.

375. *Rivington's New-York Gazetteer*, #78, October 13, 1774.

New-York, Oct. 7. Run away the 6th Inst. from MORICE SIMONS, A Negro Man, named PRINCE, about Five Feet nine Inches high, twenty Years old, had on when he went away a new Suit of brown Thickset, wears a Silver Loop, Button, and Band on his Hat; he also wears his Hair tied up behind, and a large Tupee before.

Whoever will deliver the said Servant to his Master, at Mrs. Smith's near the Fly-Market, or Mr. Stephen Rapalje, shall receive a Reward of twenty Dollars.—All Masters of

Vessels are hereby forewarned not to ship the said servant, as he may probably attempt to pass for a Freeman.

376. *Rivington's New-York Gazetteer*, #81, November 3, 1774.

Eight Dollars Reward. Run-away from the subscriber, living near Princeton, in New-Jersey, A Negro man, named Constant, ABOUT the age of twenty-six; he is a well-built, likely, black, active, sensible fellow, and has been accustomed to attend a gentleman: Had on, and took with him the following cloaths, viz. Two brown broad cloth coats; one of them rather too large and long for Him, with silver plated buttons, the other very short, with plain buttons; a blue surtout coat; one brown Holland and one fustian short coat; one pair of sustian, and one ditto of leather breeches; one pair of striped, and one ditto of check trowsers; one sustian, one striped gingham, and two white waist-coats; one pair of old boots; a pair of new and a pair of old shoes, with a pair of neat Pinchbeck buckles; one or two old beaver hats, cut in the fashion; two white and three check shirts; with sundry other things. Whoever takes up and secures said Negro in any of his Majesty's gaols, so that his Master may get him again, shall receive the above reward, with all reasonable charges, by applying to the subscriber, near Princeton, to Dr. Samuel Duffield at Philadelphia, to Mr. Lloyd Daubney at New-York, or to Dr. Bates Williams Peterson, near Elizabeth-Town. JOHN WILLIAMS SANDERS.

N.B. It is imagined he may have a forged pass, and go towards New-York or Philadelphia, with a view of procuring a passage to the West-Indies, from whence he came; therefore all masters of vessels or others, are forewarned not to take him off, or any ways harbour him at their peril. He is learning to play on, and is very fond of the fiddle.

377. *Rivington's New-York Gazetteer*, #82, November 10, 1774.

ARGYLE, October 15, 1774. Run-away from the subscriber, A Negro Man named Gassee, ABOUT twenty-six years old, five feet six inches high; had on a dark brown jacket, blue frize trowsers, new shoes, and a white shirt; he also took with him, a striped linen shirt, and wore a felt hat. Any person that apprehends said Negro, and secures him, so as his master may have him again, shall receive the reward of TEN DOLLARS. and all reasonable charges paid by the subscriber, DUNCAN McARTHUR.

378. *Rivington's New-York Gazetteer*, #86, December 8, 1774.

Ten Pounds Reward. RUN away from the Subscriber, a Negro Slave, named John Rattan, he sometimes passes by the Name of John Manley, about thirty-three Years of Age, five Feet five of six Inches high: Had on when he went away, a light colour Cloth Coat, and blue Cloth Waistcoat and Breeches; he is a likely Fellow, speaks very good English, and is very sensible.
    Whoever delivers him to Mess. Hugh and Alexander Wallace, Merchants, in New-York, shall receive the above Reward, and all reasonable Charges. ROBERT CATHERWOOD.

379. *The New-York Journal; or, The General Advertiser*, #166, January 5, 1775.

THREE DOLLARS REWARD. RUNAWAY from the subscribers, the 10th instant, two indented Mulatto boys; one named SIMEON, might be taken for a white boy; about 20 years of age, four feet two inches high; had on when he went away, a dark gray suit of kersey clothes, stockings of the same colour, shoes nailed with hob nails, supposed not to have any hat. The other named SAM, middling dark complexion, about 18 years of age, five feet 2 inches high, had on when he went away, a light gray suit of kersey clothes, a white flannel shirt and good felt hat; supposed to have other clothes with him. Whoever returns or secures said boys, giving proper notice, so that their masters may have them again, shall be entitled to the above reward, and all reasonable charges, paid by

SAMUEL PHILIPS
WILLIAM ARTHUR.

Smith Town, Long Island,
Dec. 21, 1774,

380. *The New-York Journal; or, The General Advertiser*, #167, January 12, 1775.

FIVE POUNDS Reward, And all reasonable charges. RUN away from the House of Major Prevost, in Bergen County, on the 29th of September last, a Negro Man and his Wife: The Fellow is serious, civil, slow of Speech, rather low in Stature, reads well, is a Negro Preacher, about 40 Years of Age, he is called MARK. The Wench is smart, active and bandy, rather lusty, has bad Teeth, and a cast in one Eye; she is likely to look upon, was brought up in New-London, is called Jenny: as she had a Note to look for a Master, its likely she may make a travelling Pass of it—Whoever takes up said Negroes, and brings them to the Subscribers, or secures them in any of his Majesty's Gaols, or gives such Information of them as they may be had again, shall be entitled to the above Reward, and all reasonable Charges paid, either by Major Prevost, Archibald Campbell, in Hackinsack; or Thomas Clarke, near New-York.

381. *The New-York Journal; or, The General Advertiser*, #177, March 23, 1775.

Four Pounds Reward. Run away from the subscriber, living in East Chester, on the 6th instant, a Negro man named Robin, about 5 feet 7 inches high, a well set fellow, of a

yellow complexion, part Indian, a great bushy head of hair, somewhat different from a Negro, speaks good English, and can speak Dutch, no particular mark, if he can get liquor is apt to get drunk; it is imagined he has got a pass, being very intimate with a Negro fellow, who can write, had on a felt hat half worn, a blue duffle great coat, a tann coloured over jacket, and an under one, frize, a buck skin pair of breeches, took along with him two pair of black woollen stockings, and two pair of shoes; it is imagined he has directed his course toward the North River, to get over among the Indians; he lived at the Fish Kill, on Phillips's Manor, and on York Island. Whosoever takes up and secures the said Negro fellow, so that his master may have him again, (in any of his Majesty's goals) shall have the above reward, if taken in this county, (five pounds, if taken in any other county) and seven pounds if taken among the Indians, with all reasonable charges paid by ISAAC WARD.
East Chester, March 7, 1775.

382. *The New-York Gazette: and the Weekly Mercury*, #1233, May 29, 1775.

THREE POUNDS REWARD. RUN-AWAY about 14 Days ago, from the Subscriber, living at Paramas, Bergen County, and Province of New-Jersey, a Negro Man named Joe, 21 Years old, 5 Feet 6 Inches high, and of yellow Complexion: Had on when he went away a brown Broad Cloth Jacket, Leather Breeches, pale blue Stockings, a new Wool Hat, and good Shoes. Whoever takes up and secures said Run-away, so that his Master may have him again, shall receive the above Reward, and all reasonable Charges, from ISAAC VAN BLARCUM.

383. *The New-York Gazette: and the Weekly Mercury*, #1233, May 29, 1775.

FOUR DOLLARS Reward. RUN-AWAY from Abraham Lawrence, of Flushing, on Long-Island, Queen's county, on the 18th of March, a negro man named OLIVER, (belonging to Samuel Smith, on the north side of Staten Island) but may have changed his name, as it is said he has called himself Jerry: He is about 22 years of age, 5 feet 7 or 8 inches high, has something of a yellow cast in his colour: Had on and took with him when he went away, two old blue coats, one long skirts, the other short, a striped jacket, a pair of old homespun breeches, a pair of stockings, one pair deep blue, the other grey, and an old beaver hat. It is thought he has money, and likely may have change his cloaths: He has been seen at Elizabeth-Town and in New-York, in company with Col. Morris's negro man named Jerry. Any person that secures said negro, so that his master may have him again, shall have the above reward, and all reasonable charges, paid by Samuel Smith, on the north side of Staten Island, Abraham Lawrence, at Flushing, Jonathan I. Dayton, at Elizabeth-Town Point, or Simon Hellers, at the White-Hall, in New-York.

He is very still, having but few words to say to any body; his hair is something bushy, and it is thought he has got on board some boat or sloop belonging to the East or North River, or the Jersies.

N.B. All masters of vessels, and others, are hereby forwarned from concealing or carrying off said negro at their peril.

384. *The New-York Gazette: and the Weekly Mercury*, #1236, June 19, 1775.

RUN-AWAY from on board the Sloop Seaflower, a young Negro Fellow named America, about 20 years old, very black, pitted with a small Pox, and his under Lip very thick: Had on a striped Shirt and Trowsers, red Cap, and is supposed to be secreted in this city. Five Dollars Reward will be given to any Person who brings the said Negro to the Printer hereof, or JOHN SEBRING.

385. *Rivington's New-York Gazetteer*, #116, July 6, 1775.

RUN away, on Saturday night the 24th of June, from the subscriber, at Flushing on Long-Island, a Negro man named CATO, about 30 years old, much addicted to strong liquor, and when drunk, talks much; he is about five feet four inches high, had on when he went away, an old beaver hat, tow shirt and trowsers, and some woollen cloaths, with white yarn stockings. he is gone to New-York by water, in a small craft that rows with two oars, with a small square-sail, and was seen to land at New-York. Whoever takes up said Negro, and secures him so that his master may get him again, shall be entitled to TWENTY SHILLINGS Reward, and all reasonable charges paid by me, STEPHEN LAWRENCE.

386. *The New-York Gazette: and the Weekly Mercury*, #1239, July 10, 1775.

FIVE DOLLARS Reward. RUN-AWAY from the subscriber living in the city of Albany, the 4th of June last, a negro man named CATO: He had on when he went away, an old ozenbrigs waistcoat, an old pair of patched tow-cloth trowsers, and an ozenbrigs shirt: He took with him a mix colour'd homespun cloth coat, with white metal buttons on it, a nankeen pair of breeches, a pair of stockings, one of them thread, the other white cotton, with a square cut out of the top of each of them to take out the former mark; and a new ozenbrigs shirt. He is about 25 or 26 years of age, 5 feet 6 inches high, tall, thin and raw-bon'd; he has remarkable white teeth, of a low slow speech, and shows his upper teeth when he smiles. Whoever takes him up and secures him, so that his mistress may have him again, shall have the above reward, and all reasonable charges, paid by me, FRANCES HOLLAND.

387. *The New-York Gazette: and the Weekly Mercury*, #1241, July 24, 1775.

FOUR POUNDS Reward. RUN-AWAY on the second day of July, from his master living near Coryell's ferry, Amwell township, Hunterdon county, a negro man named TOM, about 22 years of age, 5 feet 7 inches high, this country born, likely featur'd and well made: It is supposed that he has a forged pass. Had on and took with him when he went away, a lightish-colour'd sagothee coat, a white striped silken jacket, a white linen shirt, sagothee breeches, worsted stockings, good shoes, with brass buckles in them, a felt hat, a new pair of tow cloth trowsers, a tow and linen shirt, and an old claret colour'd jacket patch'd with brown broad cloth. Whoever takes up and secures said slave in any of his Majesty's goals in America, or delivers him to his said master, shall have the above reward, and all reasonable charges, paid by JACOB HOLCOMB.

388. *The New-York Gazette: and the Weekly Mercury*, #1243, August 7, 1775.

FOUR DOLLARS Reward. RUN-AWAY from the subscriber, living in the borough of Elizabeth-Town, New-Jersey, a negro fellow named STEVE, near 6 feet high, has a sower look, and is a supple spry fellow: He formerly belonged to one Mr. Ludlow, up the North River, and it is thought he is gone that way, and taken a mulatto wench with him. Any person that may take up either or both of them, and secure them in goal, or bring them home, shall have the above reward, and all reasonable charges, paid by CORBET SCUDDER.

389. *Rivington's New-York Gazetteer*, #118, August 24, 1775.

Run away from the subscriber at Brookland, Long Island, on Tuesday morning the 22nd instant, a negro man named

Prince, aged 19 years old, very black, about 5 feet 9 inches high, walks stooping, one leg smaller than the other, plays on the fife; had on with him when he went away, an old outside winter coat, double breasted, with brass buttons, an under brown thread jacket, without sleeves, an old white shirt, a new pair of oznabrigs trousers and breeches, brown thread stockings and shoes with plated buckles and a good beaver hat. Whoever brings the negro to me at Brookfield aforesaid shall receive Forty Shillings reward and all reasonable charges. Christopher Sweedland.

390. *The New-York Gazette: and the Weekly Mercury,* #1228, September 11, 1775.

TEN DOLLARS Reward. RUN-away from the subscriber, early on Tuesday morning the 5th instant, a negro man named TITUS, about 25 years old, and about 5 feet 8 inches high, well made and proportioned every way, and is very likely for a negroe: he had on when he went away, a short brown coat, made of coating; an old homespun blue and white striped linen jacket with sleeves; and a blue and white striped homespun trowsers, almost new. The hat he is supposed to have took with him is very remarkable, (unless since changed) having no brim round it, it is very much worn. He can play a little both on the fiddle and fife. Whoever takes up and secures said servant, so that his master may have him again, shall have the above reward if took out of the colony of Connecticut, and Eight Dollars if within the colony, and all reasonable charges paid by HENRY VAN DYCK.

391. *The New-York Gazette: and the Weekly Mercury,* #1254, October 23, 1775.

FIVE DOLLARS REWARD. RUN away from this city, some days ago, a Negroe boy, the property of Lieut. Colonel Turnbull, about twelve years old, well looked., and very black, whoever will deliver him to John M'Adam and

Co. will receive the above reward and reasonable charges. All persons are forbid to harbour him on pain of prosecution.

N. B. It is supposed the boy is on Long-Island.

392. *The New-York Gazette: and the Weekly Mercury*, #1254, October 23, 1775.

FIVE DOLLARS REWARD. RUN away, on Thursday the 16th instant, from the subscriber, a negro man named HARR, 16 or 17 years of age, about 5 feet 7 inches high, was formerly the property of Jacob Van Wincle of Acquacanock; had on, when he went off, a check shirt, osnabrug trousers, olive coloured short coat lined with striped homespun; has a smooth face, not very black, his wool lately cut, and his hat remarkable by the letters H H painted on the crown. He pretends to be free, but it is hoped he will find no encouragement from any Gentleman whatever. Any person in whose custody he is found after this notice may depend on being dealt with as they should be. Whoever delivers said negro at his Majesty' naval brewery on Long Island, or gives information so as he may be recovered, shall have the above reward, from ROBERT HARGRAVE.

393. *The New-York Gazette: and the Weekly Mercury*, #1257, November 13, 1775.

RUN-away from the Subscriber, a Negro Man called Mingo, 20 Years of Age, of a yellow Cast, round Face, and middling flat Nose, about five Feet two Inches high: Had on when he went away, a Felt Hat cut in the Fashion, a brown Sirtout, a homespun streaked Jacket, homespun chequered Trowsers, a Pair of blue Stockings speckled with white; carried with him a Pair of mix'd blue home knit Stockings. Whoever takes up and secures the said Fellow, so that his Master may have him again, shall receive Four Dollars

Reward, and all reasonable Charges paid by me, Benjamin Hutchinson, of Southold, Suffolk County, Long-Island.

394. *The Pennsylvania Gazette* (Philadelphia), November 22, 1775.

Three Pounds Reward. Runaway from the Subscriber in the County of Monmouth, New Jersey, A Negroe man named Titus, but will probably change his name; He is about 22 years of age, not very black, near 6 feet high; had on a grey homespun coat, brown breeches, blue and white stockings, and took with him a wallet, drawn up at one end with a string, in which was placed a quantity of clothes. Whoever takes up said Negroe, and secures him in any gaol, or brings him to me, shall be entitled to the above reward of *Three Pounds* proc. and all reasonable charges, paid by John Corlis, November 8, 1775.

395. *The New-York Gazette: and the Weekly Mercury*, #1259, November 27, 1775.

Forty Shillings reward, with all reasonable charges will be given to any person who will bring to JOHN DE LANCEY, in the delivery, or secure in the city of New-York or county of Westchester, a Negro man, who has left his mistress. He is a good looking fellow, about five feet eight or nine inches high, civil spoken, a great cockscomb, and one of the best waiters at a table in this country; plays upon the French horn, is a tolerable good cook, coachman and groom, but his vanity proving more powerful than his honesty, he fraudulently obtained a silver watch, which being discovered it is imagined occasioned his going off. He has several suits of good cloaths, was generally called Cæsar, but names himself Joseph Low.

396. The New-York Gazette: and the Weekly Mercury, #1269, February 5, 1776.

THREE DOLLARS Reward. RUN AWAY from Richard Harris in Little Queen-street, next door to the Scotch meeting house, a young negro boy named Daniel, about nine years of age, the top part of his left ear is thicker than his right, his hair on his head very thin, and is very small for his age; had on when he went away, an old brown surtout coat, and a cotton check shirt. Whoever will bring the said negro boy home to his master shall have the above reward.

397. The New-York Gazette: and the Weekly Mercury, #1289, June 25, 1776.

TEN DOLLARS Reward. RUN-away last Thursday from the Subscriber, at Newark, a certain Negro Fellow named Jack, about 25 years old, a square well-built Fellow, pretty black, Guiney born, and spoke bad English: He took with him several Sorts of Cloths, his Master's Gun, and a Grenadier's Sword, with Brass Mountings: He is supposed to have had on a good Beaver Hat cocked in the Fashion, a light coloured fine Cloth jacket, without Sleeves, and may wear a Blanket Coat, he has a Scar right down his Forehead to his Nose, his country Mark, can handle a File, and understands the Brass Founder's Business. Whoever takes up the said Fellow, and delivers him to Mrs. Wilkins, near Ogden's Furnace, in Newark, shall have the above reward; or in New-York, to JACOB WILKINS.

398. The New-York Gazette: and the Weekly Mercury, #1292, July 15, 1776.

RUN-away from the Subscriber, livings in King's County, Long-Island, a short Time ago, two Negro Men, one named Nathaniel, a very handy Fellow, about 5 Feet 6 Inches high, straight and well built, 24 Years old, of a yellow Complexion, with long Hair tied up with a Ribbon; born at

Newton, Queen's County, and lived at Flatbush. Had on when he went away, a brown Linen Jacket, with an under one double breasted, one Side red Cloth the other Homespun; also homespun Trowsers, and a half worn Hat. The other Fellow that he went away with belonged to Jeromus Remsen, at Newton, and are very like each other, being Brothers; he was well cloathed, and went by the Name of Jacob, and is a Cooper by Trade. Whoever secures the above Runaways in any Goal so that their Masters mat have them again, shall have Eight Pounds Reward, and all reasonable Charges paid by HENRY WYCKHOFF.

399. *The New-York Gazette: and the Weekly Mercury*, #1292, July 15, 1776.

TEN DOLLARS Reward. RUN away from the Subscriber, on Monday the first Inst. a Negro Man, about 21 Years of Age, named Prince, five Feet seven Inches high, thin made: Had on when he absconded, a blue Cloth Jacket, a white Homespun Shirt and Trowsers, and is a Butcher by Trade. He is supposed to have gone towards Rye, or entered the Army. Whoever will bring him to his Master in Roosevelt's Street, near the Tea Water Pump, shall have the above Reward for their Trouble. GOODHEART SIEGLER.

400. *The New-York Gazette: and the Weekly Mercury*, #1293, July 22, 1776.

RUN-AWAY, a Negro Man named JAMES, tall and thin, the whites of his Eyes remakably red, and his Face full of Eruptions: He is a talkative plausable Fellow, and had on when he went away an old grey Bearskin short Coat, Check Shirt, Linen Breeches, and worsted Stockings, and is supposed to be gone towards the East End of Long-Island. Whoever takes up and secures the said Negro, so that his Master may get him again, or brings him to Doctor Samuel Bard, in New-York, shall receive TEN DOLLARS Reward, and all reasonable Charges paid by SAMUEL BARD.

401. *The New-York Gazette: and the Weekly Mercury*, **#1294, July 29, 1776.**

Three Dollars Reward. RUN-away the 20th Instant, from the Subscriber, in the Borough of Westchester, a Negro Fellow named CATO, about 24 Years of Age, 5 Feet 6 Inches high; he is very black, remarkable large Mouth with broad Teeth, and wrinkled Forehead; is plausible and smooth in speaking, and may pass himself for a Sailor, having been used to a boat. He took with him when he went away, a green short Coat with red Collar and Cuffs, short brown Frize Coat, one brown and one white Linen Waistcoat, one brown Linen Breeches, two Pair homespun Trowsers, Two homespun Shirts and one white ditto, and may have other Cloaths with him that is not known, Whoever takes up the said Negro and secures him, shall have the above Reward, and reasonable Charges paid them by JOHN SMITH. Frog's Neck, in Westchester, July 22, 1776. He has got a Pass as a Freeman, and passes by the Name of Thomas Jackson.

402. *The New-York Gazette; and the Weekly Mercury*, **#1297, August 19, 1776.**

FIVE DOLLARS Reward. RAN-AWAY from the subscriber, on Tuesday, the 30th of July, 1776, a negro man, named CASTER, about five feet nine inches high, thin make, walks very upright, about 35 years old. Had on when he went away, a pair of white linen trowsers, tow shirt, one pair old shoes, and brass buckles; he is of a pleasant countenance, and is well pleased and elevated when one speaks to him about war. If taken on the island of New-York, the above reward shall be paid, with all reasonable charges; and if taken out of the county of New-York, Eight Dollars reward and reasonable charges. All masters of vessels, and others, are requested not to harbour or carry the said negro off. PHILIP KISSICK.

403. *The New-York Gazette; and the Weekly Mercury,* #1300, September 9, 1776.

FIVE DOLLARS Reward, RUN-AWAY, from the Subscriber, a Negro Man named TOM, about 50 Years of Age, 5 Feet high; Thick Set, yellow Complexion, Lisps some little (hardly perceiveable) Had on when he went away, a Pair of brown tow Trowsers, strip'd woollen Shirt, a felt Hat about half worn, a Pair of new Shoes with Buckles, a Waistcoat with the Fore Parts Brown, the Back Parts White. Whoever takes up the said Negro Man, and brings him to the Subscriber, shall have the above Reward, and all reasonable Charges paid; by me JOHN VAIL.

404. *The New-York Gazette; and the Weekly Mercury* (Newark), #1302, September 28, 1776.

TEN DOLLARS REWARD. RUN away from the subscriber, living in Ulster county, two mulatto slaves, remarkably white, on the 22nd inst. both well set, about 5 feet eight inches high, black hair, blue eyed, one of them stoop shouldered, and long chinned; one took with him a grey short coat, with yellow buttons, a brown jacket, a double breasted red streaked jacket, with white homespun trowsers, a pair of speckled stockings, with a Kalmarnock cap; the other took with him, two suits, the one black wilting, and the other brown cloth, made regimental fashion, with a beaver hat, marked on his cheek with gunpowder, and both brothers.—Whoever takes up said mulatto slaves, and secures them in any goal on this continent, so that their masters may have them again, shall be intitled to the above reward, and all reasonable charges, paid by Col. JAMES MCCLUGHERY, and JOSEPH HOUSTON, Hanover, Ulster county, Sept. 24, 1776.

405. *The New-York Gazette; and the Weekly Mercury* **(Newark), #1303, October 14, 1776.**

RUN-away from the Guard at Newark Goal, a Negro Man named SAM, about 5 Feet 6 inches high, formerly belonged to Mr. Lot, of Long Island—Had on a striped Jacket without Sleeves, and a Pair of Tow Trowsers. Whoever takes up said Negro and returns him to Newark Goal, or secures him so that he can be had by the Subscriber, shall receive Five Dollars Reward, paid by me JOSIAH BRYAN, Lt. Col.

406. *The New-York Gazette; and the Weekly Mercury* **(Newark), #1303, October 14, 1776.**

Three Pounds Reward. RUN-away the 8th inst. a negro man named Cato, about 23 or 25 years old, middling stature, well set, very black eyes, will often lap his tongue over his under lip and chin: Had on when he went away, a reddish brown cloth waistcoat, tow cloth trowsers, blue worsted stockings, and check shirt. The above reward, with all reasonable expences, will be paid to any person, for taking up and securing said negro in prison, and informing his mistress thereof; and the expences for bringing him to Mrs. Deborah Gomez, at the house of the subscriber, in Second street, near Walnut street, Philadelphia; or of Mr. Francis Basset, at the house of Doctor Burnet, in this town. MATTHIAS GOMEZ. It is supposed the above negro is gone towards the regulars. Newark, Octo. 9, 1776.

407. *The New-York Gazette; and the Weekly Mercury* **(Newark), #1303, October 14, 1776.**

RUN-AWAY from the subscriber, living at Jamaica on Long-Island, a young Negro fellow named YORK, tall and very black. He had on when he went off (which is about

Advertisements 191

three weeks ago) a blue [ ] waistcoat, a pair of coarse tow trowsers, and pinchbed buckles in his shoes. Whoever secures the said Negro so that his master may have him again, shall receive EIGHT DOLLARS reward, and all other reasonable charges, paid by CHARLES ARDING. N.B. He affects to laugh when he speaks. Jamaica, Long-Island, October 12, 1776.

408. *The New-York Gazette; and the Weekly Mercury* (Newark), #1303, October 14, 1776.

RUN-AWAY the third instant, a Negro lad named YORK, supposed to be lurking about the camps or [shipping], Any person giving intelligence where he may be found, shall have a reward of Five Dollars, and a further reward of Five Dollars more if brought to me, the proprietor, in Wall-Street. WILLIAM MAXWELL. N.B. YORK is about 19 years of age, 5 feet 7 or 8 inches high, rather thinly made, had on when he eloped, an old brown cloth jacket, with plain yellow metal buttons and red cloth collar, a brown cloth waistcoat, with small yellow metal buttons, a check shirt, brown linen trowsers, shoes with yellow buckles, and no stockings, and old round hat with tarnish'd gold edging, speaks good English, and may pretend to be free. New-York, October 12, 1776.

409. *The Pennsylvania Journal, and the Weekly Advertiser* (Philadelphia), #1767, October 16, 1776.

SIX DOLLARS Reward. RAN AWAY from the subscriber living in Bethlehem township, Hunterdon county, New-Jersey. A NEGRO MAN named Ben, about three and twenty years old, five feet six inches high, country born, lived lately in the lower parts of Maryland. He is lame in one of his feet. Had on an old hat, an old blue coat, a red jacket and buckskin breeches. Whoever secures said Negro so that the subscriber may have him again, or brings him home, shall receive the above reward with reasonable charges paid by THOMAS SCOTT.

N.B. Whoever takes up said Negro, is desired to acquaint the subscriber by advertising him in the Pennsylvania Journal.

410. *The New-York Gazette; and the Weekly Mercury* **(Newark), #1305, October 28, 1776.**

Brooklyn-Ferry, 16th October, 1776. FIVE DOLLARS REWARD. RUN AWAY on the second instant, from the Subscriber, living at Brooklyn-Ferry, on Long-Island, a Negro Boy named PEONCE, about 17 years of age, five feet, six or seven inches high, stoops in his walk, when pleased is apt to show his teeth very much, is very fond of strong liquor: Took with him a pale blue broad cloth coat and waistcoat, a leather jockey cap, a striped yellow and blue linsey woolsey waistcoat, two pair of tow trowsers, and a pair of old shoes. If any person will take up the said Negro, and secure him so that his Master can get him again, shall have the above Reward, and all reasonable charges paid; or if they can inform his Master where he is, so that he can get him again, shall have FOUR DOLLARS Reward. JOHN RAPALJE.

411. *The New-York Gazette; and the Weekly Mercury* **(Newark), #1305, October 28, 1776.**

RUN-AWAY some time ago, from Philip Skeene, Esq; of Skeensborough, a Spanish Negro man named Ned, near six feet high, of a yellow Complexion, about 40 years old.

He was taken a few days ago, on board the City of London, Capt. McFadzean, where he was in the capacity of a cook; since which time he has made his escape, supposed thro' bad advice, as he has lately been received and slept on

Advertisements 193

board said ship. Yesterday he was seen in town, waiting an opportunity to get on board some vessel. It is therefore requested that no person in this city, or master of vessel will conceal said Negro, as they will answer for the consequence.
  A reward of Forty Shillings will be given to any person that will take up said slave, and bring him to his master, at Mrs. Airy's, or to Capt. Vardill, near Burling's-Slip.
  New-York, October 26, 1776.

412. *The New-York Gazette; and the Weekly Mercury*, #1306, November 4, 1776.

FIVE DOLLARS Reward. RUN-away on Thursday night the 31st ult. from the subscriber, a negro man named TITE, about 40 years of age, about 5 feet 8 inches high, well shaped, a down-cast look, snuffs, smokes, and drinks immoderately when he can obtain liquor. Had on when he went off a flopped beaver hat, a brown or green double breasted jacket, check trowsers or black breeches. Whoever takes up and secures the said negro, shall have the above reward paid by the subscriber, at Mr. Ezekiel Ball's, near Springfield. JAMES STEWART.

413. *The New-York Gazette; and the Weekly Mercury*, #1307, November 11, 1776.

TEN DOLLARS Reward. RUN-AWAY, a Creole Negro fellow, named WILL, aged 19 years, about 5 feet 9 inches high, very well made, of a sallow complexion, and open countenance; was dressed when he went off in a white linen jacket with sleeves, blue cloth breeches, white stockings, and a hat half worn; he carried with him a white broad cloth coat, a mixed grey coloured cassimer jacket, linen shirt, and a pair of red striped trowsers. He speaks English very fluently, and will probably endeavour to pass for a free man, as it is suspected that he has made for the camp. Some time ago he was absent three days, and was detected with a knapsack, marked No. 49, containing the following articles, viz. 1 linen shirt, marked I.R. No. 14; 1 lapelled white linen vest; 2 linen handerchiefs with blue borders; 1 old white Barcelona handerchief; 1 pair of white worsted stockings; 2 hair combs; 1 blanket; 1 small black handled knife and fork, and an Officer's sash.

All which are now in the custody of his Owner, Finlay Nicholson, who is ready to deliver them to the proprietor, at Mr. Thomas Hepburn's store, in Mr. Bogart's house, Dock-Street; and as there is reason to suspect the fellow has again made for the camp, all Gentlemen of the Army are earnestly requested to stop him, and any person who will bring him to said Thomas Hepburn's store, shall have the above reward, and all charges paid.

414. *The New-York Gazette; and the Weekly Mercury*, #1309, November 13, 1776.

RUN-AWAY, from the subscriber, the 19th instant, living at Brower's wharf, near the New Crane, a negro boy, named Ned, about twelve years of age; this country born, and speaks very good English: Had on when he went away, a blue under jacket, a whiteish Wilton coat, a new pair blue duffle trowsers, a check shirt, a pair of new shoes and whiteish stockings. Whoever secures said negro boy, so that his master may have him again, shall receive four Dollars reward, and all reasonable charges paid by JOHN BRYSON.

415. *The New-York Gazette; and the Weekly Mercury*, #1310, December 2, 1776.

RUN-away, from Samuel Sackett, living near the Fly-market, a negro man named Joe, about 6 feet high, about 30 years old, of a yellow complexion, stout fellow; a negro wench, with a young child about 5 months, the wench about 24 years old, of a yellowish complexion, stout and well set; likewise a negro wench middling tall and slim, middling

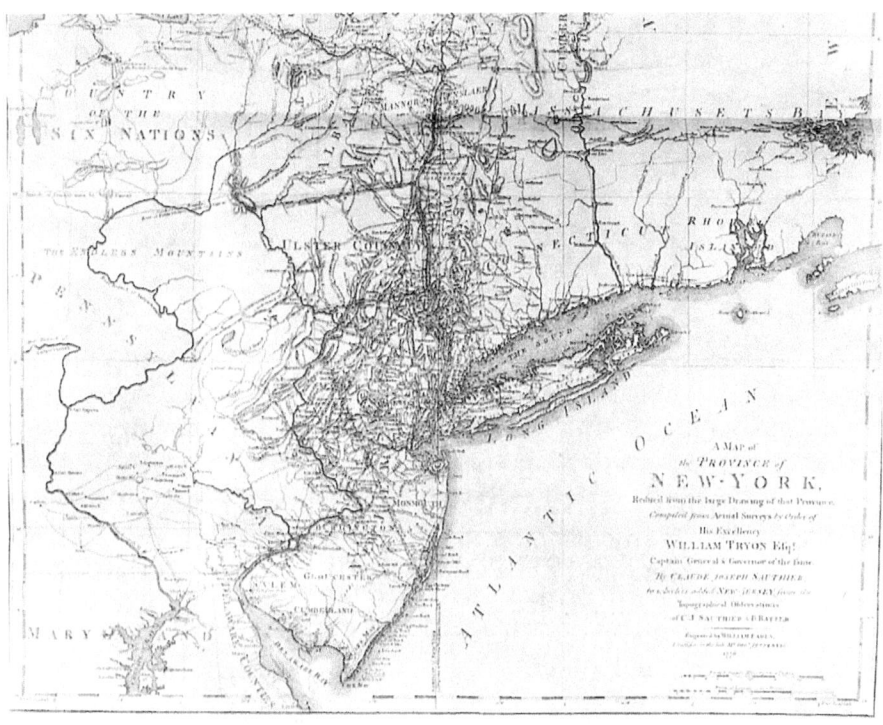

*A Map of the Province of New-York...*by Claude Joseph Sauthier. This revolutionary war map of New York, New Jersey, and the surrounding region illustrates the territory most runaways used to escape from their masters.

RUN AWAY

THE 18th Inftant at Night from the Subfcriber, in the City of New-York, four Negro Men, Viz. LESTER, about 40 Years of Age, had on a white Flannel Jacket and Drawers, Duck Trowfers and Home-fpun Shirt. CÆSAR, about 18 Years of Age, cloathed in the fame Manner. ISAAC, aged 17 Years cloathed in the fame Manner, except that his Breeches were Leather; and MINGO, 15 Years of Age, with the the fame Clothing as the 2 firft, all of them of a middling Size, Whoever delivers either of the faid Negroes to the Subfcriber, fhall receive TWENTY SHILLINGS Reward for each befide all reafonable Charges. If any perfon can give Intelligence of their being harbour'd, a reward of TEN POUNDS will be paid upon conviction of the Offender. All Mafters of Veffels and others are forewarn'd not to Tranfport them from the City, as I am refolved to profecute as far as the Law will allow. WILLIAM BULL.

N. B. If the Negroes return, they fhall be pardon'd. - 88

New-York Gazette; or, the Weekly Post-Boy, October 27, 1763. This advertisement, replete with an image signifying runaways, is a useful example of collective slave flight.

RUN away on Saturday the 23d of August last, from Nathaniel Richards, at Newark,—a negro Man named BEN, about 5 feet 8 or 9 Inches high, aged 28, slim made, thin Visage, yellow Complection, likely lively cunning Fellow, speaks good English, and can speak Low Dutch. He formerly belonged to Thomas Budue, at Morris-Town in New-Jersey, who two or three Months ago sold him to the Widow Mrs. Elizabeth Finn, at Prakenas in the County of Bergen, from whom he run-away soon after, and being advertised, was taken and brought Home to his Mistress, by whom he was soon after sold to the Subscriber.—When he went away he pretended he was going to Swim, and as he never return'd, and next Day his Clothes were found near toe Stone, he was supposed to be drown'd, till his Character was known which gives Reason to suppose he took that Method to deceive his Master and prevent a Search. It is not known whether he had any Clothes with him or not.——Whoever returns him to his Master, or secures him in any Goal, shall receive Eight Dollars Reward. and all reasonable Charges. NATHANIEL RICHARDS

New-York Gazette; or, the Weekly Post-Boy, September 4, 1766. This wonderful notice exemplifies the extreme means slaves took to elude recapture.

THIRTY DOLLARS REWARD.

RUN-AWAY from the Subscriber, the 16th of September last, a Negro Man named BOOD, about 38 Years old, 5 Feet 10 Inches high, yellow Complexion, thin Visage, has had the Small Pox; his great Toes have been froze, and have only little Pieces of Nails on them: He is much addicted to strong Liquor, and when drunk very noisy and troublesome. Whoever takes up said Slave, and brings him home, or secures him in Gaol, so that his Master may get him again, shall be intitled to the above Reward of THIRTY DOLLARS, paid by   WILSON HUNT.

Any Person who takes up said Negro, is cautioned to be particularly careful that he does not make his Escape, as he is a remarkable stout, cunning, artful Fellow.

Hunterdon-County,
Maidenhead, December 20, 1766.

New-York Gazette; or, the Weekly Post-Boy, December 25, 1766. Bood's third (possibly fourth) getaway may have been successful, as we hear no more of him. This notice also shows the harsh effects of exposure to nature on a runaway.

TWELVE DOLLARS Reward.

RAN away from the subscribers, the 2d day of July instant, a Negro man slave, who calls himself by the several names of *James, Gaul, Mingo, Mink,* and *Jem*; his real name is JEM; he is about 5 feet 6 inches high, thick set, and not very black; he has a scar in his face, and is about 35 years old; he took with him two oznabrigs shirts and trowsers, a broadcloth coat, a coating waistcoat, a felt hat, and a violin. He is supposed to have gone off with a certain PATRICK JOHNSON, who was born in Ireland, about 5 feet 10 inches high, and 30 years old; he is thin in flesh, having been lately sick; had on, and took with him, one new check and two new oznabrigs shirts and trowsers, a felt hat, narrow brim'd, and bound with black ferreting, an old fustian waistcoat without sleeves, fine short brown hair, and is much addicted to strong liquors.—They stole, and took with them, a large brown Horse, about 12 years old, near 15 hands high, very strong made, paces and trots, and is branded, either on the shoulder or thigh, with some letters not remembered. Whoever takes up the said Negro and Horse, and delivers them to the subscribers at Newark, in New-Jersey, shall be intitled to the above reward, and well paid for extra charges, or Eight Dollars for the Negro, and Four Dollars for the Horse.   ISAAC WILKINS,
      Newark, July 4, 1771.   SAMUEL OGDEN.

Pennsylvania Chronicle, July 1, 1771. Changing his name and running away with an Irish companion, Jem's runaway advertisement shows slave use of masquerade and the collective resistance of slave and indentured servant.

FIVE POUNDS Reward,
And all reasonable charges.

RUN away from the House of Major Prevost, in Bergen County, on the 29th of September last, a Negro Man and his Wife: The Fellow is serious, civil, slow of Speech, rather low in Stature, reads well, is a Negro Preacher, about 40 Years of Age, he is called MARK. The Wench is smart, active and handy, rather lusty, has bad Teeth, and a cast in one Eye; she is likely to look upon, was brought up in New-London, is called Jenny: as she had a Note to look for a Master, its likely she may make a travelling Pass of it.— Whoever takes up said Negroes, and brings them to the Subscribers, or secures them in any of his Majesty's Gaols, or gives such Information of them as they may be had again, shall be entitled to the above Reward, and all reasonable Charges paid, either by Major Prevost, Archibald Campbell, in Hackinsack; or Thomas Clarke, near New-York.

6s—

New-York Journal; or, The General Advertiser, January 12, 1775. This notice gives us a rare insight into the development of an African American itinerant clergy.

THREE POUNDS Reward.

RUN away from the fubfcriber, living in Shrewfbury, in the county of Monmouth, New-Jerfey, a NEGROE man, named TITUS, but may probably change his name; he is about 21 years of age, not very black, near 6 feet high; had on a grey homefpun coat, brown breeches, blue and white ftockings, and took with him a wallet, drawn up at one end with a ftring, in which was a quantity of clothes. Whoever takes up faid Negroe, and fecures him in any goal, or brings him to me, fhall be entitled to the above reward of *Three Pounds* proc. and all reafonable charges, paid by

Nov. 8, 1775. § JOHN CORLIS.

Pennsylvania Gazette, November 12, 1775. Titus fled south to join Lord Dunmore's Ethiopian Regiment, then returned to New Jersey the following year as Colonel Tye to begin his guerrilla war against the state's slave masters.

Eastman Johnson, *A Ride for Liberty – The Fugitive Slaves.* The women and children fleeing from slavery as portrayed in this Civil War-era painting were a prominent part of the slave exodus during the American Revolution.

black and pitted with the small-pox; it is thought they are all in the army. Whoever takes up said negroes, or any one of them, and delivers them safe to Samuel Sackett, or secures them in any Goal, so that he may get them again, shall have ten dollars a piece. SAMUEL SACKETT.

416. *The New-York Gazette; and the Weekly Mercury*, **#1311, December 9, 1776.**

RUN-AWAY from the subscriber, living in New-York, a negro lad about 20 Years of age, goes by the name of Fortune Brookman, about 5 feet 3 inches high, squat shape, his right knee bends inwards, wants some of his fore Teeth: Had on when he went away, a red plush waistcoat, and snuff coloured long trowsers. Whoever secures said runaway, shall have FOUR POUNDS reward paid by, THOMAS BROOKMAN, At Mr. Nicholl's near [ ] Market.

417. *The New-York Gazette; and the Weekly Mercury*, **#1315, January 6, 1777.**

A NEGRO WENCH, RUN-AWAY, supposed to Flatbush, on Long-Island, where she was lately purchased of Cornelius Van Der Veer, jun. is about 2[ ] years old, call'd BETTY, can speak Dutch and English, is of a stubborn disposition, especially when she drinks spirituous liquors, which she is sometimes too fond of; is a pretty stout wench, but not tall, smooth fac'd and pretty black; 'tis probable she may be conceal'd in this city. Whoever harbours her will be prosecuted, but such as give information to Wm. Tongue, her owner, in Hanover-Square, shall receive FIVE DOLLARS with thanks. She usually wore a striped homespun pettycoat and gown.

418. The New-York Gazette: and the Weekly Mercury, #1315, January 6, 1777.

Eight Dollars Reward. RUN-away on Monday the 22nd of December, a negro man named CÆSAR, about 30 years of age, very short, well-set, bandy leg'd, of a grave countenance, speaks civilly, and wants some of his fore teeth, wears commonly a dirty looking cloth coat with buttons of the same colour, a new round hat with high crown, and a set of silver shoe and knee buckles of open work; in wet weather commonly wears boots, and has a variety of cloaths. He passes himself for a free man and a glasier by trade. Whoever takes him up and secures him in any Goal so that his master gets him again, shall receive Eight Dollars reward, and reasonable charges, on application to the printer, or the subscriber, at the ordnance-office in New-York. All persons are forewarned not to harbour, employ, or carry of said negro. WILLIAM WOOD.

419. The New-York Gazette: and the Weekly Mercury, #1316, January 13, 1777.

RUN-away on Wednesday the first inst. from on board the ship Union, William Hamilton, master; lying at wharf, a black man named Prince, about twenty-one or twenty-two years of age, speaks good English, and formerly lived with a Mr. Lashel or Lasher, in the Broadway; is well known in this place, and had on when he went away a blue jacket and pair of fearnothing trowsers. Whoever will give intelligence of him to the printer, so that he may be secured; or brings him on board the said ship, shall receive two guineas reward and every other charge.

420. The New-York Gazette: and the Weekly Mercury, #1320, February 10, 1777.

FIFTEEN DOLLARS REWARD. RUN AWAY from the subscriber on Long-Island, a Negro Man, named JAFF, who now calls himself, Jeffery Johnson, is about five feet nine inches high, yellowish complexion and bushy hair, is a pretty forward chap, very free in his discourse, and had on when he went away, a claret coloured coat and breeches and a scarlet jacket, is supposed to be somewhere at Brunswick or Amboy. Any person who secures the said negro, so that the subscriber, his master, gets him again, shall be entitled to the above reward, and all reasonable costs and charges, paid by, REM COUWENHOVEN, in King's County.

421. *The New-York Gazette: and the Weekly Mercury*, #1322, February 24, 1777.

RUN-away from George Bevoïse, a negro man named FRANK, about 19 years of age, between 5 and 6 feet high, has lost two of his fore teeth, stutters in his speech and has thick lips: Had on and took with him a blue sailor's jacket, an old grey coat-tee, a pair of blue stockings, two pair of grey ditto, and three or four blankets. Whoever takes up said negro man and brings him to his master, living near Brooklyn-ferry, shall have THREE DOLLARS reward.

422. *The New-York Gazette: and the Weekly Mercury*, March 3, 1777.

TEN DOLLARS Reward. RUN away, the 16th instant, a Negro man named LOUI, about 20 years of age, 5 feet 8 inches high, strait made, a gruff look, and speaks like the West India Negroes, appears a civil innocent fellow when spoken to, wears a short blue coat lapelled, with yellow metal buttons, white waistcoat and breeches, or white flannel trowsers, good shoes and stockings, white shirt and a black silk stock, and commonly wears a white cap bound with red on his head; came lately from St. Vincents with the 6th regiment. Whoever delivers him to the printer, or gives information where he may be got again, shall receive the above reward and charges paid.

N. B. Any person harbouring or employing said Negro, will be prosecuted, and a reward of TEN GUINEAS paid to the person that makes a discovery of his being taken out of the country.

423. *The New-York Gazette: and the Weekly Mercury*, #1323, March 3, 1777.

WENT off on Sunday the 26th ult. from his master Archibald Hamilton; late Captain in his Majesty's 31st regt, a negro named CUFFY, a short thick-set fellow. If he applies to any officer to serve him, it is requested he will secure him; and if any other secures him they shall have two guineas reward.

424. *The New-York Gazette: and the Weekly Mercury*, #1325, March 17, 1777.

RUN-AWAY on Saturday, the 8th inst., a negro man about 50 years of age, goes by the name of Joseph Thompson: He is about 5 foot 11 inches high, has a remarkable black spot under his eye. Had on when he went away, a grey watchcoat, claret coloured breeches, and plain silver buckles; he often wears boots, can play upon the violin, and work at the carpenters trade.—Whoever will bring him to Jacob Bennet, jun. at Bushwyck, or confines him, shall have Ten Dollars reward, and all expenses paid.

425. *The New-York Gazette: and the Weekly Mercury*, #1330, April 21, 1777.

RUN-away from Powles-hook, a negro Man called Osborn, about five feet four inches high, twenty-seven years of age, has a remarkable small waist and bad legs, of a plausible address, pretends to a knowledge of cooking, has a down cast look when he is spoke to by strangers, seemingly the effect of bashfulness. Had on when he went off, a brown coat, white waistcoat, breeches and Stockings, and a new round hat. Whoever will secure him, or give information to the Printer, so that he may be secured, shall receive Five Dollars Reward. And 'tis requested that no person will employ him.

426. *The New-York Gazette: and the Weekly Mercury*, #1331, April 28, 1777.

ABSENTED from the service of Thomas Martin, the 16th inst. JOE, a negro man; he is a stout well made young fellow, about five feet nine inches high, can shave and dress hair pretty well: He had on when he went away, a green cloth coat and waistcoat, and a pair of leather breeches. Whoever apprehends and brings the said negro to his master, in Hanover-square, New-York, shall receive EIGHT DOLLARS, reward.

N.B. It is requested that no person will employ the said fellow, and all masters of vessels are desired not to suffer him on board their vessels, or to carry him from this country.

If he returns voluntarily, his fault will be forgiven.

427. *The New-York Gazette: and the Weekly Mercury*, #1334, May 19, 1777.

ABSENTED from his service, a negro man called SAM, a thick heavy set fellow, 5 feet 6 or 7 inches high, about 28 years old, and the property of the heirs of the late widow Hester Weyman. Whoever will bring him to the subscribers, executors to said Mrs. Weyman's estate, shall be entitled to a reward of Five Dollars. All masters of vessels and others, are requested not to take said fellow off, as the loss will fall on orphan children. PETER GORLET, GABRIEL H. LUDLOW.

428. *The New-York Gazette: and the Weekly Mercury*, #1335, May 26, 1777.

RUN-away on Thursday the 15th instant, from the subscriber, living at Corlear's-Hook, a negro lad named CHESS: He is about 20 years of age, speaks thick, is fond of dressing his hair high before, has remarkable large feet, and his eyes of a reddish cast; had on a blue coat and breeches, and is fond of dress. Whoever will deliver the said negro to the subscriber, or to Mrs. Yates, living in Wall-street, or lodge him where his master may have him again, shall receive HALF A JOE reward. All persons whatever are forbid harbouring him at their peril. STEPHEN SKINNER.

429. *The New-York Gazette: and the Weekly Mercury*, #1335, May 26, 1777.

RUN-away from Thomas Harriot, living at Jamaica South, on Long-Island, a negro man named Wilkes, about 5 feet 7 inches high, well-set, smooth face, speaks bad English, is apt to blunder, has remarkable large eyes, and is about 19 or 20 years old: Had on when he went away, a short gray coat with brass buttons, brown jacket, homespun trowsers, and a beaver hat cock'd. Whoever apprehends the above fellow so as his master may get him again, or delivers him to Capt. John Hitchin's, near John Wood's, Esq; shall have 4 dollars reward, and reasonable charges paid. All persons are requested not to harbour or employ him, and masters of vessels are desired not to ship or carry him off. He has been bred to the sea.

430. *The New-York Gazette: and the Weekly Mercury*, #1336, **June 2, 1777.**

Five Dollars Reward. RUN-away from the subscriber, the 30th of May, a negro boy named POMPY, about 17 years old, and well-made: Had on when he went away, a red jacket, ozenbrigs shirt and trowsers, shoes and stockings, with a kind of jockey cap, and is supposed to be gone in the Queen's Rangers, or some other department. Its hoped no gentleman in the army or navy, or master of vessel will inlist or carry him off: and whoever will bring him to the subscriber, shall have the above reward, and all reasonable charges paid by JOHN MOWATT, cabinet and chair maker, in William-street, New-York.

431. *The New-York Gazette: and the Weekly Mercury*, #1337, June 9, 1777.

RUN-away on Saturday the 24th of May, from the subscriber, living at Brooklyn Ferry, a negro man named PETER, about 25 years of age, 5 feet 9 or 10 inches high: Had on when he went away, a gray surtout coat, woollen shirt, and tow trowsers, and is supposed to be lurking about the city. Whoever will deliver the said negro to his master, shall have 4 dollars reward. JACOB HICKS.

432. *The New-York Gazette: and the Weekly Mercury*, #1337, June 9, 1777.

SIX POUNDS Reward. RUN-AWAY on the first day of June instant, three NEGROES, two men and one woman, the property of George Shaw, of the city of New-York, tanner. One is about 6 feet high, or upwards, and goes by the name of JAMES RICHARDS, or RICHARDSON, the other negro named HARRY ROBBINS, of a middling stature, yellow complexion, and mighty complaisant in discourse, but very deceitful and given to liquor. The other a negro woman, of a coal black complexion, named ANN, very nimble and brisk on her feet, but bold and impudent behavior, born in New-Castle county, on Delaware.

The two negro men have entered into his Majesty's service as waggon drivers, and their names are on the Commissary's books, but are my property. Whoever will take up the said negroes, and bring them to me the subscriber, shall have the above reward, or FORTY SHILLINGS for each, and all reasonable charges paid by GEORGE SHAW.

433. *The New-York Gazette: and the Weekly Mercury*, **#1338, June 14, 1777.**

THREE DOLLARS Reward. RUN-AWAY from the subscriber on the night of the 8th instant, a negro lad named FRANK, about 18 or 19 years of age; he stutters very much, has thick lips, and a great stock of impudence; has lost two of his upper fore teeth. Had on a brown coat with a cape, and old black breeches, but 'tis supposed he will alter his dress, as he has taken two check shirts and a pair of trowsers with him. It is imagined he has gone to the fleet at Staten-Island, as he stole a canoe, stretch, paddle, and oars. Whoever apprehends said negro, and returns him to his master, shall receive the above reward from GEORGE DEBEVOISE.

434. *The New-York Gazette: and the Weekly Mercury*, **#1340, June 30, 1777.**

FIVE POUNDS Reward. RUN-away from the subscriber, on Tuesday the 15th of April last, a negro man, of a yellow complexion, part Indian, well set, walks with his knees wide apart, flat nose, about five feet eight or ten inches high, forty five years of age, or thereabouts, goes by the name of Abraham: Had on when he went away, a brown homespun jacket, tow shirt, a pair of buckskin breeches, black and white yarn stockings, and a new pair of shoes.

The said negro took with him a small mulatto wench, by the name of Moll, which he claims as his wife, and two negro children; one a boy three years old, the other a girl five months old. The above negroes were seen on Long-Island, not long since. Whoever apprehends the said run-aways, and brings them to Thomas Bartow, in New-York, or to the subscriber, or secures them so that the owner may get them

again, shall receive the above reward, or Three Pounds for the negro, and Two Pounds for the wench and children, and all reasonable charges paid by THOMAS PELL.
Manor of Pelham, June 23, 1777.

435. *The New-York Gazette: and the Weekly Mercury*, #1342, July 14, 1777.

TEN DOLDARS Reward. LEFT Brigadier General De Lancey's service, from his farm at Bloomingdale. a negro fellow named HARMAN, of a yellowish colour, broad face and shoulders, hollow back, big buttocks, and remarkable strong well shaped legs, with a very large foot, is about 25 years of age, understands farming. Had on a Dutch Thrumb'd cap, a blue sailors jacket, speckled or white shirt, good trowsers and shoes, with a spare buckskin breeches. This is his second elopement, and by his dress may induce masters of ships to entertain him, who are requested to deliver him to New-York goal. Whoever takes him up shall have the above reward paid by General DeLancey, the printer, or Mr. Joseph Allicocke.

436. *The New-York Gazette: and the Weekly Mercury*, #1344, July 28, 1777.

RUN-AWAY from the subscriber the 17th ult. a negro man named Plymouth, to which he may add the name of John, having sometimes assumed that name. He is about twenty-six years of age, fond of dressing his hair high before, has large feet, and is fond of dress, of low stature, stoops, of very black complexion, and thick lips : had on when he went away a round hat with silver loop and tassel; a thick set coat, waistcoat and breeches, but may vary his dress, having carried other cloaths with him ; it is apprehended he is going towards the army in the Jersies, having lived with Capt. Drewry, of the 63d regt. last fall and part of last winter. If any of the gentlemen in the army should meet with him, it is requested they will stop him; any other person that will

deliver said negro to Mr. Thomas Lynch, merchant, in Duke-Street, New-York, to the subscriber on Staten-Island, or lodge him where his master may have him again, shall receive five dollars reward. All masters of vessels and others are forbid carry him off, or harbouring him, at their peril.
TERRENCE KERIN.

437. *The New-York Gazette: and the Weekly Mercury*, #1344, July 28, 1777.

Twenty Dollars Reward. RUN-away on the 26th of March, from Francis Conihane, living at Peck's-Slip, No. 999, a negro fellow named DICK, about 5 feet 6 inches, a baker by trade, and has followed that business with one Naugle, near Kingsbridge, and has waited a while on a gentleman in the Queen's Rangers ; speaks thick, has a mark over one of his eyes, and a scar on his breast ; was born in St. Kitts, walks sometimes as if he was lame, and is troubled a little with the rheumaticks. Took with him a dark gray coat and jacket, with white and check shirts, sundry strip'd trowsers, and a red and white striped jacket. It is supposed he keeps about Kingsbridge. Whoever brings him to his said master shall be entitled to the above reward.

N.B. All persons are forewarned not to harbour said fellow, at their peril.

438. *The New-York Gazette: and the Weekly Mercury*, #1345, August 4, 1777.

RUN-AWAY from the subscriber, a few days ago, living in this city, a mulatto fellow who lately had the small-pox, named JERREMY, about 25 years old, 5 feet 9 inches high, and pretty well made, but was crooked about the shoulders: Had on when he went away, a black [ ], breeches and stockings, a white cloth coat with [ ]d buttons, a beaver hat, and silver buckles in his [ ]. Whoever takes up and secures the said fellow, [ ] that his master may have him again, shall have five dollars reward, paid by RICHARD BAYLEY.

439. *The New-York Gazette: and the Weekly Mercury*, #1345, August 4, 1777.

RUN-AWAY on Saturday the 5th instant, from the subscriber living on Long-Island, a negro lad named DUKE, (but it is thought he has changed his name to Dick) he is about 20 years of age, about 5 feet 4 inches high, has thick lips and large eyes : Had on when he went away, a white swanskin double-breasted jacket, white drilling breeches, a tow cloth shirt, and blue and white stockings. He crossed Dennis's ferry to Staten-Island, and has most likely imposed himself upon some of the gentlemen of the army for a free man.—Whoever will deliver the said negro to the subscriber, or to the printer hereof, or lodge him where his master may have him again, shall receive Five Dollars reward.—All persons whatever are forbid harbouring him at their peril. NICHOLAS OGDEN.

440. *The New-York Gazette: and the Weekly Mercury*, #1347, August 18, 1777.

TEN DOLLARS Reward. RUN-AWAY from the subscriber, on Wednesday the 6th inst. a negro fellow named FORTUNE, but probably may change it to that of Dick, as he did when he absented at a former time : He is about 23 years of age, of a middling stature, slender made, his right knee bent inwards, a lengthy visage, yellowish complexion, a slender long nose, and has lost some of his fore-teeth.—Had on a pair of osnaburgh Trowsers, and spotted flannel jacket. Whoever will take up and secure the said negro, so that his master may have him again, shall receive the above reward. THOMAS BROOKMAN.

N. B. He was seen last Saturday [ ] night in this city, and it is supposed he is lurking in or about it at present, all persons are therefore forbid to harbour said negro, and all masters of vessels are forewarned not to carry him off.

441. *The New-York Gazette: and the Weekly Mercury*, #1347, August 18, 1777.

EIGHT DOLLARS Reward. RUN-AWAY on Thursday last the 14th instant, a negro man named WARE, this country born, of a dark complexion, well made, about 5 feet 7 inches high, 24 years of age, has a large scar in his forehead, and one on his lip : had on when he went off, a white jacket without sleeves, white breeches, and a pair of mixt coloured stockings. Whoever takes up and secures said fellow, or gives any information where he is, so that he may be had, shall receive the above reward from the subscriber, living at Newton, on Long-Island. ABRAHAM LENT.

442. *The New-York Gazette: and the Weekly Mercury*, #1350, September 8, 1777.

RUN-AWAY from the subscriber, on the 26th day of August last, a negro man named BRISTOL, about 5 feet 9 inches high, and upwards of 27 years old: had on when he went off, a reddish coloured jacket, a white waistcoat, and linen trowsers, supposed to be gone to New-York with the regular troops, or on board some vessel. Whoever takes up said negro fellow and secures him in any of his Majesty's goals, or elsewhere, so that his said master can have him again, shall have EIGHT DOLLARS reward, and reasonable charges paid, by me, PETER HOUSEMAN.
    All masters of vessels are forewarned to carry off or harbour said fellow.
    Staten Island, Sept 3d, 1777.

443. *The New-York Gazette: and the Weekly Mercury*, #1352, September 22, 1777.

RUN away on Thursday, the 14th instant, a Negro boy named TOM, the property of Doctor Donald M'Lane, at No. 6, six doors west of the Coffee-house; Said Negro is a remarkable well made boy, about 14 years of age; had on a striped jacket, and trowsers, and check shirt, no shoes nor stockings, his jacket tied with pieces of tape in place of buttons. Whoever secures the above deserted Negro, or gives intelligence of him to his said master, shall be entitled to a reasonable reward.

N. B. It is earnestly requested and presumed no gentlemen will harbour the said run away negro.

444. *The New-York Gazette: and the Weekly Mercury*, #1356, October 20, 1777.

FIFTY DOLLARS Reward. RUN-away from the subscriber, three negro fellows, viz. PRIMUS, a very likely fellow, about 22 years of age, speaks very civil and mild; went away the first of October, 1776. SYPHAX, about 34 years old; speaks broken English, very easy and slow; went away some time in November, 1776. SCIPIO, about 18 years old, went away on Wednesday night the 8th inst. he is a very handy fellow, stoops when he walks, and is apt to stammer when he talks quick.—Whoever takes up said negroes, and brings or sends them to their master, shall have the above reward for the three, or seperately for Primus 25 dollars, and for Syphax and Scipio, 12 each. P. STUYVESANT.

Peterfield, near New-York, Octo. 13, 1777.

445. *The New-York Gazette: and the Weekly Mercury*, #1356, October 20, 1777.

SEVEN DOLLARS Reward. RUN-away, the 14th inst. a Negro Wench named BET, born at Flatbush, Long-Island:

Had on when she went away, a homespun pettycoat, and callico short gown. Whoever shall secure the said wench, or give information of any person harbouring her, shall receive the above reward, by me, PHILIP LENZI, Confectioner, No. 517, Hanover-Square.

446. *The New-York Gazette: and the Weekly Mercury*, #1358, November 3, 1777.

Forty Dollars Reward. RUN away from the subscriber, the 5th of August last, a negro boy named PETER, about 13 or 14 years of age, of a yellowish complexion, lisps, and holds down his head when he speaks to any body. He has been seen a number of times with an officer of one of the new corps, and no doubt imposed himself on the Gentleman as a free negro. If he is still in the possession of that, or any other officer, it is expected he will be given up immediately. When he left my service, he had on, and took with him, a new suit of brown fustian, a suit of claret coloured fine cloth two thirds worn, a round hat, several pair of striped trowsers, &c. Whoever will secure the said negro boy, or bring him to me at No. 21, King street, shall be paid the above reward immediately. HENRY W. PERRY.

447. *The New-York Gazette: and the Weekly Mercury*, #1362, December 1, 1777.

RUN-AWAY from the subscriber, living at New Lots, King's county, on Long-Island, the 16th instant, a negro fellow named NAT; has lost his right eye, about 24 years old, pitted with the small-pox, 5 feet 8 inches high, Indian hair, and of a yellow complexion: Had on when he went away, a whitish surtout coat, a homespun coat, and light coloured jacket.—Whoever takes up and secures the said fellow, so that he may be had again, shall receive Five Dollars reward, and all reasonable charges, paid by HENRY WICKOFF.

448. *The New-Jersey Gazette* (Burlington), #5, December 31, 1777.

December 4, 1777. TWENTY DOLLARS REWARD. RAN AWAY yesterday the third instant from the subscriber, living in Mountholly, a negro man named QUASH, but may probably change it for YERRAH, by trade a cooper, about 26 years of age, 5 feet 8 or 9 inches high, speaks plain: had on, and took with him, a London brown broadcloth lapelled coat not much worn, with white metal buttons; an old whitish coloured ditto broken at the elbows and breast; a pair of leather breeches much worn; a pair of ditto striped linen; two pair of striped linsey trowsers; two tow shirts, one quite new; a beaver hat not much worn; two pair of shoes and two pair of stockings, one white cotton, the other yarn mixed red and white. It is thought he will endeavour to get to Philadelphia, or the American Camp, as he is fond of the soldiery. Whoever takes up and secures said servant, so that his master may get him again, shall have the above reward and reasonable charges, paid by JOHN JONES.

N.B. As he has a large bundle with him, and without a pass, it is thought he will be easily detected: It is therefore earnestly requested of the American gentlemen, officers and soldiers, as they are frequently travelling, to use their utmost endeavours to apprehend him.

449. *The Royal Gazette* (New York), #150, January 3, 1778.

RUN AWAY on the 25th instant, a Negro boy named ALICK, about fifteen years of age. Had on when he went away, a check shirt, reddish coloured jacket, Oznaburg trowsers, and a leather cap. He is branded on the breast with the letters R.W. Whoever shall secure the said boy, or give information of any person or persons harbouring him, shall receive Four Dollars reward from Richard Wright, at Mr. William Cross's, in George Street, No. 11. All master of vessels are forbid harbouring or carrying off said boy at their peril.

450. *The New-Jersey Gazette* (Trenton), #7, January 14, 1778.

Cumberland County, West New-Jersey, Jan. 21. TWENTY DOLLARS REWARD. RAN AWAY from the subscriber, on the 20th of August last, an indented MULATTO BOY named Levi, eighteen years of age; he has a down look, slim and straight built: Had on and took with him five shirts, two of them striped flannel; three pair of trowsers, one pair of them striped; three vests, one a light colour, the other a pale red; one pair of light coloured cloth breeches; a cloth coloured great coat. He passes for a free negro, says he has worked about Cohansey Bridge. Any person securing said servant, so that his master may get him again, shall have the above reward paid by ABIJAH HOLMES.

451. *The Royal Gazette* (New York), #153, January 24, 1778.

Run away on Monday the 19th. inst. a negro boy, 13 years old, pitted with the small pox, had on a red coat, turned up with green, green trowsers, and a blue jacket, a coarse hat with a gold band and a stone buckle. It is supposed he is in some of the houses behind the College, as his mother lives there. Whoever secures the said boy in a guard-house, or the Provost, shall receive Two Dollars reward, by applying to the printer. And all persons whatsoever are forbid harbouring him at their peril.

452. *The New-Jersey Gazette* (Trenton), #8, February 14, 1778.

THIRTY DOLLARS REWARD. RAN AWAY in June 1776, from the subscriber, living in Amwell township, a Negro man named LUN, but it is probable he may change his name: He is about 30 years of age, about five feet eight or nine inches high, a thick set fellow, has a remarkable scar on his upper lip of a cut, and is thought to have a pass with him. He is the Negro that formerly belonged to John Severns. Whoever takes up and secures him so that his master may get him again, shall have the above reward, and reasonable charges, paid by ISSAC JOHNSON.

All persons are forbid to counsel or harbour this Negro at their peril.

453. *The New-Jersey Gazette* (Trenton), #18, April 1, 1778.

TEN DOLLARS REWARD. RAN AWAY from the subscriber the 20th instant, a negro fellow named BEN, 22 years of age, remarkably stout and well made: Had on, when he went away, a homespun bearskin coat and jacket, leather breeches, and white stockings. He is supposed to be lurking about the neighbourhood of Trenton, Whoever takes up and secures said negro in any gaol so that his master may have him again, shall have the above reward, and all reasonable charges paid by ELISHA LAWRENCE.

454. *The New-Jersey Gazette* (Trenton), #23, April 23, 1778.

EIGHT DOLLARS REWARD. WAS taken away last winter by the Hessians, from near Bordentown, a Negro LAD about 14 or 15 years of age, middling thick set, of a yellow colour, his name DORUS, belonging to the subscriber, who has been informed he hath made his escape from the enemy at Philadelphia, and was seen at Bristol some short time since. Whoever will secure the above Negro lad, and deliver him to James Esdale at Burlington, to Thomas Watson at Bordertown, or to the subscriber at the New-Mills, shall have the above reward and reasonable charges. HENRY BUDD.

Burlington County, April 13, 1778.

455. *The New-Jersey Gazette* (Trenton), #23, April 23, 1778.

200 Dollars Reward. WAS stolen by her mother, a NEGRO GIRL about 9 or 10 years old, named Dianah—Her mother's name is Cash, and was married to an Indian named Lewis Wolis near 6 feet high, about 35 years of age—They have a male child with them between three and four years old. Any person that takes up the said Negroes and Indian and secures them, so that the subscriber may get them, shall have the above reward and all reasonable charges.
  Any person that understands distilling rye spirits, may find encouragement by applying to the subscriber at his own house. KENNETH HANKINSON.
Penelapon, East New-Jersey, April 15, 1778.

456. *The Royal Gazette* (New York), #167, May 2, 1778.

TEN DOLLARS REWARD. RUN away from his Master, JOHN BARTOW, Jun. of the Borough Town of Westchester, a Negro Man named FRANK, about 5 feet high, is a good tempered handy ingenious fellow, has a pleasant look, and a low soft speech, has got a scar on his left leg, which has been lately cut; Had on when he went off, a brown watch coat and vest, yarn stockings and new shoes. Whoever takes up said fellow, and brings him to his said master, if upwards of ten miles from home, shall receive the above reward, and all reasonable charges, and in the some proportion for a less distance paid them by the said JOHN BARTOW, jun.

457. *The New-Jersey Gazette* (Trenton), #23, May 6, 1778.

Ten Dollars Reward. RAN-AWAY from the subscriber, living in Great Egg-harbour, Gloucester county, on the 23th of April last, a NEGRO MAN, named Sambo, a well built

fellow, about twenty-seven years of age; had on and took with him, a homespun great coat of a whiteish colour, a drab coloured jacket with sleeves, and one without sleeves, dowlas trowsers, black yarn stockings, old shoes, round hat, and three shirts, two of them new. 'Tis supposed he will endeavour to get to Philadelphia. Whoever takes up the said Negro, and secures him in any gaol, so that his master may get him again, shall have the above reward, and reasonable charges, paid by me JOSEPH M'CULLOH.
Great Egg-harbour, May 4, 1778.

458. *The New-Jersey Gazette* (Trenton), #24, May 13, 1778.

FOUR DOLLARS REWARD. RAN-AWAY on the 25th of April, a MULATTO WENCH named PATT; had on two striped lincey petticoats, a striped linen short gown, a black bonnet, handsome check handerchief and a short brown bearskin cloak, half worn shoes and white yarn stockings with blue clocks. Whoever secures said wench in any gaol, so that her master may have her again, shall have the above reward and reasonable charges. GEORGE EVANS.
May 10, 1778.

459. *The Royal Gazette* (New York), #170, May 16, 1778.

RUN away from the Subscriber, on Friday the first of May, a young black girl, about 18 years of age named DIONA; had on when she went away, a blue and striped waistcoat, blue petticoat, black hat, short red cloak with ermine on the fore part; she may attempt getting on board some vessel. whoever apprehends said girl, and will bring her to me, at No. 169, in Queen-street, shall be handsomely rewarded. All masters of vessels and others, are hereby forewarned harbouring or carrying her off. JOSEPH POTTER.

460. *The Royal Gazette* (New York), #170, May 16, 1778.

RUN AWAY from the subscriber, a NEGRO LAD named JEM, about 14 Years old, five Feet six inches high, had on an hat and a brown vest and trowsers: Whoever will secure the said Negro, that he may be recovered by the proprietor, shall receive FIVE DOLLARS, from JOHN PORTOUR, And Co. It is requested that all Master of vessels will carefully avoid carrying him from this port.

461. *The Royal Gazette* (New York), #172, May 20, 1778.

FIVE DOLLARS REWARD. WILL be paid by the Printer of this paper to any person who will give information of a Mulatto Man, named James Hulse, who has lately absconded from his proprietor; he is about five feet nine inches high, straight made, about 30 years of age; was a few weeks since discharged from his Majesty's service in the forage department, at Turtle Bay; and, as he plays on the violin it is probable that he may be skulking in some part of this city.

462. *The Royal Gazette* (New York), #176, June 6, 1778.

Three dollars reward, run away on Thursday June the 4th, a negro wench named Phillis, she is about 5 feet seven inches high, remarkably stout, about 25 years of age, had on when she went away a black and white striped wooly jacket and petticoat, and a white bonnet. Whoever apprehends said wench and delivers her to Hugh Miller opposite the fly market shall receive the above reward.

Advertisements 215

463. The New-Jersey Gazette (Trenton), #29, June 17, 1778.

RAN AWAY from the subscriber, living in Kingwood, Hunterdon county, on Tuesday the 9th of this instant, a NEGRO MAN, named JEM, of middle stature, and marked with the small-pox; had on when he went away an old flannel waistcoat, striped flannel shirt, a pair of cloth trowsers or over-alls, and old shoes, but may have changed his dress, as he also took with him a new livery homespun cloth coat of a drab colour, sleeves and collar turned up with scarlet cloth, a nankeen vest coat, old leather breeches, two white shirts, one a new homespun the other old Holland, and a beaver hat smartly cocked. Whoever secures said Negro fellow, so that his master may have him again, shall receive Forty Dollars reward and reasonable charges, paid by CHARLES COXE.
June 14, 1778.

464. The Royal Gazette (New York), #188, July 18, 1778.

Deserted from his Majesty's ship *Phoenix's Tender* the third instant, a negro man named George Watkins, aged about 21 years, had on when he went away, a blue jacket, check shirt, and long trousers with a round hat, about 5 feet three inches high, smooth faced, with a small cast in one of his eyes; he may attempt getting on board some of the shipping; whoever apprehends the said man and will lodge him on board one of his majesty's ships and aquaint the printer shall receive five dollars reward. All masters of ships and others are hereby strictly forewarned at their peril from harbouring or carrying him off. Wm. Furnivall.

465. *The Royal Gazette* (New York), #189, July 22, 1778.

King's county, Flat Bush, July 20, 1778. Run away on the 12th instant, from the subscriber living at New Lotts, on Long Island, a negro man named Hector, about 40 years of age, 5 feet 5 inches high, had on when he went away a blue jacket without sleeves, a white shirt and tow trousers; can speak English and Dutch. Whoever takes up and secures said negro so that his master might have him shall receive five dollars reward and all necessary charges paid by Jacobus Cornell.

466. *The Royal Gazette* (New York), #192, August 1, 1778.

Two dollars reward, run away a Virginia born mulatto girl named Hannah, 14 years old, slim made, has lately had the smallpox, accustomed to house work; had on when she went away, an ozenbrig petticoat and shift, brown and blue short gown, and an old green bonnet. The above reward will be given to any person that will bring her to her master in Duke Street, No. 6. John Myers. N.B. All masters of vessels and others are forwarned from harbouring or carrying her off.

467. *The Royal Gazette* (New York), #195, August 12, 1778.

One Guinea reward, Sarah, a mulatto wench, the property of Mrs. Reid, has absconded from her mistress, on being accused of theft, and is known to be secreted in the city. Whoever will aprehend her shall have the above reward, on applying to Mrs. Reid in King Street.

468. *The Royal Gazette* (New York), #196, August 15, 1778.

Run or strayed away the 11th instant from the King's Wharf, near the North River, a mulatto boy named Sam, about 11 years old, strait hair, had on only a shirt and a pair of trousers. Whoever will deliver said boy to the subscriber living near Beckman Slip shall have two guineas reward payed by Jesse Smith.

469. *The Royal Gazette* (New York), #197, August 22, 1778.

Two Guineas reward. Run away from the subscriber the 20th instant a Mulatto servant boy named Priam, 23 years old, about five feet five or six inches high, his hair of a remarkable light coloured woolly sort. Whoever secures the said boy and will inform or deliver him to the subscriber at Flatbush, Long Island to Mr. John Taylor in Queen Street, no.15, shall be entitled to the above reward. All masters of vessels are forwarned to carry him off or conceal him, as they will answer the consequences. A. Bainbridge, Surgeon, N.J.V.

470. *The New-Jersey Gazette* (Trenton), #42, September 23, 1778.

One Hundred Dollars Reward. WAS stolen out of the subscriber's stable, in Lower Makefield township, Bucks county, near Yarley's ferry, State of Pennsylvania, on the night of the 29th of April last, a red or strawberry roan HORSE, about 14 hands and a half high, 5 years old, paces and trots well, black mane and tail, his legs also black, well made, and had neither mark or brand when stolen. He was taken to Philadelphia while the enemy has possession of it. Also,

RAN-AWAY on the 15th of June, a NEGRO BOY named Tom, 16 years old, slim made, of a yellow

complexion, and something knock-knee'd, supposed to have gone to Philadelphia, to the enemy. Whoever takes up said horse or Negro, and secures them so that the owner may get them again, or brings them home, shall have the above reward, or Fifty Dollars for either, and reasonable charges, paid by PETER ROBERTS.
Sept. 21, 1778.

471. *The New-Jersey Gazette* (Trenton), #42, September 23, 1778.

Thirty Dollars Reward. Salem, New-Jersey, September 12, 1778. RAN-AWAY on the 26th of February last, with the British light infantry, a NEGRO MAN named Harry, but it is probable he may change his name; he is about 28 years of age, five feet 8 or 9 inches high, a stout well made fellow, born at Salem, at one of Jost Miller's; has a large nose. He went as waiting-man to Capt. Hambleton, of the 52d light-infantry. It is thought he will leave the soldiers and go into the country, and may perhaps endeavor to pass for a free man: Had on when he went away, a fustian coat with a red collar, light broadcloth breeches, two coarse shirts, one fine ditto, a good hat cut maccaroni fashion, good stockings and shoes. Whoever takes up the said Negro, and secures him in any gaol, so that his master may have him again, shall have the above reward, and reasonable charges, paid by ROBERT JOHNSON.
N. B. All persons are forbid to harbour said Negro at their peril.

472. *The New-Jersey Gazette* (Trenton), #47, October 28, 1778.

Fifty Dollars Reward. RAN-AWAY on the evening of the 7th inst. from Trenton ferry, a likely MULATTO slave, named Sarah, but since calls herself Rachael; She took her son with her, a Mulatto boy named Bob, about six years old, has a remarkable fair complexion, with flaxen hair: She is a

lusty wench, about 34 years of age, big with child; had on a striped linsey petticoat, linen jacket, flat shoes, a large white cloth cloak, and a blanket, but may change her dress, as she has other cloaths with her. She was lately apprehended in the first Maryland regiment, where she pretends to have a husband, with whom she has been the principal part of this campaign, and passed herself as a free woman. Whoever apprehends said woman and boy, and will secure them in any gaol, so that their master may get them again, shall receive the above reward, by applying to Mr. Blair M'Clenachan, of Philadelphia, Capt. Benjamin Brooks, of the third Maryland regiment, at camp, or to Mr. James Sterret, in Baltimore.
    Oct. 18, 1778.   MORDECAI GIST.

473. *The New-Jersey Gazette* **(Trenton), #56, December 31, 1778.**

30 DOLLARS Reward. RANAWAY from Benjamin Vancleave's Esq. in Maidenhead, the 26th instant, (Dec.) a Negro WENCH named Dinah, 28 or 30 years of age, five feet six or seven inches high, black and very lusty. She was lately bought of Parson Van Arsdall at Springfield, and lived with Colonel Scudder, in Freehold, and it's likely is gone there. Any person apprehending said wench and applying to Mr. Phillips, innkeeper, in Maidenhead, shall be entitled to the above reward and reasonable charges, paid by WILLIAM CRAB.

474. *The New-Jersey Gazette* **(Trenton), #63, February 17, 1779.**

One Hundred Dollars Reward. RAN-AWAY last Monday night, from the house of Jesse Williams, in Philadelphia, two negro men belonging to the subscriber, in Middlesex county, New-Jersey: one named Chess, about 5 feet 8 inches high, 22 years of age, very black and well-set, and had on a sailor's blue jacket and breeches. The other named

Mark, about 5 feet 5 inches high, 24 years old, yellow and chunky;—he has hair like an Indian, except that it curls: Had on a brown old coat, striped wastecoat, old leather breeches, with striped drawers under them, and blue stockings. He usually wore a frock over his other clothes. They were lately purchased in Upper-Freehold, in Monmouth county, and it is feared they will attempt to go off to the enemy. Whoever takes up and secures said Negroes, so that their master may have them again, shall have the above reward, or Fifty Dollars for either, and reasonable charges, paid by
Feb. 12, 1779   RICHARD BRITTON.

475. *The New-Jersey Gazette* (Trenton), #68, March 24, 1779.

Twenty Dollars Reward. RAN-AWAY from the subscriber, on Monday the 8th inst. a negro man named TOM; a well set fellow, about 5 feet 8 or 9 inches high. Had on when he went away, a short bearskin coat, white vest, buckskin breeches, a round hat; he likewise took with him a brown coat lined with brown shalloon, one striped Damascus vest, and sundry other clothes.
    Whoever takes up said negro man, and brings him to his master, in Trenton, or secures him in any gaol so that his master may have him again, shall be entitled to the above reward. SAMUEL HENRY.
    N. B. He is supposed to have gone the York road, and endeavouring to get to the enemy.

476. *The New-Jersey Gazette* (Trenton), #75, May 12, 1779.

RUN-AWAY the 4th day of April last from the subscriber, living in Hunterdon county, State of New-Jersey, a mulatto negro man named Jupiter, a likely, tall, slim fellow, about 20 years old: Had on when he went away a French wool hat, about half worn, black and white mixed homespun coattee, brown waistcoat, buckskin breeches, flannel shirt, mixed

black and white homespun stockings, good shoes, and strokes his hair back. Whoever takes up the said Negro and secures him in Trenton gaol, or delivers him to his master in the township of Amwell, shall receive Forty Dollars reward if taken in the county, if out of the county Sixty Dollars.
     April 26, 1779.   DAVID JONES, Captain.

477. *The New-Jersey Gazette* (Trenton), #76, May 19, 1779.

Bergen county, State of New-Jersey, May 19, 1779. TAKEN up on his way from the enemy's lines and committed to the gaol of said county, a NEGRO MAN, who says that his master's name is John Howlet, that he resides in Gloucester county, near Popplespring church, Virginia; that he deserted his master's service and joined Lord Dunmore upwards of three years ago. Notice is hereby given, that unless the master of the said negro, or some person in his behalf, come within eight weeks from the date hereof, prove his property, pay the charges and take him away, he will be sold to pay the costs. ADAM BOYD, Sheriff.

478. *The New-Jersey Gazette* (Trenton), #79, June 9, 1779.

One Hundred Dollars Reward. Ran away from the subscriber, living in Trenton, last Saturday night, a NEGRO MAN named CUFF, about 5 feet 9 inches high, 27 or 28 years of age; he has a small blemish in one eye, and marked on his cheek with a circle or round O; is by trade a blacksmith. Had on when he went away, a yellowish brown fustian coat, scarlet vest, tow shirt and trousers, a half worn castor hat; he also carried with him two shirts, one pair of fustian breeches, thread stockings and sundry other cloathing. It is supposed he is gone towards New-York in company with another Negro man who went off the same evening. Any person bringing him to the subscriber, or

securing him in any gaol so that his master may get him again, shall receive the above reward and reasonable charges. HEZEKIAH HOWELL.
Trenton, June 8, 1779.

479. *The New-Jersey Gazette* (Trenton), #81, June 23, 1779.

SIXTY DOLLARS Reward. MADE his escape a few days ago from the Provost Guard near Raritan bridge, a Negro Man named CUFF, well set, speaks very slow but good English, about 40 years old, very black; he was confined for killing his master, Joseph Moss, of Stoney hill. Whoever secures the said Negro, so that he may be brought to justice, shall have the above reward, and all reasonable charges paid by PETER DUMONT,
June 18.   Sheriff of Somerset county.

480. *The New-Jersey Gazette* (Trenton), #81, June 23, 1779.

Kent-Island, (State of Maryland) May 15, 1779. One Hundred Dollars Reward. RAN-AWAY from the schooner Kitty, Captain John Bryan, on Saturday the 15th of April last, a Negro Man named WATT, about 5 feet 9 or 10 inches high; he is a likely straight well made fellow, remarkably black, and has a bold daring countenance: He formerly belonged to the estate of the deceased Mr. George Maxwell, and was then under the management of Mr. Samuel Nicholls, of whom I bought him; he is an artful, cunning, plausible villain, and will make use of every specious and fair tale to induce belief of his being a freeman; he is rather thin visaged, and perhaps one of the blackest Negroes in the world. I can't well describe the apparel he run off in, he had a blue jacket and breeches of coarse French cloth, shoes, stockings and a hat, all of which he took with him: He run off from the schooner while she lay at Wells's ware-house, and a few days after his going off, he was seen in the neighbourhood of Mr. Isaac Spencer, in Kent county. The rascal made an untimely effort to get on board the British fleet when they were up Chesapeak Bay; I am induced to believe that he has the like object in view, and that the villain has either made for the Delaware Bay or the Jersies, or that he designs it. I will give Fifty Dollars for securing him, if taken in this State; if taken out of it, the above reward, and reasonable charges if brought home. JAMES HUTCHINGS.

N. B. If taken in Jersey or Pennsylvania, please to apply to William Pollard, of Philadelphia.

481. *The New-Jersey Gazette* (Trenton), #83, July 28, 1779.

RAN AWAY from the subscriber, in Sussex county, a likely, short, stout Mulatto lad, aged about 20 years, American born, used to horses and waiting in the house, plays well on the fiddle and French horn; had on a white drilling coat with metal buttons, white under cloaths, and beaver hat. Lived in New-York when young, since in Carolina, and lately with Mr. Rutherford in New-Jersey; can read and write; he is a pert, saucy fellow. Whoever takes up the servant above described, and secures him so that his master can have him again, shall have Fifty Pounds reward, and all reasonable charges paid by me WILLIAM M'CULLOUGH.

July 3, 1779.

482. *The New-Jersey Gazette* (Trenton), #89, September 8, 1779.

Two Hundred Dollars Reward. RUN AWAY last Monday night, the 30th of Aug. 1779, from the subscriber living in the township of Reading, Hunterdon county, and state of West New-Jersey, a Negro Man named TONE, about 30 years old, well built, about 5 feet 10 inches high, talks good English and Low Dutch. Also another named CHARLES,

about 17 years of age, about 6 feet high, of a yellow complexion, squints very much with his eyes; he can talk good English and Low Dutch. As they took with them a number of cloaths, their dress cannot be described: It is supposed their intention is for Staten-Island. Any person that will take up said two negroes, and secure them in safe gaol, so that their master may have them again, shall receive for each Eighty Dollars, and expences paid; or if delivered to the owner at his house, the above reward, and reasonable charges paid by CORNELIUS VANHORN.
Aug. 31.

483. *The New-Jersey Gazette* (Trenton), #99, November 17, 1779.

One Hundred Pounds Reward. RUN away from the subscriber on the 2d inst. a Negro Fellow named Will, 23 years of age, a stout-built, likely man; had on when he absconded, an old beaver hat, a short brown coat half worn, made of country cloth, buckskin breeches, yarn stockings, remarkable strong shoes, and may have other cloaths with him; he formerly belonged to Mr. Wilson Hunt of Maidenhead, and was well known in that neighbourhood by the name of Minck. Whoever will secure the said negro, or give intelligence where he may be found, shall have the above reward, and all reasonable charges by applying to his master, JOHN SHAW.
Bernard's Town, Baskenridge, Nov. 4.

484. *The New-Jersey Gazette* (Trenton), #106, January 5, 1780.

Lancaster, December 14, 1779. Two Hundred Pounds Reward. RUN away from the subscriber on the evening of the 20th June last, a negro man named DAN, about 24 or 25 years of age, 5 feet 5 or 6 inches high, something pitted with the small-pox; his dress when he went off is uncertain, as he took sundry clothes with him, amongst which are, two coats, a light saggathy, and a brown with yellow buttons, three jackets, light blue, brown, and striped linen, a pair of new buckskin breeches, several pair of old striped and two pair of tow trowsers, three pair of stockings, three good shirts, and a round hat. Said negro is this country born, and talks the English and German languages, is fond of playing the fiddle, is naturally left-handed, and what is very remarkable, he bows with his left-hand when performing on the violin; he can work a little at the saddler's trade, is a shrewd cunning fellow, and will if possible procure a pass, probably change his name, and endeavour to pass as a freeman. Whoever takes up and secures said slave in any gaol, so that his master may have him again, shall receive the above reward. *CHRISTIAN WIRTZ.*

485. *The New-Jersey Journal* (Chatham), #51, February 2, 1780.

ONE HUNDRED DOLLARS Reward. RUN-AWAY from Martin Wyckoff, in Reading township, Somerset county, New Jersey, a negro boy named WILL, about five feet high, between 15 and 16 years of age. Said negro boy left his master's house under pretence of going to Jacob Wyckoff's, in Mendham, Morris County. He had on when he went away, a linsey woolsey waistcoat, a white under flannel ditto, flannel shirt, buckskin breeches, good shoes, black stockings, and a round hat with yellow binding round the crown. He likewise took with him, a red waistcoat, and a large brown linsey woolsey coat. Whoever takes up said negro, and returns him to either of the subscribers, shall have the above reward, and all reasonable charges, paid by MARTIN WYCKOFF, or JACOB WYCKOFF.

486. *The Royal Gazette* (New York), #332, February 12, 1780.

Six Dollars Reward. RUN away from the Subscriber, this morning, a Negroe Wench named Belinda, about 21 years of age, slender made and short; had on when she went away, a brown jacket, red petticoat, white hankerchief, and a high cap; has a mole on the right side of her nose; she took with her a [ ] trunk without a lock, a red and white linen gown, black hat and cloak, and a white dimity petticoat. Whoever secures the said Wench and brings her home, shall have the above reward.

HENRY GUEST,
February 10, 1780.   No. 931, Water-street.

N.B. All persons whatever are forbid to harbour her at their peril.

487. *The New Jersey Gazette* (Trenton), #112, February 16, 1780.

Two Hundred Dollars Reward Ran Away on Saturday night the 12th inst, a Negro man named Toney, a light built fellow, about 5 feet 7 inches high, his hair grows down on his forehead and is bare on the temples, speaks low Dutch and English, about 30 years old: Had on a blue broadcloth coat, green plush vest and a brown ditto over it, blue great coat with mettle buttons, a fur cap made with the Crown of a hat instead of leather, leather breeches and light blue yarn stockings. He formerly belonged to Cornelius Van Horn of Reddington —It's supposed that he is endeavouring to go over to the enemy. Any person taking up and securing the said Negro or returns him to me shall have the above reward and all reasonable charges, paid by me, Peter Dumont. N.B. He was taken up near Piscataway town and hand cuff'd but made his escape from Tunison's Tavern on Tuesday night last. Hillsborough, Somerset County, February 14, 1780.

488. *The New Jersey Journal* (Chatham), #59, March 29, 1780.

One Hundred Dollars Reward. Run-away from Jonathan Wynans at Lyon's Farms, a negro boy named Frank: He is about 17 years of age. Had on when he went away an old wool-hat, grey linsey woolsey waistcoat, much worn, a woollen shirt, a pair of calfskin breeches and a pair of grey stockings. Whoever takes up said Negro and secures him so that he may be restored to his master, shall have the above reward and reasonable charges from Jonathan Wynans. March 14, 1780.

489. *The Royal Gazette* (New York), #363, March 29, 1780.

DESERTED on the 25th inst. from the General Hospital where he has been sick with the small pox, a Negroe, named Robert Kupperth, about 19 years of age, five feet three inches high. He was a Drummer of the Hessian Regiment Landgrave, and had on when he went away his old Regimentals. He is of a pretty dark complexion, and very much pitted with the small-pox. As it is supposed that he is gone on board of a vessel, or is secreted in the city, every one is warned at his own peril, to harbour the said Negro Drummer, and whoever will secure, give intelligence, or deliver him to the said regiment Landgrave, now garrisoned in this city, will be handsomly rewarded.

de KEUDELL,
Colonel of the Regiment Landgrave.
New-York, March 29, 1780.

490. *The Royal Gazette* (New York), #370, April 15, 1780.

RUN AWAY from his master on the 11th instant, a Negro Boy called TOM, he is a stout well made Boy about 15 or 16 years of age, speaks tolerable good English; had on a brown thicksett jacket and osnaburg trowsers, an old round hat, shoes and stockings. Whoever will give information of the said run-away Negro will be thankfully rewarded, by
DONALD M'LEAN,
No. 6, near the Coffee House.

N.B. Mr. M'Lean flatters himself that none of his friends in the navy or army will countenance the above Negro, and all masters of vessels are strictly forbid to harbour him upon any pretence.

491. *The Royal Gazette* (New York), #375, May 3, 1780.

RUN AWAY yesterday morning, a *MULATTO GIRL*, 14 or 15 years old, slim made, long hands and feet; had on a flowered red and green flannel petticoat and blue cloth jacket. Any person that brings her to No. 870, Dock-street, shall be handsomely rewarded.   May 2, 1780.

492. *The New Jersey Journal* (Chatham), #66, May 7, 1780.

Ranaway from the subscriber the evening of the 2nd instant a Negro boy named Robbin, but sometimes calls himself Levi alias Leave, about fifteen years old, somewhat tall of his age, is an artful fellow, very modest in speech, has a sober look and can frame a smooth story from rough materials, naturally very lazy but capable of activity; went off in haste, having on an old felt hat, white woolen waistcoat with stocking sleeves, brown under ditto, pair of white woolen overalls, tow shirt, pale blue stockings, old shoes without buckles; supposed to have enlisted in the service or else secreted by some evil minded persons whose hearts are as black as the fugitives face. If the former should be the case, the proprietor is under no apprehensions but he will immediately be given up. A handsome reward will be paid to the person who secures him for his master besides generous payment for trouble. Noah Marsh. N.B. All persons are forewarned harbouring the said Negro at their peril. Westfield, May 9, 1780.

493. *The Royal Gazette* (New York), #378, May 13, 1780.

RUN AWAY from the Subscriber the 5th instant, a Negro Boy named JACK, aged about 17 years, pitted with the small pox, stoops in his walk, talks much like a Guinea Negro, very black, about five feet four inches high.
    Whoever secures the said Boy, so that his Master may have him again, shall receive Five Dollars Reward from me
                      JONATHAN FOWLER.
    Living in Chatham Street, at Dr. Betts's. All Commanders of Vessels are warned against carrying him off, as they will in that case be prosecuted on discovery.

494. *The Royal Gazette* (New York), #380, May 20, 1780.

ONE GUINEA REWARD, RUN away from the Subscriber on Saturday last, a Negro Boy named YORK, about 3 feet 10 inches high, tawney complexion, a scar under, or nearly under his left temple like unto a burn, well made, small bones, speaks pretty good English, is a native of the Island of Jamaica, and came here about 2 years since, has lately been employed in sweeping chimneys, is a smart talkative boy, has been out in the privateer Pollux, Capt. Rois. Had on when he went away, a short brown waistcoat, a check shirt, a kind of woollen trowsers nearly white, a blue cap, his hair wool cut short, and full of soot, is about 12 years of age, and is addicted to drinking.——Whoever brings the said boy to the Printer, or to the Subscriber, living in Duke-Strect, shall receive the above reward. All masters of ships are requested not to carry off the said boy: all other persons are forbid harbouring him at their peril.
                      PETER CREGUELL.

495. *The Pennsylvania Gazette* (Philadelphia), #2609, June 14, 1780.

Princeton, May 23, 1780. Five Hundred Dollar reward A Mullatto slave who it is supposed has been seduced to undertake to carry letters or intelligence into New York ran away from the subscriber and took off with him a dark bay horse, 6 years old 14 and a half hands high, with two white feet and a blaze and is a natural trotter. The slave is near 6 feet high, strong and well made; had on and took with him, a variety of clothes, but those he most probably will wear are a a suit of superfine mixt broad cloth, a new red great cloth, white stockings, half boots , a black velvet stock and beaver hat, but little worn. He appears to be 40 odd years of age, speaks good English, reads and writes a tolerable hand and is a decent and well-behaved ingenious fellow, capable of a variety of works. His name is Michael Hoy but he may go by some other, and it is probably he may travel as a servant to a white man who is supposed to have gone off with him and as such may change his address. He went off in the night of the 20th Inst. Five hundred dollars will be given and all charges paid for securing the slave and the horse or two hundred and fifty dollars for either paid by George Morgan. P.S. A deep blood bay mare with a black mane and tail was stolen that same night the above mentioned slave went off supposedly by him or his accomplice. She has a short dock and a lump that looks like a wind-gall or small wen, on the hindermost part of one of her thighs. She is half-blooded, pretty old, trots and is with foal. Six hundred dollars will be paid by the Rev. Mr. Smith of this town to the person who shall return the mare and convict the thief or Three Hundred Dollars for the mare alone.

496. *The Royal Gazette* (New York), #387, June 14, 1780.

RUN away the 4th inst. from JOHN AMBERMAN living at Jamaica, Queen's County; a Negro man named WILL, about 5 feet, 8 inches high, broad shouldered, has a scar on his

Advertisements 231

forehead, and one on his head just in his hair, about the bigness of an English shilling, whereon grows no hair, has thick lips, had on when he went off, a home spun grey Jacket much worn, a pair of corduroy breeches; whoever takes up said Negro, and secures him so that his master may get him again, shall have one Guinea reward, or bring him home to his said Master shall have two Guineas reward.
JOHN AMBERMAN.
Jamaica, June 10, 1780.

497. *The Royal Gazette* (New York), #388, June 17, 1780.

Six Dollars Reward. RUN AWAY on Monday the 12th instant, a Negro Boy named Toney, about five feet high, black complexion, and something pitted with the small-pox, has a remarkable scar a little above his left ear, had on when he went away a brown sailor's jacket, and striped Holland trowsers, a check shirt and a bound hat.

Whoever takes up and delivers said run-away to his master, at No. 189, Queen-Street, will be entitled to the above reward. All masters of vessels and others are hereby cautioned and forbid to take off, harbour or conceal said boy, as they will answer it at their peril.

498. *The New Jersey Journal* (Chatham), #71, June 21, 1780.

Ran-Away from the Subscriber, a very slim black Negro man named Prince, about twenty-four or five years old, can talk low Dutch, and formerly belonged to one Van Riper at Second River; if he gets a little liquor is very talkative; has on a thick homespun bluish colored short coat, an old felt hat, a pair of linen breeches, and one pair of tow trouseers and one spare shirt, is about five feet seven or eight inches high. Any person taking up and securing said Negro so that his master may get him again shall receive Twenty Hard

Dollars and all reasonable charges paid by John Blanchard. Hanover, Morris County, June 20, 1780.

499. *The Royal Gazette* (New York), #392, July 5, 1780.

RUN away last Sunday afternoon, the 2d of July instant, a Negro man named CAIN, a stout able young fellow, about 5 feet 8 inches high, had on when he went away a brown short coat, with white metal buttons, a brown waistcoat and white breeches, a cock'd hat, a black silk handkerchief about his head, and has taken with him sundry other wearing apparel; he is about 26 years of age, is but lately from Charlestown, speaks tolerable good English, has a fore head, and has lately had the small-pox. Whoever will apprehend the said runaway, and give notice thereof to Capt. Norman Tolmey, in Cherry Street, shall have FIVE DOLLARS reward, and be allowed all reasonable charges.

500. *The New-Jersey Gazette* (Trenton), #134, July 19, 1780.

Four Hundred Dollars Reward. MADE his escape on Monday the 3d instant, from the subscriber, a new Negro Man, that can scarcely speak a word of English, about 5 feet 9 or 10 inches high, who was confined in Trenton gaol, and is advertised to be sold on Thursday the 27th of July instant; had on and took with him two tow shirts, one pair tow trowsers, one pair leather breeches, a white flannel jacket, an old blue cloth jacket, old shoes, and a leather furred cap. Whoever takes up said Negro and secures him so that I get him again, shall have the above reward and reasonable charges, paid by JOSHUA CORSHON, Sheriff.
   Amwell, July 5, 1780.

501. *The Royal Gazette* (New York), #402, August 5, 1780.

RUN away Tuesday the first instant, a Negro Boy named TOM, the property of Dr. M'Lean, No. 6 Water-Street; he is a strong thick well made fellow, about 16 years of age, speaks tolerable good English, had on when he went off a thicksett jacket, and osnaburgh trowsers. Whoever apprehends and restores him to his said master shall have an adequate reward for their trouble. All masters of vessels are strictly forbid harbouring this Negro, who will probably change his name to facilitate his escape.

502. *The Royal Gazette* (New York), #403, August 9, 1780.

July 10, 1780. RUN AWAY from the subscriber, a short thick set Negro Boy, named Dick, he belonged to his Majesty's ship the Otter, and took away with him two coats, the one a dark French frock, the other a livery brown, lined, trimmed, and turned up with red; it is supposed he has let himself to some person living in the country who, if desirous of keeping him, till such time as said sloop arrives in this port, are requested to call on Mrs. M'Fadyen, at No. 2, in the Fly-Market, and without such information being given, all persons are hereby desired not to harbour him. E. M'FADYEN.

503. *The Royal Gazette* (New York), #405, August 16, 1780.

RUN AWAY, a NEGRO MAN on Saturday last, went on board a vessel in the harbour, his name is JAMES, speaks broken English, he is about five feet 8 or 9 inches high, bandy legged. The master on board whose vessel he is, may have his services, provided he will pay reasonable wages for his service. Inquire of the printer.

504. *The Royal Gazette* (New York), #406, August 19, 1780.

Five dollar Reward, Run away last Monday, a likely negro boy, about 15, he has a great impediment in his speech. James Ricketts. The boy's name is Cyrus.

505. *The Royal Gazette* (New York), #406, August 19, 1780.

TEN DOLLARS REWARD. RUN away from the Subscriber about six weeks ago, a Negro Wench named SAVINAH, she is about 30 Years of Age, slim made, of a very dark Colour, and has a small Scar on the upper part of her Nose. Also eloped from the Subscriber last Wednesday Evening, a short yellow Wench, named Grace, she carried off her Child named Harry, he is nineteen Months old, and is a very yellow Mulatto. It is imagined the above described Negroes are lurking about this City.—whoever harbours, or attempts to conceal them may depend upon being treated as they deserve, and any person who will deliver them to their master who resides at the Sign of the Crown, No. 25 Peck's Slip, shall have the above Reward, or Forty Shillings for each of the Wenches.

JAMES DUN.

August 18, 1780.

506. *The Royal Gazette* (New York), #407, August 23, 1780.

RUN AWAY, a Virginia Negro Woman called PAMELA, the property of the subscriber, aged about 18 years, and came here last summer with her mistress: she is squire built, very lusty and likely, affects to smile when she speaks or is spoken to, and is very deceitful and given to lying. She absconded about a month ago, and says she is a free Negro, tho' born in my family, and often calls herself MIRA, after her sister. As it is imagined some evil disposed persons

encourage her in this way, for wicked purposes: All persons, therefore, are hereby forwarned, not to harbour, employ, conceal, or carry off said Negro, by land or water, as they must do the same at their peril: And whoever will secure said Negro, or give timely notice who it is that secrets and entertains her, so as I may get her again, shall be handsomely rewarded, by applying at No. 30, in Roosevelt street, to
J. Agnew, Chaplain, Queen's Rangers

507. *The Royal Gazette* **(New York), #410, September 2, 1780.**

TWO GUINEAS REWARD. RUN away on Saturday the 26th of August, a Negro Boy, named SCIP, 14 years old, about four feet nine or ten inches high, he has a speck in the right eye, had on when he run away, a check shirt, a pair of striped trowsers. Whoever will give information to GIDEON CARSTANG, at the fresh water, so that his master may have him again, shall receive the above reward.

This is to forewarn all masters of vessels or others not to harbour or carry him off at their peril.

508. *The Royal Gazette* **(New York), #410, September 2, 1780.**

Ran Away from Lucas Von Beverholdt of Beverwyck near Morris Town, on the 26th of last month, a negro man, named Jack, and is supposed will go to New York; he is low of stature, very black and limps a little in his walk, though not lame, speaks broken English and some Negro Dutch; he took with him a short blue cloth coat, with red lining cape cuffs; a scarlet jacket and breeches, a light coloured homespun coat, short cut with red cape and cuffs, a darker homespun jacket and breches with black buttons; homespun shirts and trousers also some fine shirts. Whoever apprehends said fellow and secures him so that he can be delivered to said Von Beverholdt or to Mr. Patrick Darcy, shall have one thousand continental dollars reward. Beverwyck, near Morristown.

509. *The Royal Gazette* (New York), #410, September 2, 1780.

RUN AWAY from the subscriber, on the evening of the 23d ult. a Negro Lad named FORTUNE, about eighteen years of age, of a brownish cast, much pitted with the small pox, is slender made, and about five feet seven or eight inches high, came from Georgia about ten months ago with Major Drummond of the New-Jersey Volunteers, is very fond of dress, and generally wears a small round hat bound with silver lace; one of his eyes are sore and much inflamed. Whoever will apprehend said Negro, and bring him to No. 42, White-Hall, or give information where he may be had, shall receive TWO GUINEAS reward, paid by
       BROUGHTON REYNOLDS.
 N.B. All persons and masters of vessels, are forewarned harbouring or secreting said negro at their peril, as in case of conviction they will be dealt with accordingly.
      New-York, September 1, 1780

510. *The Royal Gazette* (New York), #411, September 6, 1780.

EIGHT DOLLARS Reward, RUN AWAY on Sunday night last, a Negro Girl named JENNY, about 14 years of age, a native of Georgia, from whence she came in the last fleet with her owners; she is of a very black complexion, much marked with the small pox which she had not long since; has remarkable red eyes, short curl'd eye lashes and has lost one of her fore teeth of her underjaw: She had on when she went away a black callimanco coat, a white linen wrapper and cap, and carried all her other clothes with her. The above reward will be given to any person on delivering her to Mr. Dole, No. 128, Great Dock street, or give such information so as she may be taken; She was seen yesterday with some sailors on one of the docks. Captains of vessels and others are cautioned against harbouring her.—She is a remarkable thief and liar.

511. *The New Jersey Gazette* **(Trenton), #143, September 20, 1780.**

Ran Away On the Evening of the 17th Inst. A Negro Man called Ned, a stout fellow about five feet ten or eleven inches high, speaks very low; had on and took with him when he went away, a wool hat with white loops a brown homespun coat, one woolen check and a tow cloth shirt and two pair of tow cloth trowsers. Whoever apprehends and secures the said Negro so that his master may have him again, shall be amply rewarded and all reasonable charges paid by the subscriber. J. Winters. Rocky-Hill, September 19, 1780.

512. *The Royal Gazette* **(New York), #415, September 20, 1780.**

RUN AWAY from the Subscriber on the 16th day of September instant, a Negro Wench named ROSE, she is about the middle size, is a handsome black, and has an impediment in her speech; had on when she went away a green fluff petticoat, a red and white callico short gown, a red silk handkerchief, and a black sattin bonnet. Whoever brings her to me the subscriber, or secures her, shall, upon application, at No. 55, Queen-street, receive FIVE DOLLARS REWARD, and all charges,
ALEXANDER ZUNTZ.

513. *The Royal Gazette* **(New York), #423, October 18, 1780.**

RUN AWAY from the suscriber on Monday evening, a Negro Boy called WILL, about 17 years old, five feet four inches high, remarkably marked with the small pox and scared in the face: Had on a blue jacket [ ] up with red, a canvass pair of breeches and silver plated buckle. Whoever will apprehend or secure the said Negro, shall be handsomely rewarded. All masters of ships and others are desired not to harbour said Negro, as they will be prosecuted according to the law.

JOHN SIBRELL.

514. *The Royal Gazette* **(New York), #427, November 1, 1780.**

A REWARD. RUN or enticed away a Negro Boy named BOB, about 12 years old, very black, and a remarkable flat nose, speaks good English, had on when he went away an oznaburg frock, and red jacket. Whoever secures the said negro, and brings him to the Printer, or No. 16, Maiden Lane; shall be handsomely rewarded.

Masters of vessels and others are cautioned from harbouring or concealing said Negro at their peril.

515. *The New-Jersey Gazette* **(Trenton), #151, November 15, 1780.**

One Thousand Dollars Reward from the subscriber in Princeton, on Sunday evening the 12th instant. A Negro man named Cesar, about twenty-five years of age, about five feet eight inches high, marked with the small pox; had on a blue camblet coat worn out at the elbows, a pair of new buckskin breeches, straps without knee buckels old pumps with a hole in one of the toes or a new patch, a small felt hat lopt. Whoever apprehends the said Negro and delivers him to me shall have the above reward, paid by John Denton Princeton, November 4, 1780. P. S. There is good reason to believe that he has been advised to go away any substantial evidence who will discover the fact (if the plot is by a white person) on full conviction shall have a reward of six thousand dollars, if a black person, five hundred dollars. As it is more probable that there is more people goes to market in Staten Island than ought, but if any person going there will please to call on Mr. Cubberly and enquire of his negro man Cesar who is was that advised him to leave his master and make a suficent discovery whereby the subscriber may receive sufficient damage, shall have ten guines or the exchange thereof in continental money.

516. *The Pennsylvania Gazette* (Philadelphia), #2634, December 6, 1780.

A Half Johannes Reward or the Exchange in Continental Currency. Ran Away last night from the subscriber a Negro man named Briss a well-made fellow, about 35 years old, has remarkable large feet, formerly belonged to Major Hugg of Gloucester County; had on when he went away, abrown home-spun waistcoat, ozenbrigs shirt and trousers, old shoes and an old hat. Whoever takes up said Negroe and secures him in any gaol so as his master may have him again, shall have the above reward and reasonable charge paid by. Robert Johnson, Salem, October 30, 1780.

517. *The Royal Gazette* (New York), #438, December 9, 1780.

Charlestown, South Carolina.
KIDNAPPED, inveigled, or seduced to go on board some vessel that sailed from this place in July last for New-York, a young Negro Man named Richard, but most commonly Dick, belonging to Dr. Alexander Garden, about eighteen or twenty years of age, short and stout made, but active and nimble, of a very black complexion, good features, with rather large lips, speaks good English, tho' born in Africa, has no perceivable country marks, wore a light brown coat, waistcoat and breeches when he was secuced away from his Master's house. Any person discovering and delivering the said Negro to Dr. Middleton of New-York, will receive a reward of FIVE GUINEAS.

518. *The Royal Gazette* (New York), #439, December 13, 1780.

FIVE DOLLARS REWARD. RUN AWAY (or impressed) from Thomas Skinner, No. 256, Broad Street, on Saturday evening the 9th inst. a Mulatto Slave, aged 22 years, about 5 feet inches high, a stout well made fellow, named Tony, but may call himself Anthony Frost, has a bushy thick head of hair, which he combs up very high before in the shape of a roll, round faced, has part of one of his fore-teeth broke out, a very remarkable high breast bone, is very saucy and pert, and thinks a great deal of himself; had on a short blue coat, white metal buttons, striped jacket, and a long pair of blue trowsers. Whoever will apprehend or secure said Mulatto so that his master may get him again, shall have the above reward.———All masters of vessels and others are desired not to harbour said Mulatto at their peril, as they will be prosecuted with the utmost rigour.

519. *The New Jersey Gazette* (Trenton), #157, December 27, 1780.

Two Thousand Dollars Reward. Ran Away on Sunday last from the Subscriber in Mendham township, Morris County. A Negro man named Joe, about 30 years of age, five feet eight inches high, one leg a little shorter than the other, part of one of his great toes cut off, lost some foreteeth and his back is much scarrified and in lumps by whipping. Also a handsome Negro wench, 28 years of age with her child about six weeks old, which from some of its clothes being found, she is supposed to have killed. The Negroes went off with one Slight, a soldier belonging to the 2nd Pennsylvania Regiment and they stole and took with them a variety of clothes and two horses, the one a bay, four years old the other a grey, seven years old and have switch tails. The soldier stole a written discharge in the name of William Nelson whom he will probably personate. Whoever takes up the said Negroes and horses so that the owner may get them again, shall have the above reward or Twelve Hundred

Dollars of the Negroes only or eight hundred dollars for the horses or inproportion for any or either of them and reasonable charges paid by Ebenezar Blackly, Jr. December 22, 1780.

520. *The New Jersey Gazette* (Trenton), #159, January 11, 1781.

Ran Away from the Subscribers last night. A Negro man named Joe and a Negro woman named Hester: The man is about five feet six or seven inches high, well-set, full faced of an open countenance, was formerly a servant to a British officer, speaks the German language well; had on and took with him a brown great coat badly dyed, white pewter buttons with the letters USA in a cypher, a green coat with red cuffs and cape and yellow buttons, white jacket and leather breeches a pair of boots and a pair of shoes, two or three pair of stockings and two or three shirts. The wench is small and well made and has a lively eye, being bred in Carolina and has the manners of the West-India slaves; she had on a red striped linsey short gown and petticoat and took with her a dark brown cloak and sundry other clothes. Whoever takes up and secures the above Negroes shall received Six Spanish milled dollars each and reasonable charges Robert L. Hooper, Robert Hoops, Trenton, January 8, 1781.

521. *The New Jersey Gazette* (Trenton), #160, January 17, 1781.

Philadelphia December 25, 1780. Two Thousand Dollars Reward. Ran Away this evening from the subscriber, a Negro wench named Maria alias Amoritta, she is about thirty-four years of age, tall and well-made, her face long and features more regular than are common with her colour. She had on or took with her a pale blue and white fine short linsey gown and petticoat almost new, a petticoat of tow linen, a pair of men's shoes and good shifts of brown homespun linen and aprons of the same. It is supposed she will endeavour to get into the jersey as she came from thence and once lived with Mr. Thomas Lowrey of Flemington, but it is suspected that she is now lurking in this city or concealed by some free negroes. She also took with her her female child named Jane, about four years old, well made, fat, round faced and lively had on or took with her a blue and white linsey frock. Whoever will deliver the said wench and child to the subscriber in Philadelphia, shallhave the above reward. John Duffield. N.B. All persons are forebid to harbour her at their peril.

522. *The New Jersey Gazette* **(Trenton), #161, January 24, 1781.**

RAN Away On Saturday the 20th Instant from the subscriber living in Maidenhead. A Negro man named Will, formerly went by the name of Yerrah, about twenty three years of age, five feet eight inches high, has a very remarkable hair mole on his cheek. Had on and took with him a pair of new leather breeches, two pair of stockings, a pair of new shoes, light colored home-spun coat much worn and hat. It is thought he will endeavour to get within the enemy's lines. Whoever takes up and secures said servantso that his master may get him again shall have Four Specie Dollars Reward and all reasonable charges paid by Samuel Hunt. January 22, 1781.

523. *The Royal Gazette* **(New York), #452, January 27, 1781.**

RUN-AWAY a Negro Boy, named Sim Sampson, about 18 years old, he wore a whitejacket, black hat, with a red ribbon, a pair of boots, and long blue and white trowsers. Whoever will bring him to Lieut. Le Moledar, of the Hessian Hussars, at No. 192, Queen Street, shall receive Two

Guineas Reward. All Commanders of Vessels are warned against carrying him off, as they shall answer the same at their peril.

524. *The New Jersey Gazette* (Trenton), #163, February 7, 1781.

Ran Away Bucks County, January 31, 1781 from the subscriber on the 29th ult. A mullatto girl named Agnes Beat had on when she went away, a dark linsey gown and petticoat, light colored cloak, black bonnet, low heel'd shoes and as she has taken with her sundry other clothes, she may alter her dress. Whoever takes up said Mullatto shall have three hundred dollars reward and reasonable charges paid by me Adam Van Hart. N. B. All persons are hereby forbid to harbour her; if they do so they shall be prosecuted according to law.

525. *The New Jersey Gazette* (Trenton), #164, February 14, 1781.

RAN Away on Wednesday evening the 7th Inst from the subscriber in Penn's Neck, Windsor township, Middlesex County. A Negro man named Cain, about forty years of age, very talkative and is well set about five feet five inches high. Had on when he went away a light coloured linsey coat and vest a good pair of buckskin breeches, a good felt hat blue stockings tow shirt and took other clothes with him but may change them as he is fond of trading. Any person securing said Negro man so that the owner may have him again shall have Six dollars reward and reasonable charges paid by Garret Couwenhoven February 10, 1781.

526. *The Royal Gazette* (New York), #459, February 21, 1781.

Two Guineas Reward. RUN away from his master, in Charlestown, a mustee fellow named BRAP, has bushy hair, stout made, a little bandy legg'd, marked with the smallpox, about 25 years of age, and speaks good English. Whoever will secure him, or give information of him to the Printer, & send him to his master, shall have the above reward. All persons are forbid to harbour or carry him off, as they shall answer it at their peril.

527. *The Royal Gazette* (New York), #462, March 3, 1781.

MY Negro Wench named Pleasant Queen Anne, ran away on the 18th instant, and had on a red moreen petticoat, a brown short gown, with white lining, a pair of brown rib'd stockings. Whoever will bring her to me shall receive Forty Shillings reward.

JOHN CURRY,
No. 30, William Street.

All Captains of Vessels are warned against carrying her off.

528. *The Royal Gazette* (New York), #467, March 21, 1781.

Three Guineas Reward. RUN AWAY last night from the subscriber living in Crown Street, No. 4, a Negro Girl named PRUSSIA, about 21 years of age, tall stout and well made light, complexion, thick lips, speaks good English, has been heard to say she would go on board the first ship that would take her, had a quantity of good cloaths with her. Whoever apprehends the said Negro Girl, or confines her so that her owner may get her again, shall receive the above reward. All persons and masters of vessels are desired not to

harbour or carry said Negro Girl away at their peril.
ELIZABETH DUNCAN.
March 20, 1781.

529. *The Royal Gazette* (New York), #468, March 24, 1781.

ONE GUINEA REWARD. RUN away from the subscriber, in the Township of Flushing, the 19th instant, a NEGRO MAN formerly called Oliver, but at present calls himself Joe, aged about 28 years, he is about 5 feet 10 inches high, has a thin long face, had on a blue short sailors coat, a grey homespun waistcoat and breeches. Whoever takes up said Negro Man, and secures him, so that the subscriber may have him again, shall have the above reward, and all reasonable charges paid by
WILLIAM TALMAN.
Flushing, March 20, 1781.

530. *The Royal Gazette* (New York), #475, April 18, 1781.

RUN AWAY a few days ago from the regiment of Brunswick Dragoons, at Flat-Land, on Long Island, a Black named Prince Dermen, Drummer in said regiment, about five feet ten inches high, stout built, had on a suit of light blue cloaths quite new. Whoever will secure him so that he may be brought back, or delivered over to any non-commissioned officer of the said regiment, shall receive a proper reward for so doing; and every one is forbid concealing him at their peril.

531. *The New-Jersey Journal* (Chatham), #104, April 25, 1781.

Fifteen Hundred Dollars Reward. RAN AWAY from the subscriber, the 21st instant, a Negro man named Frank, this country born, about forty-five years old; had on a brown broad cloth coat, and blue plush breeches.—Also went off at the same time, a Negro woman named Phebe, (wife of said fellow) about forty years old; her clothes cannot be described; had with her a male child, about sixteen months old.—They went off in company with a free fellow named Cuff, about twenty-five years of age; had on a light blue coat, and blue overalls. They took with them two horses, one a large forrel, and the other a bay, with a long tail, five years old this spring, fifteen hands high.—Whoever takes up said Negroes and horses, shall have the above reward, and reasonable charges, if brought home, paid by JOHN WILSON.

N. B. Though the free fellow should have a pass, it is expected he will be apprehended with the rest.

Hackett's Town, April 23. 1781.

532. *The Royal Gazette* (New York), #479, May 2, 1781.

RUN away on Sunday the 29th of April, a NEGRO BOY, named TOM, the property of Doctor Donald M'Lean, No. 20[ ], six doors from the Coffee-House, he is a stout well made fellow, speaks tolerable good English, had on when he went away, a Brown Cotton Jacket, a Black Velvet Jockey Cap, Blue Breeches, Shoes and Stockings; he may probably *change his name and dress*——Whoever brings the said Negro to his Master, will be well rewarded. All Masters of Transports, Privateers, and Merchantmen, are strictly forbid to harbour the said Negro.

533. *The Royal Gazette* (New York), #480, May 5, 1781.

A N E G R O B O Y RUN away from the subscriber on Friday the 20th April last, a Negro Boy, named Charles Macaulay, about 16 or 17 years old, near five feet high; had on when he went away, an old red jacket, and a white flannel one under it, a pair of white fearnought trowsers, and a sailor's round hat. A reward of two Guineas will be given to any person, who will bring him to the Ale Brewery, Maiden Lane, or to John Dickenson, at the King's Arms, Whitehall.

N.B. All Masters of vessels and others, are forbid to harbour or conceal the above boy at their peril.

534. *The New Jersey Gazette* **(Trenton), #176, May 9, 1781.**

One Thousand Continental Dollars Reward. Ran Away on the 24th ult. from the subscriber in Hopewell, a negro man named Toney, about 35 years of age, five feet six or seven inches high—Whoever takes him and secures him so that his master may have him again, shall have the above reward and all reasonable charges paid by Andrew Blackwell. N.B. All persons are forebid to harbour him at their peril.

535. *The Royal Gazette* **(New York), #482, May 12, 1781.**

Sunday, April 22d. 1781.
RUN AWAY from the ship Euphrates, three negro men, named Will, Paul and Duke, each marked with three marks on each side the temple, and one between the eyes, about five feet seven inches high, speak good English. Whoever will apprehend said negroes, and deliver them on board said ship, shall receive a reward of one Guinea for each.

N.B. Will is lame in one thigh.

536. *The Royal Gazette* **(New York), #483, May 16, 1781.**

RUN away from Messrs. Ray, and Fitzsimmons, two miles beyond Jamaica, a Negro and Negro Wench, about eight days ago. The Negro's name HERCULES, about 22 years of age, apt to stutter on a surprize, has thick lips, and had on a white flannel shirt, white jacket with sleeves, velvet plush breeches; the Wench young and lusty, with three scars on each cheek, both from the southward, the wench was seen in New York, and the negro at Brooklyn. Whoever secures said negro, and negro Wench, so as they may be had by the subscribers, shall receive for each Five Dollars reward, and reasonable charges paid by us. RAY and FITZSIMONS. Jamaica, May 7, 1781.

537. *The New Jersey Gazette* (Trenton), #180, June 6, 1781.

Three Pounds in Gold or Silver Reward. Ran Away on Sunday night last, the 27th of this instant, from the subscriber living in Newtown Buck's County Pennsylvania; a negro woman named Fann, a short thick wench, about 18 or 19 years of age, very black, thick lips; had on a short gown and petticoat made of linsey black and white stripes a large bundle of other cloths for herself and female child about three years old; it is expected she has been assisted by some negro or mullatto. Whoever takes up and secures said Negro wench and child, so that her master may have them again, shall receive the above reward paid by Samuel Yardley. May 29, 1781.

538. *The Royal Gazette* (New York), #495, June 27, 1781.

RUN away, a likely Mulatto Wench, called PAMELIA, 18 years old, about five feet three inches high, stout and well made, had on when she went away, a short purple callicoe gown and pink petticoat. Whoever apprehends and will conduct her to the subscriber in Dutch-Street shall be grately rewarded. All persons are cautioned from harbouring or carrying her off the Island.

ELIZABETH EVANS.
New York, 26th June, 1781.

539. The New-Jersey Journal (Chatham), #123, June 27, 1781.

RANAWAY from the subscriber living near the Cross Roads, at Lamington, the 20th instant, a yellow fellow, twenty-two years old, near six feet high, named Pomp; had on when he went away a tow shirt and trowsers, a red jacket, and had with him a black and white mixed coat.— Whoever secures said Negro in any gaol, or returns him to his master, shall have a Half Joe reward, and reasonable charges, paid by DAVID HENRY.
Hunterdon, June 27, 1781.

540. The Royal Gazette (New York), #498, June 30, 1781.

Eight Dollars Reward. RUN AWAY from the Subscriber, Matthew Daniel, living at No. 34, Duke Street, a Negro Boy, named Duff, had on when he went away a red waistcoat, check shirt and osnaburgh trowsers, no shoes nor hat. Whoever brings said boy to his master, or gives intelligence where he can be had, shall have the above reward.

N.B. All masters of vessels and others are forwarned to harbour or conceal the said Negro Boy, as they may expect to answer for the same.

541. The New-Jersey Gazette (Trenton), #185, July 11, 1781.

Eight Hard Dollars Reward Run Away a negro boy about fifteen years of age named Jack has a down look and is a very great liar. He was in Trenton last Saturday night and left it on Sunday morning. His intention is to escape to the enemy. Whoever will secure and deliver the said Negro boy to the printer hereof shall have the above reward and reasonable charges paid. Trenton, July 10, 1781.

542. *The New-Jersey Gazette* (Trenton), #185, July 11, 1781.

Ten Hard Dollars Reward Run Away from the subscriber yesterday morning; a certain negro woman named Bet, about 21 years of age: Had on a green hat, a long red strriped calico gown, a brown linsey petticoat, a striped lawn aprong. She took with her a female child of about three years of age and several other sorts of cloths. Whoever secures her and delivers her to the subscribers shall have the above reward paid by Jacob Phillips. Burlington, July 11, 1781.

543. *The Royal Gazette* (New York), #502, July 21, 1781.

Five Dollars Reward. RUN AWAY from the Subscriber, on Tuesday the 3rd instant,
A Negro Wench named LUCE, about twenty-eight years old, has a large mark on one of her cheeks which looks like a scar, she had on when she went off, a homespun short gown and petticoat. Whoever takes up the said wench and secures her, or gives information so that her mistress may get her again, shall receive the above reward, from
ANN PRICE, on Golden Hill, next door to the corner of Fair-Street.
 N.B. If the aforsaid wench will return, she will be forgiven.

544. *The Royal Gazette* (New York), #503, July 25, 1781.

RUN-AWAY on Monday night, nine o'clock, from John O'Brien, at the Four Alls, near the Ferry-Stairs, a young negro girl named Sarah, about 19 years old, she wore a white short gown and a cotton petticoat. Whoever returns her to her master, or gives information for her recovery, shall receive eight Dollars reward. All masters of vessels and others are forwarned against harbouring her at their peril.

545. *The Royal Gazette* (New York), #503, July 25, 1781.

Ten Dollars Reward. RUN AWAY from the Subscriber, about six or eight weeks ago, an indented negro man named York Revers, about one or two and twenty years of age, five feet five inches high; had on when he went away, a brown coat with red cuffs and collar, and osnaburgh trowsers.—— Also, on Saturday last a negro boy named Jack, about twelve years of age, had on when he went away, a blue coat faced with red. Whoever will secure the above negroes and bring them to the subscriber, shall receive the above reward, or five dollars for either of them. All masters of vessels and others are hereby strictly charged not to harbour or conceal either of them as they shall answer the same at their peril.
JOHN GRIFFITHS,
No. 195, Water-Street.

546. *The Royal Gazette* (New York), #506, August 4, 1781.

One Guinea Reward. RUN AWAY from the Provost Marshal, a black man named Richmon, formerly the property of the Rebel Colonel Pattison, at Christeen Bridge, in Pennsylvania: He formerly lived at Mr. Saufe's, Merchant at the Fly-market: All masters of vessels are hereby warned against harbouring him at their peril, he being the Common HANGMAN.
The above reward will be paid to any person who will secure said negro, so as the Provost Marshal may have him again, by
CAPTAIN CUNNINGHAM,
Provost Martial.

547. *The Royal Gazette* (New York), #506, August 4, 1781.

Eight Dollars Reward. RUN away from the Subscriber, a stout Negro Man named SAM IVEY, a carpenter and caulker by trade, pitted with the small pox. I forwarn all Captains of vessels, or others from harbouring or taking him away; also any other person employing him and paying him wages without an order from me, shall be answerable for the same after this date. Whoever secures said Negro Slave, or delivers him to me at No. 71, Beekman-Street, shall be paid the above reward, with every other expense.
                                    JONATHAN EILBECK
    July 30 1781.

548. *The New-Jersey Journal* (Chatham), #129, August 8, 1781.

Ten Hard Dollars Reward. RANAWAY last night, from the subscriber, a NEGRO MAN named FRANK, about 40 years of age, 5 feet 8 or 10 inches high, slender made, has small legs, remarkable large flat feet, stoops and hobbles very much in his walking; had on or took with him a long brown broad cloth coat, a pair of blue plush breeches, several cloth jackets, some tow shirts and trowsers.
    Also ranaway at same time, a Negro Wench named PHOEBE, (wife of said Negro man) about 40 years of age, very talkative, active, and smart; had on or took with her a dark brown chintz gown, a black calimanco quilt, some short gowns and pettycoats, besides several things she has stolen.—She also took with her her male child named Obadiah, about 18 months old, but small for his age; he has a very large head and crooked legs.—Whoever secures the said Negroes, that the subscriber may have them again, shall receive the above reward, and reasonable charges if brought home, paid by JOHN WILSON.
    Hackett's Town, July 24, 1781.

Advertisements 253

549. The New-Jersey Journal (Chatham), #129, August 8, 1781.

Twenty Four Hard Dollars Reward. RAN AWAY in the night of the 7th inst. from the subscriber, near Coryell's ferry, a negro man named WILL, aged about 22 years, about five feet four inches high, an artful cunning fellow, speaks good English, his hair turns up from his forehead; had on when he went away, an old blue coat, faced with red, white woollen overalls, and white breeches; it is supposed he will make for the enemies lines, and New-York. Whoever apprehends said negro, and secures him in any gaol, with giving notice, or delivers him at Morristown to Thomas Kinney, shall have the above reward, paid by either of us.
PETER CASE.
Morristown, August 8, 1781.

550. The Royal Gazette (New York), #509, August 15, 1781.

Five Dollars Reward. RUN-AWAY on Monday afternoon, from the Subscriber, living at No. 14, Golden-Hill Street, a mulatto Wench named JANE, about nineteen years of age, four feet, six or seven inches high, middling likely, had on or took with her two light coloured callico short gowns, a black callimanco skirt and old stuff shoes. Whoever secures the said wench so that her master may get her again., shall have the above reward paid by
JOSEPH THOMAS.
All persons are forewarned from harbouring her.
August 14, 1781.

551. The Royal Gazette (New York), #512, August 25, 1781.

ONE GUINEA REWARD. RUN away from the subscriber a Negro Boy, eleven years of age, small growth, thin face, had on when he went away, a coarse round hat, small strip'd jacket, without sleeves, check shirt, a pair of Russia [ ] trowsers, open at the foot. I forwarn any person to conceal or carry off said Negro Boy, at their peril. Any person bringing him to the Coffee House, shall have the above reward.

JOHN BAIN.

552. *The Royal Gazette* (New York), #512, August 25, 1781.

WENT away early on Wednesday morning the 15th of August inst. and has not since returned, a negro lad named MATTIS, he is a good looking well made lad, about 22 years of age but appears rather younger; is about five feet eight or nine inches high, has two scars just under one of his ears: he took with him three check shirts, oznaburg trowsers and frock, a pair of mottled nankeen breeches patched on the right knee, a striped jacket, and a round hat. His master is persuaded he did not mean to stay away, but has been seduced and is still secreted by someone. If the boy will return immediately he has nothing to fear; but should he not, those who detain him after this notice may depend upon being prosecuted with the utmost rigour. EIGHT DOLLARS Reward will be paid to any one who will bring him home, or FOUR DOLLARS to any person who will give the Printer information where he is.

Sometime about last fall, ran away from his master, a negro man named SAM, he is a tolerable chunkey lad, about 5 feet 6 or 7 inches high, about 22 years of age, and has a remarkable scar on one cheek. Also ran away a considerable time since a negro man named CÆSAR, but calls himself Julius Cæsar; he is about 5 feet 7 or eight inches high, by trade a sail maker, but has employed himself at times in going to sea, and in the wood boating business. Whoever will secure either of the above and give information to the Printer, that they may be had again, shall receive FIVE DOLLARS for each, and reasonable expences. It is pretty certain that both of them are lurking about this town.

553. The Royal Gazette (New York), #514, September 1, 1781.

RUN away last Monday night from his Mother in Chapel-street, a Negro Boy named JACOB, near fourteen years old, has a cut on the side of his left eye, had on a red jacket, Osnaburgh trowsers, and check shirt, but without hat or shoes.—Whoever will bring him back to his Mother Jenny, at Mr. Ludlow's, the corner of George's-street in Chapel-street, shall receive Three Dollars reward.

554. The Royal Gazette (New York), #514, September 1, 1781.

ABSCONDED a few days ago, from their owners, from the house of Mr. Ruble, at Flat-Bush: two Negro Girls, Slaves, one named Betsey, marked on the right shoulder T. A, the other named Polly, without any mark, they both speak bad English.
 Whoever may apprehend one or both Negroes, and deliver them to Alexander Forteath, No. 52, Burling Slip, shall receive for each Eight Dollars, if concealed, or harboured by any person, they may depend on being prosecuted.

555. The Royal Gazette (New York), #514, September 1, 1781.

One Guinea Reward. RUN AWAY on Thursday last, a likely Negro Boy named Jack, about fourteen years old, had on a check shirt and trowsers. Whoever will bring him to Charles Hewitt, on Hallett's wharf shall receive the above reward.
 N. B. All masters of vessels and others are forewarned not to harbour or conceal him but at their peril.

556. *The Royal Gazette* (New York), #515, September 8, 1781.

FIVE DOLLARS REWARD. RUN away from the Subscriber, Captain Charles Grant, of the 42d, or Royal Highland Regiment of Foot, a negro man named TOM, about 27 years of age, five feet five or six inches high, thick and well made, has a cut in his forehead. Whoever brings the said negro man TOM, to Captain Grant, or Mr. Hunt, at Newtown, Long-Island, or give information where he can be found, shall have the above reward.

All Masters of vessels and others are forwarned to harbour or conceal the said negro man, as they may expect to answer for the same.

557. *The New Jersey Gazette* (Trenton), #194, September 12, 1781.

Ran Away from the subscriber, living in Trenton Ferry, a Negroe Boy named Jack, between 15 and 16 years old, yellowish complexion and slim built, late the property of General Philemon Dickinson: Had on an old felt hat, small in the rim, tow shirt and long pair of trousers. Whoever secures said boy in any gaol in the state shall have eight dollars reward and reasonable charges paid by me Patrick Colvin, September 4, 1781.

558. *The Royal Gazette* (New York), #523, October 3, 1781.

TWO DOLLARS REWARD. RUN away from Major James Grant, of the King's American regiment, a negro boy named Bristol, about 14 years of age, stout made, high nose, and pretty black, his wool short, had on when he went off, a brown homespun linen shirt and trowsers. Whoever will secure the said negro boy, so as his master can have him again, is entitled the above reward.

All masters of vessels and others are forwarned to conceal the said negro, as in so doing they may expect to answer for the same.

559. *The Royal Gazette* (New York), #525, October 10, 1781.

RUN AWAY from the Subscriber Oct 1, 1781, a Mulatto Girl, named DIANA, about 14 years of age, about four feet high, stout and well made, rough face, and had on when she went away a short red callico bed gown, osnaburgh petticoat, and a blue check handerchief, she was bought of Mr. Newton the 4th of June 1781. Whoever apprehends or gives information on to the Printer, so that the said run away may be had again, shall receive Five Dollars reward. Any person or persons harbouring or concealing the said run-away, shall be prosecuted as the law directs.

560. *The Royal Gazette* (New York), #525, October 10, 1781.

DESERTED from the Civil Branch of the Royal Artillery, two labourers, viz. James Herbert, a Mulatto, about 5 feet 9 inches high, and 34 years old, he had on a brown jacket, and,

Tom Whit[ ]en, a Black, about 5 feet 4 inches high, 23 years old, he had on a green jacket. Whoever will take up the said Deserters, shall be handsomely rewarded, by making application at the Paymaster of Artillery's Office, opposite St. Paul's. All masters of vessels and others are forewarned not to harbour them on pain of prosecution. New-York, Oct 9, 1781.

561. *The Royal Gazette* (New York), #536, November 17, 1781.

RUN AWAY from the subscriber on Thursday last a Negro Wench, named Peg, about 18 years of age, born in Carolina, had on when she went away a blue cloth jacket with long sleeves, made in the form of a riding dress, with bright yellow buttons; this is to forwarn all persons from harbouring her and all masters of vessels from carrying her out of this port upon the penalty of paying whatever the law directs. Whosoever will take up the said Negro, and bring her to No. 48, Cherry Street, shall receive One Guinea reward. WILLIAM WILLSON.

562. *The New Jersey Gazette* (Trenton), #204, November 21, 1781.

Thirty Pounds Hard Money Reward Run Away from the subscribers living near Racoon Ford Orange County Virginia on Sunday the second of September, three Negro slaves, viz. George a dark mullatto fellow, about seventeen years of age, near or quite six feet tall, has a sour down look, had on or carried with him a white yearn coat, turned up with blue, one pair of green cloth breeches one pair of cotton blue coat, one striped Virginia cloth coat, one pair of green cloth breeches, one pair of cotton breeches filled in with thred;—Harry, a black Negro, about the same age as George, a very well set fellow sprightly and well-spoken; had on an old white coat and a new hunting shirt and an old maccarroni hat;—Charles, a black Negro fellow. about sixteen years of age, sparer than Harry, has a very pleasant countenance and speaks slow; had on a black hunting shirt and an old felt hat—He spins well on the foot wheel. We have reason to believe there was a white man with them who had on a white cloth coat with buttons on each side of the breast and a maccarroni hat, the other parts of his dress we cannot learn. We will give Five Pounds reward for each or either of them if taken up and secured so that we can get them or Ten

Pounds for each if delivered to us John Bledsoe, Benjamin Craig, Jeremiah Craig.

563. *The Royal Gazette* (New York), #542, December 8, 1781.

One GUINEA Reward. RUN AWAY on Thursday the 4th instant, a stout Negro Boy, named TOM, of a very black complexion, had on when he went away a long scarlet coat, double lapelled, with gilt buttons, red jacket, double breasted, white breeches, grey worsted ribbed Stockings, strong shoes, and white metal buckles, an old black velvet cap; he probably may change his name and dress. It is presumed that no person whatever, will carry off the said negro; whoever will secure the said Run-away, so that his master may get him, will receive the above reward, by applying to the Printer.
December 7, 1781.

564. *The Royal Gazette* (New York), #545, December 19, 1781.

RUN AWAY from his master Lieutenant de Bardeleben (formerly in the regiment of Diasurth) at Charlestown, and supposed to have gone on board a ship, and sailed for New York, a Negro Man named JOE, of middle size, not very black, but rather a brownish complexion, a Carpenter by trade. Whoever meets or hears of said fellow, or actually is in possession of the same, is desired to secure and bring him, or give notice thereof to Judge Advocate Heym II, quartered at Mrs. Rosevelt's, No. 20, Gold-Street, facing Ferry Street, where further information about a handsome reward will be given.

565. *The Royal Gazette* (New York), #547, December 26, 1781.

New-York, Dec. 24, 1781.
RUN away, last night, from Capt. Henry Reeve, who this morning sailed for Charlestown, in his Majesty's service, a NEGRO MAN named CUFFEE, about 23 years of age, a well made fellow, a full black, with a remarkable long scar down the middle of his forehead, had on a blue coattee, fustian waistcoat, crimson plush breeches, shoes, and black and white striped stockings, he is an old transgressor, and eloped from his said master some time ago, and came to this city, called himself Jack, and reported that he was a free man; when apprehended by his master was about indenting himself to Mr. Thomas Cotton, Peruke Maker, at the New Slip. Whoever secures him in prison, or brings him to the subscriber, who is legally empowered to act for the said Capt. Reeve, shall receive a Guinea Reward, paid by me
JOHN COX, No. 21, Wall Street.

566. *The Royal Gazette* (New York), #547, December 26, 1781.

DESERTED from her service at Greenwich, on Thursday the 27th inst. a Negro Wench called BETSEY, the property of Mr. Christopher Roberts, some time of Portsmouth in Virginia, now of London. She is a tall, good looking Wench, and lived for some time in this city, lastly in the service of Mr. Terence Kerin. Five Dollars reward will be given to any person who will apprehend her, and bring her to No. 33, Wall Street, the Office of Mr. David Campbell, who has a Power of Attorney from her Master, authorizing him to let and dispose of this Wench, in any manner he thinks proper; all persons are therefore cautioned against hiring her, or paying her any money on that account, as they will certainly be accountable to her Master, or his Attorney, for her wages.

567. *The Royal Gazette* (New York), #530, January 5, 1782.

ONE GUINEA REWARD, RUN away the 6th of December past, from on board of the ship Emanuel and Hercules, Alexander M'Dougal Master, a negro boy named Cudjoe, about five feet six inches high, stout and well made, very black complexion, speaks both English and French; had on when he went away, a blue jacket and trowsers.
 Whoever will bring him to Thomas Erskine, at Mrs. Smyth's, No. 5, Hanover-Square, will receive the above reward.

568. *The Royal Gazette* (New York), #551, January 9, 1782.

RUN AWAY from the subscriber on the 3d of January, a fat lusty Negro Wench, named Rachel, had on when she went away a dark callicoe short gown and homespun petticoat, without cloak or hat. Whoever will secure said wench so that the owner may recover his property shall receive Four Dollars reward from me
 DAVID BLAIR, No. 30, Little Dock Street.

569. *The Royal Gazette* (New York), #551, January 9, 1782.

RUN AWAY last night a Negro Girl named POLLY, about 13 years old, she went off without shoes or stockings, and wore a blue baize frock. Whoever will give intelligence where she may be recover'd shall have Two Dollars reward at Dr. Dastuge's, corner of Duke Street, in Broad Street.

570. *The New Jersey Gazette* (Trenton), #211, January 9, 1782.

Run Away from the Subscribers, the 6th instant a Negro man named Joe, about twenty-two years of age, near six feet tall; had on when he left a brown broad cloth coat, white broad cloth waistcoat and black woolen trousers. Whoever takes up the said Negro man and delivers him to the subscribers, living near Ringo's Tavern, Hunterdon County, shall have Ten Dollars reward and all reasonable charges paid by John Runyan, Jacob Williamson January 6, 1782.

571. *The Royal Gazette* (New York), #558, January 23, 1782.

A NEGRO Deserted. LEFT his Master's house the 10th inst, a negro man called ADAM, he is a tall stout made fellow, with a remarkable scar, a mark above his left eye-brow. Whoever will apprehend the said negro, and bring him to Mr. Campbell's Office, near the Coffee-House, shall have a reward of Three Guineas; and the same reward will be given to any person, who may inform where he is lurking, so as that he may be apprehended, Masters of vessels and others are hereby warned not to employ or protect him, otherwise they may depend upon being prosecuted according to law; concealing a run-away negro being as criminal as receiving stolen goods.

572. *The Royal Gazette* (New York), #560, February 9, 1782.

RUN away from her Master on Monday morning last, a NEGRO Wench, named Jane, she had on a pale green callimanco petticoat, a red short gown, a scarlet cloak with a hood on it; about fifteen years of age, very talkative and speaks very good English. Whoever takes up said Negro

Wench, and brings her to Francis Doyl, No. 63, Chatham-Street, shall have Two Dollars reward.
February 7, 1782.

573. *The Royal Gazette* (New York), #561, February 13, 1782.

Two Guineas Reward. RUN AWAY, on the 28th instant, a Negro Wench named LISSA, the property of John Carow, had on when she went away, a brown short gown, and brown serge petticoat, a blue short cloak unbound with a cap to it, and took off with her two striped callico long gowns, with some other cloathing. she has a mark on her breast, occasioned by being burnt. She speaks good English, and is rather more yellow than black, aged about 24 years old. Whoever takes up said Wench, and brings her to her master, living in Fair-street, No. 3, shall receive the above reward. All persons are forbid harbouring the said Wench.
JOHN CAROW.
N. B. The above Wench formerly belonged to Parson Burnet, on Long Island.

574. *The Royal Gazette* (New York), #507, March 6, 1782.

EIGHT DOLLARS REWARD, RUN away from the subscriber, on Sunday evening last, a likely NEGRO WENCH, nineteen years of age, named Charlottee, formerly the property of Captain Salter, she is somewhat pitted with the small pox, had on when she went away, a white gown and petticoat: Whoever takes up said Wench, and secures her so that her master can obtain her, shall receive the above reward, and all reasonable charges paid by me
JOHN VANDERHOVEN.
All masters of vessels and others are strictly forbid to carry off or conceal her at their peril.

575. *The Royal Gazette* (New York), #509, March 13, 1782.

One Guinea Reward. RUN away on Thursday the 12th instant, a stout well made Negro Boy, about five feet four inches, had on when he went away, a black super-fine broad cloth coat and waistcoat, black silk breeches and stockings, and a beaver hat with crape round it. Whoever will secure the said Negro Boy to the Printer, will be entitled to the above reward.

All Masters of vessels and others, are cautioned from harbouring or carrying off the said Negro Boy.

576. *The Royal Gazette* (New York), #572, March 23, 1782.

RUN AWAY on Thursday the 12th inst. a stout well made Negro Boy, named Tom, about five feet four inches, had on when he run off, a suit of mourning, he may probably change his name and dress. Whoever will apprehend the said Negro, or give information to the subscriber, so that he may be found, will be handsomely rewarded
      HENRIETTA M'LEAN.

It is presumed that no masters of vessels or others, will harbour or carry off the said Negro Boy, upon any pretext whatever.

577. *The Royal Gazette* (New York), #575, April 3, 1782.

DESERTED from the Ship Thomas, on Thursday last, a Negro Man named Tom, aged 25 years, had on a blue jacket with a white frock over it, a blue cap, is cropp'd of both ears, talks pretty good English, plays the fife and beats the drum, he also understands hair dressing and shaving.

Likewise deserted a Negro Boy called Cato, aged 18 years, knock-[k]need, heavy down cast look, had on a blue jacket and blue cap, and fearnought trowsers, also a Negro

Boy called Marquiss, about 18 years old, had on a blue jacket, blue cap, &c. well set, and strait made, a Creole of Grenada. Whoever will secure, or give information of the said Negroes to Capt. Casey, shall receive Three Guineas reward, or One Guinea for each of them, apply at Mrs. M'Kenny's, No. 31, Broad Street.
 N.B. It is requested that all masters of vessels or privateers, will not harbour them, but at their peril.

578. *The New-Jersey Gazette* **(Trenton), #225 April 17, 1782.**

THREE POUNDS REWARD. RUN away from the subscriber, in Trenton, a negro man, named Peter, about 5 feet 8 or 9 inches high; he had on a blue surtout coat, yellow worsted under coat, brown jacket and breeches, and blue yarn stockings, he plays on the fiddle, and uses the bow with the left hand; he made his escape the 27th of March last, and is supposed to be gone in the pines, as he formerly lived there. Whoever takes up said negro, and secures him, so that his master may have him again, shall have the above reward, and reasonable charges, paid by JON A. RICHMOND. April 16, 1782.

579. *The Royal Gazette* **(New York), #580, April 20, 1782.**

Run or taken away from the subscriber the 16th of April 1782, a Negro man named Joe, about 5 feet 5 inches high, a slit in the upper part of his left ear, lately from Charles-Town, had on when he went away a blue short jacket, and straw hat. Whoever will secure said Negro, and bring him to No. 10 John Street so that the owner may have him again, shall be handsomely rewarded for their pains.
       JENKINSON JEANES.
 All masters of vessels are forbid harbouring said Negro.

580. *The Royal Gazette* (New York), #581, April 24, 1782.

RAN-AWAY on the 21st inst. a negro boy named James; had on when he went off, a cap, one part red and the other light coloured, a short brown coat, white dimity jacket, and homespun linen trowsers. He went off under pretence of searching for some horses that were lost, having a bridle in his hand: He is about sixteen or seventeen years of age.

A reward of two Guineas and all other reasonable expences, will be paid to any person who will deliver him to STEPHEN DAVENPORT, at the New-Slip, in St. James's-Street, No. 27.

581. *The New-Jersey Gazette* (Trenton), #229, May 15, 1782.

Run Away a Negro Man named Jack, about thirty-five years old, straight and well-limbed and about five feet ten inches high, very white even teeth, has holes in his ears, understands the coopers trade and can talk French; had on a striped woolen shirt, a clothcolored jacket and waistcoat much worn and patched, a pair of buckskin breeches almost new and stained in the seat by riding bareback, grey stockings and shoes newly soaled took with him a homespun coat, buttons covered with same and lined with blue, a jacket and breeches of homespun dimity, a white linen shirt and pair of new shoes. Whoever apprehends the said Negro and delivers him to the subscriber or secures him in any gaol so that he may be had again, shall be paid three Pounds and reasonable charges by James Parker. Pitts Down, Hunterdon County, March 9, 1782.

582. *The Royal Gazette* (New York), #587, May 15, 1782.

New-York, May 14, 1782.
RUN AWAY on Friday the 10th instant, a middle sized Negro Wench named PHILLIS; had on when she went away, a brown strouding jacket, black shirt, cheque apron, blue stockings, and Men's shoes, simple in behavior.— Whoever will bring her to the Owner at No. 32, John-Street, shall receive Two Dollars reward. All persons are forbid harbouring or employing said Negro Wench, as she is a warranted property.

583. *The Royal Gazette* (New York), #594, June 8, 1782.

One Guinea Reward. RUN AWAY, from the Subscriber, on the 4th of June, a NEGRO-BOY, named BACCHUS, about twelve years old: Had on, when he went away, a white jacket, striped trowsers, no shoes nor hat. Whoever takes up the said Negro, and brings him to No. 20, Ann-Street, shall receive the above Reward.

584. *The Royal Gazette* (New York), #594, June 8, 1782.

Ten Dollars Reward. RUN AWAY, Friday the 7th of June, from the Subscriber, living at No. 7, King's Street, a tall slim yellow NEGRO-WENCH, named DINAH about 28 years of age, speaks good English. All persons are forbid concealing or employing said Negro-Wench, or they must answer it at their peril. Whoever secure the aforesaid Wench, so that her master can get her again, shall be intitled to the above Reward.
JAMES CALLOW.

585. *The Royal Gazette* (New York), #596, June 15, 1782.

DESERTED, Cæsar Augustus, black driver to the horse department of the Royal Artillery, about five feet high, very much bandy-leg'd; had on when he went away, a regimental blue coat with a red collar, red waistcoat, linen trowsers and round hat. Whoever apprehends the said deserter, shall receive one Guinea reward, by applying to the office of the horse department, No. 16, Nassau Street. It is suspected that he is gone to Bergen Point, or on board some of the vessels in the harbour. Whoever harbours or conceals the said deserter, shall be prosecuted as the law directs.

586. *The Royal Gazette* (New York), #596, June 15, 1782.

Five Dollars Reward. RUN AWAY from his Master, on Sunday night, the 2d of June, a NEGRO-BOY, named JACK, about 15 years of age, quite black, well set; and speaks broken English. Had on, when he went away, a blue and white striped linen Jacket; a pair of parson's grey broad cloth Trowsers; white homespun linen Shirt; and a small round Hat. He was lurking about town for two or three days, and it is imagined he is since got on board some vessel. Whoever brings said boy to his Master, at No. 198, Queen-Street, or secures him and gives information, so that his said master gets him again, shall receive the above Reward. And all masters of vessels and others are forbid harbouring, concealing, or carrying off said Negro-Boy, as for so doing they shall be prosecuted with the utmost severity.

WILLIAM RHINELANDER.

587. The Royal Gazette (New York), #596, June 15, 1782.

Ten Dollars Reward. RUN AWAY, on Wednesday the 12th instant, a NEGRO-BOY, named FRANK, about 5 feet high; aged 19 years, not very black: He may be known by one of his great toes which has been much bruis'd: He took with him a pale blue broad cloth Coat and Jacket; a brown Coat; corduroy Jacket and Breeches; a pair of fustain and striped Trowsers; a new castor Hat, and some other articles. It is imagined he intends going on board some privateer. The Masters of all vessels are warned not to take him, as they must answer it at their peril. Whoever will apprehend the said Negro-Boy, or give information to the Subscriber, at Jamaica on Long-Island, shall receive the above Reward.
DOUWE DITMAN.

588. The New-Jersey Journal (Chatham), #177, July 3, 1782.

MISTAKEN the road from Philadelphia to Morristown or the North-River, PETER, a Negro man who was born at Hartford, and is the servant of Mr. David Sears, of Boston. He was mounted on a sorrel horse with a white face, had a small portmantua and pistols. If any person has stopped said servant, upon suspicion of his being a runaway, it is desired that he may be released to pursue his journey.—The Negro man is desired to call on Col. De Hart, or Mr. Eleazer Miller, at Morristown, for directions to his master.
Morristown, June 18, 1782.

589. The Royal Gazette (New York), #601, July 3, 1782.

RUN AWAY from the subscriber a Negro wench named Venus, about 26 years old, this is to warn all masters of vessels and others from harbouring or carrying off the said Wench, as they shall answer for it as the law directs.

Whoever will apprehend the said Wench, shall be handsomely rewarded by bringing her to No. 27, Roosevelt-Street.
         Charles Boardwi[ne].

590. *The Royal Gazette* (New York), #602, July 6, 1782.

ONE GUINEA REWARD TO any person who will apprehend a certain black fellow of the name of SQUASH, who came from Rhode-Island, he belonged to a vessel called the Supple Jack, burnt at Sandy Hook, the said fellow stole to the value of Forty Pounds from Humphrey Wadey of Sandy Hook, consisting chiefly of womens cloaths, viz. 1 Green Silk Gown, 1 Brown Silk do. 1 Brocaded Silk, 1 Chrystal Buckle set in Silver, and several other articles, also Seven or Eight Pounds in cash. Enquire of the Printer.

591. *The Royal Gazette* (New York), #605, July 17, 1782.

Ten Dollars Reward. RUN from the Subscriber, on Friday the 12th Instant, a MULATO BOY, named DAVID, about 13 or 14 Years old, round Visage, and stares much when questioned; had on when he went away, a scarlet Waistcoat and Trowsers. The above Reward will be paid any Person that brings him to No. 39, Dock-street. All Persons are forwarned harbouring or employing him at their Peril.
         JOHN GOODRICH, jun
June 16, 1782.

592. *The Royal Gazette* (New York), #605, July 17, 1782.

Ten Guineas Reward. RUN AWAY from their master's service, and are known to be lurking about this city the four following Negroes, viz. CATO RAMSAY, a stout able bodied man, formerly lived with Mrs. Willoughby Morgan, in Dover-Street.

DANIEL FISHER, a tall stout man somewhat marked with the Small Pox, and of a yellowish complexion 'tis said he lives on Staten Island where he has a wife and children.

LUKE WILSON, a short man, has a wife somewhere in town, and is well known among the blacks.—The above three Negroes were all of them out in the privateer brig Fair American on her last cruize.

SAM, a short chunky man, about twenty five years of age, and has often been seen at Ellis's Island.——Whoever will secure the above Negroes, and give information to the Printer, that they be had again shall receive the above reward, or in proportion for either of them.

593. *The Royal Gazette* (New York), #608, July 27, 1782.

Four Guineas Reward. RUN AWAY from the subscriber, a Negro Wench, about 24 years of age, middle sized, has a scar over her left eye. Had on when she went off a shift and under petticoat. She is well known in this city, having for several years carried Biscuit through it, she was formerly the property of John White Baker.

Also a NEGRO MAN, Named CÆSAR, about five feet four inches high, twenty eight years of age—he is much addicted to strong liquors, formerly the property of Mrs. Cromeline, of Long-Island, and is well known, by his having carried Bread through the city.

Whoever takes up said Negroes, and delivers them to their master, shall have the above reward or TWO GUINEAS for each.

RICHARD JENKINS,
No. 23, John Street

594. *The Royal Gazette* (New York), #611, August 3, 1782.

TWO DOLLARS Reward. RUN AWAY from the Subscriber, a young NEGRO GIRL, about thirteen or fourteen years of age; had on when she went away, a white short gown, and black calimanco skirt, no cap, but a black bonnet; of a fair complexion, with three specks of the small pox on her nose, and has two of her upper teeth out, and a pair of gold bobs in her ears. I forwarn all masters of vessels or others from harbouring or concealing her at their peril. If any person will deliver her to her Mother, living at theWhite-Hall, shall be paid the above reward, by me,
                      ELIZABETH WALKER.

595. *The Royal Gazette* (New York), #615, August 17, 1782.

TEN DOLLARS REWARD. RUN AWAY, or impressed, on Sunday evening the eleventh instant, from Thomas Skinner, No. 47, Broad-Way, a Mulatto Slave, aged twenty-four years, about 5 feet 8 inches high, a stout well made fellow, named TONY, but may call himself Anthony Frost; a Baker by trade, has a bushy thick head of hair, which he combs up very high before, in the shape of a roll; he is round faced, with part of one of his fore teeth broke out, a remarkable high breast bone, is very saucy and pert, and thinks a great deal of himself: Had on a short light coloured wilton coat, a callico jacket, and a pair long brown silk trowsers, a pair of new shoes, and a round black hat. Whoever will apprehend or secure the said Mulatto, so that the owner shall get him again, shall receive the above reward.

All masters of vessels and others are desired not to harbour or conceal said Slave at their peril, as they will be prosecuted with the utmost rigour.
    August 15th, 1782.

596. The Royal Gazette (New York), #615, August 17, 1782.

New-Town, August 8, 1782.
RUN away from the subscriber, on Sunday the 4th inst. a negro named ADAM, 19 years of age, olive complexion, 5 feet 7 or 8 inches high, an impediment in his speech, wore an officers old red coat faced with white, and a gold basket button, a brown jacket and trowsers. Masters of vessels, and others, are strictly forbid to conceal or carry off said Negro. One Guinea reward will be paid to any person who secures him, and gives me notice thereof, so that I may get him again, with reasonable charges.
GARRET LUYSTER.

597. The Royal Gazette (New York), #618, August 28, 1782.

TWO GUINEAS REWARD. RUN AWAY on Tuesday morning the 20th instant, from Doctor David Brooks, of Cow Neck, on Long-Island, a Negro Boy named BEN, about five feet six inches high; he is tall, round faced, and of a yellow complexion, has a scar under one of his eyes from a burn, and has lost the first joints of three of his small toes on the left foot; he walks limping with one foot turned outward; had on when he went away, a brown homespun coat, with Pewter buttons, a black sattin lasting jacket, tow shirt and trowsers, and a round black hat.
 Whoever will apprehend or secure the said Negro slave, so that the Owner may get him again, shall receive the above reward.
 All Masters of Vessels and others, are desired not to harbour or conceal said slave, as they will answer it at their peril.
New-York, August 27th, 1782.

598. *The New-Jersey Gazette* (Trenton), #244, August 28, 1782.

EIGHT HALF-JOES REWARD. BROKE out of the gaol of this town on Sunday night last, a certain John Cumtain, of Woodbridge, with three negro fellows, viz. One that says he belongs to Count Rochambeau, a black smooth skin, narrow visage, speaks but little, about five feet eight inches high, not exceeding twenty-five years old; also one named Fortune, but now goes by the name of Jack, five feet six or seven inches high, stout, well made, and active, African born, but speaks good English, smooth skin, full-faced, and has a smiling open countenance, is a good cook and butcher, fond of strong drink, and, when drunk, very impudent and quarrelsome, has been a waiter for some time at Mr. Cape's in this town, in which he is very active, was raised by lawyer Wickham in New-York, and now belongs to Mr. William Buchanan of Baltimore town; the other not so black as the former, about five feet eight or nine inches high, not exceeding twenty years old, was brought up in a low Dutch family, which he discovers very plainly.

Any person securing the said John Cumtain, with the negroes, shall have the above reward, or in proportion for any of them, and if delivered in this place, all reasonable charges, paid by PETER HULICK, Gaoley.

N. B. A further reward of Three Pistoles will be given for the above named Fortune, if delivered to Mr. George Davis, in Trenton.

Trenton, August 28, 1782.

599. *The New-Jersey Journal* (Chatham), #187, September 11, 1782.

Three Guineas Reward. RAN AWAY, a negro wench named PEG, who formerly lived with Justice Campbell, at the Short Hills, in New Jersey, and lately with John D. Crimsheir, in Philadelphia. She is 29 years of age, low of stature, and strong made; she had on when she went away, a blue petticoat, striped short gown, a new black bonnet with

red lining, and a pair of mens shoes. It is presumed that she is gone to Chatham in New Jersey, or else is concealed in this city, or some place near it, by some free negroes or others, who wish to avail themselves of the service of other people's servants. All persons are therefore strictly forbid to harbour the said wench, or employ her, as they will not only be prosecuted for keeping her, but be sued for her work and labour. Whoever takes up the said wench, and secures her so that she may be had again, shall receive the above reward, and all expences, by applying to ELEAZER OSWALD, next door to the Coffee House in Market-Street.
Philadelphia, August 19, 1782.

600. *The Royal Gazette* (New York), #625, September 21, 1782.

Ten Dollars Reward. RUN AWAY the 20th instant a Negro Wench, named FLORA, about 24 years old, pretty tall long visaged, and has a slow mild way of talking, she was born in South-Carolina, and had a pass at Charles Town, of which she may attempt to avail herself here; this is therefore to warn all masters of transports or other vessels from carrying off said slave, and all others from harbouring or employing her, as they may depend on being prosecuted to the utmost rigour of the law.
Any person who will secure and deliver her to Mr. Charles Keeling, on the New-Dock, or the subscriber at Mr. Stone's, No. 66, Water-Street, shall receive the above reward, and all charges paid.
N. B. If the Wench will come home she shall be forgiven.	WILLIAM O'BRIEN.

601. *The Royal Gazette* (New York), #626, September 25, 1782.

A GUINEA Reward. RAN away, a week since, a Negro MAN, named John Jackson, about twenty-two years of age, an indented servant, (three years of his time unexpired) about five feet five inches high, slight made, shaves and dresses hair, and waits at table well; had on when he went away, a light coloured Fustian Jacket, Waistcoat, and Breeches, and a cock'd Hat; but he has also a Green, and a Red short outside Jacket, and a pair of Black Silk Breeches. If the Master of any Ship or Vessel, or any other person harbours, secrets, or employs him, they may depend on being punished with the utmost rigour.

Whoever will secure and deliver him to Captain Cunningham, at the Provost, in this City, shall receive the above reward.

N. B. If he voluntarily returns to his Master, ask his pardon, and promise never to leave him again, he will be forgiven, and no notice taken of his ungrateful behaviour.

602. *The Royal Gazette* (New York), #628, October 2, 1782.

One Guinea Reward. RUN AWAY from his Master a Negro Boy, named PETER, had on when he went away, a white linen shirt, white cloth waistcoat without sleeves, and striped Holland trowsers. Whoever will bring him to No. 56, Water-Street, shall receive the above reward.

B. Legrange.

603. *The Royal Gazette* (New York), #631, October 12, 1782.

RUN AWAY from George Powers, Butcher at Brooklyn Ferry, a young Negro Fellow, named CATO, about five feet six inches high, had on a blue short jacket, lined with green, and long linen trowsers. Whoever will bring him home, shall receive Two Guineas reward, by George Powers.

604. *The Royal Gazette* (New York), #632, October 16, 1782.

A Mulatto Boy, NAMED *JACK*, was taken off, on Sunday evening last, supposed by some Boat belonging to the Shipping.——He is ten years old, very likely, had on a coarse white shirt and trowsers, an old light brown cloth jacket, a round hat, and without shoes or stockings.— Whoever gives information, so that he may be found, or brings him to No. 9, Little Dock-street, shall receive FIVE POUNDS Reward, from
EDWARD NICOLL.

605. *The Royal Gazette* (New York), #632, October 16, 1782.

RUN AWAY on the 7th instant, from David Wilson, at the Sign of the XVIIth Dragoon, Broad-Way, a NEGRO BOY, named JACK, about four feet high; he had on a blue waistcoat, striped jacket, canvas trowsers, grey stockings, and without a hat.——Whoever brings him to David Wilson, as above, shall receive a genteel reward.

606. *The Royal Gazette* (New York), #635, October 26, 1782.

One Guinea Reward. RUN AWAY from the Subscriber, a NEGRO BOY, about Thirteen Years of age; had on when he went away, a check shirt, Oznabrig trowsers, an old red coat with a black collar and cuffs, has a small bare spot on one side of his forehead, a little within the hair. Whoever brings him to the Subscriber, at No. 56, between Beekman's and Burling-Slips, Water-Street, shall receive the above reward. All Masters of vessels and others, are strictly forbid harbouring, concealing, or carrying him off, at their peril.
Barnardus Legrange.

607. *The New-Jersey Gazette* (Trenton), #253, October 30, 1782.

ONE HUNDRED DOLLARS R E W A R D. RAN away from the subscribers on the night of the 22d inst. five slaves, viz. Moses, 5 feet 9 or so inches high, forty years old, strong built, and hump-shouldered; had on a striped short coat and trowsers, and a calico vest. Ben George, six feet high, strong built; had on a striped short coat, green jacket, and wollen trowsers. Syrus, a mulatto, 20 years old, 5 feet 8 or 9 inches high, slim built; had on a dark bearskin coat, a light coloured cloth vest, and tow trowsers. Tom, 20 years old, short and well set, has a down look; had on a blue sailor's jacket, with white lining, old tow trowsers, and very thick double soaled shoes almost new. And Harry, 5 feet 9 inches high, seventeen years old, very likely; had on and took with him two blue coats, one lappeled, two light cloth jackets, one pair of leather and one do. corduroy breeches, and white ribbed yarn stockings; he also carried off an English fuzee, and silver mounted ivory handled sword.— Whoever takes up the above negro men, and delivers them to their masters in Trenton, or secures them in any gaol, so that they may be had again, shall have the above reward, or in proportion for either of them, paid by A. LAMBERT, ELIHU SPENCER, JOHN BELL, WM. CHAMBERS, JAMES THOMPSON. Trenton, Oct. 29, 1782.

608. *The Royal Gazette* (New York), #636, October 30, 1782.

RUN AWAY from Laurel Hill, Sunday night the 20th instant, a Negro Boy, fourteen years old, called LONDON, had on a white woollen waistcoat, breeches, and a shirt, who is supposed to live with his mother BET, in or about town, Whoever brings them to me, or to No. 21, Princess Street, shall receive one Guinea reward. All persons are

hereby forwarned not to employ them, carry them off, or harbour them.
JOHN HEINEMAN,
Judge Advocate of the Hessian Regiment de Losberg, jun.

609. The New-Jersey Gazette (Trenton), #255, November 13, 1782.

Monckton Park, Nov. 5, 1782. RAN away from the above farm last night, a negro man, about twenty-three years old, middle-sized, bandy or bow-legged; had on a blanket or white coarse short coat, with red cape and red buttons, an iron collar about his neck, which had been on a few days on account of his concerting with another negro to rob his master and attempt for New-York. He is fond of playing on the fiddle, which he does badly, and is a great thief, liar and drunkard: Whoever takes up the said negro man, and delivers him to the subscriber on the above farm, two miles below Bristol, on the river Delaware, shall receive Thirty Dollars reward. ROBERT M. MALCOLM.

610. The New-Jersey Gazette (Trenton), #256, November 20, 1782.

RAN away from the subscriber at Middlebush, in Somerset county, State of New-Jersey, a mulatto wench, about fifteen years of age, five feet four or five inches high; had on when she went off a linen short gown and petticoat: Whoever takes up the said wench, and secures her, so that the owner may have her again, shall have Twenty Shillings reward, and all reasonable charges paid by JEROMUS RAPPELYEA.
N. B. It is supposed she went off with the French troops.

611. *The Royal Gazette* (New York), #644, November 27, 1782.

R U N A W A Y, From the Subscriber, *On Sunday last, the 17th Instant.* A Likely young Guinea NEGRO FELLOW, named NERO: He had on when he went away, an ordinary shirt, a blue frieze shooting jacket, lined with green baize, had four slack pockets and hair buttons, brown cloth trowsers, and an old flapped hat; he also carried with him a new suit of gray coating, the waistcoat and coat lined with green baize, with plain white metal buttons, and a pair of boots. Whoever will secure the said Negro, and deliver him to the subscriber, at Newtown, Long-island, or to Mr. Robert Dunbar, No. 37, Maiden-Lane, New-York, shall receive FIVE GUINEAS Reward.

Wm. GARDEN.
Newtown, Nov. 22, 1782.

612. *The New-York Gazette: and the Weekly Mercury*, #1630, January 13, 1783.

Twenty Dollars Reward. RUN away from his master, a negro boy named BILLY, lately from the island of Jamaica, about twenty years of age, and near about 5 feet 6 inches high: He was born in Guinea, and speaks bad English, is of a very black complexion, with a yellow cast in his eyes; he is branded on the breast with a D. S. He had on when he went off the common dress of a sailor, viz. a blue jacket, a pair of blue trowsers, round hat and check shirt. As he has made some voyages to sea, it is probable he may look for employment in some vessel, therefore master of vessels and others are forewarn'd not to harbour or carry him off. DANIEL McCormick.

613. *The New-Jersey Gazette* (Trenton), #268, February 12, 1783.

TWENTY DOLLARS REWARD. RAN away from the subscribers on the evening of the 26th ult. two negro men, viz. One named Elimas, 20 or 21 years old, about 5 feet 6 inches high, straight and stout built, has a lump on the second joint of one of his thumbs, lisps in his talk; had on a light yellow broadcloth coat, and jacket of the same, leather breeches, and a small round hat; the rest of his clothes unknown.—The other named Ben, near of the same age with Elimas, about 5 feet 7 or 8 inches high, a good countenanced fellow, has a scar on the right side of his forehead, stoops in his walk; had on a lead coloured fulled linsey coat half worn, and an old jacket of the same colour, leather breeches, black stockings, an almost new felt hat, with a piece of yellow binding round the crown; but 'tis suspected they may change both their names and clothes. Whoever apprehends and secures said negroes, so that their masters may get them again, shall have the above reward, or Ten Dollars for either of them, and all reasonable charges paid by JOHN LAQUEAR, TEUNIS QUICK.
Amwell, February 1, 1783.

614. *The Royal Gazette* (New York), #667, February 15, 1783.

R U N A W A Y, *On Thursday morning, the 13th instant*, A stout NEGRO WENCH, The property of Mrs. Mary Carey, named *Nancy Blond*: She had on a green baize wrapper, a light coloured petticoat, and a bundle of other clothes.

Whoever will bring her to her Mistress at the Rose and Crown, in Queen-street, shall receive Forty Shillings reward. It is ordered she shall be stopped at the Ferry, and all masters of vessels are warned not to take her on board.

615. *The New-Jersey Journal* (Chatham), #211, February 26, 1783.

Six Dollars Reward. RAN away from the subscriber, on the evening of the 10th instant, a negro man named POMP, 37 or 38 years old, about 4 feet 5 inches high, and stout built; had on and took with him a brown coloured fulled linsey coat and great coat, old leather breeches, two pair of yarn stockings, one blue the other black, old shoes, two woollen shirts, a linen coat, linen corded jacket and breeches, and other clothes. Whoever apprehends and secures said negro, so that his master may get him again, shall have the above reward, and all reasonable charges paid, by BETHUEL PIERSON.
Orange, February 25, 1783.

616. *The New-Jersey Journal* (Chatham), #213, March 12, 1783.

RAN away from the subscriber, the 19th of January last, a NEGRO GIRL, named HAGER, about thirteen years of age, likely and strong. Whoever will take up said negro, and bring her to the subscriber, shall be entitled to Three Dollars reward. ELEAZER CAMPBELL.
N. B. All persons are forbid harbouring, employing, or assisting the said girl to keep away from her master.
Springfield, March 11, 1783.

617. *The Royal Gazette* (New York), #675, March 15, 1783.

R U N A W A Y, *From the Subscriber on the 10th instant,* A Mulatto, or Quadroon Girl, about 14 years of age, named Seth, but calls herself Sall, sometimes says she is white and often paints her face to cover that deception; she staid out of her master's house for two or three nights before she went off, and was seen dancing in a house, at or near the old barracks, where, it is probable, she is still lurking.—She

had on when she went off, a red baize jacket, petticoat, and high-heel'd shoes; she has black curled hair, and a large spot of the leprosy on her right side, she is well known in town and particularly at the Fly-Market, for many wicked tricks.——Two Dollars reward will be given to any person who will bring her home, or give information so that she may be found. All Masters of vessels, and others are forewarned not to harbour the said Mulatto Girl, as they shall answer at their peril.
A. A. M'KAY,
No. 27, Maiden Lane.

618. *The New-Jersey Gazette* (Trenton), #275, April 2, 1783.

FIVE DOLLARS REWARD. Ran away from the subscriber living in Monmouth county, and township of Upper Freehold, on the 23d of March inst. a likely young negro man named Cuff, about 19 or 20 years of age, 5 feet 7 or 8 inches high; had on when he went away a black and white mixt coloured coat, butternut coloured jacket, flannel shirt, buckskin breeches, white yarn stockings, shoes half soled, and felt hat. Any person apprehending said negro and securing him, so that the owner may have him again, shall be entitled to the above reward, and reasonable charges, paid by RICHARD JAMES.
March 31, 1783.

619. *The Royal Gazette* (New York), #682, April 9, 1783.

ONE GUINEA REWARD. RUN AWAY, on Sunday the 6th instant, from his Master, a Negro Boy, eighteen years of age, about five feet six inches high, named EBB. Had on when he went off, a Brown Coat, made French fashion, Grey Cloth Jacket, Black Breeches, and a large brimed bound Hat. Whoever takes up said Negro, and returns him to Captain Joshua Pell, in the Bowery, shall be entitled to the

above Reward, and all necessary expences. All masters of vessels are cautioned not to take him away.
New-York, April 9, 1783.

620. *The New-York Gazette: and the Weekly Mercury*, #1643, April 28, 1783.

ONE GUINEA Reward. RUN-away from Mathew Daniel, living at No. 34 Duke-street, a negro boy called DUFF : Had on when he went away, a brown jacket, new fustian trowsers, and a new wool hat. Whoever apprehends said boy, or gives information so that his master may get him again, shall have the above reward. All masters of vessels and others, are forewarned to harbour or conceal said negro boy as they must answer for the same.

621. *The Royal Gazette* (New York), #688, April 30, 1783.

EIGHT DOLLARS REWARD. RUN-AWAY from the Subscriber on the 22d inst. April, a Mulatto Negro Man, named *Sam*, the property of the Subscriber, about 5 feet 9 inches high, well made, and somewhat marked with the small-pox: had on when he went off, a brown short coat and waistcoat, and cloth trowsers, speaks both English and Low Dutch, and formerly lived in Bergen.—Whoever will deliver or secure the said Negro, so that his master may have him again, or to George and Jeronimus Remsen, shall be entitled to the above reward, by applying to Rem H. Remsen, at the Wallabough, Long-Island.

622. *The Royal Gazette* (New York), #691, May 10, 1783.

ONE GUINEA REWARD. RUN AWAY the 19th of April last, from the prize schooner Swan, prize to the polac[ ] Prince William Henry, a negro boy named YORK; he is

about 4 feet 5 inches high, neat built, tawney complexion, round visage, has remarkable small ears, is a cunning smart boy, but much addicted to getting drunk; he has deserted from his master sundry times within these three years past, and has been on board of several of his Majesty's ships, viz. the Adamant, Thames, and Bellisarius frigates, and is now supposed to be on board of some ship in this harbour. All Gentlemen are requested to give notice to the Subscriber if said boy should apply to them for service; and every other person is forwarned to conceal or take him off at their peril.
Peter Creighton.

623. *The Royal Gazette* (New York), #691, May 10, 1783.

FIVE GUINEAS REWARD. RAN-AWAY from the subscriber, on Monday evening the 6th instant, a negro man named JACK; he had on when he went off a check shirt, blue waistcoat, a blue coatee with a red cape, long white trowsers, white stockings, &c. can speak very little English to be understood, stutters much in his speech, is about 23 years of age, has taken soars on his left arm, and a small scar on his nose.

All house keepers are forwarned harbouring him at their peril: Masters of vessels are forbid concealing or carrying him off, as they will be prosecuted to the utmost rigour of the law.
VALENTINE NUTTER.
N. B. Ten Guineas will be given to discover the person who enticed him.

624. *The New-York Gazette: and the Weekly Mercury*, #1647, May 12, 1783.

SIX POUNDS Reward. RUN-away from the subscriber, a negro boy about eighteen years of age, stout and well countenanced, known by the name of Frederick. He was some time waiter upon Col. Webster of the 33d regt. and is supposed to be about this city or on Long-Island. Whoever takes up said boy, and delivers him to Mr. John Vanderhoven, near White Hall, or secures him in goal so that his owner may get him again, shall have the above reward, and all reasonable charges paid. ISAAC COTHEAL.

625. *The Royal Gazette* (New York), #695, May 24, 1783.

FIVE GUINEAS REWARD. WENT off from his master on Thursday night, a Negro Wench, called VIOLET, with her male children, one about 7 years old, called Willis, the other about two years old, named Joe. The Wench is about 26 years old, tall, thin, and somewhat pitted with the small-pox. The youngest boy is rather of a yellow complection. Both boys have lately had their hair or wooll cut short. Whoever apprehends said Negroes, and brings them to the Subscriber's House, at Greenwich, shall have a reward of Five Guineas immediately paid them.
David Campbell.

626. *The Royal Gazette* (New York), #701, June 14, 1783.

ONE GUINEA REWARD. RUN-AWAY, a *Negro Man*, named Cesar, about 26 years old, 5 feet 4 inches high, an honest look, smooth face, a scar over one of his eyes: Had on when he went away, a light coloured cloth waistcoat, without sleeves, white metal hollow buttons, a pair of jean breeches, shoes and stockings, and a half worn white hat: He is well known by carrying bread and biskets about the streets. Whoever gives information where he may be found, shall receive the above reward, from the Subscriber, at No. 23, John's Street.
RICHARD JENKINS.

627. *The Royal Gazette* (New York), #701, June 14, 1783.

RUN-AWAY from the Subscriber, living at No. 110, Water-street, near the New Slip,
 A Negro Girl, named POLL, about 13 years of age, very black, marked with the Small-Pox, and had on when she went away a red cloath petticoat, and a light blue short gown, home made. Whoever wil take up and secure the said Girl, so that the owner may get her, shall be handsomely rewarded by Thomas Brinckley.
New-York, May 28, 1783.

628. *The Royal Gazette* (New York), #703, June 21, 1783.

Ten Dollars Reward. RUN-AWAY on Monday the 9th June, from Long Island, a negro man named JACK, formerly belonged to John Packer, of New-York; had on when he went away a brown coat, red jacket, and leather breeches, with a large flopt hat. Whoever secures the above negro, and delivers him at No. 174, Water-street, shall receive the above reward. All masters of vessels, and others, are hereby forwarned not to harbour or carry off said negro, as they shall answer the same at their peril.

629. *The New-Jersey Gazette* (Trenton), #287, June 25, 1783.

WHEREAS negro Adam still continues to absent himself from the service of the subscriber, in such a manner as that the constables have not been able to take him, after being publickly declared to be the property of the subscriber by a solemn adjudication had on a writ of Habeas Corpus, before the Justices of the Supreme Court: And whereas there is great reason to believe that he is still employed, protected, secreted and encouraged, by the same evil-minded advisers as formerly, having been seen on Tuesday the 17th inst. by different and indifferent creditable witnesses, mowing in the meadow of Nathan Beakes, in company with a young man who lives at his house, and not been heard to abide many minutes in one place since.

This is therefore to forbid all people from harbouring, employing, or dealing with the said negro, and to beg that they woulf apprehend and deliver him to the constable, the gaol-keeper, or to the subscriber in Trenton, give information or encourage him to return to his duty, which will prove much to the advantage of the negro, and they shall be generously rewarded by DAVID COWELL.

630. *The New-York Gazette: and the Weekly Mercury*, #1656, June 29, 1783.

Fifteen Dollars Reward. RUN away on Friday the 13th instant, a negro wench named LUCE, about 30 years of age, middling, or rather low in stature; her right cheek stained of a different colour from her natural black, carries her head remarkably high, and seems to have a difficulty to open her eyes, she is very noisy and quarrelsome in the streets; had on when she went away a green striped fluff gown that has been washed, a dark blue moreen petticoat, a gauze cap and pink ribbons, no hat, she had also with her a dark purple callicoe gown, she commonly goes by the name of Luce Price, from her having formerly lived with Edward Price, the pilot, on Cruger's wharf; she has been seen two or three times since she run away about the streets, the last time at the Fly Market, supposed to be going over the Ferry, where she sometimes used to run, as also to Harlaem and Shrewsbury: It is supposed she is lurking somewhere in this city, and is afraid to come home. Any person who will discover her to her master, at No. 49, the corner next to the Exchange, so that he may apprehend her shall receive the above reward; and if said wench will voluntarily return home, her master will forgive her.—All persons are cautioned not to conceal, harbour, or carry off said wench.

631. *The New-Jersey Gazette* **(Trenton), #288, July 2, 1783.**

Three Pounds R E W A R D. RAN away from the subscriber in Mendham, Morris county, the 25th of May, a negro fellow named Cuff, about 26 years old, five feet ten inches high, has a scar on one of his hands by the cut of an ax, from his little finger knuckle to the third finger, so that it occasions his little finger to stand in to the palm of his hand; had on when he went away a thick coat, black and white wool mixed in the cards, tow shirt and trowsers, new shoes. Whoever takes up said fellow, and secures him in any gaol, so that the owner may have him again, shall receive the above reward, and all reasonable charges by SAMUEL WELLS.
Mendham, June 18, 1783.

632. *The New-Jersey Journal* **(Chatham), #230, July 9, 1783.**

RAN-AWAY from the subscriber at New-Brunswick, the 22d day of June last, a NEGRO MAN named CUFFE, about 24 years of age, five feet six or seven inches high; is a likely fellow, speaks good English, and walks nimbly; had on a light coloured coat and jacket, corduroy breeches, checked shirt, silver shoe and stock buckles. Whoever takes him up, and secures him in gaol, or brings him to his master, shall have one guinea reward, and all reasonable charges paid, by JOHN DUNHAM.
New-Brunswick, July 8, 1783.

633. *The Royal Gazette* **(New York), #708, July 9, 1783.**

ONE GUINEA REWARD. RUN AWAY from Peter Alexander Al[   ], on Saturday the 5th instant, a MULLATTO BOY, named Jack, between 11 and 12 years of age, full and flat faced; had on when he went away, an

Osnaburg shirt and tow trowsers, supposed to be harboured by some free negroes in town. Any person who will apprehend said Negro Boy, and bring him to No. 14, in Wall-Street, shall receive the above reward.

All Masters of Vessels are forwarned to carry him off.
New-York, July 9, 1783,

634. The Royal Gazette (New York), #714, July 30, 1783.

Ran-away from the Subscriber, On the 18th of June last, A NEGRO BOY named JACK, aged about sixteen years.―― Any person taking up said Negro Boy, and delivering him to his Master, shall have one Guinea Reward for his trouble; and also a Reward of Five Guineas for discovering such person or persons, who may have employed, harboured, concealed, or entertained said Negro Boy.
                                          JEROMUS LOTT.
King's-County, July 29, 1783.

635. The Royal Gazette (New York), #715, August 2, 1783.

EIGHT DOLLARS REWARD. RUN-AWAY from the Subscriber, whilst in West-Chester County, New-York State, the 23d of July last, a Negro fellow, named JACK, 26 years old, about five feet high, thick set, he can read and write, and has served as an hostler this some time past to take care of the noted horses, *Pastime* and *Goldfinder*; and it is most likely he will make towards Rhode-Island, as he formerly came from thence: He had on when he went away, an old white short brown jacket, and a pair of striped trousers; a wool hat, bound with white, and cock'd, no shoes nor stockings on. And I desire all Captains of vessels, to beware not to take or receive such fellow on board; and whoever will take up and secure him, so that the owner may get him again, shall have the above reward and all reasonable charges, per me,

DEMAS FORD, or
JOSEPH PURDY.

636. *The Royal Gazette* (New York), #719, August 16, 1783.

RAN-Away a few days ago, a little Negro Boy, had on a blue coat with red cuffs and collar, a pair of fustian trowsers, with buttons all down the sides; he has got marks on the fingers of his left hand like a burn. All Masters of vessels and others, are warned against keeping said Negro, any information of said Boy, will be thankfully received, and all reasonable charges paid. Enquire of Mr. Rivington.
New-York August 15, 1783.

637. *The New-York Gazette: and the Weekly Mercury*, #1661, August 18, 1783.

Eight Dollars Reward. RUN-away on Sunday morning the 3d instant, a tall, stout negro wench and her child; the wench is named LUCY, the child VENUS. The wench is very much pitted with the small pox, and her feet is so large that she is obliged to ware mens shoes. She took with her two short gowns, and two petticoats, one striped bottom short gown and a yellow ground callicoe one; one black petticoat and one other supposed green, either of which she wears. The child had on a tow cloth frock, has a scar on her shoulder, and is about 5 or 6 years old. Her mother is about 28 years. Whoever gives information to the printer so as the owner may have them again, shall receive the above reward.

All persons are forewarned not to conceal, harbour or carry off the said wench and her child, as they will have to answer for it at their peril.

638. The New-York Gazette: and the Weekly Mercury, #1663, September 1, 1783.

Five Dollars Reward a Head, RUN-away from the subscriber, on Saturday the 16th inst. three negro men, who it is likely will keep together; one of them is named William, a slim fellow, 27 years of age, about 5 feet 9 inches high, has a remarkable scar across his nose, speaks very good English and Low Dutch: Had on when he went away an old brown coloured coat, and a blue cloth jacket, a pair of new spotted breeches, and linen stockings. Another fellow goes by the name of Harry, about 5 feet 7 inches high, about 30 years of age, had on a linsey woolsey coat coloured grey, a white jacket of ditto, striped over-hawls, and new shoes; took with him a short pair of white linen breeches. The third is called John, about 39 years of age, 5 feet 8 inches high, well set, has a remarkable scar on his upper lip: Had on a brown cloth coat, a blue cloth jacket, linen breeches, and black trowsers. Whoever secures the above negroes, so that their masters may have them again, shall have the above reward, and all reasonable charges, paid by us, DAVID HASBROUCK, NATHANIEL LEFEVER, ANDRES LEFEVER, jun.
New-Paltz, in Ulster County,
August 18, 1783

639. The Royal Gazette (New York), #726, September 10, 1783.

RUN AWAY, from the Widow Suydain, at Flushing, a negro Wench, named P E G, about twenty years of age, very black, thick set.—Whoever will secure the said Wench, shall receive TWO GUINEAS reward, by the Widow Suydain, and all reasonable charges paid.
September 6, 1783.

640. *The Royal Gazette* (New York), #726, September 10, 1783.

RUN AWAY from the Subscriber, a MULATTO MAN named S A M, had on when he went away, a striped jacket and trowsers, made out of a [ ]; carried off a bag of cloaths, consisting of a red waistcoat, [ ]skin pair of breeches, and two pair of white breeches.—Whoever will bring him to the Subscriber or to William Byron, the Corner of the Fly-Market, by the Ferry-Stairs, will be handsomely rewarded.
EDWARD BARDIN,
Jamaica, Long-Island.

641. *The Royal Gazette* (New York), #727, September 13, 1783.

F I V E P O U N D S Reward. RUN AWAY, about two months ago, a Negro Boy, named GEORGE SCRIBENS, free born, at Craddock Neck, in Acomack County, Virginia, from whence he was brought, with his Father, to this city, about October, 1781.—He is supposed to be gone to Nova-Scotia.——The above reward will be given on the delivery of this Boy to his Master, (to whom he is an indented apprentice.)
SHADRACK FURMAN,
Facing Oswego-market, in the Broad-Way.
The same reward will be given on delivering the Boy to Captain Wheeler, at Port-Roseway, Nova-Scotia.

642. *The Royal Gazette* (New York), #728, September 17, 1783.

ABSCONDED from his MASTER. A NEGRO MAN SLAVE, named JEM, belonging to Mr. Anthony Stewart. This Negro is well known in the City, and goes amongst his Companions by the name of JAMES BUTLER. He is a likely man, about thirty years of age; an exceeding good House Servant, and understands waiting upon a Gentleman.

Whoever apprehends and secures him so as his Master may have him again, shall receive F I V E G U I N E A S Reward, paid by applying to the Printer, or at No. 206, Water-Street.

643. *The Royal Gazette* (New York), #732, October 3, 1783.

A NEGRO GIRL, ABOUT 12 years old, named Madlane, who arrived in this Town yesterday, strayed away, having on a striped Woollen Rapper, dark blue Petticoat, with white flowers, and was bare footed.——Whoever will show her to No. 11, Little Queen-Street, shall have FOUR DOLLARS for their trouble.
October 1, 1783.

644. *The Royal Gazette* (New York), #736, October 15, 1783.

FIVE GUINEAS Reward. RUN AWAY from the Subscriber, from on board the Brig Neptune, RICHARD DAVIS, Master, lying at Murray's Wharf, F E L I X, a Mulatto Man, of a dark complexion, about 5 feet 8 or 9 inches high, stout built, large head and face, with thick short curled hair, has lost some of his fore teeth, is much inclined to drink, and when so, talks very much; he speaks French and English, and professes to be a Barber, Cook and Sailor; no doubt he will change his name, he being an artful fellow.—Whoever will apprehend the said Felix, and deliver him on board the said Brig, or to Mr. Bartholomew Anster, No. 24, Water-Street, or to Mr. Anthony Van Dam, shall receive the above reward.
JACOB HOWELL.

645. The New-York Gazette: and the Weekly Mercury, #1670, October 20, 1783.

FIVE DOLLARS Reward. RUN-away from the Subscriber, on Wednesday last, a negro wench about seventeen years of age. Whoever will apprehend and secure her so that her master may get her again, shall be entitled to the above reward, and all reasonable charges paid, by applying to Gilliam Cornell, opposite to the Fly Market, or the subscriber, at New Town, Long-Island. ISAAC CORNELL.
N.B. All masters of Vessels and others, are hereby warned not to harbour, conceal, or carry off the said wench, as they shall answer it at their peril. Oct. 11, 1783.

646. The New-York Gazette: and the Weekly Mercury, #1672, November 3, 1783.

TWENTY DOLLARS Reward. ESCAPED last night out of the Main Guard, a mulatto man named Thomas, a well set thick fellow, long bushy hair; had on a blue sailors jacket, green under waistcoat, whitish woollen, or oznabrig trowsers. Whoever will apprehend, or give information of him to the Printer, or Mr. *David Berkman*, No. 15 Smith Street, so that he may be taken, shall receive the above reward. All persons are forbid harbouring him, and all masters of vessels from carrying him off, as they may depend on being prosecuted for the same, as he has been guilty of robbing his Master.
New York, October 19th, 1783.

647. The Royal Gazette (New York), #738, October 22, 1783.

FIVE POUNDS REWARD. RUN-AWAY, on Friday 19th September, a NEGRO WENCH, named KATE, born in the family of Jacob Bennet, on Long-Island, has lived with Mr. George Hunter and Ephraim Smith, of this City: She is very stout made, about 5 feet 9 or 10 inches high, of a light black, and likely face, without any particular marks, generally wears her hair very high and straight up, over a roll, with a great deal of pomatum, a great talker and shrill voice; took with her a variety of clothes, among which there was a Callico Short Gown, with the figure of horses, carriages, and soldiers, in blue and yellow colours, particularly a row of the latter round the bottom of it; and several caps, all with long ears. Is supposed to feign the name of Boyle, an Ensign in General De Lancey's corps.

Whoever will apprehend and secure her, so that her master may get her, shall have the above reward, and all reasonable charges paid, by applying to the Printer, or No. 19, Crown-street.

All Masters of vessels and others, are hereby warned not to harbour, conceal, or carry off the said Wench, as they shall answer it at their peril.

648. *The Royal Gazette* (New York), #742, November 5, 1783.

Reward of Twenty Dollars for each. RAN away from the Subscriber, two NEGROES, viz. one went away the 4th of October last, a well-set Fellow, named Cuffey, a Taylor, speaks pretty good English; had on when he went away a brown Surtout-Coat. The other left the Subscriber the 4th of November inst. called Johannis, speaks but little English; had on when he went away a blue and white striped Linen Jacket, with Shoes and Stockings: They are both from St. Croix. Whoever apprehends the said Negroes, or either, shall be entitled to the above Reward, by bringing them to Mr. TOBIAS STOUTENBURG, just behind the main Guard, or to me the Subscriber at the Said Mr. Stoutenburg's.
P. H. LOORBURGH.

649. *The Royal Gazette* (New York), #743, November 8, 1783.

FIVE DOLLARS Reward. RUN-AWAY, on the 3d day of this instant, from his Master, HENRY STANTON, living at Brooklyne, Long-Island, a NEGRO BOY, named JESS: Had on when he went away, a brown homespun coat, vest and breeches, and a red silk handkerchief about his neck, has a great turn at whistling.—Whoever takes up said Negro Boy, and brings him to his Master, shall receive the above Reward.
N. B. All Masters of Vessels are strictly forbid harbouring or carrying off said Negro, at their peril.
HENRY STANTON.
November 7, 1783.

650. *The New-York Gazette: and the Weekly Mercury*, #1673, November 10, 1783.

RUN-AWAY on Tuesday night the 4th instant, from the subscriber at Hampstead, in Queen's county, Long-Island, a negro man slave named ANTHONY, about 35 years old, of a middling stature, a black complexion, very talkative, speaks good English, and pretends to be a preacher, and sometimes officiates in that capacity among the Blacks. Had on when he went away a bearskin great coat, and the rest of the cloaths chiefly of the same kind, and partly worn, and may very likely have changed his clothes. Any person who will apprehend said negro man, and delivers him to the subscriber, or secures him so that his master may have him again, shall receive a reward of FIVE DOLLARS, if taken in Queen's county; and TEN DOLLARS if taken elsewhere to be paid by me.
N. B. All masters of vessels, and others, are hereby forbid to carry him off, &c. S. CLOWES.

651. *The Political Intelligencer and New-Jersey Advertiser* (Trenton), #5, November 11, 1783.

Eight Dollars Reward. RUN-AWAY, two weeks ago, a NEGRO MAN named George, 42 years of age, a small slim made fellow, speaks bad English, a very great liar, he is a regular bred gardener, much addicted to liquor, went off in a drunken fit, leaving all his best cloaths behind him, had on an old short blue coat, and a round hat.—He is the property of a gentleman in this neighbourhood.—If taken within six miles of this place four dollars will be paid, if at a greater distance eight, by JACOB BENJAMIN.
Trenton, November 2, 1783.

652. *The Royal Gazette* (New York), #744, November 12, 1783.

FOUR GUINEAS Reward. ABSCONDED from the Subscriber, a NEGRO WENCH, named FLORA, also a NEGRO MAN, named JAMES, usually called JAMES JACKSON.—The Wench about 44 or 45 years of age, middle size, generally wears striped Homespun.——The Man about 21 years old, rather short, slender make, has bow shins, wears dark brown, turned up with scarlet; plays on the German Flute and Fife.

Any person that apprehends the above Negroes, and delivers them to the Subscriber, shall receive a reward of FOUR GUINEAS, or TWO GUINEAS for either of them.—All Masters of Vessels and others, are forbid to take away said Negroes, or harbour them.
M. BROWNEJOHN,
No. 24, Hanover-Square.
N. B. They may be both in black.

653. The Royal Gazette (New York), #745, November 15, 1783.

TWO GUINEAS Reward. RAN away from the Subscriber, on Sunday the 9th instant, a N E G R O M A N, named PETER, about 5 feet 7 inches high, very black, has a downcast look; had on when he went away a short brown coat, lined with green baize, a double-breasted waistcoat, dark brown, lined with striped linsey woolsey, a pair of red cloth trowsers, quite new, and an old felt hat; and took with him a pair of brown trowsers. Whoever takes up said Negro, and returns him to the subscriber near Brooklyne, on Long-Island, or to Mr. R. S U Y D A M , No. 9, Little Dock-street, shall have the above reward, and all Charges paid.

N. B. All Masters of Vessels and other persons are forbid harbouring said Negro, as they may depend answering for the same at their peril.

654. The Royal Gazette (New York), #745, November 15, 1783.

FIVE DOLLARS Reward. RAN away, on Friday Night last, from the Subscriber, living in East-Jersey, Essex County, a NEGRO LAD, about 19 years of age; a tall, thin built fellow, a little on the yellow cast; had on when he went away a sailor's jacket, with a red one under it. Whoever will take him up, and send him to his Master, living within a few miles of Elizabeth-Town, shall receive the above reward, and all reasonable charges, paid by me,

JOHN ROSS, jun.

November 14, 1783.

655. The Royal Gazette (New York), #746, November 19, 1783.

TEN POUNDS *Reward.* RAN away from the Subscriber, some time ago, a stout young NEGRO MAN, aged 22 years, about 5 feet ten inches high, his name formerly was

NEPTUNE, but now goes by the Name of JOHN NEPTUNE. Any person delivering him at No. 12, in Crown-street, shall be entitled to the above reward.

All Masters of Vessels are forbid carrying him away, as they may depend on being prosecuted, by

THOMAS GUION

New-York, Nov. 17, 1783.

656. *The Royal Gazette* **(New York), #745, November 19, 1783.**

TEN POUNDS Reward. RUN-AWAY from the Subscriber, on Sunday night the 16th inst. a NEGRO WENCH, named ISABEL; had on when she run-away, a short whitish Cloth Cloak, with a hood, about 5 feet 6 inches high, very black colour, speaks pretty thick. She was taken away by her Husband, a Negro Man, called Peter Longster, about 6 feet high, pretty stout, formerly lived with Col. Lutwyche, at Brooklyne-Ferry, Long-Island.—Whoever will secure either of them, or give information to the Subscriber, or to William Bryan, at the Fly-Market Stairs, so that he may get his property again, shall receive the above reward, and all reasonable charges paid.

EDWARD BARDIN,
at Jamaica, Long-Island.

N. B. All Masters of Vessels and others, are hereby forewarned not to harbour them, but at their peril.

657. *The Royal Gazette* **(New York), #745, November 19, 1783.**

TWO GUINEAS Reward. RUN-AWAY from the Subscriber, on the 14th instant, a NEGRO BOY, named HECTOR, about eighteen years of age, four feet six inches high, speaks tolerable good English: Had on when he went away, a round hat, a short coatee, of a light colour, cloth waistcoat, much the same, a watch-coat, with a velvet cape, a coating pair of trowsers, of a grey colour, a pair of white stockings.—He is a well-set fellow.—Whoever secures the said Negro, and brings him to the Subscriber, living near the Provost, in Great George Street, No. 7, shall be entitled to the above reward, and all reasonable charges paid.

N. B. All Masters of Vessels, and others, are forbid taking him off, or concealing him, as they shall answer it at their peril.

PHILIP RUCKEL.

658. *The Political Intelligencer and New-Jersey Advertiser* (Trenton), #7, November 25, 1783.

Five Pounds Reward. RUN-AWAY from the subscriber at Delaware-Mills, Bucks County, and State of Pennsylvania, two NEGROES, the one named JIM, about five feet six or seven inches high, thirty years of age, well made, a smart active fellow, of a yellowish complexion, had on when he went away a light coloured coat with a red cape, brown jacket and overalls—The other a WENCH, wife to Jim, about thirty years of age, small in stature, slow in motion and speech, some scars in her face, had on when she went away a striped linsey petticoat and short-gown; they both have changes of cloaths.—Whoever takes up and secures said Negroes shall have the above reward and reasonable charges paid by MARK BIRD.

November 10, 1783.

659. *Rivington's New-York Gazetteer and Universal Advertiser*, #751, December 6, 1783.

RUN-AWAY from the Subscriber this morning, about nine o'clock, Two Negro Lads, called STEPNEY and PRINCE: The first 20 years of age, about 5 feet 8 inches high, well made genteel fellow, has a small impediment in his speech, red eyes from an inflamation in them, and has taken clothes with him of various kinds, but generally wears a green short coat, a blue under waist-coat, and buck-skin breeches, with a blue surtout-coat, and has been used to wait in a Gentleman's family.—PRINCE is about 5 feet 5 inches high, 17 years of age, has thick lips, and a remarkable large mouth; he is talkative and impudent; had on a pair of blue cloth trowsers, a reddish sailors jacket, and dark brown great coat; he has been used to work at the Ship-Carpenters Business, and understands caulking and mast-making pretty well. It is supposed they have gone on board some vessel immediately bound to sea.

All Masters of vessels are requested not to harbour or take them off. Any person delivering them to Capt. Nicholson, No. 92, William street, shall have Five Guineas Reward for each.

New-York, Dec. 2, 1783.

660. *Rivington's New-York Gazetteer and Universal Advertiser*, #754, December 17, 1783.

TWENTY DOLLARS REWARD. RUN AWAY from the Subscriber, at Yongkers, near Kingsbridge, about two months since, a negro man named YAFF; but goes generally by the nickname of MINK, about 20 years of age, 5 feet 6 inches high, thick set, yellow complexion, a scar upon his cheek, and another upon his forehead, given very much to drink; had on when he went away a blue coat, with a white lining, a clouded velvet waistcoat, and white plush breeches. The above reward will be paid to any person who can give such information that he may be found again, by applying to Edward Huestis, Shoe-maker, the upper end of Queen street, near the Tea-Water Pump, or to the Subscriber.

JESSE HUESTIS.

December 16, 1783.

661. Rivington's New-York Gazetteer and Universal Advertiser, #754, December 17, 1783.

TWO GUINEAS REWARD. RUN-Away from the Subscriber, the 24th day of November last, a likely Negro Woman, named Sarah, brought up in the family of Mr. Deycay, deceased, where she went by the name of Clarender, about thirty years of age; she is pretty tall and slender made, her complexion being very black, has a remarkable wart on her right eye-lash. Had on when she went away, a callicoe short gown, black skirt, and a black hat trimmed with edging, but as she has a great number of good cloaths, which she carried away with her, it is impossible to describe the dress she may now be in. It is supposed, that she is kept concealed somewhere in this city, she having a great many relations and acquaintances here. This is to forewarn all persons from harbouring her, as they will answer it at their peril. Any person who will apprehend the said Negro Woman, and secure her so that her mistress may have her again, shall receive the above reward, paid them by me, living at No. 385, Murray-Street.
ELIZABETH MILLER.
N. B. All Masters of vessels are forewarned not to harbour or carry off the said Negro Woman.

662. Rivington's New-York Gazetteer and Universal Advertiser, #756, December 24, 1783.

ABSCONDED from his Master, since Sunday morning, an INDIAN BOY, of a yellow colour, about 13 years of age, had on a blue short jacket, and trowsers of the same cloth. It is imagined he was inticed away by a white boy, who went about the city offering some gold rings for sale, and said he run away from a ship of war. Whoever will apprehend said Negro Boy, and bring or send him to his Master, at Mr. Stoutenberg's, shall have Four Dollars Reward. All masters of vessels are requested to search for him on board their vessels, and are also forbid carrying him off, under penalty of the law.

Appendix 1
Tables

Table 1

Gender of Fugitive Slaves, 1716–1783

	1716–1740		1741–1750		1751–1760		1761–1775		1776–1783		Total	
	N	%	N	%	N	%	N	%	N	%	N	%
Male	37	92.5	48	87.3	106	92.2	209	91.3	250	79.6	650	86.3
Female	3	7.5	7	12.7	9	7.8	20	8.7	64	20.4	103	13.7
Total	40	100	55	100	115	100	229	100	314	100	753	100

Table 2

Age of Fugitive Slaves, 1716–1783

	1716–1740		1741–1750		1751–1760		1761–1775		1776–1783		Total	
Age	N	%	N	%	N	%	N	%	N	%	N	%
0–15	2	8	1	2.7	4	6	7	4.35	47	21.27	61	11.94
16–25	9	36	21	56.8	36	53.7	73	45.34	114	51.58	253	49.51
26–35	8	32	8	21.6	22	32.8	58	36.02	44	19.91	140	27.40
35+	6	24	7	18.9	5	7.5	23	14.29	16	7.24	57	11.15
Total	25	100	37	100	67	100	161	100	221	100	511	100

Table 3

African-American Population Table for New York and Eastern New Jersey, 1703–1775

New York		Total Population	White (%)	Black (%)	Black Male/Female	Black Ratio Male/Female	Mean Annual % Black Increase
1703	New York	4375	3745 (85.6%)	630 (14.4%)	233/397	59/100	—
	Kings	1912	1569 (82.1%)	343 (17.9%)	207/136	152/100	—
	Queens	4392	3968 (90.3%)	424 (9.7%)	215/209	103/100	—
	Westchester	1946	1709 (87.8%)	198 (10.2%)	124/74	168/100	—
	Richmond	504	407 (80.8%)	97 (19.2%)	64/33	194/100	—
	Total	13129	11398 (86.8)	1692 (13.2)	843/849	99/100	
1723	New York	7248	5886 (81.2)	1362 (18.8)	628/734	86/100	5.81
	Kings	2218	1774 (79.8)	444 (20.2)	254/190	134/100	1.47
	Queens	7191	6068 (84.4)	1123 (15.6)	621/502	124/100	8.24
	Westchester	4409	3961 (89.8)	448 (10.2)	247/201	123/100	6.32
	Richmond	1506	1251 (83.1)	255 (16.9)	150/105	143/100	8.15
	Total	22572	18940 (83.9)	3632 (16.1)	1900/1732	110/100	

1731	New York	8622	7045 (81.7)	1577 (18.3)	785/792	99/100	1.98
	Kings	2150	1658 (77.1)	492 (22.9)	270/222	122/100	1.35
	Queens	7995	6731 (84.2)	1264 (15.8)	702/562	125/100	1.58
	Westchester	6033	5341 (88.5)	692 (11.5)	445/247	180/100	6.81
	Richmond	1817	1513 (83.3)	304 (16.7)	162/142	114/100	2.4
	Total	26617	22288 (83.7)	4329 (16.3)	2364/1965	120/100	
1737	New York	10664	8945 (83.9)	1719 (16.1)	903/816	111/100	1.5
	Kings	2348	1784 (76.0)	564 (24)	294/270	109/100	2.43
	Queens	9059	7748 (85.5)	1311 (14.5)	714/597	120/100	0.62
	Westchester	6745	5894 (87.4)	851 (12.6)	457/394	116/100	3.83
	Richmond	1889	1540 (81.5)	349 (18.5)	184/165	112/100	2.47
	Total	30705	25911 (84.4)	4794 (15.6)	2552/2242	114/100	
1746	New York	11717	9273 (79.1)	2444 (20.9)	1140/1304	87/100	4.69
	Kings	2331	1686 (72.3)	645 (27.7)	339/306	111/100	1.6
	Queens	9640	7996 (82.9)	1644 (17.1)	892/752	119/100	2.82
	Westchester	9235	8563 (92.7)	672 (7.3)	394/278	142/100	−2.33

Table 3 cont.

	Richmond	2073	1691 (81.6)	382 (18.4)	193/189	102/100	1.06
	Total	34996	29209 (83.5)	5787 (16.5)	2958/2829	105/100	
1749	New York	13294	10926 (82.2)	2368 (17.8)	1111/1257	88/100	-1.03
	Kings	2283	1500 (65.7)	783 (34.3)	497/286	174/100	7.13
	Queens	8040	6617 (82.3)	1423 (17.7)	729/594	123/100	-4.47
	Westchester	10703	9547 (89.2)	1156 (10.8)	639/517	124/100	24
	Richmond	2154	1745 (81.0)	409 (19.0)	218/191	114/100	2.37
	Total	36474	30335 (83.2)	6139 (16.8)	3194/2845	112/100	
1756	New York	13040	10768 (82.6)	2272 (17.3)	1140/1138	100/100	-.59
	Kings	2707	1862 (68.8)	845 (31.2)	447/398	112/100	1.13
	Queens	10786	8617 (79.9)	2169 (20.1)	1199/970	124/100	7.49
	Westchester	13257	11919 (89.9)	1338 (10.1)	791/547	145/100	2.24
	Richmond	2132	1667 (78.2)	465 (21.8)	267/198	135/100	1.96
	Total	41922	34833 (83.1)	7089 (16.9)	3844/3251	118/100	
1771	New York	21863	18726 (85.7)	3137 (14.3)	1500/1637	92/100	2.54

	Total Population	White (%)	Black (%)	Male/Female (Black)	Black Ratio Male/Female	Mean Annual % Increase Black
Kings	3623	2461 (67.9)	1162 (32.1)	606/556	109/100	2.5
Queens	10980	8744 (79.6)	2236 (20.4)	1156/1080	107/100	0.21
Westchester	21745	18315 (84.2)	3430 (15.8)	1777/1653	108/100	10.43
Richmond	2847	2253 (79.1)	594 (20.9)	351/243	144/100	1.85
Total	61058	50499 (82.7)	10559 (17.3)	5390/5169	104/100	
New Jersey						
1715 New Jersey	22500	21000 (93.3)	1500 (6.7)			—
1726 Bergen	2673	2181 (81.6)	492 (18.4)	273/219	125/100	—
Essex	4230	3922 (92.7)	308 (7.3)	162/145	112/100	—
Middlesex	4009	3706 (92.4)	303 (7.6)	163/140	116/100	—
Monmouth	4879	4446 (91.1)	433 (8.9)	258/175	147/100	—
Somerset	2271	1892 (83.3)	379 (16.7)	213/166	128/100	—
Total	18062	16147 (89.4)	1915 (10.6)	1069/845	127/100	

Table 3 cont.

Year	County						
1738	Bergen	4095	3289 (80.3)	806 (19.7)	443/363	122/100	5.32
	Essex	7019	6644 (94.7)	375 (5.3)	198/177	112/100	1.82
	Middlesex	4764	4261 (89.4)	503 (10.6)	272/231	118/100	5.5
	Monmouth	6086	5431 (89.2)	655 (10.8)	362/293	124/100	4.28
	Somerset	4505	3773 (83.8)	732 (16.2)	425/307	138/100	7.76
	Total	26469	23398 (88.4)	3071 (11.6)	1700/1371	124/100	
1745	Bergen	3006	2390 (79.5)	616 (20.5)	379/237	160/100	-3.37
	Essex	6988	6543 (93.6)	445 (6.4)	244/201	121/100	2.67
	Middlesex	7612	6733 (88.5)	879 (11.5)	483/396	122/100	10.69
	Monmouth	8627	7728 (89.6)	899 (10.4)	513/386	133/100	5.33
	Somerset	3239	2896 (89.4)	343 (10.6)	194/149	130/100	-7.59
	Total	29472	26290 (89.2)	3182 (10.8)	1813/1369	132/100	

Source: Evarts B. Greene & Virginia D. Harrington, *American Population Before the Federal Census of 1790* (New York, 1932), 88–112; Peter O. Wacker, *Land & People, A Cultural Geography of Preindustrial New Jersey: Origins and Settlements.* (New Brunswick, NJ, 1975), 189–205.

Table 4

Origin and Destination of Runaways

Origins	1716–1750	1751–1760	1761–1775	1776–1783	Total
Rural NJ	38	39	95	87	259
Rural NY	18	39	41	61	159
New York City	19	30	53	153	255
Ship	2	3	4	16	25
Other	2	1	17	14	34
Total	79	112	210	331	732
Destinations					
New York City	—	—	—	—	—
From NYC	—	3	7	12	22
Outside NYC	—	—	8	8	16
Rural NY	2	—	4	5	11
New Jersey	—	2	6	6	14
Sea	1	3	2	10	16
New England	—	4	—	—	4
Indians	—	2	2	1	5
Pennsylvania	1	—	4	3	8
Military	1	—	—	26	27
Total	5	14	33	71	123

Table 5

Month of Escape by Runaways

	1716–1740	1741–1750	1751–1760	1761–1775	1776–1783	Total (%)
January	3	—	7	4	11	25 (4.99)
February	—	1	4	7	13	25 (4.99)
March	—	—	8	6	14	28 (5.59)
April	—	2	2	7	20	31 (6.19)
May	2	5	11	16	16	50 (9.98)
June	4	5	12	18	22	61 (12.18)
July	3	6	7	16	20	52 (10.38)
August	4	5	9	19	27	64 (12.77)
September	1	2	5	24	11	43 (8.58)
October	1	5	5	14	22	47 (9.38)
November	3	2	6	10	20	41 (8.18)
December	—	—	9	11	14	34 (6.79)
Total	21	33	85	152	210	501 (100.00)

Table 6

Listed Skills of Runaways

Skills	1716–1740	1741–1750	1751–1760	1761–1775	1776–1783	Total
Runaways with listed skills	12	7	26	34	44	123
Musician	4	4	14	19	10	51
Fiddler	4	4	14	15	7	44
Other	0	0	0	4	4	8
Servant/Housekeeper	—	—	3	14	12	29
Sailor/Privateer	1	—	4	3	10	18
Husbandry/Farming	1	1	2	6	2	12
Carpenter	4	1	1	1	5	12
Metalsmith	1	—	3	2	2	8
Cooper	3	—	2	—	3	8

Table 6 cont.

Soldier	—	—	1	—	4	5
Cunning Person*	1	—	1	3	—	5
Baker	—	1	—	—	2	3
Caulker	—	—	1	—	2	3
Gardener	—	—	—	1	1	2
Preacher	1	—	—	—	1	2
Chimney Sweeper	—	1	—	1	—	2
Shoemaker	—	—	1	1	—	2
Taylor	—	—	—	1	1	2
Butcher	1	—	—	—	—	1
Shipwright	1	—	—	—	—	1
Wheelwright	1	—	—	—	—	1
Mason	—	1	1	—	—	1
Weaver	—	—	1	—	—	1

Longshoreman	—		1	
Grist Miller	—		1	
Watchmaker	—		1	
Potash Maker	—		1	
Mast maker	—		—	1
Glazier	—		—	1
Hangman	—		—	1
Sailmaker	—		—	1
Total Skills	19	8	35	56	59	177

* Doctor, Dentist, Magician, Mathematician, Slight of hand tricks

Table 7

Escape Strategies of Runaways

	1716–1750	1751–1760	1761–1775	1776–1783	Total
Has old pass	—	4	2	4	10
Forged pass	1	3	17	3	24
Pretends to be free	—	13	17	11	41
Stolen goods					
Clothing	3	7	7	13	30
Horses	2	1	2	4	9
Guns	—	1	3	—	4
Money	1	4	2	1	8
Dogs	—	1	1	—	2
Jewelry	—	—	—	2	2
Boat	4	1	2	3	10
Food	—	1	—	—	1
Travelling with other slave	1	9	16	23	49
With white indentured servant	3	4	3	1	11
Total	15	49	72	65	201

Table 8

Linguistic Capabilities of Fugitive Slaves

	1716–1750		1751–1760		1761–1775		1776–1783		Total	
	Well	Poorly	Well	Poorly	Well	Poorly	Well	Poorly	Well	Poorly
Dutch	1	—	—	—	4	5	2	—	7	5
English	19	2	18	3	35	27	21	10	93	42
Both	6	—	11	—	26	—	7	—	50	—
French	—	—	3	—	10	—	3	—	16	—
Spanish	—	—	2	—	6	—	—	—	8	—
African	3	—	1	—	—	—	1	—	5	—
Indian	4	—	—	—	1	—	—	—	5	—
German	—	—	—	—	1	—	2	—	3	—
Literate	4	—	6	—	10	—	3	—	23	—
Negro Dutch	—	—	—	—	—	—	1	—	1	—
Total	37	2	41	3	93	32	40	10	211	47

Table 9

Master's Comments on Slave Appearance and Personality

	1716–1750	1751–1760	1761–1775	1775–1783	Total
Appearance					
Black	4	5	14	24	47
Mulatto	13	8	9	17	47
Yellow	5	3	11	10	29
Indian	8	3	3	3	17
Scarred	2	7	27	18	54
Pock-marked	9	7	22	13	51
Disabled	4	6	12	8	30
Missing Teeth	2	2	5	7	16
Total Appearance	47	41	103	100	291
Personality					
Bold	—	1	2	5	8
Down Look	2	2	4	5	13
Smooth-tongued	1	3	4	4	12
Stutters	—	—	2	4	6
Smoker	—	2	1	1	4
Drinker	1	—	6	11	18
Total Personality	4	8	19	30	61

Appendix 2
Hues and Cries

A warrant for a Negroe run away

Sept. 26 Whereas Thomas Mathews of Yarmouth in New England, hath had a Negroe Servant run away from him lately from this place, These are to require and comand all persons within my Government to bee ayding and assisting to him the said Thomas Mathews, or his Assignes in finding out the said Negroe, and if hee shall bee found in any of your parts to seize upon him and cause him to bee sent or secure him and send word thereof unto Thomas Powell at Huntington on long Island, who hath order to pay all necessary Expences or charges relataing thereunto; And all neighboring Colonyes are likewise desired that the like order may bee taken throughout their Jurisdictions, Given under my hand at Fort James in New Yorke etc. Sept. 26.1664.

R. Nicholls.

The Negroe is a lusty young fellow about 20: years of Age, hee was cloathed in a red wastecoate, with a sad colour'd cloath Coate over it, a paire of linen breeches, somewhat worne, and a grey felt hat, but no shoes or stockings.

To all Constables or other officers whom these may concerne, beginning at West Chester to bee sent with dispatch to all other places along the Coast, without any lett or stop whatsoever.

Another warrant to the same effect was sent through Long Island.

A warrant for Mr. Stuyvesants 4 Negore servants lost.

Oct. 6th.

Whereas Complaint is made by Mr. Peter Stuyvesant, that hee hath lost 4 Negroes (men servants) These are therefore to desire you to bee ayding and assisting to the bearer or bearers hereof in the apprehending the said Negroes and to cause them to bee brought with safety to New Yorke upon the Manhatans, where they shall receive full satisfaction for their labour and charge, Given under my hand this 6th day of Oct. 1664 At Fort James in New Yorke etc.

R. Nicholls.

To all Governors, Deputy Governors Magistrates and other Officers whatsoever, in any of his Majestyes Colonyes in America, and all others to whom these presents shall come.

Hue and Crye after a Negroe

Whereas there is lately a Negroe servant runn away from his Masters service and supposed to bee gone your way toward New England. These are to require all persons within this Government and to desire all others if the said Negroe can bee found within your libertyes orprecincts that you forthwith seize upon and secure him, and cause him to bee safely conveyed to this place, or to his Master Daniel Tourneur at Haerlam upon this Island. Given under my hand at Fort James in New Yorke this 28 day of June 1669

To the Constable of West Chester to be sent forward if occasion require

The Negroe is bigge and tall about 25 or 26 yeare old and went away from his Master 4 or 5 days since.

[HUE AND CRY AFTER JACOB, RUNAWAY SLAVE OF SWEER TEUNISSEN OF SCHENECTADY]

You are hereby Required in his Majesties name to Persue and follow after with all speed a negro man about 25 Yeares of age, not Very Taal but of a Very dark Complexion, haveing a dark Colloured Serge Coat, with Pocketts before, and an old Coat of Light Colloured Serge, and dark Collourd Breeches, a half wore gray hatt buttond up on one Side, he Speakes good English and Dutch, and can read Dutch, he Speakes good Maquase and Mahikanders Indian Langadge his name is Jacob, he Runn away from his Master Sweer Teunise of Schinnechtady the 22th of August Last, and if any man or Person can bring him to his Master, or Tydings where he is, hee or they that shall doe the Same whither Christian or Indian Shall have Sufficient Reward for his or there Paines to ther Content. And hereof you are not to fail upon your Perrills given under our handes in our Court hall of albany this 2d day of September 1679

To all his Majesties officers both Civill and Militare or others whom these may Concerne

Dirk Wesselsz
Corn Van Dyck

[ENDORSED:] Albany
Hue and Cry
against
A Negro

[HUE AND CRY AFTER SEVERAL ESCAPED PRISONERS AND RUNAWAY SERVANTS (PARTLY FROM MSS INDEX)]

[   ]mander in Cheife.

[   ]reas nicholas Hardwall a Prisoner in [   ] of this City on Suspicion of Fellony Robert [Weefer] A

Runnaway Servant and two Negro men Like [   ]ken up as Runnaways the one Called Joseph Savig[ ] other Robert Scary and Prisoners in the Said Together with A Negro Man Called Peter another [ ]egro Man Called Cane and the other Negro Men called [ ]bram. a Negro woman Called Elizabeth and a Negro Boy Called Peter all Slaves belonging to Severall persons in this Citty are Runnaway and Absented themselves From their Masters Service and taken with them an open Boate And SOme Provissions and Neccessaryes. These are therefore in his Majesties name to Require and Command you to make Huee and Cry Dilligent Search and Enquiry [   ] Fresh Persuite after the said Prisoners and Negroes both by Land and by Water and if theey or any or Either of them Cann be Found that you Cause them to be Apprehended Secured and Safely Conveyed to the Sherrife of [E33:8] [several lines lost]

[   ] Mr. Robert Alding or any others to whom this Shall Come.

[A mittimus for Severall R[un]awayes.

By the commander in Cheife.

Forasmuch as Robert Spencer Godfrey W[   ]ward Samll. Streete Tho: Lane and A Negro boy Called Charles who were Lately taken up at Sea in A small Sch[   ] or Yoale by A Sloope bound from Delleware to this Po[   ] And braught in here have on their Examinacion Confes[   ] [E33:67] [2 lines lost] RObert Spencer who app[   ] or and Contriver therein. [   ] Majesties name to Require and Co[   ]our Custody the Bodyes of the s[   ]oodward   Samll. Streete Thomas [   ] Boy and them Safely keepe [   ] them forthcomeing when Required [   ] Authority and for soe Doeing this Shall be your warrant [   ]ven under my hand in New Yorke this 23th Day of Jun[ ]683.

[   ]pt. John Colier Sheriffe   A:B:
[   ] the Citty of New Yorke.

Sources of Hues and Cries

State Library Bulletin History, #2, May 1899: Colonial Records of New York, General Entries, 1664-1665 (Albany, 1899), 122 and "New York State Library Miscellaneous Manuscripts," 101 vols. New York State Library, XXVIII, 127, 129, 142; XXXVIII, 3; XXXV, 113. For other hues and cries see Peter Christoph, et al. eds. *The Andros Papers 1674-1688: Files of the Provincial Secretary of New York During the Administration of Governor Sir Edmund Andros, 1674-1688.* 3 vols. Syracuse, N.Y.: Syracuse University Press, 1989-1991. II, 189, 191-192, 200, 202, 204; III, 140-141, 440 and Christoph, ed. *New York Historical Manuscripts: English. Books of General Entries of the Colony of New York, 1664-1673.* 2 vols. Baltimore, Genealogical Publishing Co., 1982, II, 250, 277, 279.

Glossary

This glossary serves as a brief introduction to the innumerable references to clothing fashions and local idioms used in the runaway advertisements. Because the authors of the ads used phonetic spellings and regional variations freely, we have included the correct spellings, accompanied by versions used in the notices. Definitions are drawn from Elisabeth McClellan, *Historic Dress 1607 to 1800*, London: John Lane: the Bodley Head, 1896; Billy G. Smith and Richard Wojtowicz, *Blacks Who Stole Themselves: Advertisements for Runaways in the Pennsylvania Gazette, 1728-1790*, Philadelphia: University of Pennsylvania Press, 1989, 179-83; Peter F. Copeland, *Working Dress in Colonial and Revolutionary America*, Westport, Ct.: Greenwood Press, 1977; Richard M. Lederer, Jr. *Colonial American English: A Glossary*. Essex, Conn.: A Verbatim Book, 1985; *The Canting Academy; or Villanies Discovered ... A Compleat Canting Dictionary, ...* 2nd. ed. London: Printed by F. Leach, for Mat. Drew, 1788, and the *Oxford English Dictionary*, Compact Edition. 2 vols., New York: Oxford University Press, 1971.

Baize: A coarse woollen material with a long nap.

Beaver: the fur of the rodent, used generally in making hats. Can also refer to a heavy woollen cloth like beaver fur.

Brevet: a rank in the army, without the appropriate pay.

Britches (breeches): Short trousers, especially fastened below the knee. Early colonists wore breeches of dressed leather; later they were made of every material.

Broadcloth: A fine wollen cloth with a smooth surface, mostly used for men's garments and always regarded with respect by the lower classes.

Buckskin: Leather made from a buck's skin; may also refer to a thick smooth cotton or woollen cloth.

Callimanco: A glazed linen fabric showing a pattern on one side only; described by some writers as a fashionable woolen material with a fine gloss.

Camlet (chamblet): A fabric made of wool or silk, sometimes of both, much used for cloaks and petticoats. Name derived from the place of manufacture on the River Camlet in England.

Cassimir: A thin, twilled woolen cloth used for making men's clothes. From Kashmir, India.

Castor hat: Refers to a hat made of beaver skin or another animal. As rabbit fur and other substitutes were employed in hat manufacture, the term *castor* came to be used to distinguish such models from true beaver hats.

Chintz: Cotton printed in several colors.

Chitterling: A frill on the breast of a shirt. Such a frill resembled the mesentery which connects the intestines to the abdominal cavity.

Clocks: The plaits of a ruff, also ornaments on stockings.

Damascus: A fabric woven in elaborate patterns of silk, wool, or linen.

Dimity: A fine ribbed cotton fabric made first in Damietta, used throughout the colonial period.

Dowles (dowlas): A heavy linen originally from Brittany.

Drugget: A fabric of wool used for heavy coats.

Duck: A strong linen fabric without a twill.

Duffil (duffel): A woolen stuff originally made in Flanders, used in the colonies after 1672.

Duroy: A variety of coarse woolen cloth produced in the west of England — but not synonymous with corduroy.

Everlast: A sturdy woolen material used in clothing, especially ladies' shoes.

Fearnought (fearnothing, fearnot): A heavy woolen material often used in harsh weather aboard ships as protective outer wear.

Felt: A fabric made of wool and hair.

Ferret: A narrow ribbon or tape of cotton or silk; used mainly for binding, such as buttonholes.

Firkin: a small cask for liquids, butter, or fish; about eight or nine gallons.

Frize (freize): A thick and warm woolen cloth in use since the fourteenth century.

Frock: a long gown with loose sleeves.

Fustian: A species of cloth, originally made at Fusht on the Nile, used for jackets and doublets as early as the fifteenth century. It has a warp of linen thread and a woof of thick cotton.

Fuzee: An American variant of fusee, a large-headed match for lighting a fire in the wind.

Gad: A cut on the ear of cattle or a slave as a sign of ownership.

Gaol: Variant spelling of jail.

Garlix: A sort of linen fabric originally from Gorlitz, Silesia.

Grogham: A rough fabric of silk and wool with a diagonal weave. Often used by country women to make gowns.

Guinea cloth: Coarse woollen cloth used for slaves.

Half joe: Slang for a Portuguese coin, the Johannes.

Heckling: The splitting and separating of flax and hemp fibers.

High Dutch: An eighteenth-century term for German.

Holland: A linen fabric named after the Netherlands' province of Holland, from which it originates.

Homespun: Any cloth made of homespun yarn.

Howell-hovel: A plane with a convex side, used by coopers for smoothing the insides of casks.

Inst. (Instant): The current calendar month.

Jockey cap: A cap with a peaked front and round crown, usually decorated with a ribbon around the crown.

Joseph: A lady's riding habit buttoned down the front. When worn open this garment was popularly called a "flying Josie."

Kersey: A fine woolen material.

Linsey Woolsey (lincey): A coarse woolen stuff first made at Linsey in Suffolk, England and very popular in the colonies.

Logwood: An Indian tree, producing a substance used in dyeing.

Low Dutch: Referred to the Germans along the sea coast and the northern and northwestern flatlands, including the Netherlands and Flanders.

Lugs: Ear lobes; wattles.

Maccaroni: A nickname for a London fop, satirically based on a pretentious craving for the Italian dish. Refers to hair or hats shaped like the noodle.

Manchester velvet: A fine cotton used in making dresses.

Nankeen: A cotton cloth of a yellow color imported from China and named for Nankin where it was made.

Nap: Initially describing the projecting fibers found on fabric surfaces, the term subsequently described the purposeful raising of short fibers on the surface of a textile followed by trimming and smoothing.

N.B.: The abbreviation for *nota bene*, which means to pay particular attention to what follows.

Negro Dutch: A dialect composed of Dutch and a variety of African tongues.

Ozenbrig (oznaburg, oznabrig): A coarse linen made in Hanover and named for a province of that name. The commonest material purchased for slave clothing.

Pea jacket: A stout, short overcoat of coarse woollen cloth, now commonly worn by sailors.

Pomatum: An unguent used mainly for hair dressing; pomade.

Penniston: A coarse woolen stuff made in England.

Pettycoat: A woman or girl's skirted undergarment hanging from the waist or shoulders. Worn universally and made of every sort of material.

Piece of Eight: The Spanish peso of eight *reals*.

Pinchbeck: a piece of cheap jewellery.

Pistole: A Spanish coin, worth four pieces of eight.

Plush: A cloth comprised of silk, cotton, or other materials, alone or in s ome combination, with a nap longer and softer than velvet.

Pothook: a hook over a hearth for hanging a pot.

Prunella: A light-weight stuff used for clergyman's gowns, usually in a dark color.

Pumps: A shoe with a thin sole and low heel, often worn by seamen as part of their shoregoing finery.

Ratteen: A heavy woolen material something like drugget.

Russet: A twilled woolen stuff like baize, common in the colonies.

Russia duck: A fine, imported bleached linen used for summer clothing.

Sagathee: A durable woolen stuff.

Sartout (surtout): A man's greatcoat or large overcoat.

Shag: A heavy woolen cloth with a long nap.

Shalloon: A woolen fabric not unlike modern challis and made in Chalons, France.

Stroud: A coarse blanket cloth. From Stroud, in Gloucestershire, England.

Stuff: Textiles in general, and especially a lustrous, English fabric of cotton or wool.

Swanskin: A fine type of flannel, thick and warm.

Thickset: A material possessing a close-grained nap.

Tow: The short fibers of flax or hemp which are separated from the longer ones by heckling.

Thrumb'd: to make or cover with thrums, the unwoven end of a warp-thread, or the whole of such ends, left when the finished web is cut away.

Ultimo: The last or previous month.

Watch coat: A stout coat or cloak worn in inclement weather.

Wherry: A light rowing boat used chiefly on rivers to carry passengers and goods. A large boat of the barge kind.

Waistcoat: An underjacket or a vest.

Whitney: A heavy coarse stuff used for coats, cloaks, and petticoats.

Wilton: A type of cloth named after a town in southern England.

Worsted: A woolen cloth first made at Worstead, England.

Selected Bibliography

Unpublished Primary Sources

Emmet Collection, New York Public Library.

New York State Library Historical Documents, 101 vols., New York State Library.

Parish Transcripts, New-York Historical Society.

Printed Primary Sources

Brodhead, John Romeyn, comp; O'Callaghan, E.B. and B. Fernow, eds. *Documents Relating to the Colonial History of the State of New York*. 15 vols. Albany, N.Y.: Weed, Parsons, 1856–87.

The Canting Academy; or Villanies Discovered ... A Compleat Canting Dictionary, ... 2nd. ed. London: Printed by F. Leach, for Mat. Drew, 1788.

Christoph, Peter. et. al. eds. *The Andros Papers 1674-1688: Files of the Provincial Scretary of New York During the Administration of Governor Sir Edmund Andros, 1674–1688*. 3 vols. Syracuse, N.Y.: Syracuse University Press, 1989–1991.

Christoph, Peter, and Christoph, Florence C. *New York Historical Manuscripts: English. Books of General Entries of the Colony of New York, 1664–1673 ...* 2 vols. Baltimore: Genealogical Publishing Co., 1982.

Colonial Laws of New York from the Year 1664 to the Revolution. 5 vols., Albany, N.Y.: James B. Lyon, 1894–96.

Davis, T. J. ed., *The New York Conspiracy by Daniel Horsmanden*, Boston: Beacon Press, 1971.

"Eighteenth-Century Slaves as Advertised by their Masters," *Journal of Negro History* 1 (1916): 163–216.

Minutes of the Common Council of the City of New York, 1765–1776. 8 vols. New York: Dodd, Mead and Company, 1905.

Nelson, William. *Documents Related to the Colonial History of the State of New Jersey (New Jersey Archives)*, "Extracts from American Newspapers Relating to New Jersey, 1704–1775," 11 vols. Paterson, N.J.: The Press Printing and Publishing Company, 1894–1923.

O'Callaghan, E.B. ed. *Calendar of Historical Manuscripts: English.* 2 vols. Albany, N.Y.: Weed, Parsons, 1865.

_____ . *Laws and Ordinances of New Netherland, 1638–1674.* Albany, N.Y.: Weed, Parsons, 1868.

State Library Bulletin History, #2, May 1899: Colonial Records of New York, General Entries, 1664–1665. Albany, N.Y.: University of the State of New York, 1899.

Stryker, William S. *Documents Related to the Colonial History of the State of New Jersey (New Jersey Archives)*, "Extracts from American Newspapers Relating to the History of New Jersey," 2nd ser. 5 vols., Trenton: John L. Murphy Publishing and State Gazette Publishing Company, 1901–1917.

Secondary Sources

Andrews, William. *To Tell A Free Story: The First Century of Afro-American Autobiography, 1760–1865.* Urbana, Il.: University of Illinois Press, 1986.

Aptheker, Herbert. *American Negro Slave Revolts.* New York: Columbia University Press, 1943.

_____ . *To Be Free: Studies in American Negro History.* New York: International Publishers, 1948.

Archdeacon, Thomas F. *New York City, 1664–1710 Conquest and Change.* Ithaca, N.Y.: Cornell University Press, 1976.

Bastide, Roger. *The African Religions of Brazil: Toward a Sociology of the Interpenetration of Civilizations.* Baltimore, Md.: Johns Hopkins University Press, 1978.

Bauer, Raymond and Alice. "Day-to-Day Resistance to Slavery." *Journal of Negro History* 27 (1942), 388–420.

Beckles, Hilary. *White Servitude and Black Slavery in Barbados, 1627–1715.* Knoxville, Tenn.: University of Tennessee Press, 1989.

Berlin, Ira. "Time, Space, and the Evolution of Afro-American Society in British Mainland North America," *American Historical Review*, 85 (1980), 44–78.

Bolster, William J. "African-American Seamen: Race, Seafaring Work, and Atlantic Maritime Culture, 1750–1860." Ph. D. diss., Johns Hopkins University, 1991.

Brigham, Clarence. *History and Bibiliography of American Newspapers, 1690–1820.* 2 vols., Worcester, Mass.: American Antiquarian Society, 1947.

Cohen, David Steven. *The Dutch-American Farm.* New York: New York University Press, 1992.

Cooley, Herbert. *A Study of Slavery in New Jersey.* Baltimore, Md.: Johns Hopkins University Press, 1896.

Copeland, Peter F. *Working Dress in Colonial and Revolutionary America.* Westport, Ct.: Greenwood Press, 1977.

Creel, Margaret Washington. *"A Peculiar People" Slave Religion and Community-Culture Among the Gullahs.* New York: New York University Press, 1988.

Dillon, Merton. *Slavery Attacked: Southern Slaves and Their Allies, 1619–1865.* Baton Rouge, La.: Louisiana State University Press, 1990.

Ekirch, Roger. *Bound for America: The Transportation of British Convicts to the Colonies, 1718–1775.* Oxford, U.K.: The Clarendon Press, 1987.

Fields, Barbara Jeanne. *Slavery and Freedom on the Middle Ground: Maryland during the Nineteenth Century.* New Haven, Ct.: Yale University Press, 1985.

Fishman, George. "The Struggle for Freedom and Equality. African-Americans in New Jersey, 1624–1849/1850." Ph.D. diss. Temple University, 1990.

Flynn, J. K. *Asante and its Neighbors, 1700–1807.* Chicago: University of Chicago Press, 1971.

Foote, Thelma. "Black Life in Colonial Manhattan." Ph.D. diss. Harvard University, 1991.

Frey, Sylvia. *Water from the Rock: Black Resistance in a Revolutionary Age.* Princeton, N.J.: Princeton University Press, 1991.

Gaspar, David Barry. *Bondsmen and Rebels, A Study of Master-Slave Relations in Antigua with Implications for Colonial British America.* Baltimore, Md.: Johns Hopkins University Press, 1985.

Genovese, Eugene. *From Rebellion to Revolution: Afro-American Slave Revolts and the Making of the Modern World.* Baton Rouge, La.: Louisiana State University Press, 1979.

Goebel, Julius and Naughton, T. Raymond. *Law Enforcement in Colonial New York, A Study in Criminal Procedure (1664–1776).* New York: The Commonwealth Fund, 1944.

Goodfriend, Joyce D. *Before the Melting Pot: Society and Culture in Colonial New York City, 1664–1730.* Princeton, N.J.: Princeton University Press, 1992.

_____. "Burghers and Blacks: The Evolution of a Slave Society at New Amsterdam." *New York History* (1978), 125–44.

Greenberg, Douglas. *Crime and Law Enforcement in the Colony of New York, 1691–1776.* Ithaca, N.Y.: Cornell University Press, 1974.

Evarts B. Greene & Virginia D. Harrington, *American Population Before the Federal Census of 1790* (New York, 1932), 88–112.

Greene, Lorenzo. "The New England Negro as Seen in Advertisements for Runaway Slaves," *Journal of Negro History* 29 (1944): 125–46.

Higgenbotham, A. Leon. *In the Matter of Color, Race & the American Legal Process: The Colonial Period.* New York: Oxford University Press, 1978.

Higham, Barry. *Slave Populations of the British Caribbean, 1807–1834.* Baltimore, Md.: Johns Hopkins University Press, 1984.

Heuman, Gad, ed. *Out of the House of Bondage: Runaways, Resistance and Marronage in Africa and the New World.* London: Cass Publishers, 1986.

Hodges, Graham R. *African-Americans in Monmouth County During the Age of the American Revolution.* Lincroft, N.J.: Monmouth County Parks System, 1990.

_____ . *African-Americans in Monmouth County New Jersey: 1784–1860.* Lincroft, N.J.: Monmouth County Parks System, 1992.

_____ . *Black Resistance in Colonial and Revolutionary Bergen County, New Jersey.* River Edge, N.J.: Bergen County Historical Society, 1989.

_____ . "Black Revolt in New York City and the Neutral Zone: 1775–83," in Gilje, Paul A. and Pencak, William, eds. *New York in the Age of the Constitution.* Cranburry, N.J.: Associated University Presses, 1992: 20–47.

_____ . *Root and Branch: African-Americans in New York and East-Jersey, 1613–1863,* forthcoming.

Johnson, Michael P. "Runaway Slaves and the Slave Communities in South Carolina, 1799 to 1830," *William and Mary Quarterly,* 3rd ser., vol. 38, (1981): 418–41.

Jones, Norrece T. Jr. *Born a Child of Freedom Yet a Slave: mMechanisms of Control and Strategies of Resistance in Antebellum South Carolina.* Hanover, N.H. and London: Wesleyan University Press, 1990.

Leaming, Hugo. "Hidden Americans: Maroons of Virginia and South Carolina." Ph.D. diss. University of Illinois at Chicago, 1979.

Lederer, Richard M. Jr. *Colonial American English: A Glossary.* Essex, Conn.: A Verbatim Book, 1985.

Linebaugh, Peter. *The London Hanged: Crime and Civil Society in the Eighteenth Century.* New York: Cambridge University Press, 1992.

Littlefield, Daniel C. *Rice and Slaves: Ethnicity and Slave Trade in Colonial South Carolina.* Baton Rouge, La.: Louisiana State University Press, 1981.

Lydon, James T. "New York and the Slave Trade, 1700–1774." *William and Mary Quarterly,* 3rd. ser. 35 (1978), 375–95.

McClellan, Elisabeth. *Historic Dress 1607 to 1800.* London: John Lane: The Bodley Head, 1896.

McManus, Edgar J. *A History of Negro Slavery in New York.* Syracuse, N.Y.: Syracuse University Press, 1966.

_____. *Black Bondage in the North.* Syracuse, N.Y.: Syracuse University Press, 1973.

Meaders, Daniel. *Dead or Alive: Fugitive Slaves and Indentured Servants before 1800.* New York: Garland Publishers, 1993.

_____. "South Carolina Fugitives as Viewed Through Local Newspapers with Emphasis on Runaway Notices," *Journal of Negro History* 40 (1975): 288–319.

Miller, Joseph C. *Way of Death: Merchant Capitalism and the Angolan Slave Trade, 1730–1830.* Madison, Wis.: University of Wisconsin Press, 1989.

Moss, Simeon. "The Persistence of Slavery and Involuntary Servitude in a Free State (1685–1900)." *Journal of Negro History* 45 (1950), 289–314.

Mullin, Gerald W. *Africa in America: Slave Acculturation and Resistance in the American South and the British Caribbean, 1736–1831.* Urbana, Ill.: University of Illinois Press, 1992.

_____. *Flight and Rebellion: Slave Resistance in Eighteenth-Century Virginia.* New York: Oxford University Press, 1972.

Narrett, David E. *Inheritance and Family Life in Colonial New York City.* Ithaca, NY.: Cornell University Press, 1992.

Nash, Gary B. *Forging Freedom: The Formation of Philadelphia's Black Community, 1720–1840.* Cambridge, Mass.: Harvard University Press, 1988.

_____. and Soderlund, Jean. *Freedom by Degrees: Emancipation in Pennsylvania and its Aftermath*. New York: Oxford University Press, 1991.

_____. *The Urban Crucible: Social Chanage, Political Consciousness, and the Origins of the American Revolution*. Cambridge, Mass.: Harvard University Press, 1979.

Nelson, William. "The American Newspapers in the Eighteenth Century as Sources of History," in *Annual Report of the American Historical Association for the Year 1908*. 2 vols. (Washington, D.C.: Government Printing Office, 1909), I: 214–15.

Okihiro, Gary Y., ed. *In Resistance: Studies in African, Caribbean, and Afro-American History*. Amherst: The University of Massachusetts Press, 1986.

Oliver, Paul. *Songsters and Saints: Vocal Traditions on Race Records*. New York: Cambridge University Press, 1984.

Olson, Edwin. "Social Aspects of Slave Life in New York," *Journal of Negro History* 26 (1941): 66–77.

Oxford English Dictionary, Compact Edition. 2 vols., New York: Oxford University Press, 1971.

Parker, Freddie Lee. *Running for Freedom: Slave Runaways in North Carolina, 1775–1840*. New York: Garland Publishers, 1993.

Parson, Henry S. *A Check List of American Eighteenth Century Newspapers in the Library of Congress* (Washington, Government Printing Office, 1936).

Patterson, Orlando. *The Sociology of Slavery: An Analysis of the Origins, Development, and Structure of Negro Slave Society in Jamaica*. London and New York: Fairleigh Dickinson University Press, 1967.

Pingeon, Francis D. "Slavery in New Jersey on the Eve of the Revolution," in *New Jersey in the American Revolution*, ed. William C. Wright, rev. ed. Trenton, N.J.: New Jersey Historical Commission, 1974.

Price, Clement A. *Freedom Not Far Distant: A Documentary History of Afro-Americans in New Jersey*. Newark, N.J.: New Jersey Historical Commission, 1980.

Prude, Jonathan. "To Look Upon the 'Lower Sort': Runaway Ads and the Appearance of Unfree Laborers in America," *Journal of American History*. 78 (1991), 124–60.

Salinger, Sharon V. *"To Serve Well and Faithfully": Labor and Indentured Servants in Pennsylvania, 1682–1800*. New York: Cambridge University Press, 1987.

Schwarz, Philip J. *Twice Condemned: Slaves and the Criminal Laws of Virginia, 1705–1865*. Baton Rouge, La.: Louisiana State University Press, 1988.

Singleton, Esther. *Social New York Under the Georges, 1714–1776*. New York: D. Appleton, 1902.

Smith, Billy G. and Wojtowicz, Richard. eds. *Blacks Who Stole Themselves: Advertisements for Runaways in the Pennsylvania Gazette, 1728–1790*. Philadelphia: University of Pennsylvania Press, 1989.

Sobel, Mechal. *The World They Made Together: Black And White Values in Eighteenth-Century Virginia*. Princeton, N.J.: Princeton University Press, 1987.

Soderlund, Jean. *Quakers and Slavery: A Divided Spirit*. Princeton, N.J.: Princeton University Press, 1985.

Stuckey, Sterling. *Slave Culture: Nationalist Theory & the Foundations of Black America*. New York: Oxford University Press, 1987.

Thornton, John. *Africa and Africans in the Making of the Atlantic World, 1400–1680*. New York: Cambridge University Press, 1992.

Wacker, Peter O. *Land & People A Cultural Geography of Preindustrial New Jersey: Origins and Settlement Patterns*. New Brunswick, N.J.: Rutgers University Press, 1975.

Warwick, Edward, et al. *Early American Dress: The Colonial and Revolutionary Periods*. New York: Benjamin Blom, 1965.

White, Shane. *Somewhat More Independent: The End of Slavery in New York City, 1770–1810*. Athens, Ga.: University of Georgia Press, 1991.

Windley, Lathan A. *A Profile of Runaway Slaves in Virginia and South Carolina from 1730 through 1787*. New York: Garland Publishers, forthcoming.

_____. comp. *Runaway Slave Advertisements: A Documentary History from the 1730s to 1790*, 4 vols., Westport, Conn.: Greenwood Press, 1983.

Wood, Peter H. *Black Majority: Negroes in Colonial South Carolina from 1670 through the Stono Rebellion*. New York: W.W. Norton, 1974.

Wright, Giles R. *Afro-Americans in New Jersey: A Short History*. Trenton: New Jersey Historical Commission, Department of State, 1988.

Wright, Marion M. Thompson. "New Jersey Laws and the Negro," *Journal of Negro History*, 28 (1943), 156–99.

Zilversmit, Arthur. *The First Emancipation: The Abolition of Slavery in the North*. Chicago: University of Chicago Press, 1967.

Subject Index

Note: The numbers refer to the case number preceding each advertisement.

Advertisements by jailers, 6,7, 9, 10, 209, 213, 229, 235, 242, 248, 256, 265, 293, 323, 324, 303

African markings: scarification, 111, 227, 268, 341, 355, 367, 397; holes in the ears, 119, 212, 581; teeth filed, 6, 214

Birthplace: Africa, 3, 6, 25, 28, 36, 42, 69, 101, 104, 106, 256, 268, 282, 290, 517; Bombay, 228; England, 323; North America, 25, 27, 29, 60, 83, 109, 144, 148,156, 186, 188, 190, 193, 200, 218, 232, 234, 245, 247, 264, 274, 275, 286, 326, 333, 336; Spanish territories, 77, 95, 158, 244, 251, 288, 289; West Indies, 44, 47, 107, 130, 142, 154, 155, 160, 210, 212, 224, 228, 230, 278, 301, 371, 437, 494

Branded, 130, 154, 301, 449, 554, 612

Escape objectives: backcountry, 94, 153, 167, 251, 252, 321, 323, 340, 437, 578; family or former home, 205, 206, 217, 258, 261, 272, 321, 336, 352, 354, 356; free blacks, 280, 522, 599; Indians, 176, 381; Long Island, 391, 400, 434, 624; military or enemy, 60, 143, 399, 406, 413, 430, 436, 439, 442, 446, 448, 472, 474, 477, 487, 492, 522, 541, 610; New England, 92, 106, 136, 143, 179, 380, 635; New Jersey, 192, 420, 453, 454, 522, 599; New York City, 190, 214, 263, 280, 294, 311, 312, 332, 357, 368, 373, 376, 384, 385, 417, 431, 440, 442, 451, 461, 467, 478, 482, 489, 505, 508, 522, 536, 599, 624, 661; Nova Scotia, 641; Philadelphia, 26, 294, 300, 376, 448, 457, 470; swamps, 130, 272; vessels, 1, 77, 162, 172, 383, 411, 433, 472, 480, 489, 517, 528, 564, 585, 586, 587, 600, 604, 612, 661;West Indies, 376

Escape Strategies: changes name, 42,182, 263, 272, 309, 327, 346, 383, 395, 401, 436, 439, 440, 448, 452, 471, 489, 495,501, 505, 519, 521, 529, 563, 617, 647; escaped previously, 58, 94, 176, 218, 244, 267, 268, 306, 308, 310, 337, 354, 435,

565; forge a pass, 99, 106, 115, 130, 152, 225, 257, 262, 264, 310, 329, 339, 359, 376, 387, 485; pass as free, 2, 169, 91, 104, 124, 156, 179, 195, 201, 204, 211, 230, 239, 250, 256, 257, 262, 289, 296, 303, 310, 322, 324, 342, 348, 366, 373, 375, 392, 408, 413, 418, 446, 450, 471, 480, 485, 506, 565; pass as White, 47, 617; use an old pass, 69, 102, 139, 158, 296, 381, 401, 452

Escaped with others: couples or families, 132, 134, 194, 388, 414, 434, 455, 472, 505, 519, 520, 531, 536, 537, 548, 593, 625, 637, 658; with Indians, 68; with other blacks, 20, 69, 111, 127, 329, 432, 444, 482, 545, 553, 554, 577, 592, 598, 607, 613, 638, 648, 659; with white indentured servants, 4, 10, 25, 80, 82, 127, 111, 292, 346; with other whites, 106, 303, 336, 345, 353, 495, 515, 519, 562, 662

Irons on, 141, 155, 183, 197, 298, 338, 609

Items stolen: boat, 4, 14, 26, 218, 385; extra clothing, 16, 47, 77, 82, 139, 152, 164, 175, 177, 201, 262, 274, 295, 296, 322, 334, 339, 365, 376, 381, 383, 387, 401, 413, 448, 457, 463, 475, 478, 485, 519, 525, 548, 615, 637, 647, 659; gun, 8, 80, 175, 176, 218, 225, 334; horse, 33, 37, 74, 115, 269, 337, 346, 470, 495, 519, 531, 588; dog, 175, 250; money, 25, 87, 114, 127, 132, 152, 201, 383, 590; tools, 176

Languages: Good English, 8, 20, 22, 24, 28, 29, 30, 33, 35, 41, 46, 59, 60, 62, 67, 70, 71, 79, 85, 87, 88, 90, 98, 106, 108, 112, 116, 128, 130, 142, 144, 154, 156, 159, 163, 164, 166, 173, 178, 186, 190, 193, 201, 202, 207, 208, 213, 227, 224, 228, 238, 245, 250, 262, 263, 264, 274, 279, 289, 301, 331, 339, 344, 348, 362, 378, 397, 408, 413, 414, 419, 479, 484, 490, 501, 508, 517, 526, 528, 532, 549, 572, 573, 598, 632, 645, 648, 650, 657; Broken or poor English, 2, 7, 58, 62, 65, 77, 100, 119, 134, 168, 197, 210, 211, 212, 214, 231, 233, 235, 242, 243, 248, 254, 267, 268, 271, 279, 281, 282, 290, 292, 299, 429, 444, 500, 503, 554, 586, 611, 623, 651; no English, 6, 101; Negro Dutch, 508; Low Dutch, 12, 34, 36, 211, 243, 248, 249, 258, 306, 598; Indian, 22; German (High Dutch), 23, 239, 484, 520; English and Dutch, 16, 23, 25, 27, 35, 53,

88, 99, 105, 117, 136, 143, 150, 165, 167, 189, 192, 195, 220, 237, 239, 298, 303, 304, 307, 319, 324, 325, 326, 329, 298, 303, 304, 307, 319, 324, 325, 326, 329, 342, 347, 351, 353, 482, 487, 621, 638; French, 25, 96, 168, 204, 232, 249, 250, 266, 295, 301, 315, 366, 581; Spanish, 58, 230, 250, 266, 288, 289, 411; multilingual, 12, 22, 23, 250, 266, 366; Literate: read, 154, 366; read and write, 21, 59, 115, 117, 135, 147, 152, 191, 201, 226, 359, 381, 495, 635

Masters' occupations: baker, 57, 593; blacksmith, 211, 281, 286; butcher, 95, 603; cabinetmaker, 430; carpenter, 27, 192; chemist, 184, 216; confectioner, 445; distiller, 168, 435; doctor, 305, 443, 532, 597; farmer, 344; goldsmith, 140;inn keeper, 196, 285, 320; iron master, 82; mason, 266; merchant, 67, 166, 191, 328; military officer, 435, 489, 509, 523, 546, 558, 560, 564, 565; miner, 153; minister, 234, 473, 495; post master, 246; shipwright, 131; storekeeper, 25; surgeon, 469; tanner, 432

Musicians: drummers, 64, 489, 530, 577; fiddlers (includes violin players) 12, 15, 20, 22, 35, 45, 48, 60, 73, 97, 108, 115, 117, 143, 150, 156, 166, 169, 171, 193, 199, 201, 205, 224, 253, 257, 270, 286, 295, 319, 321, 346, 354, 358, 376, 390, 424, 461, 481, 484, 577; french horn, 481; fifers, 390, 577, 652

Previous owners, 1, 2, 9, 28, 34, 47, 84, 87, 95, 103, 107, 109, 118, 124, 127, 144, 161, 167, 190, 194, 198, 205, 206, 218, 224, 233, 238, 245, 246, 257, 261, 266, 274, 275, 286, 293, 296, 298, 303, 306, 320, 333, 336, 343, 352, 354, 356, 373, 388, 392, 405, 417, 471, 473, 480, 487, 498, 509, 516, 546, 557, 559, 566, 574, 593, 599, 624, 628, 647, 661

Race or ethnicity (other than Negro) : Indian, 1, 20, 68; Part Indian, 22, 34, 38, 88, 111, 144; Madagascar or Malagasco, 5, 23, 28, 42, 69; Mullatto, 10, 16, 34, 38, 47, 56, 61, 68, 77, 87, 88, 96, 102, 104, 115, 116, 117, 118, 127, 128, 129, 133, 181, 195, 206, 207, 225, 226, 239, 272, 276, 277, 323, 337, 362, 388, 413, 466, 467, 468, 469, 472, 476, 491, 495, 505, 518, 524, 538, 550, 591, 595, 610, 617, 621, 633; Popaw, 6

Religious: 17, 33, 380, 650

Sex: female runaways: 16, 27, 36, 66, 84, 87, 93, 103, 142, 157, 164, 165, 181, 194, 195, 213, 220, 223, 227, 246, 248, 252, 258, 274, 280, 297, 345, 355, 360, 365, 380, 388, 415, 417, 432, 434, 445, 459, 461, 466, 467, 472, 473, 486, 491, 505, 506, 510, 512, 519, 520, 521, 524, 527, 528, 531, 536, 537, 538, 542, 543, 544, 548, 550, 554, 559, 561, 566, 568, 569, 572, 573, 574, 582, 554, 589, 593, 594, 599, 600, 610, 614, 616, 617, 627, 636, 637, 639, 643, 644, 747, 652, 656, 658, 661

Site of Escape (New Jersey, by county): Bergen, 19, 54, 72, 99, 103, 114, 123, 150, 153, 175, 189, 203, 311, 319, 369; Burlington, 2, 9, 10, 18, 48, 50, 77, 92, 197, 202, 206, 213, 259, 264, 448, 453, 543, 557, 578, 598, 607, 609, 651; Cumberland, 256, 450; Essex, 12, 15, 65, 80, 85, 109, 139, 171, 306, 324, 327, 328, 333, 334, 335, 336, 343, 344, 359, 362, 388, 397, 405, 406, 425, 615, 616, 654; Gloucester, 4, 26, 71, 207, 218, 251, 457, 472, 478; Hunterdon, 29, 43, 104, 113, 176, 236, 279, 282, 387, 409, 463, 476, 482, 500, 534, 570, 581, 613; Middlesex, 1, 5, 6, 22, 33, 35, 61, 69, 88, 100, 124, 132, 141, 158, 167, 198, 209, 223, 228, 231, 239, 240, 242, 243, 244, 246, 254, 258, 283, 302, 318, 322, 323, 329, 339, 345, 364, 366, 376, 474, 495, 515, 520, 522, 525, 541, 633; Monmouth, 3, 7, 20, 32, 36, 37, 51, 73, 81, 102, 118, 122, 127, 130, 154, 187, 235, 257, 263, 265, 267, 273, 290, 296, 299, 309, 313, 314, 316, 317, 321, 325, 330, 332, 338, 363, 394, 618; Morris, 28, 83, 112, 145, 262, 270, 277, 278, 354, 360, 488, 492, 498, 508, 519, 531, 549, 588, 631; Salem, 294, 471, 516; Somerset, 8, 24, 222, 255, 269, 310, 331, 340, 479, 485, 487, 511, 539, 548, 610; Sussex, 253, 287, 481

Site of Escape (New York, by county) : Albany, 23, 55, 250, 288, 289, 337, 370, 386, 411; Columbia, 63, 162; Dutchess, 30, 39, 52, 89, 106, 115, 143, 177, 180, 234; Kings, 304, 389, 398, 410, 420, 424, 431, 447, 465, 530, 554, 649, 653; Nassau, 40, 108, 111, 133, 138, 379; New York, 11, 14, 16, 17, 27, 31, 34, 44, 47, 53, 57, 70, 75, 78, 84, 86, 94, 95, 101, 107, 131, 135, 136, 140, 145, 148,

155, 157, 160, 161, 163,
164, 165, 166, 168, 170,
172, 174, 181, 183, 184,
188, 190, 191, 194, 195,
196, 201, 203, 204, 205,
208, 210, 212, 214, 216,
217, 220, 226, 227, 229,
230, 232, 233, 238, 241,
245, 266, 271, 274, 280,
281, 284, 293, 295, 297,
298, 301, 315, 320, 326,
341, 342, 346, 347, 352,
355, 356, 357, 361, 365,
375, 378, 390, 391, 392,
395, 396, 399, 400, 402,
403, 408, 412, 413, 414,
415, 416, 417, 418, 422,
423, 426, 427, 428, 430,
432, 433, 435, 437, 438,
440, 441, 442, 443, 445,
446, 449, 451, 459, 460,
461, 462, 466, 467, 468,
469, 486, 489, 490, 491,
493, 494, 497, 499, 501,
503, 504, 505, 506, 507,
509, 510, 512, 513, 514,
518, 523, 527, 528, 532,
533, 535, 536, 538, 540,
543, 544, 545, 546, 547,
550, 551, 552, 553, 555,
556, 558, 559, 560, 561,
563, 566, 567, 568, 569,
571, 572, 573, 574, 575,
579, 580, 582, 583, 584,
585, 586, 587, 589, 591,
592, 593, 594, 595, 596,
597, 600, 601, 602, 603,
604, 605, 606, 608, 611,
612, 614, 617, 619, 620,
621, 624, 625, 626, 627,
630, 634, 636, 637, 638,
639, 641, 642, 643, 645,
646, 647, 648, 652, 655,
657, 659, 661, 662;

Orange, 46, 59, 211, 237,
303, 350; Queens, 42, 92,
149, 186, 292, 308, 368,
383, 407, 429, 439, 496,
529, 629, 640, 650, 656;
Richmond, 79, 98, 134,
173, 192, 215, 260, 268,
312, 436; Suffolk, 68, 74,
91, 129, 147, 393; Ulster,
56, 105, 117, 120, 137,
404; Westchester, 38, 62,
66, 128, 144, 169, 178,
179, 182, 199, 261, 275,
276, 285, 286, 349, 351,
353, 358, 367, 371, 372,
374, 377, 381, 401, 434,
456, 635, 660

Site of escape (outside of
region) : Connecticut,
119, 193, 225, 249, 305;
Maryland, 480;
Pennsylvania, 60, 248,
470, 484, 524, 537, 658;
Philadelphia, 142, 200,
252, 272, 300, 521, 599;
Ship, 151, 159, 185, 224,
348, 384, 418, 464, 502,
577, 590, 622, 644; South
Carolina, 517, 526, 564;
Virginia, 373, 562

Slaves' occupations: baker, 57,
437, 595, 626; barber,
166, 426, 577, 601, 644;
blacksmith, 23, 211, 321,
478; butcher, 20, 95, 399;
carpenter, 1, 10, 17, 20,
191, 211, 424, 547, 564,
659; caulker, 191, 547;
chimney-sweep, 342;
cook, 166, 237, 274;
cooper, 20, 104, 398, 448,
581; doctor, 137, 310;
farmer, 144, 146, 154,

156, 158, 239, 262, 270, 273, 305, 435; fortune teller, 154; gardener, 651; glazier, 418; goldsmith, 140; hangman, 546; hostler, 239, 481, 635; magician, 321; mason, 144; mast maker, 659; miller, 304; potash maker, 362; saddler, 484; sailmaker, 552, 651; sailor, 30, 41, 77, 105, 136, 162, 262, 264, 300, 401, 464, 552, 644; servant, 239, 344, 348, 376, 395, 520, 624; shoemaker, 88; silversmith, 163; soldier, 143, 153, 436, 448; spinner, 562; taylor, 95, 348, 648; teamster, 432, 585; weaver, 150; wheelwright, 20

smallpox-pitted, 18, 25, 43, 50, 57, 94, 115, 172, 182, 229, 484, 493, 497, 513, 526, 547, 557, 637

stutters, 186, 403, 433, 444, 446, 504, 613, 623, 659

Vices: drinkers, 25, 34, 40, 308, 310, 319, 330, 366, 373, 381, 385, 410, 417, 494, 498, 593, 598, 622, 644, 651; snuff, 412; tobacco users, 75, 106, 113, 172, 263, 412

whip-scarred, 13, 155, 211, 250, 519

Name Index

Note: Numbers refer to case number, not page number.

Abeel, James, 223
Aberdeen, 240
Abraham, 187, 257, 434
Abrahams, John, 268
Acton, John, 319
Adam, 571, 596, 629
Adonia, 211
Aesop, 123
Agar, Edward, 247
Airy, Mrs., 411
Alick, 449
All, Peter Alexander, 633
Allaire, Alexander, 62
Allen, 242
Allen, Adam, 63
Allen, Henry, 133
Allen, John, 213
Allen, Joseph, 338
Allicocke, Joseph, 435
Amberman, John, 496
America, 383
Amoritta, 521
Amos, 256
Andrew, 49, 105
Andrewson, David, 199
Ann, 432
Anster, Bartholomew, 644
Anthony, 97, 116, 650
Anthony, Joseph, 261
Antony, Elizabeth, 25

Arch, 340
Arding, Charles, 407
Armstrong, George, 146
Arthur, William, 379
Ash, 110
Aten, Derrick, 113
Atkins, Charles, 371
Bacchus, 583
Bacher, John, 370
Backman, Jacob, 248
Baddeley, John, 155
Bagley, Daniel, 15
Bain, John, 551
Bainbridge, A., 469
Baird, Francis, 255
Ball, Ezekiel, 124, 412
Banks, James, 80
Baptist, Jean, 233, 315
Bard, Mr., 252, 294
Bard, Dr. Samuel, 400
Bardin, Edward, 640, 656
Barkley, Robert, 269
Barnard, James, 285
Barnes, Richard, 182
Barnes, Roger, 188
Barnett, William, 336
Bartow, John, 456
Bartow, Thomas, 434
Bassett, Francis, 406
Bates, Solomon, 12, 15

Bayard, Captain Samuel, 194
Bayard, William, 96, 288, 344
Bayley, Richard, 438
Beat, Agnes, 524
Beekman, Henry, 30
Belinda, 486
Bennet, Jacob, 424
Beezley, Captain, 58
Begill, 279
Bell, 66
Bell, John, 27, 607
Ben, 270, 278, 305, 329, 334, 337, 363, 409, 453, 597, 613
Benjamin, 327
Benjamin, Jacob, 651
Bennet, Jacob, 647
Benson, Alderman, 274
Benson, Robert, 136
Benson, Samuel, 349
Berkman, David, 646
Bernard, James, 196
Bet, 445, 542, 607
Betsey, 554, 566
Bethall, Benjamin, 151
Betts, Dr., 493
Betts, John, 76
Betty, 252, 417
Bill, 179, 298
Billy, 612
Billow, Thomas, 41
Bird, Mark, 658
Blackley, Ebenezar, Jr., 519
Blackwell, Andrew, 534
Blackwood, Jane, 252

Blair, David, 568
Blanchard, John, 498
Blauveldt, Johannes, 211
Bledsoe, John, 562
Blond, Nancy, 614
Bloodgood, Francis, 69
Boardwi[n]e, Charles, 589
Bob, 472, 514
Bodkin, Mr., 191
Bolton, 75
Bon, 337
Bond, 337
Bond, Elijah, 92
Bonnell, Edward, 345
Bood, 176, 222, 308
Boon, Richard, 4
Boshirks, 194
Bowne, Samuel, 172
Boyd, Adam, 477
Boyle, 647
Brap, 526
Bradford, William, 2
Bradstreet, Colonel, 337
Bradt, Arent, 23
Bram, 370
Brasier, Henry, 326
Breese, John, 34
Brested, Andrew, 152
Brett, Colonel Francis, 56
Brinckley, Thomas, 627
Brinkerhoff, Alderman, 293
Briss, 516
Bristol, 109, 139, 170, 176, 347, 442, 558

Name Index

Britt, 336, 343, 359
Britton, Richard, 474
Brookman, Fortune, 416, 440
Brookman, Thomas, 416, 440
Brooks, Captain Benjamin, 472
Brooks, Dr. David, 597
Brownejohn, M., 652
Brown John, William, 174
Brown, Thomas, 189, 363
Brott, Captain Peter, 362
Bruyne, Jacobus, 105
Bryan, John, 358
Bryan, Captain John, 480
Bryan, Lt. Colonel Josiah, 405
Bryson, John, 414
Buchanan, William, 598
Buck, Aaron, 263
Budd, Bern, 262
Budd, Henry, 454
Budde, Thomas, 306
Bull, William, 241
Burge, William, 2
Burnet, Dr., 406
Burnet, Parson, 573
Burns, George, 230, 238
Burtus, Paul, 291
Bush, Hannes, 303
Bush, Dr. William, 305
Butler, James, 642
Byron, William, 640
Cæsar (Cesar), 4, 26, 85, 91, 100, 126, 129, 141, 186, 241, 292, 293, 373, 395, 418, 515, 552, 593, 626

Caesar Augustus, 585
Cain, 499, 525
Calder, Joseph, 176
Callow, James, 584
Campbell, Archibald, 380
Campbell, David, 566, 625
Campbell, Eleazer, 616
Campbell, James, 172
Campbell, Justice, 599
Campbell, Mr., 192, 286, 571
Cannon, Arnout, 270
Cannon, John, 14
Cape, Mr., 598
Carey, Mary, 614
Carnes, Richard, 283
Carpenter, Elizabeth, 125
Carrey, Mary, 58
Carrol, James, 157, 162
Carrow, John, 573
Carver, Joseph, 197
Casey, Captain, 577
Cash, 455
Castello, 287
Cate, 280
Caster, 402
Catherwood, Robert, 378
Cato, 25, 130, 154, 239, 265, 267, 314, 335, 352, 385, 386, 401, 406, 577, 603
Chambers, William, 607
Charles, 65, 148, 190, 201, 301, 313, 344, 482, 562
Charlottee, 574
Chess, 428, 474
Christopher, Aristoblus, 10

Cip, 363
Clarender, 661
Clark, Thomas, 71
Clarke, Thomas, 380
Clause, 12, 15, 35, 152, 351
Clawson, John, 302, 318
Clement, Moses, 149
Clopper, Cornelius, 298
Closs, 374
Clows, S., 650
Clowse, Samuel, Jr., 45
Cock, Samuel, 253
Cocker, Emanuel, 65
Codiments, George, 189
Coffey, John, 82
Colvin, Patrick, 557
Comes, Solomon, 80
Conihane, Francis, 437
Constant, 376
Coombs, John, 261
Cooke, Gabriel, 31
Cooke, William, 331
Cooper, Daniel, 197
Cooper, John, 85
Cooper, Robert Lettis, Jr., 202
Corlis, John, 394
Cornell, Gilliam, 645
Cornell, Isaac, 645
Cornell, Jacobus, 465
Cornwell, Thomas, 292
Corshon, Joshua, 500
Coryell, John, 55
Cotheal, Isaac, 624
Cotton, Thomas, 565

Couwenhoven, Gerret, 525
Couwenhoven, Rem, 420
Coward, Joseph, 257
Cowell, David, 629
Cox, John, 187, 257, 565
Coxe, Charles, 463
Coyler, Hendrick, 321
Crab, William, 473
Craddock, Mr., 191
Craig, Benjamin, 562
Craig, Jeremiah, 562
Creighton, Peter, 622
Cregier, Simon, 84
Cretia, 220
Cromeline, Mrs., 593
Creguell, Peter, 494
Crook, 96
Cross, William, 449
Cubberly, Mr., 515
Cudjoe, 567
Cuff, 106, 150, 302, 318, 479, 618, 631
Cuffe, 632
Cuffee, 565
Cuffy, 423, 648
Cumsheir, John D., 599
Cumtain, John, 598
Cunningham, Captain, 546, 601
Cunningham, Waddel, 159
Curry, John, 527
Cuyler, Henry, 107
Cyrus, 243, 504
Duley, Philip, 161
Dan, 484

Name Index

Daniel, 225, 231, 396
Daniel, Mathew, 620
Darcy, Patrick, 508
Darlington, William, 315
Dastuge, Dr., 569
Davenport, Stephen, 580
David, 591
Davies, Captain Thomas, 181
Davis, George, 598
Davis, Richard, 644
Daubney, Lloyd, 376
Dauchey, Mary, 220
Dawson, Roper, 215
Day, Thomas, 81
Dayton, Elias, 321
Dayton, Jonathan, 383
Deall, Samuel, 210
de Bardeleben, Lieutenant, 564
Debevois, George, 421, 433
Decay, Mr., 661
Decker, John, 134
De Hart, Colonel, 588
De Klerk, Theunis, 46
de Keudel, 489
De Lancey, Brig. General [Oliver], 435, 647
De Lancey, James, 238
De Lancey, John, 395
De Lancey, Peter, 78, 128
De Peyster, Cornelius, 11
De Peyster, John, 352
Demeld, Abraham, 136
Denton, John, 515
Derman, Prince, 530

Desbrosses, Elias, 343
Devenport, Samuel, 169
De Vore, David, 195
Dewery, Captain, 436
Diana, 559
Dianah, 66, 455
Dick, 177, 339, 357, 437, 439, 440, 502, 517
Dickinson, John, 534
Dickinson, General Philemon, 557
Dinah, 473, 584
Dionah, 459
Ditmas, Dow, 307, 587
Dixon, Thomas, 224
Dole, Mr., 510
Domingo, 58
Donbar, James, 251
Dorus, 454
Douglass, William, 260
Douw, Abraham, 289
Doyle, Francis, 572
Drummond, Major, 509
Dublin, 215, 285
Duca, 211
Duff, 540, 620
Duffield, John, 521
Duffield, Dr. Samuel, 376
Duke, 140, 439, 535
Dumont, Henry, 145
Dumont, Peter, 479, 487
Dun, James, 505
Duncan, Elizabeth, 528
Dunham, John, 632
Durham, Jane, 205

Ebb, 619
Edgar, David, 339
Edward, Mark, 193
Elimas, 613
Elliston, Mary, 135
Emlen, Mr., 257
Emons, Hendrick, 356
Ernest, John, 288
Erskine, Thomas, 567
Esop, 81,
Evans, Elizabeth, 538
Evans, George, 458
Everson, Nicholas, 88
Ewing, William, 373
Exceen, Mary, 355
Ezekiel, 283
Fann, 537
Fanny, 164, 181
Farmer, Brook, 246
Farral, Mr., 191
Felix, 644
Ferrari, Mary, 280
Ferris, Caleb, 144, 156
Field, Francis, 263
Finn, Elizabeth, 306
Fisher, Daniel, 592
Fitzherbert, Captain William, 185
Fitzsimmons, Mr., 536
Flora, 600, 652
Foote, Moses, 179
Ford, Demas, 635
Ford, Standish, 218
Ford, Jacob, 83

Forman, Stephen, 218
Forteath, Alexander, 554
Fortune, 111, 255, 509, 598
Fowler, Jonathan, 493
Frost, Anthony, 518
Fowler, Samuel, 120, 137
Francois, Lewis, 107
Francois, 168
Frank, 45, 53, 132, 151, 168, 203, 209, 272, 332, 421, 433, 456, 488, 531, 548, 587
Franklin, John, 295
Frederick, 624
Freeman, Isaac, 126, 141
French, Philip, 35
Frost, Anthony, 595
Fu-Fu Negro, 326
Fuetter, Emory, 300
Furman, Moore, 202
Furman, Shadrack, 641
Furnivall, William, 464
Gaine, Hugh, 359
Galloway, 34
Garden, Dr. Alexander, 517
Garden, William, 611
Gassee, 377
Gaul, 346
George, 77, 149, 260, 368, 562, 651
George, Ben, 607
German, 201
Gillet, Joel, 180
Glasgow, 185
Gomez, Matthias, 406

Name Index

Goodrich, John Jr., 591
Gorlet, Peter, 427
Goy, John, 373
Grace, 505
Graham, Reverend Chauncy, 106, 234
Graham, Dr., 178
Grant, Major James, 558
Grant, Captain Charles, 556
Grant, Thomas, 124
Green, Jack, 180
Griswold, Joseph, 168
Grover, Joseph, 257
Guest, Henry, 486
Guion, Thomas, 655
Hack, 311
Hager, 360, 616
Hall, Edward, 9
Hall, Captain, George, 44
Hallet, Samuel, 223
Halsted, Benjamin, 204
Halsted, Josiah, 127
Hambleton, Captain, 471
Hamersley, Thomas, 140
Hamilton, Alexander, 159
Hamilton, Archibald, 423
Hamilton, Colonel, 87
Hamilton, William, 419
Hank, 192
Hankinson, Kenneth, 455
Hanlon, Patrick, 258
Hannah, 165, 245, 466
Hannibal, 63, 128, 160, 300
Harman, 435

Harr, 392
Hargrave, Robert, 392
Harriott, Thomas, 429
Harris, Joseph, 117, 143
Harris, Richard, 82, 173, 396
Harry, 39, 52, 54, 89, 173, 183, 202, 237, 243, 253, 266, 319, 362, 471, 505, 562, 607, 638
Hart, John, 176
Harvey, Arthur, 80
Hasbrouck, David, 638
Hastier, John, 163
Hatheway, Shadrack, 83
Hatfield, Abraham, 178
Hatfield, Cornelius, 293
Hatfield, Joshua, 178
Haughwout, Widow, 134
Hawkhurst, Benjamin, 74
Hawkhurst, Joseph, 40
Hawkhurst, William, 74
Hayes, Judah, 87
Haynes, Joseph, 64
Heard, Nathaniel, 323
Hector, 79, 86, 98, 465, 657
Heday, Joseph, 111
Heddin, Joseph, 109
Heineman, John, 608
Hellers, Simon, 383
Hendricks, John, 265, 267, 314, 316
Hendrickson, William, 309
Henry, 169
Henry, David, 539
Henry, Samuel, 475

Herbert, James, 560
Hepburn, Thomas, 413
Hercules, 536
Herriot, Samuel, 279
Hester, 520
Hewitt, Charles, 555
Hewlings, Abraham, 236
Heym, Judge Advocate, 564
Heysham, Christopher, 208
Hicks, Dennis, 131, 179
Hicks, Jacob, 431
Hicks, Whitehead, 95
Hile, Peter, 227
Hitchin, Captain John, 429
Hobart, John, 292, 293
Holcomb, Jacob, 387
Holiday, 90, 121
Holland, Francis, 386
Holmes, Abijah, 450
Holt, John, 201
Hooper, Robert L., 520
Hoops, Robert, 520
Hopper, Andrew John, 369
Hopper, Colonel, 256
Horton, Silas, 350
Hosmer, John, 348
Housman, Peter, 442
Houston, Joseph, 404
Howell, Hezekiah, 478
Howlet, John, 477
Hoy, Michael, 495
Huestis, Edward, 660
Huestis, Jesse, 660
Hudson, John, 303

Huff, Leonard, 51
Hugg, Major, 516
Hughes, Hugh, 287
Hughes, John, 287
Hulet, Daniel, 265
Hulick, Peter, 598
Hulse, James, 461
Hunlock, Thomas, 10
Hunt, Chariss, 205
Hunt, John, 29
Hunt, Mr., 556
Hunt, Samuel, 522
Hunt, Thomas, 47
Hunt, William, 176
Hunt, Wilson, 222, 308, 483
Hunter, Captain, 194
Hunter, George, 647
Hutchings, James, 480
Hutchinson, Benjamin, 393
Hutler, James, 642
Hyer, Victor, 53
Hyer, William, 325
Inglis, Charles, 357
Isaac, 48, 76, 111, 241
Isaacs, Ralph, 249
Isabel, 66, 656
Ishmael, 83, 321
Ivey, Samuel, 547
Jack, 3, 18, 30, 43, 59, 64, 68, 99, 104, 113, 150 (2), 174, 176, 206, 208, 210, 224, 248, 249, 261, 283, 304, 329, 356, 364, 366, 367, 397, 493, 508, 541, 545, 555, 557, 565, 581, 586, 598, 604, 605, 623,

628, 633, 634, 635
Jackson, James, 652
Jackson, John, 601
Jackson, Thomas, 226, 401
Jacob, 250, 263, 326, 398, 553
Jaff, 420
James, 7, 32, 37, 207, 347, 348, 400, 503, 580, 652
James, Richard, 313, 618
Jane, 249, 550, 572
Janneau, 66
Jasper, 163, 273
Jeanes, Jenkinson, 579
Jem, 346, 460, 463, 642
Jenkins, Richard, 593, 626
Jenney, 27, 380, 510, 553
Jennings, Joseph, 106
Jeremy, 116
Jerremy, 438
Jerry, 279, 383 (2)
Jess, 649
Jeste, John, 158, 244
Jim, 286, 305, 325, 658
Joe, 138, 144, 156, 217, 270, 275, 278, 309, 382, 415, 426, 519, 520, 529, 564, 570, 579, 625
Johannis, 648
John, 295, 333, 335
Johnny, 25
Johnsey, 21
Johnson, Isaac, 226, 452
Johnson, Jeffrey, 420
Johnson, John, 206
Johnson, Patrick, 346

Johnson, Robert, 471, 516
Johnson, William, 281
Jones, David, 476
Jones, John, 286, 448
Jones, Nicholas, 175
Joseph, 288
Jupiter, 31, 476
Kean, Thomas, 345
Kearney, Philip, 345
Keen, George, 200, 218, 236
Kelsall, Johanna, 21
Kelly, William, 191, 330
Kemble, Mr., 258
Kemble, Peter, 61
Kennedy, Robert, 233
Kent, David, 100
Kerin, Terrence, 436, 566
Keteltas, Peter, 356
Kip, Jacobus, 161
Kingsland, Isaac, 103
Kingsland, John, 203
Kinney, Thomas, 549
Kissick, Philip, 402
Klein, John, 298
Knap, Benjamin, 237
Kortwright, Lawrence, 371
Kupperth, Roberta, 489
Lambert, A., 607
Lane, Gizebert, 310
Lanen, William, 95
Lank, 316
LaQuear, John, 613
Lashel, Mr., 419
Lasher, Mr. 419

Lawrence, Abraham, 368, 383
Lawrence, Daniel, 98
Lawrence, Elisha, 453
Lawrence, Lawrence, 166
Lawrence, Stephen, 385
Leake, John, 232
Leave, 492
Lee, Charles, 323
Lefever, Andres, 638
Lefever, Nathaniel, 638
Leggett, Gabriel, 38
Leggett, Isaac, 351
Legrange, Bernardus, 602, 606
Le Moldar, Lieutenant, 523
Lens, 195
Lent, Abraham, 441
Lenzi, Philip, 445
Leonard, John, 6
Leonard, James, 8, 33
Leonard, Samuel, 22
LeRoux, Mr., 192
Lester, 241
Letson, Thomas, 242
Leversage, 274
Levi, 450, 492
Lewis, 66, 107
Lewis, Charles, 183
Licum, 133
Linch, John, 303
Linden, 30
Linley, Joseph, 106
Lissa, 573
Lister, William, 259
Livingston, John, 67

Livingston, Philip, 101
Livingston, Robert, 103
Lock, James, 345
Longster, Peter, 656
London, 322, 608
Lott, 92
Lott, Jeromus, 634
Loui, 422
Low, Cornelius, 239
Low, Joseph, 395
Low, Peggy, 148
Low, Peter, 342
Low, Rachel, 148
Lowery, Thomas, 521
Lucas, Frind, 153
Luce, 543, 630
Lucretia, 220
Lucy, 258, 637
Ludlow, Gabriel H., 427
Ludlow, Mr., 388, 553
Lun, 452
Lutwyche, Colonel, 656
Luyster, Garret, 596
Lyell, David, 1
Lynch, Thomas, 436
M' Adam, John, 391
M'Clenachan, Blair, 472
M'Culloh, Joseph, 457
M'Cullough, William, 481
M'Dougall, Alexander, 567
M'Intosh, Lochlin, 235
M'Kay, A.A., 617
M'Kenney, Mrs., 577
M'Lane, Dr. Donald, 443

Name Index

M'Lean, Henrietta, 576
M'Neil, Arthur, 229
MacClughery, Colonel James, 404
McArthur, Duncan, 377
McCormick, Daniel, 612
McFadzean, Captain, 411
McFadyen, Mrs. E., 502
McLean, Dr. Donald, 490, 501, 532
Macaulay, Charles, 533
Madlane, 643
Malato, John, 10
Malbone, Godfrey, Esq., 116
Malcolm, Robert M., 609
Man, Isaac, 297
Mando, 69
Manley, John, 378
Manuel, Fransh, 2
Maria, 521
Mark, 380, 474
Markham, Governor, 9
Marple, George, 77
Marth, Widow, 132
Marquiss, 577
Martin, 177
Martin, John, 112
Martin, Thomas, 426
Marston, John, 95
Martin, Hugh, 43
Mathews, Roger, 9
Matthews, Edmund, 162
Mattis, 552
Maxwell, George, 480
Maxwell, William, 408

Meeker, Samuel, 221
Meredith, Reefe, 172
Mersereau, Jacob, 150
Mersereau, John, 192, 312
Meyer, Ide, 165
Middleton, Dr., 517
Miller, Benjamin, 324
Miller, Eleazer, 588
Miller, Elizabeth, 661
Miller, Hugh, 462
Millers, Josh, 471
Milligan, David, 245
Mills, Dr., 118, 127
Mills, James, 75
Mills, John, 82
Minck, 483
Mingo, 41, 241, 268, 286, 346, 354, 393
Mink, 346, 660
Minors, Norton, 191
Mira, 507
Moll, 434
Molly, 142
Money Digger, 326
Moore, Colonel, 190
Moore, Benjamin, 296
Moore, James, 1
Morehouse, Rebecca, 274
Morgan, Alexander, 4, 26
Morgan, Caleb, 353
Morgan, George, 495
Morrel,, Jacob, 360
Morrel, Silyar, 254
Moore, Samuel, 69

Morris, Anthony, 26
Morris, Colonel, 383
Morris, John, 290
Morris, Mr., 224
Moses, 200, 218, 236, 607
Mott, Patrick, 108
Mott, William, 138
Mount, 269
Mowatt, John, 430
Mugguire, Philip, 82
Mumford, George, 111
Murray, Alex, 82
Myer, Andrew, 301
Myer, Johan Jeremiah, 127
Myers, John, 466
Nap. Daniel, 170
Nat, 447
Nathaniel, 398
Ned, 147, 411, 414, 511
Neilson, James, Esq., 223
Nell, 103, 246
Nelson, William, 519
Neptune, 655
Neptune, John, 655
Nero, 290, 299, 611
Neville, Samuel, 69
Newcome, Mr., 86
Newell, Robert, 104
Newkerk, Cornelius, 152
Newton, Mr., 559
Nicholl, Edward, 604
Nicholl, Mr., 416
Nichols, William, 7
Nicholson, Captain, 660

Nicholson, Finlay, 413
Nicholls, Samuel, 480
Nim, 1
Nixon, Mr. 167
Norris, John, 353
Norway, 320
Nutman, Sam, 139
Nutter, Valentine, 623
Nutus, John, 88
Nutus, Thomas, 88
O'Brien, William, 600
Ogden, David, Esq., 109, 361
Ogden, Nicholas, 439
Ogden, Samuel, 354
Ogden, Samuel, 346
Ohnech, 165
Okeson, Samuel, 364
Oliver, 529
Osborn, 425
Oswald, Eleaser, 599
Packer, John, 628
Palmer, Mr., 261, 275
Pamela, 506, 538
Pamper, Lodewick, 136
Parker, James, 581
Parr, Samuel, 218
Parsco, Simon, 167
Parmeter, Par., 19
Patt, 458
Pattison, Colonel, 546
Paul, 535
Peakes, George, 214
Peet, 29
Peg, 561, 599, 639

Pegg, 274
Pell, John, 66, 274
Pell, Captain Joshua, 619
Pell, Thomas, 434
Penell, Mr., 224
Peonce, 410
Pero, 212
Perry, Henry W., 446
Peter, 56, 175, 182, 431, 446, 578, 588, 602, 653
Peterson, John Williams, 376
Petty, John, 68
Philips, Francis, 107
Philips, Jacob, 542
Phill, 223
Phillipse, Col., 34
Phillips, Ephraim, 264
Phillips, John, 94
Phillips, Mr., 473
Philips, Samuel, 379
Phillis, 223, 355, 462, 582
Phoebe, 84, 531, 548
Pierot, 371
Pierson, Bethuel, 615
Pierson, Robert, 18
Pitts, Henry Jacob, 220
Pleasant Queen Ann, 527
Plymouth, [John], 436
Poll, 627
Pollard, William, 480
Polly, 554, 569
Pomp, 539, 615
Pompey, 131, 136, 184, 216, 229, 290, 299, 361, 430
Pool, Lawrence, 279

Popaw, 6
Porteur, John, 460
Potter, Joseph, 459
Powell, Howell, 256
Powelse, Jacob, 19
Powers, George, 603
Pratt, James, 263
Prevost, Major, 380
Price, Edward, 630
Price, Luce, 630
Price, William, 159
Priam, 369
Prime, 312
Primus, 42, 113, 444
Prince, 167, 194, 338, 369, 375, 389, 399, 419, 498, 659
Price, Ann, 543
Provest, William, 320
Provost, David, 312
Prussia, 528
Purdy, Joseph, 635
Quaco, 197
Quash, 11, 448
Quaw, 44
Quayne, Mark, 191
Quick, Teunis, 613
Quinby, Isiah, 282
Quit, Toby, 337
Rachel, 472, 568
Ralph, 159, 172
Ralsten, William, 320
Ramsay, Cato, 592
Ramson, Jores, 70
Rantus, 146

Rapelje, John, 410
Rapelje, Stephen, 375
Rappelie, Mr., 45
Rappelyea, Jeromus, 610
Rattan, John, 378
Ray, 536
Raymond, John, 2
Read, Colonel John, 225
Reade, Charles, Esq., 77
Reade, Joseph, 16
Reed, Andrew, 48
Rees, John, 244
Reeve, Captain Henry, 565
Reick, 145
Reid, Augustine, 270, 278
Reid, Captain John, 28
Reid, John, Jr., 158
Reid, Mrs., 467
Remsen, Aris, 266
Remsen, George, 621
Remsen, Jeromus, 398, 621
Remsen, Rem, 621
Renier, Mr., 9
Revers, York, 545
Reyerse, George, 114
Reynolds, Broughton, 509
Rhea, George, 296
Rhinelander, William, 586
Richard, 57
Richmond, 546
Richmond, Jon A., 578
Richards, Captain, 229
Richards, James, 432
Richards, Nathaniel, 305, 327,
334, 337
Richards, Paul, 34
Richardson, James, 432
Richardson, Widow, 322
Ricketts, James, 504
Risoer, George, 209
Rivington, Mr., 636
Robin, 37, 72, 114, 189, 198, 381
Robbin, 60, 492
Robbins, Harry, 432
Robert, 322
Roberts, Charles, 201
Roberts, Christophe, 566
Roberts, Peter, 470
Robinson, Henry, 296
Robinson, Joseph, 296
Robinson, Thomas, 147
Rochambeau, Count de, 598
Rogers, Daniel, 256
Rome, William, 36
Roosevelt, Mrs., 564
Rose, 157, 512
Rois, Captain, 494
Ross, James I., 177
Ross, John, Jr., 654
Rouse, James, 55
Rowen, James, 132
Ruble, Mr., 554
Ruckel, Philip, 657
Runyan, Jonathan, 240, 570
Rutgers, Cornelia, 86
Ryckman, Isaac, 152
Ryder, Barnabus, 186
Ryerson, George, Jr., 54

Name Index 365

Ryerson, Luke, 175
Ryersz, Adrian, 79, 98
Sackett, Samuel, 415
Sal, 297, 617
Salem, 208
Salmon, Nathaniel, 336, 343, 359
Saltar, Captain, 574
Saltar, Joseph, 330
Salvanus, 214
Sam, 50, 78, 238, 358, 379, 405, 427, 468, 552, 592, 621, 640
Sambo, 242, 282, 294, 353, 457
Sampson, 94, 221
Sampson, Sim, 523
Sanders, John Williams, 376
Sandy, 160
Sarah, 16, 87, 467, 472, 544, 661
Sargeant, Jonathan, 80, 81
Savinah, 505
Saufe, Mr., 546
Saxon, Andrew, 17
Schenk, Abraham, 304
Schmerhorn, Captain John, 155
Scipio, 335, 444
Scott, Thomas, 410
Scramschaire, Thomas, 164
Scribins, George, 641
Scudder, Colonel, 473
Scudder, Corbet, 388
Sears, David, 588
Sebring, John, 384

Seth, 617
Severns, John, 452
Sharer, Robert, 39, 52
Sharp, 281
Sharp, Joseph, 294
Shaw, George, 432
Shaw, John, 483
Shepherd, John, 127
Shippen, Joseph, 82
Sibrell, John, 513
Siegler, Goodheart, 399
Simeon, 379
Simon, 33, 67
Simons, Morice, 376
Sippee, 46
Siro, 219
Skeene, Philip, 411
Skinner, Stephen, 428
Skinner, Thomas, 595
Skinner, Thomas, 518
Slidell, John, 341
Slight, 519
Smith, Abner, 193
Smith, Ephraim, 647
Smith, Gilbert, 263
Smith, Jacamiah, 336, 343, 359
Smith, James, 206
Smith, Jesse, 468
Smith, John, 401
Smith, Lawrence, 102
Smith, Mary, 102
Smith, Mrs., 375
Smith, Philip, 89

Smith, Reverend, 495
Smith, William, 23, 107
Smith, William Peartree, Esq., 167, 333, 355
Smyth, Mrs., 567
Squire, Jonathan, 335
Spencer, Elihu, 607
Spier, 341
Squash, 590
Stanbury, Samuel, 106
Staniard, Joseph, 257
Stanton, Henry, 649
Stanton, Jeremiah, 243
Stanton, Mr., 297
Starne, Jacob, 283
Start, James, 263
States, Adam, 220
Stelle, Gabriel, 3
Stelle, Isaac, 3
Stephen, 350
Stephany, John Sebastian, 184, 216
Stepney, 659
Sterret, James, 472
Steve, 388
Stevenson, John, 273
Stewart, Anthony, 642
Stewart, James, 412
Stiles, Daniel, 47
Stillwell, Richard, 130, 154
Stites, John, 324
Stockholm, Aaron, 347
Stoffels, 20
Storde, 47
Stout, Samuel, 213

Stout, Zebulon, 24
Stoutenburg, Tobias, 648, 662
Stow, Jonathan, 21
Stuyvesant, P., 444
Suck, 194
Sue, 258
Suydain, Widow, 639
Suydam, Mr. R., 653
Swan, James, 166
Sweedland, Christopher, 389
Syme, 342
Symon, 342
Symonson, Rem, 150
Syphax, 444
Syrus, 607
Talman, John, 263
Talman, William, 529
Tallman, Stephen, 363
Tamar, 66
Tappen, Isaac, 366
Taylor, Joseph, 37
Taylor, Joshua, 303
Teabrooke, Mr., 297
Ten Eyck, Barent, 288, 289
Thomas, 646
Thomas, John, 275
Thomas, Joseph, 550
Thompson, James, 28, 607
Thompson, Joseph, 424
Throckmorton, John, 102, 296
Tiebout, Cornelius, 160
Tim, 354
Tindall, Thomas, 50
Tingley, Samuel, 49

Name Index

Tite, 412
Titus, 71, 135, 225, 390, 394
Toby, 130, 257, 284
Tolmey, Captain Norman, 499
Tom, 5, 24, 40, 61, 69, 74, 88, 108, 115, 117, 118, 127, 143, 161, 173, 176, 188, 199, 205, 230, 277, 289, 349, 387, 403, 443, 470, 475, 490, 501, 532, 556, 563, 576, 577, 607
Tone, 95, 482
Toney, 68, 276, 487, 498, 534
Tongue, William, 417
Tony, 73, 122, 259, 307, 518
Tooker, Charles, 352
Trace, 234
Traile, George, 233
Traso, 253
Tucker, Samuel, 303
Turnbull, Lt. Col., 391
Tuthill, John, 68
Tyng, Eleaser, 60
Vail, John, 403
Valleau, Peter, 25
Van Arsdall, Parson, 473
Van Beverholdt, Lucas, 509
Van Blarcum, Isaac, 382
Van Buskirk, Abraham, 99
Van Buskirk, Jacob, 150
Van Buskirk, Lawrense Janse, 123, 311
Van Cleek, Barent, 115, 117
Van Cleek, Leonard, 115, 117
Van Cortlandt, Jacobus, 17
Van Dam, Anthony, 644

Vandervere, Cornelius, 73, 417
Vanderhoven, John, 574, 624
Van Dike, Roelof, 340
Van Dollsen, Mr., 266
Van Dorn, Abraham, 122
Van Dorn, Anne, 123
Van Dorn, 278
Van Dyck, Henry, 390
Van Dyke, Lambert, 258
Van Gelder, Alderman, 53
Van Harlingen, Ernestus, 329
Van Hart, Adam, 524
Van Horne, Augustine, 284
Van Horn, Cornelius, 5, 482, 487
Van Horne, Jacob, 150
Van Houten, Johannes, 36
Van Kleek, Balrus, 143
Van Mater, Cyrenius, 317
Van Mater, Daniel, 332
Van Riper, Mr., 498
Van Schaick, Jacob, jr., 145
Vantile, Otis, 150
Van Wincle, Jacob, 392
Van Wyck, Cornelius, 84
Van Wyck, Thomas, 91
Van Wyngard, Luykas, 67
Vardill, Captain, 411
Varien, Michael, 365
Vaughn, Jason, 13
Veile, Myndert, 115, 117
Venture, 111, 125
Venus, 213, 589, 637
Vermilye, John, 276

Violet, 345, 365, 625
Vincent, Judith, 20
Vrendeburg, William, 46
Waddell, John, 190
Wadley, Humphrey, 590
Waldren, Captain John, 47
Waldren, Peter, 29
Waldron, Leffert, 329
Waldron, Resolved, 57
Walker, Elizabeth, 594
Wallace, Alexander, 378
Wallace, Hugh, 378
Wan, 22, 57, 153, 232
Ward, Isaac, 381
Ward, Nathaniel, 80
Wardell, John, 110
Ware, 441
Waters, Anthony, 219
Waters, Edward, 219
Watkins, George, 464
Watson, John, 25
Watt, 480
Webb, Joseph, 119
Webster, Colonel, 624
Well, Samuel, 374
Wells, Obadiah, 68, 85
Wells, Samuel, 631
Wescot, Richard, 207, 251
Weston, Richard, 214
Weyman, Hester, 427
White, John, 593
White, Thomas, 32
Whit[t]en, Tom, 560
Wickham, Lawyer, 598

Wickham, Samuel, 59
Wickoff, Henry, 447
Wilkes, 429
Wilkins, Isaac, 286, 346, 354
Wilkins, Mrs., 397
Wilkinson, Philip, 47
Will, 8, 178, 372, 413, 483, 485, 496, 513, 522, 535, 549
Willet, John, Jr., 42, 90, 93, 121
Willis, 625
William, 638
Williams, Benjamin, 170, 171
Williams, Jesse, 474
Williams, John, 335
Williamson, Jacob, 570
Willing, Mr., 224
Wilson, David, 605
Wilson, John, 531, 548
Wilson, Luke, 592
Willson, William, 561
Windsor, 196
Winters, J., 511
Wirtz, Christian, 484
Witherspoon, Thomas, 272
Wolis, Lewis, 455
Wood, Elias, 198
Wood, John, 429
Wood, William, 418
Woodruff, Isaac, 328
Wray, George, 250
Wright, Richard, 449
Wyckoff, Henry, 398
Wyckoff, Jacob, 485

Wyckoff, Martin, 485
Wynans, Jonathan, 488
Wynkoop, Cornelius, 25
Yaff, 660
Yard, William, 2
Yardley, Samuel, 537
Yates, Mrs., 428
Yerrah, 448, 522
York, 51, 70, 166, 175, 317, 407, 408, 494, 622
Youngs, Christopher, 129
Zabriskie, John, 72, 198
Zenger, John Peter, 30
Zepperly, Frederick, 30
Zuntz, Alexander, 512

www.ingramcontent.com/pod-product-compliance
Lightning Source LLC
Chambersburg PA
CBHW022103290426
44112CB00008B/535